SOME KIND OF PARADISE

A Florida Sand Dollar Book

Also by Mark Derr

The Frontiersman (1993)
Dog's Best Friend (1997)

SOME KIND
OF PARADISE

A Chronicle of Man and the Land in Florida

Mark Derr

University Press of Florida

Gainesville/Tallahassee/Tampa/Boca Raton
Pensacola/Orlando/Miami/Jacksonville

08 07 06 05 04 03   7 6 5 4 3 2

Library of Congress Cataloging-in-Publication Data
Derr, Mark.
Some kind of paradise: a chronicle of man and the land in Florida / Mark Derr.
p. cm.
Originally published: New York: W. Morrow, c1989.
Includes bibliographical references (p.) and index.
ISBN 0-8130-1629-0 (pbk.: alk. paper)
1. Florida–History. 2. Florida–Economic conditions. 3. Ecology–Florida.
4. Environmental policy–Florida. I. Title.
F311.D47   1998
975.9–dc21   98-8860

The University Press of Florida is the scholarly publishing agency for the State
University System of Florida, comprising Florida A & M University, Florida
Atlantic University, Florida International University, Florida State University,
University of Central Florida, University of Florida, University of North Florida,
University of South Florida, and University of West Florida.

University Press of Florida
15 Northwest 15th Street
Gainesville, FL 32611
http://www.upf.com

For Gina

CONTENTS

MAPS

ACKNOWLEDGMENTS

Among the many people and institutions who have helped to make this book possible, I should like to thank Lou Toth, Jim Millenson, and Ginger Creighton of the South Florida Water Management District; Pat Tolle, Sonny Bass, and William Robertson, Jr., of the Everglades National Park; Fred Fagergren and Bruce Freet of the Big Cypress National Preserve; Tom Moses and Fred Hardin of the Reedy Creek Improvement District; David Webb of the Florida State Museum, Gainesville; Charlotte Porter, also of the Florida State Museum. Sandy Dayhoff, director of the Loop Road Interpretive Center for the Everglades National Park, helped me understand the uniqueness of south Florida. David Girardin of the St. Johns Water Management District took me on the trail of William Bartram.

For excellent work on the maps, I should like to thank Peter Krafft of the Florida Resources and Environmental Analysis Center at Florida State University. Joan Morris and her assistant at the Florida State Archives, Joanna Norman, collected the photographs. Joan Runkel, curator of the Henry Morrison Flagler Museum, helped me search through their abundant material.

Barney Karpfinger, my agent, had faith in the story of Florida when no one else did and encouraged me throughout the two and one-half years of the writing with his wisdom and kindness. My editor at William Morrow, Harvey Ginsberg, refined and defined the text with skill and sensitivity.

My mother, Mary Derr, ran a one-woman clipping service on all aspects of Florida, from central Florida.

I could not have written this book without the love and support of my wife and friend, Gina Maranto. Editor, critic, boon companion, she never faltered.

What is good and enduring in this volume belongs to those who helped make it possible. The rest is mine alone.

Madison
Madison
Hamilton
Jasper
Perry
lor
Live Oak
Suwannee
Mayo
Lafayette
Lake
City
Columbia
Baker
Nassau
Fernandina
Beach
Duval
Macclenny
Jacksonville
Union
Lake
Butler
Bradford
Starke
Clay
Green
Cove
Springs
St. Johns
St. Augustine
Cross City
Dixie
Gilchrist
Trenton
Gainesville
Alachua
Palatka
Putnam
Flagler
Bunnell
Bronson
Levy
Marion
Ocala
Volusia
Daytona Beach
DeLand
Citrus
Inverness
Sumter
Lake
Tavares
Sanford
Seminole
Titusville
Hernando
Brooksville
Bushnell
Orlando
Orange
Dade City
Pasco
Kissimmee
Osceola
Brevard
Clearwater
Pinellas
Hillsborough
Tampa
Polk
Bartow
Indian River
Vero
Beach
Wauchula
Hardee
Sebring
Ft. Pierce
Manatee
Bradenton
Okeechobee
St. Lucie
Sarasota
De Soto
Arcadia
Highlands
Okeechobee
Stuart
Martin
Sarasota
Charlotte
Punta
Gorda
Glades
Moore
Haven
LaBelle
Palm Beach
Lee
Ft. Myers
Hendry
Palm Beach
Broward
Ft.
Lauderdale
Collier
Naples
EVERGLADES
Miami
Monroe
Dade

Note: All the
keys south of
this line are part
of Monroe County

Key West

PROLOGUE

Sometime in the next century or two, the sea will cover Florida as it has periodically for the past 250 million years, and sometime, assuredly, the sea will retreat, leaving a peninsula dotted with lakes and marshes, ringed by a new beach of glistening sand. It is an anomalous land, jutting southward like a thumb splayed from the North American mainland. Shielded by barrier islands and caressed on its southeast flank by the Gulf Stream, the peninsula divides the Gulf of Mexico from the Atlantic Ocean and brings the North American mainland in touch with the tropics. Strange and exotic to all who encounter it, Florida is fast becoming a victim of its allure, with 300,000 people a year rushing to make it their home and another 44 million coming to visit. This book is an examination of the natural state, which, although poorly used by its human inhabitants, continues to prove irresistible.

In human terms, Florida is as much a state of mind as of being, a land of imagination where fantasies come true, although the nature of the dreams, like the land itself, has changed with shifting social fashions. Now tourists arrive to visit the Magic Kingdom of Walt Disney World or to view the trained porpoises and whales of Sea World, whereas a century ago they came to cruise rivers, coast the shore, and visit resorts built around wondrous springs. In these past one hundred years, man has reshaped and relandscaped the peninsula, leveling forests, draining its marshes. The process continues at such a rapid rate that many residents of more than a decade barely recognize the areas around their homes.

The tale of Florida's development is often sordid, marked by the greed of people intent on taking whatever the land offered and leaving nothing in return, yet it is leavened by men and women who found the place special and called it paradise. Their love and respect are responsible for the preservation of what remains of the natural state. Without their diligence, there would be only artificial playgrounds attempting to imitate wilderness.

This study begins late in the last century when the state's leadership pursued a policy of resource exploitation and development for the economic gain of a few individuals and corporations. The greatest of the capitalist investors in Florida during this period was Henry Flagler, the partner of John D. Rockefeller in the Standard Oil Company and the founder of the Florida East Coast Railway. Investing his own fortune, Flagler laid his tracks 522 miles down the Atlantic coast of the peninsula from Jacksonville to Key West, joining that island city to the mainland for the first time. Along the way he built hotels and cities that defined resort living at the turn of the century.

Flagler and his contemporaries—among them Hamilton Disston, who once laid claim to a third of the state, and Henry Plant, who developed resorts and constructed railroads from Jacksonville across the peninsula's midsection to Tampa—literally carved up the state. The late nineteenth and early twentieth centuries also witnessed the birth of modern citriculture, of commercial production of vegetables for the winter market, and of phosphate mining; the full and grotesque flowering of the logging and naval stores industries; the first campaigns to drain the Everglades; and the beginnings of mass tourism. The same era set patterns of population growth and urban development in the state and triggered the earliest calls for conservation of natural resources. Americans began to lust after Florida real estate as if it were gold. That craving resulted in a real estate boom that, when it went bust, threw the state into economic collapse. The first section of the book ends with those bizarre events.

Before shifting to an account of developments over the past six decades, the narrative looks at what existed prior to development, going back 250 million years to the beginning of the landmass now known as the Floridan Plateau and proceeding to the eve of the Flagler period. Individual chapters examine the peninsula's evolution through the appearance of Paleo-hunters 15,000 to 20,000 years ago, and the unique cultures of pre-Columbian tribes and their fate at the hands of European conquerers. William Bartram, the brilliant and eccentric botanist from Philadelphia whose *Travels* is required reading for all who would understand the state, journeyed through much of Florida during the time of British rule in the 1770s, before humans thoroughly transformed it. His descriptions of the flora and fauna and of the Indians just then coming to be known as the

Seminole are unexcelled—as are his paintings from the period. Following the discussion of Bartram are sections on the American seizure of Florida and the campaign—known as the Seminole Wars—to obliterate colonies of free blacks and extirpate the Indian; and on plantation slavery, the Civil War, and Reconstruction. The focus, as throughout the book, is on the land and its inhabitants.

The final four chapters review the events of the last six decades, from the Great Depression through the present, when even the state's most avid promoters recognize that it suffers from too many people, too much trash and pollution, too few parks, schools, roads, and other public amenities. The severity of the state's problems has repeatedly forced its leaders to adopt legislation to protect the environment, especially water and wildlife. Yet too often those laws have proved inadequate to the task, and the state has remained a victim of its popularity. Looming over the state's growth during the past two decades is Walt Disney World in central Florida, and the last chapter deals with both its impact and the different responses to it.

Politicians appear only as their actions have materially affected the look and feel of the land and water. During the nearly 170 years of American possession of Florida, state officials have been most noteworthy for their eagerness to give away or sell for a pittance the natural endowments of the peninsula whose stewardship they claimed as their duty. Those few elected officials who have worked on behalf of preservation have distinguished themselves for their courage and foresight more than for their lasting accomplishments. In addition to the politicians, there are government workers—national, state, regional, and local—who have dedicated their lives to Florida, keeping their faith in its potential through times of hostile as well as friendly leadership. Through their reports, interviews, and educational programs, they have taught Floridians about the need to nurture their unique environment.

ONE

The End of the Line

Flagler's railroad links Key West to peninsular Florida and the island city prospers, then declines, contrary to expectations. His "domain" stretches down the east coast, from Jacksonville to Land's End.

The band played Sousa. Navy gunships rocked in the harbor. Bombs burst, whistles blew, and a thousand schoolchildren in their Sunday best waved flags and sang for the grand old man. The place was Key West, the southernmost city in the United States and now the end of the line for the Florida East Coast Railway. The year was 1912, and although trains were commonplace through much of the nation, many of the local residents, who knew every type of boat from a sharpie to a battle cruiser, had never seen a locomotive. Assorted socialites, gadflies, corporate officials, and politicians from Tallahassee and Washington, D.C., had gathered for a three-day celebration in praise of one man and the completion of his aptly named Overseas Railroad, 128 miles of track laid from the tip of mainland Florida to this island city at a cost of $20 million and perhaps as many as seven hundred lives. The old man with blurred vision and bad hearing, white hair and mustache, frail but still handsome, reveled in the applause and adulation. On January 22, 1912, ten days into his eighty-third year, Henry Morrison Flagler could look back on his accomplishments with pride. He could track his trains for 522 miles from Key West to Jacksonville, with a straight shot from there to New York. Flagler told the crowd his

17

dream was fulfilled, and he could die a happy man.

He lived barely more than another year, long enough to hear, while crossing the Keys, his steam locomotive whistle a warning at preoccupied walkers so they could dive into one of the wire cages strategically hung from the bridges. (Necessary for maintenance, the cages were a godsend to crusty natives and wandering naturalists who used the tracks as the only ground link between the Keys.) Whether he died a happy man, no one can say. He certainly died a rich one, among the wealthiest in the world, and he died knowing that his Overseas Railroad ranked as one of the great engineering feats in history, perhaps the greatest planned, financed, and executed by a private individual relying on his own resources.

Today, seventy-five years after his death, Flagler is regularly invoked in histories and newspaper accounts as the man who "tamed the wilderness," the former partner of John D. Rockefeller in the Standard Oil monopoly who "philanthropically" devoted his final three decades and $50 million of his personal fortune to changing Florida into a tropical playground for tourists and winter residents. By 1908, his eight Florida hotels—the Continental in Fernandina; the Ponce de Leon, Alcazar, and Cordova in St. Augustine; the Ormond at Ormond Beach; the Royal Poinciana and Breakers at Palm Beach; and the Royal Palm in Miami—along with his fishing camp at Key Largo—could house up to forty thousand people at a time. He ran steamships to his two hotels in the Bahamas—the Colonial and Royal Victoria—and to Havana, where he had declined to build.

He was credited with building the cities of West Palm Beach, Palm Beach, Fort Lauderdale, Miami, and the south Florida farming communities of Modello, Holland, Delray Beach, Deerfield Beach, Dania, Ojus, Perrine, Homestead, Kenansville, and Okeechobee. Considered one of the great capitalist builders of the turn of the century, he viewed his accomplishments with the pride of ownership. "My domain," he boasted, "begins in Jacksonville."[1]

The Henry Morrison Flagler who reshaped Florida was the same man John D. Rockefeller once called "the brains behind the Standard Oil Company." Several times in his life, he diligently labored to master a field of business, and after having done so, made a seemingly sudden switch to a new enterprise.

He worked with calculated boldness, and drove through or beat down whatever opposed him. In 1844, aged fourteen, he left home near Medina, New York, passed through Buffalo, and headed for Ohio, the home of his half brother Daniel Harkness. Dan, seven years Henry's senior and his hero, managed the Harkness family general store in Republic and had arranged a job for Henry as his assistant. In 1852, Flagler was awarded a full partnership in Harkness and Company and one year later married Dan's young cousin Mary. He prospered along with the business.

Like many another entrepreneur, Flagler saw a chance to make money from the Civil War. After taking advantage of a provision in the draft law of 1862 that allowed men of means to avoid conscription by hiring someone else to fight for them—Rockefeller did the same—Flagler sold his interest in the booming Harkness and Company back to the family and threw his profit and life savings into salt mining in Michigan. The war had brought incredible demands for salt, and the mine flourished until the armistice, when salt prices crashed and Flagler was left with a $50,000 debt, no savings, and a family to support. At thirty-six, he was broke.

He returned to Ohio and had begun to settle into a career in the grain and distillery business when John D. Rockefeller, whom Flagler had befriended before the Civil War, asked the Harkness family, through Henry, to invest in his Cleveland oil business. In 1867, Stephen Harkness, Mary Flagler's cousin, agreed to put $100,000 into Rockefeller's enterprise, providing Henry would control the investment as a partner. According to all reports, Flagler provided the strategic genius while Rockefeller managed the details. Flagler suggested incorporation of the Standard Oil Company and drew up the appropriate document; Flagler pressed for control of all aspects of the business—production, transport, refining, packaging, and marketing. The goal, he told the *Bellevue* (Ohio) *Gazette* in 1906, was to make "good oil as cheaply as possible" and to sell it "for all we could get."[2] Through the height of his Florida ventures, Flagler remained active in the company he had created. The experience he gained in building a corporate monopoly, he applied with a vengeance to constructing his tropical empire.

Henry Flagler first visited Florida in 1876 while seeking a healthy climate for his wife, Mary Harkness, who suffered from chronic bronchitis. One daughter, Jennie Louise, had recently married a young financier; another had died in early childhood fifteen years before; and a third child, Henry ("Harry") Harkness Flagler, was seven. Although the family had not escaped tragedy (few did in this age without vaccines and advanced sanitation), it was by the measure of any day prosperous and privileged. But each northern winter further weakened Mary, and the family physician advised that a change of climate was crucial.

In the 1870s, Florida, because of its warm, relatively dry winters, was the favored wintering ground for people from the Northeast and Midwest suffering respiratory problems. Health spas and rest homes dotted its north and central regions. Despite the state's growing popularity, there was at that time no way to travel from New York to Jacksonville—Florida's major city—quickly, reliably, and comfortably. The train from New York to Savannah was acceptable, but the connection to Jacksonville took sixteen hours and offered no sleeping cars. As alternatives, one could take the longest route and sail from New York or ride the rails to Savannah and then board a steamship for Jacksonville. The Flaglers chose the latter course. Once in Jacksonville, they took a steamer south, up the north-flowing St. Johns River to the little hamlet of Tocoi where they transferred to a slow-moving narrow-gauge train bound for St. Augustine. The landscape was flat and sandy, filled with monotonous scrub and longleaf pine forest.

St. Augustine, already renowned as the country's oldest city, pleased Flagler no better than did the transportation. The town's promoters claimed—inaccurately—it was the site of Ponce de León's first landfall in 1512. Whatever its origin and history, Flagler found that its hotel lacked amenities, the food was poorly prepared, and his fellow guests were predominantly hopeless consumptives.

Despite the urging of her physicians and of Henry, Mary Harkness Flagler did not return to Florida. She refused to leave her husband, and he would not leave New York, loath to lay aside his work at Standard Oil for a place he disliked. Ironically, Henry returned to Florida in 1882, a year after Mary's death. With the permission of his physician, he traveled for recuperation from a liver ailment to St. Augustine, for reasons he never explained.

In an 1887 interview, he said of his second visit to the three-hundred-year-old city:

I was surprised when I got here. There had been a wonderful change in the former state of things. Instead of the depressing accommodations of the years before, I found the San Marco one of the most comfortable and best kept hotels in the world and filled, too, not with consumptives, but that *class of society one meets at the great watering places of Europe*—men who go there to enjoy themselves and not for the benefit of their health. . . .

. . . I liked the place and the climate, and it occurred to me very strongly that someone with sufficient means ought to provide accommodations for that class of people who are not sick, but who come here to enjoy the climate [and] have plenty of money. [Emphasis added][3]

As a widower, Flagler moved to reestablish a social life he had neglected for nearly two decades, and in June 1883, he married Ida Alice Shourds, the former actress who had served as Mary's nurse. They spent that winter in St. Augustine and returned the following year to find a new hotel under construction and to observe a festival commemorating Ponce de León's landing. Sometime during that trip, Flagler decided to build the Hotel Ponce de Leon, establishing a pattern of operation that he followed with little deviation in all his Florida business ventures. He arranged for a resident, the physician Andrew Anderson, who became his closest friend and confidant, to serve as his agent in St. Augustine in purchasing property and navigating the intricacies of local politics. Early in his work with Standard Oil, he had used the same approach to avoid unwanted publicity and to hold down land prices that inevitably soared whenever rumors about his interest began circulating. His second line of defense was more telling than the first: When sellers did attempt to charge him exorbitant prices, he simply walked away from the deal and built his hotel or laid his tracks elsewhere. (Walt Disney applied these same principles ninety years later in putting together land for Disney World.)

Having selected a locale, Flagler would do all that he felt necessary to assure that his hotels had adequate and competent staff and support facilities, even if this meant he had to finance and build an electric company, waterworks, streets, harbors, or an entire town. He spared no expense to guarantee that his guests were properly served because he knew if they were not they would leave as surely as he had once fled St. Augustine and Jacksonville.

Flagler hired two young New York architects, John Carrère and Thomas Hastings, to design the Ponce de Leon as a luxury hotel that complemented the sixteenth-century buildings of St. Augustine while containing the conveniences of the late nineteenth century. They drew up plans for a Moorish-style structure that would be one of the earliest and largest cast-concrete buildings in the country—poured from a mixture of sand, cement, and coquina, a distinctive form of limestone that dominates the coast around St. Augustine. At one point, they employed twelve hundred black laborers from along the St. Johns River to tamp the concrete into wooden forms. Work began in December 1885 and was completed the end of May 1887 at a cost of $2.5 million. The Ponce de Leon opened officially in January 1888, the beginning of the next tourist season.

The hotel occupied four and one-half acres, with a third of that devoted to the dining hall, white servants' quarters (blacks being relegated to more distant shanties), kitchen, and storage facilities. There were two water towers, holding sixteen thousand gallons each, in case of fire; writing and smoking rooms; a barber shop; ladies' billiard room; artesian wells to supply healthful if somewhat sulfuric drinking water; electricity throughout; and 540 guest rooms and suites. Louis Tiffany—at the time relatively unknown—designed the windows. The place lacked only one amenity—private bathrooms, which were soon added. Although to fashion-conscious resort goers the Ponce de Leon never quite lived up to the glory of that first season, for eight decades it opened every winter to receive guests. Now the home of Flagler College, it is one of only four Flagler hotels still standing. (Of the rest, the Alcazar is the St. Augustine City Hall and museum; the Cordova, the St. Johns County Courthouse; the Breakers, a luxury hotel.)

The Ponce de Leon catered to the wealthy, with rooms ranging from $39 a day up to $75 or more. For tourists of somewhat more modest means Flagler constructed across the street the three-hundred-room Alcazar, a smaller hotel designed, again, by Carrère and Hastings, and featuring an indoor swimming pool with gallery and casino with Roman, Russian, and Turkish baths. Both the Alcazar and its larger neighbor drew rave notices in the travel press, which said that Flagler had transformed the sleepy old town of two thousand, the resting place of consumptives and other respiratory invalids, into the Florida Newport.

That assessment proved premature. During the 1890s—the Gay Nineties—cold winters, yellow fever epidemics, and a deterioration (because of overlogging) of the physical beauty of north Florida drove Flagler south, where he developed new, larger resorts. Again, wealthy winter visitors rushed to them. Yet the construction of the Ponce and Alcazar and Flagler's purchase and improvement of the two-hundred-room Casa Monica (rechristened the Cordova) brought to St. Augustine increased recognition and a prosperity that has persisted to the present.

The degree to which Flagler succeeded in bending St. Augustine to his will indicates the validity of his notion that few public officials and civic leaders, when presented with a choice, opt for freedom over financial gain. Flagler built the Alcazar on a site his principals had led people to believe would be a park. Protest was damped to a whimper by construction, within the new hotel, of a shopping arcade. In 1889 he blocked construction of a streetcar line in the city because it would compete with a transportation system he contemplated building. And when he wanted the land—for the Alcazar—on which a church sat, he acquired it by offering to build a new church and parsonage in a different location. According to one report:

> Flagler built the Grace Methodist Episcopal Church on the new site from materials similar to the ones used on the Ponce de Leon. [But] he made it clear to his contractors that the church was not to have the same careful attention as the hotel: "I see that you are wheeling the muck into the church lot. Country sand is good enough for them."[4]

That Flagler would order the use of sand in that situation is sadly indicative of his contempt for those he considered his inferiors. Both malaria and yellow fever were believed caused by miasma, or swamp gas, that was supposed to emanate from dirty, standing water of the sort that may settle in excavations for new buildings or in low-lying land. During the construction of the Ponce, Flagler, worried about a malaria outbreak, demanded that special care be taken in preparing the foundation and filling the marsh around it. However, the Methodist Episcopal churchpeople, being local residents and of a different religious denomination, did not warrant such elaborate precautionary measures. He was a churchgoing man, the son of a Presbyterian preacher, but charity when related to business had its limits. (On the other hand, when his daughter Jennie Louise

Benedict, after divorce and remarriage, died in 1889, he constructed the St. Augustine Presbyterian Church in her honor. A
mausoleum, added in 1904, holds the remains of Jennie Louise,
her child, Mary Harkness, and Henry Flagler.)

Transportation was vital to the success of all of Flagler's
Florida ventures. Within a month of breaking ground for the
Ponce de Leon, he purchased, with several partners, the Jacksonville, St. Augustine and Halifax River Railroad, a short line
that served roughly the area for which it was named. This
shrewd move enabled him not only to monopolize land routes
to his hotel but also to begin to acquire land. For each mile of
track or waterway a railway or canal company completed, the
Florida state government pledged tens of thousands of acres.
Although technically "submerged," or swamp, lands, the parcels were frequently flatwoods inundated during the height of
the rainy season—if at all. The railroad increased the value of
the land to settlers at least five times over, but even in its natural
state the acreage was rich in potential for logging and turpentine
manufacture.

In addition to the inducements offered by the state government, property owners would trade real estate to railroad companies for the laying of their tracks along specific routes or to
agreed-upon locales. Trains were the fastest, most reliable vehicles for transportation of produce and goods; the alternatives,
steamships or sailboats, were subject to the vagaries of tides,
weather, and shifting channels. Railroads thus represented to
wealthy capitalists a shrewd investment for the short and long
term. In the view of most late-nineteenth-century business and
political leaders, railroads also represented a way to improve
society and enhance the prestige of their builders—an ego in-
ducement of great power. The critic Larzer Ziff said in his book
The American 1890s that the goal of many late-nineteenth-
century capitalists "was to hoist Darwin up one side of the locomotive and the Bible on the other and run a railroad that would
never go bankrupt."[5]

Over a three-year period, in addition to the Jacksonville, St.
Augustine and Halifax River Railroad, Flagler bought two other
local lines, which were owed more than a million acres of land.
(He ultimately collected only 250,000 of those, forced by the
state to settle for less.) By 1889, though, he had literally reached
the end of the line. What lay south of Daytona on the east coast

of the peninsula was beyond the reach of existing rails, a land served, if at all, by small steamships and shallow draft sailing vessels, a region of scattered settlements and homesteaders who lived by hunting, fishing, and garden-plot farming. Inland lay the vast, unfenced cattle ranges, where large profits could be made from trade with Cuba—and few places could be found to spend them. Brigands and fugitives roamed every desolate area, and in some cases their crimes were as great as the tales about them. South lay the sawgrass marshes of the Everglades, which originated on their northern extremity at Lake Okeechobee and ran down to Florida Bay at the tip of the peninsula. Largely unexplored and unmapped, they were a haven for no more than five hundred people: outcasts, hunters, hermits, and Indians. A few tourists went as far south as the Everglades, interested in hunting and fishing for sport; bold ones among them even built winter homes along the coasts. But if the 'Glades entered the consciousness of polite company at all, they did so as vast and ominous wilderness, to be claimed through drainage for civilization.

In 1892, Flagler merged his lines into the Jacksonville, St. Augustine and Indian River Railway Company and simultaneously received a charter to extend rail service from Daytona to Miami at a rate of eight thousand acres a mile. In reorganizing the railroad, Flagler severed a business relationship between his lines and the Jacksonville, Tampa, and Key West Railroad of Henry Plant, with whom he would later run a steamship service. At the same time, Flagler hired as vice president for his company the former general counsel of Plant's railway, Joseph F. Parrott, who almost immediately established himself as Flagler's top lieutenant in the state. Flagler also retained another Plant official, James E. Ingraham, to serve as head of his land department. The hirings were something of a preemptive strike. Just a few months earlier Plant had dispatched Ingraham on a survey of the upper Everglades to determine whether he could bring his railroad south along the Gulf coast from Tampa to Fort Myers, the old cow town and army post where Thomas Edison had his winter home, and from there cross the peninsula past Lake Okeechobee to Fort Dallas at the mouth of the Miami River, the trading village that became Miami. Although a highway now runs from Fort Myers to Fort Lauderdale and farms and roads cross the drained upper Everglades, Ingraham found them inhospitable to Plant's plans and the project was abandoned until the 1920s when the successor to Plant's railroad company made the crossing.

In four years, Flagler pushed his railway down the coast, stopping at New Smyrna in 1892, Rockledge, near Titusville, in 1893, West Palm Beach in 1894, and Miami in 1896, employing laborers fetched by fair means and foul from around the state, from New York, and from Caribbean islands. His contractors, following the practice of the day, leased convicts (most commonly black men) from the state and worked them under conditions worse than those of the most inhumane plantation, punishing waywardness with whippings and imprisonment in sweatboxes. The goal was to get the work done as fast as possible in order to meet state-mandated deadlines and claim those valuable acres. In laying the eighty miles of track from Daytona to Titusville, his company employed fifteen hundred men, who completed the task in seven months. In lives and money, it was a costly endeavor, the work of a man who would not accept that something could not be done. Significantly, the tracks were laid to stay, unlike those of some railways of the period that were slapped down simply to qualify for the state land bonuses. Flagler was building for the long term. Neither the insubstantial sand and swamps nor the economic panic of the 1890s that threw one third of the state's railroads and many of its largest investors into bankruptcy slowed Flagler's advance.

He paused after reaching Miami to consolidate his east coast domain and plan for his assault on the Keys. Flagler weighed the rewards of his plan against its risks. He placed in his will a provision that his estate should not undertake the project: He didn't want his heirs to lose his empire on such an uncertain venture. By 1905, two years after bringing his tracks to Homestead, a small agricultural community south of Miami near the tip of the east coast of the peninsula, he had determined that the Florida East Coast Railway would go to Key West regardless of whether he was living or dead, and changed his will.

With just over seventeen thousand residents, Key West was the state's third largest city and one of the most prosperous communities in the nation. Some hyperbolic politicians liked to call it the American Gibraltar because of its position at the confluence of the Atlantic Ocean and Gulf of Mexico and its strategic view of the Straits of Florida, the major shipping lane in the region. As seat of an admiralty court and the dominant port in the region, it had served as an international bazaar of salvaged goods for more than eighty years. Since the 1860s, it had also produced cigars for a smoke-happy world, hosting a thriving community of Cuban exiles and émigrés to match its black and white populations. The sponge beds that surrounded the island supported in 1895 alone fourteen hundred men working on three hundred boats, hooking $385,000 worth of the creatures out of the shallow water for sale around the world. It was, in short, a distinctly unusual American city, but also one beset by problems that worsened in the decades to come.

Key West's gradual decline began around the turn of the century. Construction of lighthouses and the advent of steam engines had combined to reduce the number of ships foundering on the barrier reef, and the growth of national salvage and insurance companies operating through agents assigned to specific areas had cut out independent wreckers who had roamed the Straits of Florida and lower east coast. Meanwhile, many of the factories that had moved from Cuba in the 1860s and 1870s and made the city the largest producer of cigars in the world had relocated to Tampa. (To reverse the trend, in 1899 Flagler, who fancied cigars, offered a $50,000 bonus to any major manufacturer willing to relocate from Tampa to Key West, to help guarantee a steady income for his planned projects; no one took the inducement.) A U.S. Navy base, a few drydocks, turtle kraals (pens near shore where the captured sea turtles were kept alive until killed and cooked), fish and sponge markets, salt pits, and a smattering of guesthouses rounded out the economic base.

Flagler believed his railroad would revitalize Key West by providing reliable transport of coal and provisions for Navy ships and by allowing freighters passing through the planned canal across the Isthmus of Panama to transfer their cargoes at the city docks onto trains—his trains —for rapid shipment north. His ferries would be within ninety miles of Cuba, ready to carry people and goods to that tropical island. He also expected to profit from the lime and pineapple growers of the upper Keys, as well as from the loggers who were taking out mahogany, mangroves, buttonwood, and anything else that could be used for furniture, ships, or charcoal.

Except for Key West most of the islands were barely populated; some held a settler or two, maybe a few families. Many of those people were, in modern parlance, dropouts. They lived in rude, often dirty shacks built of salvaged wood, with palmetto-thatched roofs. They were content in their isolation, raising fruit and some vegetables; taking the fish they needed; hunting and picking up odd jobs as guides or smugglers when they felt like making money. Lacking wells, all residents used cisterns to collect rain and dew; some stacked rocks around the roots of trees to encourage condensation. By the time the railroad arrived, cisterns for the houses of poorer residents were Standard Oil cans placed under the eaves and fed by a wooden gutter. Boats provided the only means of travel between keys or to the peninsula. The islanders thus lived a kind of subsistence existence that Flagler and tourists who came to fish found difficult to understand, especially after experiencing their first fierce mosquito attack.

The islands were exceedingly fragile ecologically, many scarcely land at all. The thin layer of nutrient-poor sand that covered the coral in the upper Keys and the oolitic limestone around Key West provided barely enough soil to grow lemons and limes—including the distinctive Key limes that can be found in the United States only on the Keys and in Dade County—sisal, pineapples, coconuts, and other tropical fruits and a few vegetables. Commercial agricultural was, however, precarious. The soil of the Keys rapidly lost its nutrient value when heavily cultivated; rain, which provided the islands' only fresh water, could fall in quantities measured in feet per day or not at all—for weeks.

Nearly everyone who spent time on the Keys met at least one of their veteran, singular inhabitants. Some of Flagler's officers became their suppliers, agents, and friends. William Krome, while chief engineer for the Overseas Railroad, befriended Nicholas Mateovitch, a hermit on No Name Key who raised tropical fruit. In 1912, David Fairchild, the founder of the U.S. Department of Agriculture Section of Foreign Plant Introduction, went with Krome to meet the Russian émigré, and examine his trees. Fairchild wrote in his memoirs, *The World Was My Garden:*

> Mateovitch was a picturesque old fellow, with a great shaggy beard, large head and perfectly enormous hands. After fighting in our Civil War, he had homesteaded a hundred and sixty acres on the Key in 1868, and, although he had a wife and son in Key West, he had lived as a hermit on this little island for forty-three years. In a haphazard way, he had planted patches of fruit trees and vegetables, and as he was

particularly fond of sapodillas, he had many trees of this delicious fruit. More than once he had nearly starved to death and doubtless would have done so had it not been for Mr. Krome's kindness in sending him food from time to time. He was morbidly suspicious and set gun traps in the brush, stretching invisible wires about, so that visitors to the Key were in danger of being shot. . . . [His] shack was incredibly disorderly and unkempt.[6]

Offshore from the Keys was an aquatic wonderland, lush and hypersensitive to changing conditions. Coral reefs buffering the islands from the deep water of the Straits of Florida and the Atlantic housed fish and crustaceans in quantities that seemed limitless to settlers. Green turtles flocked in the aquatic grass. Manatee were there, and for some years the Caribbean monk seal. Manatee are hard to find anywhere in Florida now, and when they appear they've often been carved by boat propellers. The last monk seal was sighted forty years ago. Green turtles struggle to survive. Pollution from decades of development, ship groundings, and human divers have taken their toll on the reefs, leaving many of them diseased and weak.

Unfortunately, no census of wildlife on the Keys was conducted before the railroad builders came, and after they had finished, no accurate counts could be made—the changes were that great. The upper Keys—those closest to the mainland—hosted rich hardwood forests, called there and throughout the state, hammocks. Like their name, these woodlands are distinctively Floridian, readily identifiable yet difficult to define, ranging in size from tens to thousands of acres and capable of containing more than three hundred types of trees, flowers, and shrubs. Most assuredly *hammock* is a variant of the English *hummoch*, a word of obscure origin that refers to a forested area raised above a marsh, although over the years scholars have suggested alternative derivations, most prominently that its root lies in *hamaca*, an Arawak word meaning a mass of vegetation floating in a river. There are several varieties of hammock in Florida, identified by tree type and soil moisture content, but all represent the climax forest of the state and generally occupy its richest soil, which their decaying leaves and limbs enrich.

The hammocks of the southern end of the peninsula and the Keys consist of a unique mix of tropical and temperate hardwoods—mahogany, live oak, royal palms, gumbo-limbo, and dozens more—found nowhere else in North America. They also host *Liguus* tree snails, brightly colored prizes of collectors and scientists who tried to determine how each hammock, each Key, could support a different species. *Ligui* also inhabited the tree islands of the Everglades—the Everglade Keys, as they were called—but otherwise were found nowhere else on the continent. No one was—or is—quite sure how they arrived from Cuba. On and around Big Pine Key resided the dwarf key-deer, a subspecies of the whitetail that when grown weighs about fifty pounds, or as much as a medium-sized dog. The deer lives nowhere else in the world. The whole stretch of islands was a birder's paradise.

Charles Torrey Simpson, a naturalist for the Smithsonian Institution, lived in, and tramped through, south Florida and the Keys for more than fifty years, observing and collecting wildlife and plants. In his 1932 book, *Florida Wild Life,* he wrote, "Looking back to the days when South Florida was a beautiful wilderness filled with magnificent wild life [*sic*] and then contemplating the wreck of today, is enough to sicken the heart of a lover of nature, yes, even of any sensible person who has a true valuation of the useful and beautiful."[7] Flagler's railroad invaded that wilderness, from Daytona Beach to Key West, and the last 128 miles were in many ways the wildest and most desolate.

Once he decided to proceed, Flagler wanted to move quickly, driven by awareness of his advancing age and by the terms of the state charter that required completion of the railway by May 1912. William J. Krome, the young engineer, conducted a survey to determine the best route—whether to build south from Homestead and across the Keys as if they were stepping-stones; or to cross the sawgrass prairies of the Everglades southwestward to Cape Sable and then construct a bridge across the shallow, shielded Florida Bay before island-hopping to Key West. The cost of the second option was judged prohibitive and thus, for economic reasons alone, the area now known as Everglades National Park was spared. Construction would proceed from Homestead to Key Largo and then by bridge and causeway to Key West.

Flagler's initial intention was simply to fill the southeast Everglades from Homestead to Key Largo and the channels between the Keys because that was the most economical and direct construction method. But federal government engineers challenged this plan because they feared, as did people familiar with the geography of south Florida, that by preventing the flow of water between Biscayne Bay, the Atlantic, and Florida Bay, the causeways would force the Gulf Stream to change its course, thus altering the climate of the area. They worried as well that hurricane damage would become more severe if tidal surges accompanying those storms were blocked outright or forced through tight channels between keys, which would amplify their power. Flagler compromised—a little—by agreeing to put in eleven miles of concrete viaducts and just over seventeen miles of deep-water bridges.

Because the only contractors bidding for the project had demanded "cost-plus," rather than providing a fixed estimate— an absurd condition given the uncertainty involved in the work—Flagler determined that his Florida East Coast Railway Company would handle the construction itself. He hired Joseph Meredith as chief engineer, with Krome serving as his assistant and field supervisor. Work crews finally moved out of Homestead toward Jewfish Creek, across the southeastern Everglades in May 1905.

Flagler's international work force, which had reached four thousand men by early 1906, was composed of blacks from Florida, Georgia, Alabama, and other southern states; Swedish, Italian, and Irish immigrants; divers from Greece by way of Tarpon Springs, Florida; shanghaied Bowery bums; California drifters; Cubans; Conchs, as the native Key Westers of Anglo-Saxon origin by way of the Bahamas were known; Crackers, the sometimes derogatory name for poor Florida whites from the piney woods of the peninsula; West Indians; Minorcan steamboat pilots from St. Augustine; and assorted others. The census is detailed because in 1907 the Florida East Coast Railway and its construction bosses had to defend themselves against charges of forced labor. In the process, Flagler produced a statement analyzing the relative merits as workers of each group, singling out the Conchs, Crackers, and Florida and southern blacks for his opprobrium because they were unwilling to perform hard labor for low pay. Chief Engineer Meredith, his assistant Krome, a third railroad employee, and a New York labor contractor were indicted in New York for violating anti-slavery and kidnapping laws. Although charges against Meredith were dismissed and the others were acquitted, a stigma remained, and for years Flagler was accused by his detractors of employing slave labor.

The work camps were rough affairs. Mosquitoes and other insects swarmed over everyone who bled or drew breath; and isolation, heat, humidity, and long terms of labor proved physically and mentally numbing. Flagler banned alcohol from the camps but entrepreneurs brought floating saloons and bordellos to the Keys and moored them nearby. Many of the workers deserted as soon as the paymaster arrived and they could arrange passage on the first flimsy craft for Miami or Key West. Despite the difficulties, the work progressed. The crews drained and filled a lake near Key Largo that had appeared on no map and, therefore, was named Surprise. They hacked down and burned out hardwood hammocks for fuel, housing, and railroad ties. They clear-cut islands of Dade County pine, whose heartwood was prized for fence posts, ties, and housing because it was impervious to termites and rot. It also made good fuel for locomotives because it burned hot and long.

In 1906, a hurricane ripped across the Keys, killing two hundred workers and delaying the project for a year, during which time three thousand men were laid off. Most of those furloughed drifted to Miami or Key West where they added new escapades to the boom-time tales of those cities. Miami especially was known for the jook joints and bordellos that sat just outside its "dry" boundaries. Hurricanes struck again in 1908 and 1909, causing further construction delays but resulting in less loss of life because the railroad had learned to take precautions to shield men and equipment from high winds and storm tides.

Though few considered it at the time, the natural cost of building the railroad was as high as the human toll. In his 1920 book, *In Lower Florida Wilds,* Simpson described some of the effects:

A few years ago a hammock that was perhaps the finest and most extensive in the lower part of the state covered [Key Largo] for several miles in the vicinity of Cross Key. The Florida East Coast Railway cut a right of way through this for the Key West extension of its line and piled the felled timber along the edge of the clearing. When it was fairly dried out it was set on fire by sparks from the locomotives (so claimed) and this unfortunately communicated to the forest. For

months the fire slowly ate its way through the peat-like soil
and as it crept along its ruinous way the grand old giants of
the hammock toppled and fell. Every vestige of the soil was
consumed and today the charred ruin glints in the sun as a
silent and pathetic protest against useless waste and folly.[8]

Farmers contributed to the destruction. They razed forests
in order to plant pineapples, which the train carried to northern
markets. The hurricane of 1906 smashed the industry and
twenty years later the same hurricane that flattened Miami and
other southeast Florida towns battered the lime groves that
farmers had planted in place of pineapples. Cheaper Mexican
limes that flooded United States markets during the Depression
ruined what remained of the islands' citrus industry, and Key
limes became a dooryard fruit in south Florida.

Because it was the work finally of one man and his fortune,
the railroad had an economic life independent of struggling
farmers and natural disaster. Inexorably the construction progressed. Overworked, Chief Engineer Meredith died in mid-
project, and Krome, at only thirty-two years of age, assumed full
command. From Knight's Key to Bahia Honda Key, bridges
were thrown across seven miles of water with only a few touch-
downs on small islands; and from Bahia Honda to Big Pine Key
a bridge spanned two miles of deep, open water. From June
1911 to January 1912, twenty-five hundred men worked around
the clock not only to meet the terms of the state charter but to
do so in time for Flagler's eighty-second birthday.

The Overseas Railroad and the opening of a railroad-car
ferry to Havana led to a brief revival in the sagging fortunes of
Key West, whose population climbed to twenty-two thousand.
Expansion of the naval base during World War I further bol-
stered its economy. During Prohibition, the smuggling of liquor—and sometimes drugs and people—brought instant cash
to local skippers and federal law-enforcement dollars to the
county and city governments. Overall, though, the end of
the war ushered in a long decline. Trade with Cuba slipped, the
Navy cut its forces, and the last of the cigar factories closed.
The Depression ruined tourism and fishing; a blight devastated
the sponge beds. By 1934, Key West's population had fallen by
half, and the city was bankrupt. It was during this period that
Ernest Hemingway made the city his home and built the island's

first private swimming pool (his former home, now a museum, is one of the city's most popular tourist attractions). Other writers and painters came for the calm, the weather, and tropical flavor of the place but they couldn't reverse its fortunes.

At one point, the Federal Economic Recovery Administration contemplated evacuating the city, then decided to turn it into a tourist mecca, a plan that had begun to work when a hurricane severed Flagler's masterwork, the city's only link to the mainland. Raging in from the Atlantic the storm tore across the middle of the Keys on Labor Day, 1935. It was one of the most vicious on record, with wind speeds estimated at 200 to 250 miles an hour—74 is the minimum for hurricane force; 150 is considered large. Barometers in the area fell to 26.35 inches— the lowest sea-level reading on record at the National Weather Service until Hurricane Gilbert smashed across Jamaica and the Yucatan Peninsula in September 1988.

A rescue train was dispatched by the Florida East Coast Railway to Upper Matecumbe Key to pick up crews working to close a forty-mile gap in the Overseas Highway, which the federal government was building. The workers were World War I veterans who had marched on Washington as members of the "Bonus Army" demanding promised, but never delivered, payment for their military service. Their protest gained them jobs in the Keys, where they received thirty dollars a month for harsh toil. The hurricane knocked the relief train off the tracks and ripped through the veterans' shanty-camp, killing nearly eight hundred; only five hundred corpses could be found.

Although the trestles and arches of the Overseas Railroad withstood the winds, the tracks were ripped off. As conservationists and old seadogs had predicted, miles of embankments and causeways were washed out. Most of the forty-mile stretch between Upper Matecumbe and Big Pine was lost.

Bankrupt, the Florida East Coast Railway, which became part of the Alfred I. Du Pont Estate holdings in Florida, could rebuild nothing. For $640,000, the state purchased the remaining causeway and right of way and used the railroad's trestles and arches to complete the Overseas Highway. But for two years, there was no land route from Key West to the rest of the peninsula—for the first time in over two decades. The isolation increased the city's financial problems and made life difficult for its ten thousand residents, who had grown accustomed to receiving goods by train.

The new highway opened on July 4, 1938. Motorists on U.S. Highway 1 could drive from Maine's northern border to Key West—eventually, dreamers thought, the road, with ferry links, would stretch from Labrador to Guatemala. Joining Miami to Key West, the highway was expected to help yank the islands from bankruptcy and south Florida from Depression. The trip took five hours; tourists began to make the road hum.

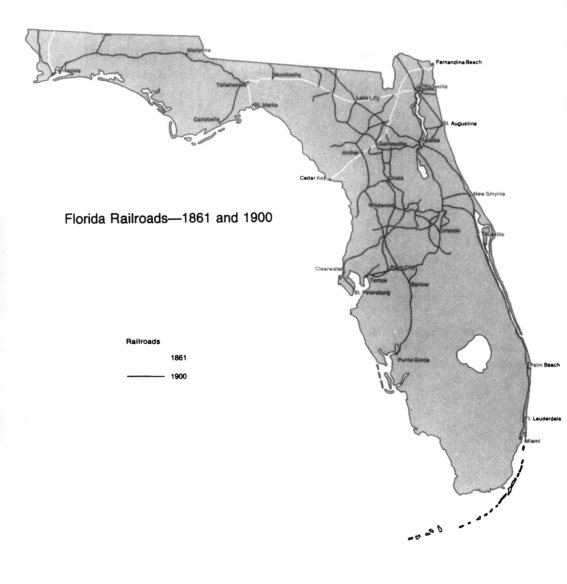

Florida Railroads—1861 and 1900

Railroads

1861

——— 1900

Institute of Science and Public Affairs, Florida State University, *Atlas of Florida,*

TWO

The American Riviera

Flagler's railroad and resort hotels open the tropical southeast coast to tourists and settlers. A handful of residents begin to speak of paradise lost. Desire for profit and pleasure win out.

In taking his railway down the east coast into south Florida, Flagler brought to reality a dream of Florida's promoters, who had long considered the region prime for agricultural and resort development. The problem had been transportation, with the place accessible only by boat, usually from Key West. "If large settlements, towns and cities were founded there, and regular communications opened," said one enthusiastic publicist, "it would be one of the most delightful regions of America, healthy, agreeable, while the products of the salt-water coast, fresh-water lakes and rivers, fields, gardens, and groves would furnish mankind, in all seasons, the best and most delicious of all foods the human nature craves."[1] There weren't many freshwater lakes there, but little matter; hearsay determined people's knowledge of the region.

In south Florida, Flagler created the communities that, more than his railroad, marked his place in the annals of Florida development: Palm Beach, West Palm Beach, and Miami. He created them and for a time ruled them with a firm hand though he held office in none. They grew devoted to the twin gods of money and pleasure, and in the process they helped define America's notion of the good life.

After completing his railroad to Rockledge in February 1893, Flagler announced his intention to make a tiny village on the northeast shore of Lake Worth the site of a huge new resort hotel. The Coast Guard called the place the Lake Worth Settlement; in 1887, its three residents named it Palm City so they could qualify for a post office. Flagler declared it Palm Beach, the future capital of his Florida domain and the southern mecca for his wealthy peers. His announcement set off a frenzy of land speculation that caused the settlers on the lake to think they had, indeed, discovered paradise. Contrary to his usual practice, Flagler paid the asking price for the real estate he wanted. In 1893, he bought for $75,000 a homestead that had sold seven years earlier for $10,000; the new owner had not improved it substantially. But Flagler wanted that site on the lake's eastern shore for a new hotel, the Royal Poinciana. It would be the largest and most luxurious resort in the world, built in a city devoted solely to the wealthy. For the one-hundred-acre parcel he put together for the hotel and its grounds, he paid $300,000—an average of $3,000 an acre—which was at that time in that area an exorbitant price. Flagler bought additional lots for houses. On the west shore of the lake, he purchased land for a workers' town, which he named West Palm Beach.

The four hundred or so people calling the shores of Lake Worth home were aghast and agog. Those living on the north end, where the Palm Beaches would grow, sought to cash in on the land rush and speculative fever. Those to the south, near and on an island named Hypoluxo—which they interpreted to mean "water all around; no get out"—wondered whether the boom would bring them any profit at all. It did not, but it did confirm that their life of relative ease, common on both coasts of Florida but primitive by standards of the day, was gone. Charles Pierce, one of the earliest settlers of Hypoluxo, said in his memoirs:

> By 1893, before the coming of the railroad, the people of the lake, especially those who had arrived in the seventies, no longer thought they were living on the frontier. . . . [T]here were eight post offices on the lake . . . , four general stores, three hotels, two large boarding houses and a weekly newspaper published at Juno. Nonetheless, the hotels, and the founding of the city of West Palm Beach brought an end to an era.[2]

Flagler was enamored of the lush tropical vegetation, especially the coconut palms that graced his resort and inspired its name. They came from the Spanish barque *Providencia,* which ran aground offshore in 1878 and jettisoned its cargo, and a project that Ezra Osborn and Elnathan T. Field launched a few years later to plant coconuts from Miami to Jupiter—an eighty-mile stretch of the peninsula's southeast coast, thinking the palms would grow to produce a fortune. Rabbits ate most of the seedlings, but a few survived; more important, the campaign employed many young men for some months—and paid them cash wages.

For the settlers from Lake Worth to Biscayne Bay, cash was a rare commodity. Theirs was an isolated region, where people traveled by boat or beach-walking, sometimes a combination of the two. The journey from Hypoluxo—just above Boca Raton—to William Brickell's general store on the Miami River, a distance of approximately sixty miles, took three days of walking along the sand and crossing several rivers. Mail traveled that way, in its first and final legs. From Biscayne Bay, it would go to Key West by schooner, then steamer to Tampa and train to Jacksonville, and it would come into Biscayne Bay by the same route. From the early 1870s to the opening of Flagler's railroad, Lake Worth's mail carrier walked barefoot along the waterline—the most consistently solid footing in south Florida.

For several centuries following the extirpation of the indigenous tribes by the Spanish, it was a region of scattered settlers and a few Seminole clans. Lake Worth boasted two settlers in the 1860s, a German immigrant named Lang and his wife. Lang fled his home—some reports say it was on the Indian River, others, in Georgia—to avoid the Confederate draft, and built a palmetto-thatched hut on the shores of Lake Worth. In 1867, Michael Sears and his son George sailed out of Miami for the Jupiter Inlet and found the Langs living in ignorance of the war's outcome. After hearing news of its end, the Langs left, presumably to return home, and the Searses sailed back to Biscayne Bay. Apparently, no one settled in the area again until 1872, when Charles Moore moved up from Miami and occupied the old Lang homestead. Families drifted in from around the country after that, staking claims and making the arduous trip to the state land office in Gainesville to record them. Among those early settlers—pioneers they liked to call themselves—were Hannibal Pierce, his wife Margretta, and their family, including their son Charles. Hannibal Pierce had been shipwrecked in the Keys and was a bit of a roustabout, like many of his fellow settlers. For him the place was ideal, and he became assistant keeper of the lighthouse at Jupiter Inlet before taking the family farther south on Lake Worth to Hypoluxo Island.

The southeast coast was so little known that in 1873, a shipwrecked crew nearly starved to death between Biscayne Bay and the Little River, a distance no greater than twenty miles. Within three years of that disaster, the U.S. Life Saving Service was building houses of refuge along the unsettled shore. The Gulf Stream, racing north parallel to the peninsula's east coast, passed within three miles of Lake Worth. Ships cruising south had to stay between the stream and the coast; those sailing north would catch a ride in its strong current. The weather and the necessity of running close to shore made wrecks and groundings frequent occurrences.

The Gulf Stream and trade winds brought a tropical exuberance to the southeast coast. The region was so rich in fish, game, and vegetation it is hard to imagine how people could come close to dying of hunger there. Dunes and mangroves forming the shore gave way along the coast to hardwood hammocks jutting like islands from pine forests that covered the Atlantic Coastal Ridge, an ancient marine terrace that provided the highest land around. West of the ridge, the land grew damp; pine flatwoods flourished. That was the eastern edge of the Everglades. The blend of tropical and temperate trees and shrubs that defined those hammocks made them unlike any found in north and central Florida, made them, in fact, unique in the world. The cities along the coast—Boca Raton, Fort Lauderdale, Miami, Coconut Grove (which despite its annexation by Miami continues to think of itself as a distinct community)—began as settlements in the hammocks, where the land was fertile and relatively dry.

People built their homes with scavenged lumber and thatched palmetto roofs, which kept the rain out but harbored insects, particularly the palmetto bug or cockroach—an inch-long creature that has been known to terrify unsuspecting newcomers to Florida as it glides on its stiff wings toward their beds. Mosquito nets were preferred for sleeping in the absence of windows and screens, although Bahamians and others in the Keys were known to use heavy wood shutters to close their homes, day and night. While effective against mosquitoes, the practice turned the houses into dark, sweltering boxes. Cook fires were outdoors, under—at most—a thatched cover. People ate what they could catch, shoot, or scratch from the ground.

Settlers gathered sea turtle eggs and often ate the turtles themselves. Fresh fish were had in all seasons, and Indians would bring venison from the inland for trade, along with hides, pelts, and produce. Pumpkin and sweet potatoes were staples when provisions ran low, with the latter being used for bread and coffee as well as being stewed, baked, fried, and poned. Coconuts provided fresh milk, cabbage palm was cut down for its heart, and the native cycad—coontie—was converted to starch and sold as arrowroot for eight to ten cents a pound in Key West.

Looking for cash to buy essential dry goods and equipment, the settlers turned to whatever seemed workable and productive. Although their numbers were few, their impact on the environment was often great. Around Biscayne Bay, for instance, their starch-making destroyed the coontie fields and nearly drove the ancient plant to extinction. Pierce reported that one Cracker hunter in just a year shot out the largest rookery on the north end of Lake Worth—a place called Big Pelican at Munyon's Island. "When the first settlers came to the lake," Pierce said, "they found the woods fairly alive with game. Bears were plentiful in the beach hammock and deer could be found everywhere, as well as wildcats, coon and possum, and an occasional panther."[3] Alligators and crocodiles filled the available waterways. Within a dozen years the bear, deer, herons, and curlews were hunted out of the area, although only twenty families lived there.

The federal Department of Agriculture sent the settlers seeds for wheat and barley, which would not grow in the tropics. The people learned to cultivate tomatoes, peppers, and eggplant during the winter season and to raise pineapples and citrus. They hauled their produce, plumes, hides, and salvage by boat to Titusville for transshipment north aboard steamboats. Tourists were trickling into the north end of the lake in search of warmer weather and more plentiful fish and game—stocks in north Florida having been severely depleted already. Most travelers stayed at the first Palm Beach inn, the Cocoanut Grove House of Elisha Newton Dimmick, which he opened to visitors in the late 1880s and gradually expanded. Dimmick's guest house later became the site of Whitehall, the $2.5-million gilded-marble mansion Flagler built in 1902 for his third wife, Mary Lily. The Flaglers occupied Whitehall for the last months of the winter season—roughly January through March—after spending Christmas in St. Augustine and the rest of the year in New York and Long Island. With $35,000 rugs and, in Mrs. Flagler's suite, the country's first sunken bathtub in a private residence, the Palm Beach estate possessed every luxury. One of its special effects, a pneumatic bathroom door, is believed to have closed suddenly on the elderly Flagler, causing him to lose his balance and tumble down several stairs. He broke his hip in the fall and suffered other injuries from which he never recovered. (After Mrs. Flagler's death, Whitehall became a first-class hotel and is now the Henry Morrison Flagler Museum.)

Palm Beach began, then, as a home for people looking for a climate that would mend broken respiratory systems, or allow them to live an easy, uncluttered life; as another way station for hunters, fishermen, and winter cruisers. Flagler began the rapid transformation of the place into something else entirely. In 1952, Cleveland Amory said of the nation's reigning winter resort: "To the extreme Right Wing of Old Guard Society . . . , Palm Beach has long been regarded, at best, as the country's social back door—at worst, as a kind of Buffet Society Babylon which some socially ill-advised soul unfortunately carved out of the wilds of a state which should never have been admitted into the Union, let alone into society, in the first place."[4] Drink and fornication, in that view, were the chief sport and occupation of Palm Beach residents—wealthy men, women, and spoiled children from nearly everywhere but Florida.

In May 1893, Flagler broke ground on the Lake Worth side of Palm Beach for the six-story, Colonial-style Royal Poinciana Hotel. A workers' slum sprouted immediately near the site to house the bulk of the one thousand laborers thrown at the task. They dubbed their shantytown the Styx—perhaps a reflection of their feeling toward what they built or of the exorbitant rent they paid or of their belief that they were in "the sticks," a remote and wild region. The Styx lasted until Flagler built his company town for all but his most favored white workers across Lake Worth in a two-hundred-acre enclave. On this land—considered the least desirable in the area for settlement because of its dampness—James Ingraham laid down the grid for West Palm Beach. Perhaps reflecting his own bias, he named the streets after native plants. Over the years the temporary housing was replaced with more durable structures. A city hall, post office, schools, fire station, courthouse, hospital, even a Catholic church—Flagler built them all for his company town. He developed the water-works because he needed a fresh supply for his resort, in the process charging West Palm Beach for what it used. The workers rowed across Lake Worth to Palm Beach at dawn and back at dusk until 1896 when the railroad bridge was completed and they could cross on foot after paying a toll. By then West Palm Beach already had one thousand residents and was officially incorporated. But it remained Flagler's town for years.

The Royal Poinciana opened in February 1894 with seventeen guests for its 540 rooms, 125 private bathrooms, elevators, and electricity. It opened without the gaudy display of wealth that had marked the debut of the Ponce de Leon and of Plant's Tampa Bay Hotel, but the following year it drew more guests and achieved more renown than either. The hotel had consumed 500,000 board feet of indigenous Dade County pine and of Georgia yellow pine, which was transported, like nearly all the building supplies, by rail to Jupiter and then by boat to Palm Beach. When all its wings were spread, it had seven miles of corridors, 1,150 rooms, and a full-occupancy capacity of two thousand. The fourteen hundred employees were so attentive—one worked full time filling water bottles—that they earned for the hotel the name Royal Pounce-on-'em.[5] The white staff had separate quarters, dining facilities, and even an orchestra for entertainment; the blacks lived in West Palm Beach. The grounds held beautiful and extensive gardens that endured after the hotel was razed in 1928, following a hurricane that torqued its upper floors and left the hotel cantilevered over its foundation.

As the Royal Poinciana rose, the railroad moved south. Flagler had, in fact, set his crews in a race to see whether the hotel would be completed before the tracks reached Lake Worth. The game, which the railroad lost by a little more than a month, cost the lives of twenty men. For two years after the tracks were completed to West Palm Beach, visitors crossed Lake Worth by ferry to docks at the Royal Poinciana. Then, in 1896, the private train of Flagler's friend Cornelius Vanderbilt rolled across the recently completed bridge over Lake Worth to the door of the hotel.

In the summer of 1895, less than six months after the most brutal and destructive freeze in sixty years, Flagler began construction of the Palm Beach Inn, which opened on the Atlantic shore of the island the following winter. In 1901, it was expanded to four hundred rooms, twice its initial size, and renamed the Breakers. The Breakers—made of pine heartwood like its larger mate, the Royal Poinciana—burned in 1903 and again in 1925, when it cost $7 million to rebuild. It alone, of all Flagler's chain, remains a working hotel.

Construction of the two hotels had cost Flagler more than $4 million, but they represented only part of his Palm Beach investments. For selected white employees, he built lakefront and oceanfront cottages. For his imbibing guests, he induced the formerly "dry" Palm Beachers to get "wet" and approve the sale of liquor. Since no resort at the time was complete without a casino, Flagler brought to Palm Beach Ed Bradley, the operator of the Bacchus Club at his St. Augustine Ponce de Leon Hotel, and installed him in what was to become the Bradley Beach Club. Gambling was illegal in Florida at the time, but Flagler and his wealthy friends felt free to ignore the prohibition. Membership in the gambling parlor was restricted to men until 1899 when women were admitted, over Flagler's protest, as long as they had a male escort. Other rules remained unchanged for years: "No native of Florida, no man who did not look twenty-five, no man who was under the influence of liquor, and no man not in evening clothes was permitted to gamble."[6] Palm Beach was a bastion of race and class prejudice. Blacks were kept out, unless servants or laborers, and anti-Semitism was an article of faith.

Palm Beach owed its early success as much to its fabricated insularity from poverty, disease, and labor unrest as to its lush vegetation, beautiful waters, and warmth. The resort community embodied the spirit of the Gay Nineties, a time of play and enjoyment because science, technology, and industry were generating vast new wealth. Few places were more "sporting" than Palm Beach with its beaches, its heated pools, casino, yachts, polo club, golf course, tennis courts, excursions into the wilds of Florida, gossip, and games of musical beds between mates and lovers. Adventurous, wealthy youth staged an elaborate winter ritual—starting at the opening of the tourist season at the Ponce de Leon and then hopping down the coast to Ormond Beach, which had a reputation as a young lovers' haven, and then to Palm Beach. Even travel within Palm Beach exuded an air of exotic luxury while harking back to an imagined antebellum world of smiling faces and laughter. People rode in Afromobiles, rickshaws initially pulled and then pushed—so passengers could have a better view—by uniformed black men on specially adapted bicycles. (Afromobiles remained in use until after World War II when even Palm Beach couldn't fully ignore the new racial consciousness that was sweeping the country.)

In its January 1901 issue the Florida East Coast *Homeseeker* declared, "What a great thing it will be when such monopolies as ours get control of the whole State, opening up the now worthless thousands upon thousands of acres of land, building railroads, towns, paying good wages, taxes, and making things 'get' generally." The Model Land Company published the *Home-seeker* as part of a major, well-orchestrated campaign to encourage new settlers, especially on land purchased from the Florida East Coast Railway. Flagler had established the Model Land Company in 1896 to handle sales of acreage granted him for extension of his tracks down the coast. By 1897, nearly 415,000 acres were available, with approximately a million more claimed for miles of rail laid. Shying away from one-time sales of large tracts to speculators, the company concentrated on promoting colonies for groups, homesteads for individual families.

Flagler sought to create a society that would ensure his long-term profit. Control meant selecting new settlers carefully so they would be responsible and hardworking, preferably white, Protestant families from the northern or midwestern United States or Europe. A Japanese colony was established near Boca Raton and called Yomato, but that was an exception. Modello, a farming community established north of Miami for four hundred Danish families, more neatly fit the rule. Land prices varied according to soil type and proximity to the railroad, with muckland—the richest for agriculture—initially commanding $100 an acre and pinelands $77. Although large reductions were made soon after Modello was platted, Flagler in general preferred to hold out for his asking price. Ingraham, president of the Model Land Company, was occasionally criticized by Joseph Parrott and Flagler himself for his willingness to cut prices to promote sales and help people. In the early days of Miami, for example, he wanted to offer discounts for lots to help alleviate an acute housing shortage. He was overruled.

The Flagler grand plan called for each settlement to produce cash crops the Florida East Coast Railway would then haul to market. From the earliest years of his Florida venture, Flagler promoted citriculture and truck farming as useful enterprises for new settlers. In the aftermath of the disastrous freezes of 1894–95 and 1896–97, he acted decisively to rebuild the ruined citrus industry and, in the process, restore the confidence of investors and homesteaders alike. The first of these freezes ruined north Florida groves and caused Flagler to push his railroad south immediately rather than wait a few years as he had once planned.[7] Growers recovered and planted new groves farther south, where killer frosts, they hoped, would not descend.

In February 1897, a month after Flagler's Royal Palm Hotel opened at the mouth of the Miami River, frigid weather swept down the peninsula freezing groves and gardens. Crops were ruined throughout Dade County and into the Keys. The damage threatened to drive into bankruptcy farmers and growers who had not yet fully recovered from the icy assaults of 1894–95. Again Flagler acted without hesitation. He sent Ingraham into the countryside to loan people whatever money they needed to replant—at 6-percent interest but with no time limit for repayment. It was a shrewd and timely business move. Ingraham said:

> When I wired my associates and told them what Mr. Flagler had told me to do, they were tremendously revived, their courage was restored, their energies renewed and they realized what a great thing it was to do and why they chose to stay by Mr. Flagler and work with him and for him rather than independently. Within seventy-two hours of the time that the first relief check was issued, vegetables, tomatoes, snap beans began to move, first by express, then by carload, then by trainload, and I want to tell you that this season was so good a one as to price and quantity as to establish permanently the trucking industry in Florida.[8]

In addition to allaying people's fears and keeping many from quitting their farms, which he, no less than they, could ill afford, Flagler's decisiveness reinforced in his senior staff the belief that they were engaged in a great enterprise that would bring civilization to the wilderness.

To generate profits for his Florida East Coast Railway, Flagler offered free and cut-rate round trips on his trains to prospective settlers, and his ticket agents often doubled as realtors for his Model Land Company. Flagler's own calculations indicated that each new settler was initially worth $300 to his railroad alone, with more recent analyses placing the figure closer to $400.[9] Tourism also meant profit. At the turn of the century, the price of a regular five-week Florida vacation featuring round-trip coach fare on Flagler trains and accommodations at any Flagler hotel was $350—not a small sum in a time when laborers earned $1.25 a day. The charge for each private railroad car making the round trip from Jacksonville to Palm Beach for the winter season was $342. In the late 1890s, approximately one hundred private cars a year made the journey.

Precise figures for Flagler's total earnings in the state are elusive because he established corporations for each division of his empire—the Florida East Coast Hotel Company, the Florida East Coast Railway, the Model Land Company, the Miami Electric Light Company, the West Palm Beach Water Company, the Florida East Coast Car Ferry Company. Smaller land companies were created to serve specific communities—the Fort Dallas Land Company in Miami, for example. This arrangement permitted utilization of creative and secretive accounting practices to obscure profits and losses as well as hide assets. It also served to shield from potential creditors Flagler's personal fortune and holdings in Standard Oil, which he nonetheless could use to finance his ventures. Flagler seldom owned less than 90 percent of his companies, often granting minority shares to his trusted lieutenants only to meet the demands of incorporation and to preserve their allegiance. Parrott and Ingraham each owned 15 shares of the Model Land Company; Flagler held the remaining 4,970. In an exception to the general rule, he gave each of his two senior aides 10 percent of the Fort Dallas Land Company, while retaining 80 percent. Until 1909, when he floated a $40-million bond offering to pay all outstanding debts—primarily those his companies owed him—and finance completion of the Overseas Railroad, he bore all railroad construction himself. The Flagler system by 1901 was a major monopoly beginning and ending with one man, controlling life along the Florida east coast.

Flagler continued to exercise power through subalterns in his various enterprises and politicians beholden to him directly or indirectly. Parrott, while president of the Florida East Coast Railway, belonged to a Jacksonville law firm that included Duncan U. Fletcher, first a political ally and later a bitter foe of Napoleon Bonaparte Broward, the governor who in 1906 launched the first major campaign to drain the Everglades around Lake Okeechobee. Fletcher served as one of Florida's United States senators from 1908 through 1932.

In the towns Flagler built—chiefly the Palm Beaches, as they are sometimes called, and Miami—his influence was direct and considerable. In West Palm Beach he made his wishes known through communiqués sent to the mayor and city council. In Miami he owned the water and electric works, the beachfront, and most of the land in the town. According to his wishes, the city was dry (an illusory condition, to be sure: Guests—but not locals—were allowed to drink at Flagler's Royal Palm Hotel, and saloons flourished just north of the city limits until 1902 when Flagler approved a charter amendment and the bars moved south). John Sewell, head of Flagler's work gangs in 1896 when the town was laid out and the hotel constructed, boasted that his "Black Artillery," one hundred black workers brought in and registered for the first municipal election, had ensured victory for the railroad. Sewell himself served as mayor from 1903–07. The city's first newspaper, the *Metropolis,* was a Flagler mouthpiece; and he eventually owned or controlled nearly all the major newspapers along the east coast, from Jacksonville to Key West.

Political opposition came at various times from the Farmers' Alliance, which flourished briefly during the late 1880s in north Florida; populist politicians subscribing to its anticorporate views; and individuals dispossessed in one way or another by railroad expansion and population growth. Many Floridians complained that the state government was delivering to railroad and canal companies millions of acres of land that should have gone to homesteaders. That was, in fact, one of the major policy battles of the time, and although they accepted less land than they legally claimed, the corporations won. The operative principle was simple: Suffer occasional political losses and abuse from candidates if that was necessary for preserving an economic structure favorable to corporate interests. A case in point was the Florida Railroad Commission, reestablished in 1898 to regulate the industry, its rates, terminals, and depots. The lines had ignored the first commission, which was abolished in 1891 (before Flagler began his major building); they learned to live with the second.

For politicians, association with Flagler could cause defeat at the polls. The Flagler divorce bill, introduced for his benefit and pounded through the legislature in 1901 with a $135,000 hammer, became a major campaign issue in 1904. The special law, which made insanity a grounds for divorce following Flagler's change of his legal residence from New York to Florida, offended the rigid Protestant morality of many Floridians, who watched as he jettisoned his second wife and married young Mary Lily Kenan within months of its passage. Doubtless, too, the bill served as a focal point for anticorporate sentiment. Even Napoleon Bonaparte Broward had to cover his tracks to ensure his election as governor. No evidence suggests that Broward, who said that as a state senator he voted for the bill because he thought it fair, received any gratuities from Flagler. He nonetheless promised to seek and sign a repeal, which he did. But Flagler had what he wanted.

Other opponents were less organized and more troublesome because not for sale. The independent and often disagreeable Cracker cowmen, who fought any threat to their open range, found themselves in regular conflict with the railroads over rights of passage and the slaughter by locomotives of their cattle. On occasion, they fired on the trains in retaliation for an accidental death. The residents of Coconut Grove on Biscayne Bay rejected Flagler's advances when he determined to push his railroad through Miami into their patch of the tropics, and they later protested against the environmental damage wrought by his activities.

Psychological explanations for Flagler's actions are almost too obvious to state, but the fact remains that the more control he sought to exercise on the peninsula, the less he could manage in his personal life. Early in the 1890s, as he prepared to move south of Daytona with his railroad, Flagler brought his son to St. Augustine to manage the hotels and learn about railroads. He intended for Harry to assume command of the budding empire after his death. But Harry quit after two years of halfhearted effort and drifted so far from his father that he barely saw him for twenty years. (After his father's death, Harry, who had married Annie Louise Lamont, the daughter of financier Charles Lamont, became a leading philanthropist in the New York music world.)

At the same time as his son was foiling his grand plan, his second wife Ida Alice discovered the Ouija board and began to communicate with spirits. They told her the czar of Russia was passionately in love with her and planned to kill Henry in order to marry her. Or that she should kill Henry to free herself for the lustful monarch. When she tried to mail jewels to the czar, Henry intercepted them. She spoke with imaginary people. She was troubled by her infertility and Henry's infidelities. Psychiatrists diagnosed her malady as "delusionary insanity," and she was committed to a sanatorium in Pleasantville, New York, in 1895. She was released in time for her thirteenth wedding anniversary on June 5, 1896, but she wasn't cured of whatever troubled her mind. That winter, she tried to cut one of her doctors with a pair of scissors. In March 1897, she was committed to the Choate Sanatorium, and Flagler never saw her again. In 1899, a New York court declared her insane, and she lived in the asylum in her own cottage with her private car and maids until 1930. Flagler had placed $1.4 million worth of Standard Oil stock in trust for her care; by the time of her death the fund's value was $15 million.

Ida Alice Flagler certainly suffered delusions. But, in the case of Henry's infidelities, they were not baseless. In 1901, Flagler was named corespondent in a divorce suit filed in Syracuse by C. W. Foote against his wife, Helen Long. Foote claimed she had been Flagler's mistress from December 1896 to December 1897, or beyond.[10] The suit stated that Flagler's gifts to Mrs. Foote included a town house on East Fifty-seventh Street in Manhattan and Standard Oil stock worth $400,000. Before Foote's divorce was granted, Flagler vanished as a corespondent, but he never denied the charges. By the time Ida Alice was permanently committed in 1899, Flagler had commenced his affair with Mary Lily Kenan, a young southerner and a friend of his favorite niece.

While Flagler worked to build up the Palm Beaches, continued to help Rockefeller solidify the Standard Oil monopoly, and struggled to deal with a deteriorating personal life, a marginal businesswoman and hustler named Julia Tuttle badgered him from Fort Dallas, the Seminole War-era base that became Miami. It is an article of faith that the widow Tuttle birthed Miami by virtue of her imagination, drive, and—not coincidentally—her offer to Flagler of land in exchange for a railroad station. She certainly played a major role in encouraging Flagler to choose the confluence of the Miami River and Biscayne Bay as site for a new hotel, but to call her, as some do, "the mother of Miami" is to denigrate motherhood and ignore several major truths.

Developers schemed a rail connection to Biscayne Bay before Julia Tuttle set eyes on the area in 1875, four years after her parents, Ephraim and Frances Sturtevant, had moved there with William and Mary Brickell to establish a store catering to Indians and a handful of settlers. The notion throughout Florida was that all the area needed to become a sort of tropical paradise was transportation—and fewer insects.

Flagler obtained the charter for a rail link to Fort Dallas in 1892 and clearly planned to build there even before Mrs. Tuttle began pleading with him to do so. She had bought 640 acres on the north side of the Miami River, at the site of Fort Dallas, a year after the death of her husband from tuberculosis in 1886. Finally in 1890, aged forty-one, she moved there permanently with her two children—a daughter, Frances, twenty-one, and son Henry, nineteen. She had already approached Ingraham, then working for Plant, about the South Florida Railroad coming to Fort Dallas but, receiving no commitment, turned to Flagler. She had a connection to him through Rockefeller, who attended the same church as she did in Cleveland. For a time, Flagler demurred, claiming he was not yet ready.

According to legend, Tuttle finally caught Flagler's attention when, after the freeze of 1894–95, she sent him a sprig of oranges and blossoms to show that the Miami River region had been spared; intrigued, he visited her at Fort Dallas and struck a deal. In fact, James Ingraham gathered the citrus blossoms and fruit, and Flagler's state charter—like all the others for railroad and canal construction—required him to complete service to Fort Dallas within a specified period of time in order to claim land bonuses. What Tuttle did offer Flagler was 100 acres plus alternating sections along the Miami River, which amounted to another 250 acres or so, in exchange for bringing his railroad across that land and for clearing up her rather confused titles, a result of grants dating back to Spanish colonial days and a common phenomenon in Florida. At least one potential buyer had already turned down a land deal with Tuttle because of that confusion, but Flagler had the resources and lawyers to straighten out the situation. Later, after the Brickells donated 100 of their acres on the south bank of the river to the cause, he extracted a like amount from Tuttle, in addition to what she had already promised. She was eager and greedy enough to consider that a bargain.

The Brickells seem to have been ambivalent about Flagler's

plans, perhaps because Julia Tuttle got to him first. Although the family donated 100 acres, Mary Brickell was known to dislike Flagler and his railroad, and she opposed his plans and policies. William objected vigorously to spoil from Flagler's harbor-dredging operations being thrown on his property and obstructing his view of river and bay until his wife sold the heap to road builders. For all their opposition, the Brickells clearly wanted a railroad to Miami; moreover, in anticipation of it, they had as early as 1890 begun charging as much as $1,000 an acre for prime home sites.

William Brickell, a roustabout who had traveled much of the world and—according to most reports—lived to lie about it, and his wife Mary, who for years had nursed and aided local Indians, whites, and blacks alike, appear on reflection to embody more of the spirit of the place than Tuttle. That they have received less attention than she is due no doubt to the fact that they withdrew from the public eye and that their four unmarried daughters refused to open the family records for years.

Flagler also received inducements of 10,000 acres a mile from the Boston and Florida Atlantic Coast Land Company and 1,500 acres a mile from the Florida Coast Line Canal and Transportation Company for the 66-mile West Palm Beach to Fort Dallas portion of the Florida East Coast Railway, which brought him more than 100,000 acres with agricultural potential.[11]

Through Ingraham, if no one else, Flagler was aware that south of the Miami River lay the rich soil of the Redland and that between the coastal hammocks and the Everglades, just west and north of Fort Dallas and Coconut Grove, stretched the forests of Dade County pine, valuable as building material and fuel. Since the land—once clear-cut—was prime for agriculture, the railroad company stood to profit greatly.

Finally, Biscayne Bay offered a beautiful, if shallow, harbor, well positioned for steamboats running to the Bahamas and other Caribbean ports. One area resident, Ralph Middleton Munroe, suggested that Flagler build his docks and hotel offshore, on Key Biscayne, where he would be closer to deep water, but he refused. Tuttle offered free land, and it cost less to build on the peninsula than to span the bay. Flagler did not realize that the channel he would have to dredge would need constant maintenance and would destroy much of the bay's beauty and charm.

* * *

Having decided to take the mouth of the Miami River, Flagler moved with his usual speed and decisiveness. Men, money, and material were thrown at the project, as if they were troops and it were a battle. Years later, Ingraham described the process in a speech before the Women's Club of Miami. He said that on his first visit to Fort Dallas in 1895, Flagler struck his deal with Tuttle and the Brickells, selected the site for the Royal Palm Hotel, ordered its construction, told Joseph Parrott—president of the railroad—to begin laying the tracks from West Palm Beach, and authorized Ingraham to draw up plans for the new city by Biscayne Bay. The land did not surrender easily.

One of Flagler's chief subalterns in the battle against nature was John Sewell, a Georgian, who had started work in 1882 at age nineteen for land mogul Hamilton Disston on the Kissimmee River and then drifted into the Flagler camp in 1892. Sewell led the assault on the hammocks that gave the area its tropical splendor. He took over the whole process of their clearance from Ingraham and his contractors who had proved incapable of rooting the massive hardwoods out of the limestone. "When starting to make Miami a city," Sewell irreverently recalled in his memoirs, "I had twelve black disciples." One of them, the Reverend A. W. Brown, "threw the first shovel of dirt starting . . . Miami."[12] Giving recognition to black workers was not common practice in the various Flagler enterprises, so Sewell, for all his other faults, deserves some credit for that.

Convict labor was first pitted against the Miami landscape—150 prisoners leased from the state for something on the order of forty cents a day per man and woman. They cleared the pinelands but balked at the dense, nearly impenetrable hammocks. After Sewell assumed command of the endeavor, he sent the convicts off to another project and hired free black workers to supplement his "disciples." When ironwood proved too hard for axes and saws, he and his crew blew the trees to pieces with dynamite. They burned out the two species of poisonous tree—manchineel (*Hippomane mancinella*) and Jamaica dogwood—and destroyed groves of naturalized coconut palms, oranges, guavas, bananas, and Key limes growing along the Miami River, which formed the major part of a dugout trail from Lake Okeechobee for Indians coming to hunt, fish, and trade on the shores of Biscayne Bay. Originally, the Calusa called Lake Okeechobee "Mayaimi," which means "Big Water." After the Calusa perished, the Seminole renamed the lake Okeechobee (also "Big

Water"), and the ancient name floated downstream where promotional-minded business leaders thought it more exotic and poetic than Fort Dallas.

The most significant destruction from a historical and archaeological point of view occurred at the site of the Royal Palm Hotel where there squatted an ancient Indian mound, measuring some one hundred feet long and seventy-five feet high. The mound was perhaps a burial site for the Tekesta Indians, a pre-Colonial tribe that had settled southeast Florida and whose last remaining members left with the Spanish in 1763. Sewell and his men leveled the mound to make room for the Royal Palm's veranda. They screened the soil to form a bed for the lawn and used the shells, rocks, and shards as road material and landfill. They found fifty or sixty skulls and partial skeletons at the level of the surrounding ground, most of which Sewell gave away—to anyone who asked. The remainder he stored in his tool shed until the hotel was finished. Then, he "took about four of my most trusted negroes and hauled all of these skeletons out near by where there was a big hole in the ground, about twelve feet deep, and dumped the bones in it, then filled the hole up with sand and instructed the negroes to forget about this burial and whereabouts of same."[13] The richest source of information on a lost people thus passed into sand, for a hotel for the rich.

The first train rolled into Miami in 1896. Along the way, the Florida East Coast Railway Company turned Fort Lauderdale, a small way station and Indian trading post, into a workmen's town. In January 1897, the Royal Palm Hotel opened with 450 rooms, two elevators, a swimming pool, and a staff of three hundred people. It was hardly luxurious in the style of the Royal Poinciana, but it was commodious. A newly dredged, nine-foot-deep channel through Biscayne Bay provided access for pleasure yachts. A charter boat took guests on deep-sea fishing excursions. The bay and ocean waters were so rich with fish that boats invariably returned overloaded to the dock where the anglers could pay to have their pictures taken with their prizes.

The person who most wanted to cash in on the railroad failed miserably to do so. Julia Tuttle bought vacant land to sell at exorbitant prices and sent boats to intercept lumber being shipped from Key West so she could have a monopoly; instead, she mired herself in debt and created a shortage of building material that retarded the town's growth. So did a lack of provisions—of dry goods and staples like flour—that became acute before the railroad rolled to town. The newcomers flooding to Miami, looking to cash in on the boom, were ill-prepared to live off what the land provided, the way the early settlers did.

Flagler himself was distracted by family matters and disgusted with the avarice of Tuttle, who regularly requested loans to cover cash-flow problems arising from her faltering business ventures. He also disagreed with the engineers who laid out the town, claiming that their grid design provided for streets that were too wide, although they were universally considered too narrow. He objected as well to the Bahamian schooners that ran up the river with supplies and to black laborers who were clearing the hammocks to build the town he didn't like. The boats offended him, the way tramp steamers running the channelized river offend the protectors of tourism today. He declined to have the city named for him, in part—one may suppose—because of his disgruntlement and in part to keep his privacy, for his business was conducted better that way.

But the town grew despite its poor design, and Flagler built the electric company, waterworks, schools, and churches, as well as homes his workers could rent. In 1897, he brought the Florida East Coast Steamship Company's new electric boat, the *S.S. Miami,* to town, and two years later added two more for pleasure, business, and the run to his Bahamas' hotels—the Colonial, which he built, and the Royal Victoria, which he bought from the government. The pair gave him effective control of tourism in Nassau. He persuaded the U.S. Congress to appropriate $100,000 for completion of the dredging of a channel through Biscayne Bay, a process that destroyed much of its vegetation and charm.

Ralph Munroe, recalling the bay before the railroad and hotel launched the first of the area's many population explosions, said:

> No sea-lover could look unmoved on the blue rollers of the Gulf Stream and the crystal-clear waters of the Reef, of every delicate shade of blue and green, and tinged with every color of the spectrum from the fantastically rich growths on the bottom, visible to the last detail through this incredibly translucent medium. It scarcely resembles northern seawater at all—a cold, semi-opaque, grayish-green fluid, which hides the mysteries of the bottom. Drifting over the Florida Reef on a quiet day one may note all the details of its tropical

luxuriance twenty feet below, and feels himself afloat on a
sort of liquid light, rather than water, so limpid and brilliant
is it.[14]

Munroe was one of a small band of Biscayne Bay residents
steadfastly opposed to Flagler's expansionism, his disregard for
the landscape and the way of life there; others were the naturalist Charles Torrey Simpson; the unrelated Kirk Munroe who
wrote popular children's adventure stories and founded the
League of American Wheelmen bicycling club; Kirk Munroe's
wife Mary; the Brickells; and later, David Fairchild.

Salt water began to rush into wells drilled into the freshwater Biscayne aquifer as the water was pumped out to supply the
growing population. Raw sewage and sludge choked the Miami
River and the bay; sediment despoiled the shoreline. Wood and
coal smoke from power plants, trains, and steamboats befouled
the air. The railroad campaigned actively to have troops biv-
ouacked in Miami during the war against Spain in 1898, and the
soldiers brought with them social chaos and disease.

Ralph Munroe and other dissenters cared as little for Flagler the man as for his work. "What an extremely lucky thing
that I did not go along with Standard Oil," the Staten Island
émigré wrote in his memoirs. "At best I would have been nothing but a money-grubber all my life."[15] When the master builder
visited Coconut Grove on his trip to Miami to bargain with Julia
Tuttle in 1895, he stopped by Munroe's house on the bay and
saw his majestic Royal Palms. Flagler mentioned that he considered calling his new hotel the Royal Palm and asked whether he
could buy Munroe's. Munroe flatly refused to sell.

The growing population changed everything. Wildlife vanished as the woods were cut; turtles were driven from the
beaches; fish populations dropped as more people sought larger
catches for pleasure and profit. The Seminole, whose trade had
brought wealth to the Brickells and other storekeepers, found
themselves unwelcome among the majority of the newcomers.
So, too, did the community of Bahamian blacks who had lived
in Coconut Grove for decades, and the more recent black residents who labored to build the city.

Newcomers tore out the native vegetation to plant fruit
trees or create a landscape more closely resembling their northern forests and gardens or their notions of the tropics. They
spared only native plants easily identified with the exotic lands

of popular imagination—the palms and bamboo, the delicate orchids and bright-spiked bromeliads. In replacing the indigenous flora of south Florida, people have introduced nearly a thousand new species of plants, and while most of those imports have enhanced the area, a few have dramatically altered its environment.

Casuarina—the so-called Australian pine, although it is no pine at all—appeared in Key West around 1860, brought by mariners and planted to create windbreaks. Flagler ordered them transported to the mainland in the late 1890s to adorn the streets of Palm Beach and Miami; two species appeared— *Casuarina equisetifolia,* which inhabits coastal dunes and beaches, and *lepidophloia,* which prefers canal banks and inland areas. Both are tall, ill-shaped, fast-growing trees with a pronounced tendency to topple in high winds and to shade out all other vegetation, creating forests of little more than casuarina, a monotonous and unproductive community. On Key Biscayne and other Miami-area beaches, the trees completely replaced the native sand pine scrub community. On Cape Sable, after Hurricane Donna spread seeds there in 1960, casuarina ruined one of the rare green turtle's few nesting grounds remaining on the peninsula. At Sanibel and Captiva islands on the Gulf, at Jupiter on the Atlantic, on old Indian mounds, casuarina has also driven out native pine and mangroves.

Another Australian import, the melaleuca, is even more invasive and damaging than the casuarina. Also called cajeput, melaleuca was introduced in 1906 by John Gifford, who found it in Cuba where it was planted around houses. Like chinaberry in north and central Florida, the trees were used to dry marshes in the belief they would prevent miasma from carrying malaria and other diseases into nearby homes. Gifford, thinking it an ideal plant for drying the Everglades, brought seeds to Miami and started sowing. On the west coast, plantsmen began promoting and cultivating the tree as well, so that it began to lock the Everglades in a botanical pincers. The danger was spread from the air in the late 1940s when county and state officials bombarded the east Everglades with millions of seeds.

In south Florida today, the melaleuca has invaded fifteen different plant communities and exterminated from 65 to 95 percent of the indigenous species within them, according to Bruce Freet, resources manager at the Big Cypress National Preserve. No animals live in the stands of melaleuca, not even birds. The resin of the tree is poisonous; pollen from its blossoms is a potent allergen that troubles thousands of people throughout south Florida. Melaleuca has no apparent practical or economic use, yet it cannot be destroyed. Fire races to the crowns of the trees and then roars across them scattering seeds but not burning the plants. "The melaleuca," Freet says, "is the toughest thing I've ever come across to control."[16]

An equally invasive plant is the Brazilian pepper, *Schinus terebinthifolius,* an ornamental introduced for landscaping in 1898 that loves to colonize abandoned farmland and construction sites. It grows quickly and produces masses of seeds, which birds and animals help scatter. Shade tolerant, it grows under a wide range of conditions, but seems especially to love logged pinelands where it will, in the absence of fire, become the dominant plant. Many abandoned fields today invite *Schinus* but will not accept the pine trees that once covered them. Those lands were rock-plowed during the 1950s and 1960s, a technique that literally turned up and pulverized the limestone lying under the soil. Now more than one hundred native prairie plant species appear incapable of returning to their former homes. Researchers at the Everglades National Park Research Station have warned that by the year 2000, *Schinus* may destroy all of the Miami rock-ridge pineland surviving in Dade County outside the confines of the national park, where officials work diligently to protect the pine. Only 2 percent of the original stretch of pineland remains, "one of the most endangered ecosystems in the United States."[17]

Little more than a decade before *Schinus* appeared on the south Florida scene, another South American import entered the state's waters. Mrs. W. F. Fuller, a winter resident of San Mateo, visited the New Orleans Cotton Exposition in 1884 and purchased some lovely Venezuelan water hyacinths for her fishpond. They rapidly filled the pool and so she did what people through the ages have done with unwanted plants and animals—she threw the excess into the nearest river. Within a few years, water hyacinths had covered millions of acres of the St. Johns and its tributaries and become such a menace to navigation that steamboats enclosed their wheels in an effort to keep them free of entangling leaves and stalks. Soon few waterways in the state were free.

Various attempts at control have either failed or proved more damaging than the plants themselves. In the 1890s, cowmen experimented with hyacinths as cattle fodder only to find they lacked a full range of nutrients. By the time wildlife biologists discovered that manatees ate them, the sea cows were so few that they couldn't keep pace. Scooping the plants out mechanically is costly and ultimately ineffective while dynamite blows them to pieces but kills every other living thing in the area. Although the herbicide 2,4-D—Agent Orange—destroys the plants, it remains in the environment for years, causing various mutations in fish, other marine animals, and birds. Regardless of the way the plants are destroyed, they sink to the bottom, depriving the water of oxygen as they decay and overloading it with organic matter.

Recently, chemists discovered new ways to turn hyacinths scooped from the lakes and rivers into more nutritive cattle feed and into fertilizer. Unfortunately, these cost too much to produce, especially when measured against the price of inorganic fertilizer and chemical-laced feeds. The day is approaching, however, when the cost to the environment of hyacinths and herbicides will have to be figured into the equation, and then people will conclude they can no longer afford not to make and purchase the products.

Hydrilla, a fast-growing marine grass brought into the peninsula to adorn aquariums, has joined the hyacinth in recent years and in some areas has supplanted it as the prime hazard to freshwater aquatic life. The grass craves nutrients that run into lakes and rivers from farms and heavily fertilized lawns. When present in 10 to 40 percent of a lake or river, according to biologists, it can help increase fish populations by providing havens for them and the organisms they consume. Above that threshold of coverage, however, hydrilla becomes a threat to the life it previously harbored, and in most Florida lakes and rivers nothing short of repeated spraying with copper sulfate retards its growth; and that treatment often damages other organisms more than it does hydrilla.

Since the turn of the century, successive waves of settlers have transformed the natural marshes and border swamps surrounding most lakes into sandy beaches or manicured lawns through filling and building of bulkheads. Those marshes and swamps cleansed water running into the lakes, which, in their absence, have become, in extreme cases, little more than receptacles for the wastes of people and breeding grounds for pestiferous plants. Many rivers have suffered, as well, becoming choked and cloudy.

Over the years exotic animals have joined the plants in

transforming the look of south Florida. Among the most damaging have been the fish—oscar, talapia, and walking catfish—that were deliberately or accidentally introduced by man at the expense of the native species. Poison toads, whose toxin is strong enough to kill small dogs, have become a hazard, as have armadillos, which arrived four decades ago and began feasting on the eggs of ground-nesting birds. Parrots and parakeets have taken to the air above south Florida cities; often they live on mangoes and avocados, like the foxes introduced during the Depression.

The list of changes grows in a depressingly mechanical way to match the machine age that bore them to America's piece of the tropics. The Miami River rapids, where water from the Everglades rushed across the edge of the Atlantic Coastal Ridge for Biscayne Bay, were dynamited in 1909 to provide water for guests at Flagler's Royal Palm Hotel. And the tourists didn't care: That winter, 125,000 people—twelve times the resident population—visited the new city on the bay.

The Miami River is a canal now, walled in and polluted from Lake Okeechobee to Biscayne Bay. In 1987, as it has periodically since Miami was built, it served as a conduit for untreated sewage from a broken pipe. When Ralph Munroe first saw the river little more than a century ago, it was "a beautiful clear-water stream, its banks lined with towering coco-palms and mangroves."[18]

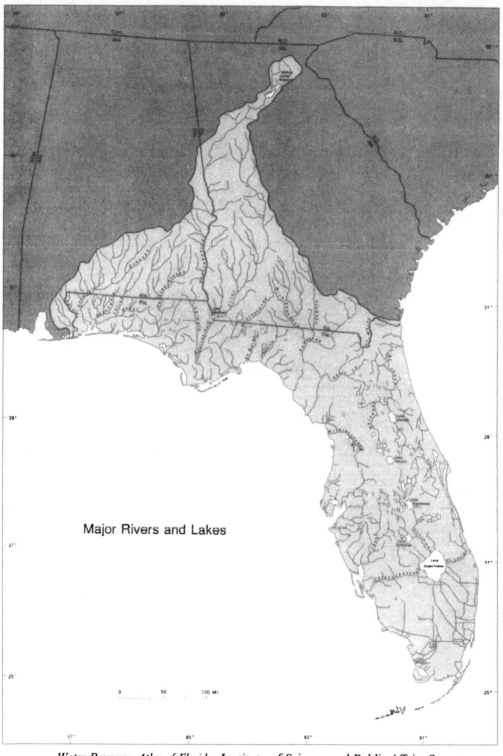

Major Rivers and Lakes

Water Resources Atlas of Florida, Institute of Science and Public Affairs State University

THREE

Alligators and Oranges

Viewed as a backwoods Eden, Florida becomes the mecca of sportsmen, invalids, immigrants, and the hybrid snowbird. Boats carry the load. Henry Sanford buds a grove; towns spring up. Oranges, oranges, oranges.

Henry Flagler's opening of the east coast to rail travel and his resort hotels in Palm Beach and Miami marked the establishment of Florida's greatest modern industries—tourism and citriculture. No depressions or freezes, however damaging or painful, could destroy them, and in the following decades they would become as identified with the state as palm trees and alligators. Trains carried people and produce in greater quantities and in more timely fashion than any other form of transportation yet seen in the state. People began flocking in sickness and in health to the state, which was, to many of the newcomers, a backwoods Eden, lush and ready for taking. "To the rough, practical Northern mind," said one observer, "Florida is a land of dreams, a strange country full of surprises, an intangible sort of place, where at first nothing is believed to be real and where finally everything is considered possible."[1]

Through the 1870s and 1880s a lack of adequate transportation forced people to communities served by boat. New settlement was most concentrated along the St. Johns River and its tributaries flowing out of the elevated ground forming the peninsula's spine. The region is comprised of a series of ancient marine terraces known collectively as the Central Highlands, although its greatest peak is less than 300 feet above sea level. Pressure for prime land became enormous, driving prices to levels only the wealthy could afford. Harriet Beecher Stowe, a winter resident since the early years of Reconstruction, was a promoter of Florida through her writings. Stowe, like many later advocates of growth, frequently found the result of rapid growth disheartening. In her book, *Palmetto Leaves,* she described what she saw on a tour up the St. Johns from the winter home she had purchased in the riverfront hamlet of Mandarin: "The wild, untouched banks are beautiful; but the new settlements generally succeed in destroying all Nature's beauty, and give you only leafless, girdled trees, blackened stumps, and naked white sand, in return."[2]

The population of Florida doubled from 188,000 in 1870 to 391,000 in 1890, with a 35-percent increase in the following decade. The numbers seem slim by today's standards, but Florida was a poor land. Only three communities boasted enough people to rate as cities—Key West, Jacksonville, and Pensacola—and none topped 10,000 even as late as 1880. Dade County, whose borders reached north from the peninsula's southern tip to Lake Worth, had an official population of 257. Tampa, when Henry Plant's railroad arrived in 1884, could claim 800 citizens.

By that time more than 25,000 people were visiting the peninsula each winter, with another 10,000 to 15,000 taking up permanent residence each year. The tourists were primarily Yankees; the settlers a mixed lot from the United States and abroad. Many craved nothing more than escape from foul winter weather or, more profoundly, from a ruined life. The resettlement followed an identifiable geographic pattern, with northerners and midwesterners predominating in the St. Johns region and Central Highlands and ex-Confederates clustering in the old plantation country of the Panhandle and along the Gulf coast. The two groups mixed, in places like Fort Myers and Sarasota, where a smattering of wealthy northerners admired the climate, fishing, and isolation.

The results of the intermingling of newcomers with Florida's natives proved as disruptive as productive. Like the other states of the defeated Confederacy, Florida possessed an antebellum social and political structure. Former slaves and their descendants comprised 40 percent of the population, even more in the old plantation counties across the Panhandle and north Florida. Granted freedom and citizenship during Reconstruction, they nonetheless could not bend the course of Florida's development to their advantage or even prosper through their own labor. When unreconstructed whites regained political power in 1876, they moved to limit blacks' civil rights by instituting literacy tests and poll taxes as requirements for voting, by discriminating in housing and the allotment of funds for education, and by legalizing segregation in public and private life. Blacks were considered suitable only for menial work as laborers or domestic servants, sharecroppers on the old plantations, serfs in turpentine camps, or migratory hands in the fields and on construction sites. Echoing prevailing wisdom, even among liberal defenders of equal rights, Harriet Beecher Stowe wrote: "[The] negro is the natural laborer of tropical regions. He is immensely strong; he thrives and flourishes physically under a temperature that exposes a white man to disease and death."[3] Stowe and a number of other northerners tried through education and various economic schemes to help Florida's freedmen improve their circumstances, but such efforts met with minimal success. The chief leverage of black workers came from the demand for their labor, but they often could exercise that power only by walking off a site that treated or paid them poorly and moving to another.

Florida's white natives lacked even that leverage—employers wanted their labor as little as they desired to give it. In the class-conscious society of the late nineteenth century, poverty could be nearly as great an impediment to social advance as race, for to be poor was to be genetically flawed. The two most unique groups of Florida whites were the Crackers and the Conchs. In the Old South, Crackers were poor whites who lived in the pine barrens and swamps, on any infertile soil. They were Anglo-Saxon, Celtic, Scottish on the east side of the Atlantic, half-wild backwoodsmen of the same origins on the west. At their worst, they were "white trash," bigoted and violent toward each other and blacks whose economic stratum they shared, whose similarity they could not admit for fear they then would have no status. At their best they possessed what social historian W. J. Cash called "perhaps the most intense individualism the world has seen since the Italian Renaissance and its men of 'terrible fury.' "[4] In Florida the term *Cracker* applied not only to the poor whites of the piney woods but also to descendants of whites, often Tories, who had settled in Florida during the

American War of Independence and to the sons and daughters of later "pioneers" from various states and nations who made their living off the land.*

Conchs colonized the Keys and little Singer Island on the east coast near Jupiter early in the nineteenth century, as fishermen and wreckers. They were descendants of American Tories who fled to and then from Florida during the American Revolution, English Cockneys, and Africans. Despite miscegenation, the whites generally considered themselves the only true Conchs and segregated themselves from their black relatives and neighbors. According to legend, they earned the name *Conch* during a rebellion in the Bahamas when, flagless, in mid-uprising, they raised conch shells stuck on poles as their insignia; an alternative suggests that the rebels communicated with conch-shell horns. (Contemporary usage defines a Conch as any Caucasian born in the Florida Keys. In the 1930s, Cracker honorably referred to any Caucasian born on the Florida mainland, but it was discredited in the 1950s and 1960s, when it became synonymous with bigot and now takes second place to the word *native.*)

For much of the late nineteenth and early twentieth centuries, these natives held little in common with new settlers or winter residents. The publicist for the state immigration office in the 1870s, George Barbour, fulminated in his guidebook against "the genuine, unadulterated 'cracker'—the clay-eating, gaunt, pale, tallowy, leather-skinned sort—stupid, stolid, staring eyes, dead and lusterless; unkempt hair, generally tow-colored; and such a shiftless, slouching manner; simply white savages— or living mummies."[5] Other observers regarded the Crackers' devotion to their kin and their unwillingness to travel far afield to work for scant wages at a lumber or railway camp as negative attributes. They were content, their detractors said, to survive on salt pork from the wild razorback hogs and grits, like black people (who were called then "niggers," or Negroes if one was being proper) and to attend their dances and fairs, which decent folk of Barbour's class considered rude excuses for drinking and courting. Many of the same characteristics were attributed to Conchs, although the tale-tellers recognized that they ate grunts

---

*Other theories hold that *Cracker* is derived from "cracked corn"—the common food of poor white southerners—or that it comes from the Scottish *Crocker,* meaning braggart. I have adopted the explanation Floridians preferred because it seems as valid as any other.

(a fish) and grits. Those who were wreckers were considered pirates in polite society, just as their landbound cousins were considered cattle rustlers and rogues even if they were ranchers.

In many rural areas, the land adequately supported its residents—black and white—if they steadily hunted for fresh meat or brought home fresh fish and worked at keeping the garden free of raiding birds, rabbits, raccoons, and deer. The hogs were real enough, too. Lean and mean descendants of domestic stock brought by Spanish explorers and settlers, they roamed the woods eating snakes and bird eggs and attacking any man or dog who stepped in their path. The first cold spell of winter brought the start of hog-slaughtering season. So prevalent and so ingrained was this backcountry practice that the state legislature in 1937 declared *wild* razorbacks nonexistent in order to end thieving of farm-raised hogs. (It was a typically retrograde legislative act that was later reversed when it became clear that wild hogs not only existed but also had multiplied so rapidly that populations had to be controlled through hunting.) Across the prairies of the peninsula's interior, scrub cattle also provided meat, as did deer and bears. On the coasts and along lakes and rivers, there were fish, clams, and turtles. Miami forester and historian John Gifford reported that early in the present century "[t]he Conch and Cracker lived on the natural resources of the great out-of-doors with little or no restraint. That is now about ended with the exhaustion of those resources."[6]

Life in the backcountry could be as hardscrabble as it was bountiful. Gardens failed during droughts, freezes, or plagues of insects or disease; game and fish became periodically scarce from overhunting and overfishing or epidemics among particular species; staples such as coffee, sugar, and grits failed to appear when ships were wrecked or remained locked in port during stretches of bad weather. Since most crops ripened in the winter, summer almost always brought shortages of fresh vegetables and even game. At those times families subsisted off cabbage palm and coontie supplemented by whatever else they could grub.

For cash, rural Floridians unwilling to work the mines, construction or timber camps bartered; hunted furs and plumes; collected moss, vanilla beans, and salvage; sold excess crops; worked the cattle drives; and served as fishing and hunting guides for the traveling sportsmen. As tourism grew, so did the inclination of many natives to live off tourist dollars during the winter season; the different cultures clashed, with stereotypes created on both sides—the slothful Cracker, shiftless Negro, and rapacious Conch; and the naïve, stupid, and profligate Yankee.

In the nineteenth century, equipment and money weren't available for building decent roads on the loose sand of the scrub, across the low-lying savannas, or through the flatwoods. Even with the use of specially adapted, single-axle, wide-wheeled carts, moving supplies and material was difficult and time-consuming. Oxen frequently drew the carts of natives because they had proved well suited to the climate and country, but they were slow. When traveling cross-country without much baggage, people walked or rode horses if they had them and kept watch for rattlesnakes. Stagecoaches with reinforced springs ran on deeply rutted sand and corrugated log roads. People took the stage only out of necessity.

Floridians' traveled whenever possible by boat. The craft were as varied and idiosyncratic as their owners: Some were beautifully designed sailing vessels, others homemade yachts adapted to steam. There were salvaged lifeboats, dugouts, and luxury steamships with staterooms. Sharpies—shallow-draft sailing craft similar to the skipjacks of the Chesapeake Bay— were favorites among dwellers on both coasts and the Keys. By the 1870s, steamboats dominated the commercial trade along the state's navigable rivers and the major intercity coastal routes—from Jacksonville south to Titusville and from Cedar Key on the Gulf of Mexico to Tampa and Key West.

Steamboating in Florida began around 1830, well over two decades after Robert Fulton's *Clermont* belched down the Hudson on her maiden voyage. Jacksonville and Palatka became important ports with shipbuilding facilities in the 1850s, and, after the disruption of the Civil War and Reconstruction, blossomed again in the 1870s, with the period 1875–87 being called the golden age of steamboat travel in Florida. In 1880, some one hundred boats, stern-wheelers and side-wheelers, plied the St. Johns River and its tributaries, hauling people and cargo. Perhaps that many more served the state's other rivers—the Suwannee, Apalachicola, and the Indian. Steamers came to Lake Okeechobee, the Kissimmee, and Caloosahatchee early in the decade. On major waterways, the boats were capable of holding hundreds of people and sailing from Jacksonville to New York or to Havana or the Bahamas. Small, specially built stern- and side-wheelers carried passengers through the narrow, twisting channels of the state's more scenic, spring-fed rivers.

Steamboat captains and pilots became dominant figures in the life not only of the river but of the interior as well. Captains served as middlemen for settlers and merchants, transporting produce to market, arranging its sale, purchasing and returning with provisions. Everywhere in the state, a ship captain's signature was as good as money. When landings closed for the evening, pine logs were placed on platforms for night-running boats to take on as fuel. After loading, the captain would sign a chit indicating how much wood he had taken, which was negotiable for cash or good for barter. It was a system based on mutual trust, personal contact, and, when necessary, rough frontier justice that allowed a wronged man to make right through vengeance. Especially in the more sparsely settled regions of west and south Florida, persons—not laws or institutions—mattered.

Steamboating declined during the decades of the 1890s as a result of a yellow fever epidemic in Jacksonville, the expansion of railroads throughout the state, and the crop-killing freezes. A resurgence occurred in 1898 when fifty steamboats assembled at Tampa for the invasion of Cuba, but from then on, steamboats mainly carried resort-bound tourists. The paddle wheelers experienced a last hurrah of sorts during the 1920s' real estate boom, when they hauled goods and materials the overloaded railroads couldn't handle. After that, the internal combustion engine and economic chaos of the Depression relegated them first to memory, then to history.

Today, one can purchase a ticket to that time past and take a diesel-powered paddleboat ride down the St. Johns from Sanford or along the channelized Caloosahatchee to Lake Okeechobee or across the waters of Biscayne Bay. Disney World offers a riverboat adventure, on an artificial waterway through a man-made forest inhabited by mechanical creatures, and riverboat haute cuisine on a docked sternwheeler called the *Empress Lily*. More people probably visit the amusement park's craft during a busy week than rode all the St. Johns steamboats combined in, say, 1875.

In the 1870s, tourism was an infant enterprise, stunted by war and economic depression. True tourists—people coming for pleasure and play instead of rest and recuperation—repre-

sented to investors and the state's officials a potentially limitless
market, and they set out to cultivate it. Promotional material
boasted the peninsula's charms and often anticipated improvements in transportation and facilities by several years. Special
appeals were made to sportsmen—"devotees of the rod and
gun"—suggesting to them that Florida was the nearest thing to
paradise, overflowing with birds, fish, and alligators.

Women, children, and less trigger-happy men made excursions either by boat, horseback, or, if the primitive roads permitted, carriage, to picnic and collect flowers. (Walking was
considered difficult and unpleasant on the loose sand soil and
wet lowlands that characterized much of northeast and central
Florida. A stroll on the beaches, on the other hand, was acceptable.) In Jacksonville, St. Augustine, Palatka, and the spas, collecting curios was popular; shops offered caged raccoons, otters,
squirrels; stuffed rattlesnakes, water moccasins, and birds, complete with eggs and nests. In Jacksonville, mockingbirds usually
sold for $10 to $50, with spectacular singers fetching $500.
(They became protected by law and were named the state bird
early in this century.) There was also a large trade in palmetto
hats, canes carved from orange wood or mangrove, shells, trin-
kets, alligator teeth—plain or carved into charms and whistles—
sea beans for buttons, live baby turtles and alligators, caged
birds and colorful plumes. Stereographs of Florida scenes were
runaway best-sellers.

Those visitors who found the peninsula a delightful place
to winter built homes, planted gardens and groves, and grew
numerous enough to form their own distinctive tribe, "snow-
birds," who migrated to Florida in December and returned
north in May, the start of the rainy season. Growing up to serve
them and the shorter-lived tourists, Florida resorts and their
employees became locked in an economy of extremes: flush
winters and barren summers. Fear of disease did as much as the
heat, humidity, and rain to drive those who could afford it to
migrate during the summer months. Malaria was commonplace
throughout the state and yellow fever was frequently epidemic
in Florida ports: Travelers often faced quarantine or fear that
their destination might be a stricken town, their ship a carrier
of death. Superstition and ignorance were widespread, often
dividing families and communities. During outbreaks, inland
counties regularly instituted "shotgun quarantines"—a quite
literal description—to keep from their communities people

from afflicted cities and towns. After an epidemic in Tampa in 1871, during which he lost his wife and small daughter, local physician John Perry Wall began intensive investigations and within two years concluded that *Aedes aegypti,* the yellowhammer or treetop mosquito, was the carrier of yellow fever. But in an age that blamed the disease largely on miasma or filth or God, his discovery met with no response, even after Havana physician Carlos Juan Findlay confirmed it in 1881. Until Walter Reed rediscovered the truth in 1900, people from all walks of life wondered in times of outbreaks which breath of air would lay them low.

The appetite of tourists was insatiable. They laid waste landings all along the river, stripping them of flowers, clearing them of wildlife. They slaughtered animals they considered beautiful, like herons and egrets, as frequently as those they considered instruments of the devil or worse, like alligators and snakes. A favorite male pastime involved lining the decks of steamboats and firing at everything in an orgy of noise, gunpowder fumes, and death that offended nearly everyone who witnessed it. A correspondent for *Forest and Stream* magazine boarded a St. Johns steamer in 1876 and joined his boatmates in shooting alligators. He wrote of the reptiles:

> Their scaly backs, when dry, are precisely the color of bark, and lying on or by fallen trees, their form assimilates so closely to the decaying trunks, that we are unable to distinguish them at first, even when our small imp-of-all-work would grimace like a monkey in a tree to point them out. We did not admit with candor that we did not see them, and bravely fired away, and kept up an expression of entire wisdom, even when, in response to hurried shots, chips flew from logs that were not very near the splash made by the escaping saurian. One or two were hit and when wounded gave a display of power that increased our respect for them.[7]

The "monkey," the black deckhand, must have enjoyed the foolishness of the hunters who belittled him, but his was a private joke. The reporter boasted, "We were on the highway [the St. Johns], where from the forward decks of every steamer a fusillade of small arms is kept up on every living thing, from alligators to the useful buzzards that clustered upon the floating carrion." Before the killing started, he had seen those "useful

buzzards" perched in pine boughs overhanging the river and
described them as "unmindful of rifle-balls; safe in worthless-
ness as they surveyed the scene their repulsive forms marred."

By the late 1870s, game populations along the middle St.
Johns and its major tributaries had become so depleted that a
number of captains acted independently of an inept and uncon-
scious state government to prohibit shooting from the decks of
their ships. The sportsmen went farther into the interior or
along the coasts in search of game. The hunts became adventures, subject to the vagaries of weather and transportation, the
whim of guides, the lack of accommodations, and the threat of
illness or injury from poisonous snakes, animals, and their own
guns. Wherever they traveled, the hunters and fishermen left a
trail of spoiled meat. Like their counterparts in the American
West who were laying waste the herds of bison and antelope, the
flocks of passenger pigeons, these Florida sportsmen cared primarily for blood.

One of their favorite destinations was the Indian River, a
lagoon on the middle east coast. Travelers would journey to
Lake Harney, nearly the last navigable stretch of the St. Johns,
on small steamers, then take a mule-drawn train to Titusville
(sometimes called Sand Point), a hamlet at the head of the
Indian River. Its main guesthouse and point of interest was the
Titus Hotel, named, like the village, for another of the colonels
who seemed nearly as common in Florida as mosquitoes. ("Colonel" was a southern honorific denoting socioeconomic status
for certain white males, some of whom had earned the proper
military rank in the Confederate Army.)

H. T. Titus is a shadowy figure, like so many of those who
planted themselves along the lower Florida coasts. Reportedly,
as a proslavery partisan, he had fought in Kansas against John
Brown and his abolitionist allies; raided in Nicaragua and Cuba;
and run the federal blockade along the Florida coast during the
War Between the States. Those activities proved lucrative
enough for him to open a hotel catering predominantly to Yankees—the people he had despised most of his life. When state
publicist George Barbour encountered Titus in 1879, he was
"old, a helpless invalid," and an uncompromising supporter of
the Republican party he had "so viciously fought in his younger
days."[8]

Whatever his background, Titus ran a famous hotel. Barbour said it was "built in what may be called the tropical style—a

large main building with two long wings, all one story high, forming three sides of a square neatly laid out in a garden, and with rooms opening off the wide verandas like a row of houses in a city block."[9] The food amounted to a tropical cornucopia— oysters, clams, fish, shark steaks, sea turtle steaks and soup, fruit and vegetables, all from local waters and farms. In this respect, the Titus Hotel was similar to other guesthouses along the Atlantic and Gulf coasts, all of which were known for their good food and good company.

Titusville might have become Palm Beach, but was spared the distinction by an act not of heroism or compassion but of greed. Early in the 1890s, when Flagler was hunting for a southern, frost-free, and tropical location for a resort to end all resorts, he looked to the renowned Indian River, specifically to a chunk of Sand Point owned by a crusty settler named Louis Coleman. When Coleman learned that the master builder had designs on his mangrove swamp and coastal prairie, he demanded a price high enough to make Flagler decline and move south to the shores of Lake Worth.

Less intrepid tourists satisfied their desire for adventure by riding a paddle wheeler up the Oklawaha from its confluence with the St. Johns River at Palatka to Silver Springs. This small, twisted river with banks so low as to be almost nonexistent and its dense, moss-draped, overarching forest of cypress, oak, and palm, ranked among the top attractions in Florida and subsequently achieved nearly mythic status as one of the nation's most exotic waterways.

The poet and musician Sidney Lanier, down from Baltimore in 1875 to fulfill a contract with the Great Atlantic Coastline Railroad for a guidebook to Florida, cruised up the Oklawaha on the *Marion*, "a steamboat which is nothing in the world so much as a Pensacola gopher with a preposterously exaggerated back."[10] The little boat was built to crawl upstream and make turns so tight that a man was stationed on the foredeck to keep it from becoming entangled in the vegetation along the shore. The river itself was

[t]he sweetest water-lane in the world, a lane which runs for more than a hundred and fifty miles of pure delight . . . , a lane clean to travel along for there is never a speck of dust in it save the blue dust and gold dust which the wind blows out of the flags and lilies, a lane which is as if a typical

woods-stroll had taken shape and as if God had turned into water and trees the recollection of some meditative ramble through the lonely seclusions of His own soul."[11]

Lanier seldom had difficulty allowing his romantic imagination to roam. He found in the trees and vines of one stretch of shoreline a "troop of girls, with arms wreathed over their heads, dancing down into the water," and later,

> Una on her lion, Angelo's Moses, two elephants with howdahs, the Laocoon group, Arthur and Lancelot with great brands extended aloft in combat, Adam bent with love and grief leading Eve out of Paradise, Caesar shrouded in his mantle receiving his stabs, Greek chariots, locomotives, brazen shields and cuirasses, columbiads, the twelve apostles, the stock exchange.[12]

At night, when torches were set atop the steamboat's pilot house, the sight of their glow dancing across water and trees did not leave the loquacious Lanier groping for words:

> The white columns of the cypress-trunks, the silver-embroidered crowns of the maples, the green-and-white of the lilies along the edges of the stream,–these all come in a continuous apparition out of the bosom of the darkness and retire again: it is endless creation succeeded by endless oblivion. Startled birds suddenly flutter into the light, and after an instant of illuminated flight melt into the darkness. From the perfect silence of these short flights one derives a certain sense of awe. Mystery appears to be about to utter herself in these suddenly-illuminated forms, and then to change her mind and die back into mystery.[13]

The second morning of the cruise from Palatka brought a "journey over transparency," as the *Marion* entered the Silver Springs Run, as pellucid a stream as could be found in a region of transparent waters. Through centuries, travelers have marveled at being able to look overboard and through the glass bottom of boats into the world of fish, down to the bright sand, or into the springs themselves. Lanier was no exception, observing of Silver Springs, "It is as if depth itself–that subtle abstraction–had been compressed into a crystal lymph, one inch of which would represent miles of ordinary depth."[14]

Lanier undertook to write his travelogue as hackwork to provide him with money and as an opportunity to travel south and improve his fragile health. Although the tour failed to cure him of tuberculosis, which killed him in 1881, the book he produced—despite its excesses—has endured and exerted far more influence on succeeding generations than any of his poems or music. Nearly a century after *Florida: Its Scenery, Climate, and History* first appeared in print, environmentalists used the opening chapter on the Oklawaha and the voyage of the *Marion* to bolster their case against the Cross-Florida Barge Canal then under construction and threatening the river and springs with destruction.

In the heyday of steamboating, little settlements seemed to grow around every landing, spas around every spring. Wealthy northerners created vast estates comprised of farms, groves, timber operations, hunting preserves, and winter homes. The more ambitious laid out entire communities. Many of the minor hamlets founded in the 1870s and 1880s would vanish and even some of the major river towns barely survived. Palatka, for instance, once second only to Jacksonville among ports on the St. Johns, declined from its former grandeur to become an "old" Florida town, living off logging, some agriculture, a little boating, government offices. Today, it's a horizontal community of one- and two-story cinder block buildings, a Holiday Inn on the river, a public boat landing, and dock. Another example is Enterprise, a quaint town on the east shore of Lake Monroe, upriver about ninety twisted miles from Palatka. Just beginning to suffer the Disney-induced development boom that has for twenty years buffeted various parts of central Florida, the old resort community is nestled in high pinelands and hardwood- and cabbage-palm-dominated hammocks. At the crossroads stands an Episcopal chapel dating from the town's more prosperous past, when it played host to thousands of travelers a year and served as headquarters for two of the most powerful figures in Florida steamboating, Jacob Brock and Count Frederick De Bary.

Brock's shipping line, which he started in 1852, dominated St. Johns steamboating until 1876, when De Bary entered the business with greater drive and resources. The Brock Line ran large side-wheelers from Jacksonville to Enterprise, where from the Brock House groups of tourists would travel by small steamer to more southern lakes on the river—Harney, Jessup, Ponsett—to hunt and fish in the profligate style of the day. Others would travel a mile overland to Green Sulphur Springs, to partake of the waters and inhale what they considered the healing terebinthine scent of the longleaf pine.

In 1870, Count Frederick De Bary arrived in Enterprise from his American home in New Jersey. De Bary had come to the United States in 1851 to sell Apollinaire mineral water and champagne produced by G. H. Mumms and Company, owned by his brothers. He quickly became a millionaire and like many of his wealthy contemporaries decided to invest in Florida real estate after the Civil War, when prices were low and the lure of exotics high. On four hundred acres near Enterprise he built the most famous and luxurious private residence on the river, a two-story mansion with seven bedrooms surrounded by groves of citrus and bamboo fed by an elaborate, wind-driven irrigation system. There, during his winter sojourns, he entertained with lavish evenings of music, dance, skits, abundant champagne, and a table loaded with fresh game, fish, fruit, vegetables, and green-turtle soup.[15]

In 1876, De Bary entered the booming St. Johns steamboat business. In 1881, he incorporated his line and commissioned an iron-hulled sidewheeler, the *Frederick De Bary,* as his flagship. It sailed north at the end of each winter season and returned at the start of the next. In 1882, he ordered built and finished with Florida mahogany and yellow (longleaf) pine the *City of Jacksonville,* which became known almost immediately as the finest ship on the river. It had the distinction, too, of being the first coal-burner on the St. Johns, its predecessors all using turpentine-soaked pine for fuel, a commodity that was becoming scarce as demand increased with the expansion of boat and rail traffic throughout the state. After merging with a rival in the mid-1880s, the De Bary steamship company finally became part of the Clyde Line, which dominated the declining river trade early in this century.

A well-connected and influential businessman, De Bary attracted a number of prominent officials and investors from the northeastern United States to his estate in Enterprise. One of his most distinguished guests was Henry Sanford, a retired general in the Union Army, once Lincoln's ambassador to Belgium, and a leading light in the Republican party. An avid sportsman, Sanford initially came to the banks of Lake Monroe in 1870 to fish and hunt; he soon determined to exploit its timber resources and build a community and farms. He negotiated purchase from the state of a twenty-two-square-mile tract on the southwest bank of Lake Monroe near Fort Mellon, a post established during the Seminole War of the 1840s and later abandoned. As was common in that day, his plan combined social activism, Christian dogma, and profitable enterprise—believed the most appropriate combination for human advancement. Sanford soon learned that in Florida progress most frequently came by indirection and, even then, seldom matched the preconceived plan.

The general's first obstacle involved gaining clear title to his fourteen thousand acres. From the sixteenth through the early eighteenth century the Spanish crown had divided much of Florida's interior into large tracts and granted them to various loyal subjects and immigrants. These grants had to be identified and their legitimacy verified or owners found before newcomers could receive clear title. Dense forests and wetlands that covered much of the state made it difficult, if not impossible, to conduct the surveys necessary to affix precise property lines. As a result of the delays, Sanford did not take possession of his land until 1874.

Around Lake Monroe even the antebellum plantations and farms, abandoned during the war and not reoccupied, had begun to return to woodland. Sanford planned to cut and mill the timber, then turn the profit into establishing orange groves and farms. A railroad depot at the docks would receive additional produce from the interior for eventual shipment by steamboat down the St. Johns to Jacksonville.

He needed workers. Sometime around 1874, Sanford brought some sixty black laborers from the surrounding area to clear land for a citrus grove. Neighboring whites at once protested and, when words failed, turned violent. One dark night, armed white vigilantes attacked the camp of Sanford's workers, killing one and wounding a half dozen more. Those who survived fled, not to return. Race hatred, fear of losing power and privilege they never had but believed they did, and lust for vengeance against intruding, rich Yankees—all motivated the attack. Jobs were not the issue; no local whites before or after stepped forward as workers on Sanford's grant, though loggers and farmers were needed. Faced with a sudden unavailability of local labor, Sanford sent an agent to Sweden to recruit people willing to work hard for low wages in exchange for the opportunity to emigrate.

The immigrants began arriving in 1875 and commenced erecting sawmills, logging, and farming. (Sanford and his young manager James Ingraham, who had moved from Ohio because of tuberculosis and would become in twenty years the head of Henry Flagler's land company, were as much agricultural researchers as working farmers.) But the Swedes aroused jealousy and opposition, although less violent than the freedmen encountered. Agents from Jacksonville traveled upriver to encourage their desertion and flight to the city for higher wages. The men Sanford sent to bring the runaways back were harassed and even arrested. Eventually, Sanford added Italian and Polish workers to those Swedes who remained and succeeded in establishing viable agricultural operations on his land. Workers who completed their terms and elected to stay received five-acre groves and, with new arrivals from Sweden, soon made citrus the area's dominant crop.

After the freezes of 1894–95, the groves were replaced with cold-resistant winter vegetables, especially celery, for which the city of Sanford became renowned. In one of those ironies of history, the vast majority of workers in the fields and packing plants are now black; the crop they handle, cabbage. The transition to black labor brought a decline in Sanford's economic fortunes, as whites abandoned the city to the poor. Recently, the exploding population of central Florida has begun to transform the surrounding area from agricultural country to a jumble of suburbs and office complexes, with all the support stores, gas stations, and fast-food outlets that accompany the sprawl.

Wars, the chronic lack of transportation, and a disease called "long scale" retarded expansion of citriculture until Sanford became involved in the 1870s. From that time, cultivation first of oranges and later grapefruit—with limes and various exotics thrown in—grew into a major enterprise that defined Florida in the popular mind.

Douglas Dummett established the first "budded" orange grove in Florida at his estate on upper Merritt Island early in the 1830s, by taking sweet China orange buds from Mays Grove at Orange Mills near Palatka and grafting them onto wild sour-orange trees growing on his land.[16] So successful and hardy were his trees that buds from them were used to revitalize the

St. Johns citrus industry after a killer freeze in 1835. Dummett himself achieved notoriety as captain of a state militia company called the Mosquito Roarers, which plied the Indian River during the Seminole Wars. He lived in a cabin in his grove, within two hundred feet of his black mistress, the mother of his three children.[17] During his lifetime, his oranges were prized above all others in New York City markets, and after his death in 1873, his grove and others he established near New Smyrna became famous as the progenitors of Indian River oranges, which many connoisseurs consider the finest in the world. ("Indian River" oranges and grapefruit attained protected status in the 1920s when the Federal Trade Commission decreed that citrus grown outside the watershed of the lagoon could not carry its name to market.)

Renewed proof that sweet oranges could be successfully budded onto sour-orange root stock—with the hybrids producing fruit in fewer years than any plant grown from seed—set off a rush for dry hammock land. The soil was ideal for citrus—well drained and rich in organic matter—and the hammocks themselves were often laced with mature sour-orange trees descended from those that Spanish colonists had brought to the peninsula in the sixteenth century. Settlers, Indians, and animals had spread the seeds, and the plants had become so thoroughly naturalized in the hardwood hammocks that some nineteenth-century observers thought them native. Prime land for oranges, with root stock already present, fetched as much as $7,000 an acre by the early 1870s, an amount within reach of only the wealthy.

Between 1874 and 1877, Florida growers imported 200 million oranges, trees, and cuttings worth $2 million from the Mediterranean and West Indies. In 1880, approximately sixty varieties of oranges were under cultivation, of which only two or three are still grown commercially—most notably the late-maturing, quite sweet Valencia, which came from Spain by way of Rivers Nursery in England. Sanford himself introduced blood and Jaffa oranges—neither of which is extensively cultivated anymore in Florida—to his groves on Lake Monroe in the mid-1880s. Commercialization and the frozen concentrate industry that arose following World War II were responsible for narrowing the number of varieties, although recent demand in gourmet markets for exotic fruit has sparked a revival of interest in different types.

The nineteenth-century quest for new varieties produced a curious mutant of the shaddock, which Count Odette Philippe, a French physician living on Tampa Bay, introduced to the peninsula in 1823. Called a *pomelo* in Portuguese and a *toronja* in Spanish, the mutant came to be known in English as the grapefruit because it grew in grapelike clusters. Production increased through the 1880s, as markets for it expanded. In 1892, Lue Gim Gong, a Chinese horticulturalist living in De Land, a community established fifteen years earlier on the St. Johns by a baking powder manufacturer, hybridized a grapefruit, named in his honor, that withstood temperatures ten degrees colder than previous varieties. One of the peninsula's foremost horticulturalists, he also developed a new type of late-maturing orange. (Today, Florida produces nearly 75 percent of the world's grapefruit and boasts of itself as the birthplace of all named varieties but the Texas Ruby Red.)

In the early days of mass citrus production, land selection was based on observation of natural vegetation. Beginning around the turn of the century, the use for budding of rough lemon stock, often drawn from south Florida hammocks, permitted expansion of the industry into the deep, sandy soil of the Central Highlands, where abundant lakes were believed to provide some additional protection from frost. (By 1930, it was no longer possible to use native vegetation as a guide for site selection for groves. Too little remained from the axes and saws of lumber companies, agriculturalists, and developers.)

Low hammocks, with their shallow soil, marl substrate and propensity for holding water, could produce exceptional fruit, as they do in the Indian River region, if carefully prepared. But, as a rule, orange and grapefruit trees like to keep their "feet" (roots) dry and so grow poorly in that damp ground. The relatively infertile soil of the flatwoods and low-lying bayhead swamps near lakes and rivers were especially ill-suited for citrus, although more advanced technology and fertilizers have allowed growers to establish groves in some of those areas in recent decades. Soil in the scrub was too sandy and nutrient poor for commercial crops of any kind. In south Florida, where the soil might reach a maximum depth of a foot before limestone is struck, orange trees are difficult to plant, although the climate and abundant rainfall make it a region ideal for fruit. In the days before the process known as rock plowing was invented, growers used dynamite to blast holes for trees.

Capitalists from throughout western Europe joined the

press of Americans from the North and South who saw in Florida groves and timber an investment secure from financial panic and depression. In 1880, Henry Plant ran the South Florida Railroad from Sanford's Lake Monroe docks to Orlando, which soon became the peninsula's largest inland city. In the Orlando area, British investors joined with former Confederate officials, Cracker cowmen—who often cultivated oranges on the side—and wealthy northerners to create profitable citrus, vegetable, and cattle industries. Along Plant's railway, resorts and communities began to blossom—Altamonte Springs and Winter Park, Orlando's tiny sister, among them.

Like many other "new" resorts of the post-Reconstruction period, Winter Park was imposed on a small antebellum community. In 1858, it was founded as Lakeview, and in 1870, uncertain of its identity, its citizens renamed it Osceola in honor of the martyred Seminole war leader and one of the seven lakes that made it distinctive. In 1881, northerners, arriving by Plant's train, platted a town among the lakes, which they set out to connect with canals. They chose the name Winter Park to reflect their intended use of it as a retreat from the bitter cold of their homelands. In 1885, Chicago industrialist Alonzo Rollins endowed a college. A year later, Henry Plant opened the palatial Seminole Hotel, then the largest south of St. Augustine. The Seminole served twenty-three hundred people its first season and, like other luxury resorts, offered croquet, tennis, billiards, and bowling; horses and buggies; fishing and boating in the chain of lakes; and musical entertainment. More hotels and guesthouses were built to cash in on the town's beauty and charm. Winter Park today retains much of that character and consequently ranks among the most expensive and prestigious small cities in the state.

The town also figures in the annals of Florida citriculture as the home of the Temple, a fifty-fifty cross between an orange and tangerine that is one of the sweetest citrus fruits grown anywhere. According to reports, the first Temple arose from the grove of Louis A. Hakes in 1915 in Winter Park. He named his new fruit in honor of W. C. Temple, head of the Florida Citrus Exchange, and began selling it to other growers in 1919. Soon thereafter, it was discovered that the Temple was identical to the Jamaica, which had been growing since 1896 in a grove in nearby Oviedo, but the name of the fruit remained the Temple because, one suspects, of politics and friendship and a touch of jingoism.

North of Winter Park, a band of Union Army veterans planted a colony on the site of Fort Maitland, a Seminole War military outpost and antebellum plantation community. Wanting to incorporate their new town in 1884 and needing thirty voters—meaning adult men—the Yankees encouraged blacks to register, and they did. At the first election, blacks outnumbered whites and elected a black mayor and marshal. Maitland's white minority found the situation unacceptable and so offered to help the black majority found its own community—on a site the whites bought. Eatonville, the nation's first incorporated black town, named for Captain Josiah Eaton, one of the Maitland whites who sponsored it, thus came into existence in 1887.

Zora Neale Hurston, the folklorist and novelist who documented many aspects of southern life and culture that otherwise would have been forgotten, was born in Eatonville in 1901. As a child, she recalled in her autobiography, *Dust Tracks on a Road,* she lived with her family

> on a big piece of ground with two big chinaberry trees shading the front gate and Cape Jasmine bushes with hundreds of blooms on either side of the walks. There were plenty of oranges, grapefruit, tangerines, guavas and other fruits in our yard. We had a five acre garden with things to eat growing in it, and so we were never hungry. We had chicken on the table often; home-cured meat, and all the eggs we wanted.[18]

The Florida she knew was, as it had been for decades before her birth, "a country where personal strength and courage were the highest virtues. People were supposed to take care of themselves without whining."[19] And it was still a near wilderness where "bears and alligators raided hog-pens, wildcats fought with dogs in people's yards, rattlesnakes as long as a man and as thick as a man's forearm were found around back doors."[20] Eatonville became a remarkably vibrant, if poor community; Maitland became a stop on Plant's railroad and gained a measure of wealth as a resort and citrus-producing community and, later, a suburb of Orlando. Hurston herself became one of the leaders of the Harlem Renaissance before a bogus morals charge in 1948, later dropped because she had been falsely accused, drove her into depression and hiding near Fort Pierce, where she worked for some years as a maid. She died in anonymity in that Florida east coast town in 1960.

O. M. Crosby, a Connecticut Yankee, was a typical colonizer who shared the racism and classism of the period. In 1886, he chose a site about fifty miles south of Orlando and twenty west of the Kissimmee River, because of its "open pine forests studded with clear water lakes, an abundance of fish and game, freedom from malaria, mosquitoes, and Negroes." Crosby's promotional treatises claimed that the $25-an-acre homesites were a bargain "for a quiet man with a yearly income of about $500." But the man had to be responsible and possessed of the proper work ethic. "Mischief makers are not welcome," Crosby's flier, *The Home Seeker*, proclaimed, "and above all, do not come to Avon Park if you must have strong drink or questionable entertainment." The people who bought Crosby's Florida Development Company lots were recruited from England, and the Britishers did well until the freeze of 1894–95. A decade later the coming of rail service and creation of new settlements and groves revived the town.

In 1884, along the banks of the St. Johns River, some thirty-five miles above Jacksonville, Frederick Delius settled to manage a grove his father had purchased to teach him responsibility. Instead, upon hearing for the first time the music of neighboring blacks, the twenty-two-year-old attained what he later called a "state of illumination." He began to spend his evenings with the family of Elbert Anderson, learning the distinctive rhythms, chants, and melodies of their music. He studied the comingling of black, Cracker, and Indian tunes when the poor people of the area would rendezvous for a wedding, wake, or celebratory dance. Delius was one of the few immigrants of wealth and privilege who bothered to observe closely any aspect of indigenous culture and to care passionately enough about it to make it his own.

On a trip to Jacksonville to fetch a doctor for his partner, who had caught malaria, Delius met Thomas Ward, the city's organist. The encounter earned Delius a music instructor but lost him a friend and associate. Ward agreed to teach him composition and harmony; the partner, once recovered, decided to seek his fortune in another grove. Under Ward's tutelage, Delius continued to visit local black families and churches. The grove languished until his brother arrived from New Zealand, allowing Delius finally to set off for advanced study in Germany. His chamber and orchestral works incorporated into classical forms the music of Florida blacks and, to a lesser extent, Crackers. They earned for him a glowing international reputation and, although today he is largely forgotten, he influenced artists in every field, including D. H. Lawrence. Of his own inspiration, Delius said, "In Florida, through sitting and gazing at Nature, I gradually learnt the way in which I should eventually find myself."[21]

Between the early 1870s and 1893, the size of the Florida citrus crops rose from 1 million to 5 million boxes. After the freezes of 1894–95, production plummeted to 147,000 boxes. The 5-million-box level was not regained until 1910, and over the next five years it doubled, to 10 million, despite an outbreak of citrus canker, a bacterial disease imported with oranges from China to the Gulf coast. The only cure lay in burning all infected trees, and in 1915, the state legislature, responding to growers' demands for action, established a State Plant Board, which promptly launched a ten-year, $2-million canker eradication program. Dominating the economies of many areas, citriculture was too large and well organized to ignore; the state had to take precautions to protect it and assure quality crops.

The U.S. Department of Agriculture and the state had by the turn of the century established formal research programs to help growers. Researchers introduced new types, like the navel orange, and produced new hybrids, like the tangelo, a cross of the Darcy orange and grapefruit. One of the greatest of these hybridizers was W. T. Swingle, a colleague of David Fairchild in the USDA, who worked out of a grove on the New River in south Florida. The perfection of the canning process in 1921 led to an increased demand, but the greatest technological advance in the citrus industry occurred in 1945 when researchers for the Florida Citrus Commission perfected the process for making frozen concentrate. In 1949, the scientists—L. G. MacDowell, E. L. Moore, and C. D. Atkins—assigned their patent to the federal government for the free use of the American people, and the frozen juice business was born.

Almost overnight new plants devoted to the manufacture of concentrate began to create unanticipated water pollution problems in central Florida's lakes while filling the air with a distinctive, unpleasant odor, as rancid as orange blossoms are sweet. As frozen concentrate became popular, the amount of fresh fruit eaten or squeezed each year by American consumers dropped 75 percent, and certain hard-to-cultivate and -ship varieties became rare. Many groves are devoted solely to the production of oranges for concentrate, which travel by the truckful to plants owned by Coca-Cola and other conglomerates though their names remain Minute Maid and Tropicana. Within the past three years, however, producers have begun marketing at premium prices orange juice squeezed fresh either on the premises or at a nearby plant. Fresh juice is better; whether it gains a sizable share of the huge American orange market is more a question of economics than flavor.

The explosive growth of the frozen juice industry brought such demand for groves that growers increasingly were forced to plant in reclaimed soil, a costly process that nonetheless produced great dividends. In 1950, 100 million boxes were picked and by 1970, the total reached 200 million. The peak year to date in citrus production was 1979–80, when 283,550,000 boxes were picked. Severe freezes in December 1983 and again in January 1985 destroyed well over 100,000 acres of groves and production fell to 158,965,000 boxes in 1985–86. Many growers have not replanted in the northern and north-central counties because of doubts about the weather, cost, development pressure on their land from the sprawling suburbs and cities, and a new outbreak of citrus canker that resulted in a quarantine on young trees.

A USDA plant introduction center established in the Miami area in 1910 by David Fairchild moved rapidly to assist local growers not only with citrus but also with avocados and mangos, both of which became important cash crops in the region. Coconuts, whose value as a cash crop declined during the first three-quarters of this century, have begun once again to appear on grocers' shelves. Members of the Hispanic community demand them along with other tropical fruit. Around Gainesville, growers established tung nut plantations. As demand increases for particular fruit, no matter how exotic, and as profits rise, so do the number of acres devoted to that fruit, repeating the cycle of experimentation and commercial production.

The constant that binds all fruit cultivation is the cold. Each winter, warnings of freezing temperatures moving down from the north send growers into their fields and groves to light smudge pots and turn on sprinkler systems in the hope of beating back the frost. Sometimes they even use helicopters to keep air blowing through the trees. Old automobile tires burned in the pots warm the air; the running water first forestalls formation of ice, then, if the temperature drops low enough, forces formation of a thin layer of ice that insulates the fruit from the cold. The most severe blasts of cold air still overwhelm all human defenses.

FOUR

The Middle Kingdom

Hamilton Disston buys a kingdom of scrub and swamps to bail the state from bankruptcy. Cattle roam the palmetto prairie. Plant nurtures Tampa; cigars boost the bay.

Henry Sanford and other private investors of the 1870s failed, for all their acumen and resources, to cure the state's fundamental problem—insolvency born of defeat in the Civil War and three decades of incompetent, sometimes corrupt, management of public lands, its most valuable resource. The federal government welcomed Florida into the Union as a state in 1845 by awarding it 500,000 acres for use in its economic development. In 1850, the federal government passed a Swamp and Overflowed Lands Act deeding to the states wetlands deemed unfit for cultivation and decreeing that they act to reclaim those acres for productive purposes. Florida's leaders spent five years devising a mechanism for disposing of their windfall, finally creating in 1855 an Internal Improvement Fund with a board of trustees composed of the governor, comptroller, treasurer, attorney general, and registrar of state lands. (In 1979, the Internal Improvement Fund was abolished and its functions assigned to the Department of Natural Resources, with the governor and cabinet granting final approval for disposal of public land.) Florida was due as much as 22 million acres under the act, and the trustees determined to offer the land as collateral for bonds offered by various antebellum railroad and canal companies, who managed to lay 531 miles of track and several scores of ditches to link lakes and rivers before the Civil War. The policy of the Internal Improvement Fund trustees violated the Swamp Lands Act's requirement that the wetlands be diked and drained for human settlement, but the board justified its favoritism toward corporations by arguing that transportation would open the interior of the state to homesteaders. In the aftermath of the Civil War, the railroads defaulted on their loans, and their bondholders claimed the pledged Florida acreage as their due. They gained court injunctions prohibiting state officials from using public land to underwrite much-needed development projects until the claims of all creditors were satisfied either with money or land.

Lacking funds and loath to part with land worth more than the debt they owed the financiers, the trustees of the Internal Improvement Fund struggled for eleven years, 1870–81, to duck their obligation to pay off the antebellum bonds. In 1879, the state legislature passed a bill instructing the fund's trustees to award ten thousand acres of swampland in alternate sections within six miles of the right-of-way for each new mile of canal dug or railroad track laid. Florida's creditors blocked the giveaways in court. The conflict took a bizarre turn in 1881 when Governor William Bloxham, a war hero and leader in the so-called Bourbon Restoration—after the French—that brought former Confederates back to power in 1876, struck an alliance with Yankee industrialist Hamilton Disston to pull the state into solvency. Disston and his junior partners agreed to drain twelve million acres of submerged land in south Florida in exchange for half of what he reclaimed—six million acres. Disston and his associates were to "lower the level of Lake Okeechobee, to deepen and straighten the channel of the Kissimmee River, and to cut canals and ditches to connect Lake Okeechobee with the Caloosahatchee River on the west, the St. Lucie River on the east, and the Miami and other rivers on the southeast."[1] In effect, Disston was to drain the upper Everglades and create passage through Lake Okeechobee from the Atlantic to Gulf of Mexico, thereby fulfilling two dreams of Florida schemers to create waterways and land. The final configuration of south Florida's maze of canals, dikes, and channelized rivers generally follows this blueprint, but it took nearly a century and more than $500 million to accomplish.

"Ham" Disston was an odd hero. He had twice tried to join the Union Army during the Civil War only to have his father purchase his discharge and return him to work in the family business, the Keystone Saw, Tool, Steel, and File Works. After his second aborted attempt to become cannon fodder, Ham became a volunteer fireman, until he was discharged for attending too many blazes. He then settled into life as the Disston company heir apparent and directed his excess energy and financial resources toward supporting the Republican party. As a major contributor, he enjoyed considerable prestige in the party's upper echelons and in 1877 began joining Sanford and his friends on their fishing and hunting expeditions to Florida. In 1878, a year after his first visit to the state, the thirty-four-year-old Ham inherited the company his father had founded and applied himself successfully to its expansion. By 1881, he had wealth, a love of Florida, and a desire to bring the two together. According to historians Alfred Jackson Hanna and Kathryn Abbey Hanna:

> He was a creator, looking for new enterprises in which to satisfy this urge. Transforming a portion of the earth's surface stirred his imagination, and among sections of the earth needing remodeling the boggy wilderness around Lake Okeechobee held high place. The Florida development was to Hamilton Disston his own peculiar project apart from anything he had inherited.[2]

The immediate problem early in 1881 was that the Internal Improvement Fund could not finalize Governor Bloxham's deal with Disston until the state's creditors were appeased, and they had petitioned the federal court in New York, which had jurisdiction in the case, to award in settlement of their claims all the land the fund controlled—fourteen million acres. Believing that the peninsula would become the southern France or Italy of the United States, a pastoral region of resorts, spas, and extraordinarily productive farms, several groups of investors—including one led by Sanford—approached Bloxham about purchasing up to four million acres of land. Using his influence with Bloxham, Disston arranged to buy four million acres for $1 million—$200,000 upon execution of the contract and the remaining $800,000 in three installments between June 1881 and January 1882. The trustees of the Internal Improvement Fund agreed to allow Disston to choose the land he wanted in ten-thousand-acre parcels. The blocks he selected formed a sort of

triangle across central Florida, running on the Gulf coast from
Marco Island north for two hundred miles to above Tampa Bay,
then cutting across to a point above Titusville before angling
back down toward Marco.

The state's deal grabbed headlines around the country. *The
New York Times* trumpeted that Disston had made the largest
land purchase by an individual in the world. Certainly he became the owner of more land than any other person in the
United States. By scaling down the Panhandle on his marketing
maps, Disston portrayed the areas as encompassing two thirds
of the state. Even discounting his hyperbole, the amount of land
involved was astounding. When added to the land he expected
to drain, which came down the Atlantic coast and swept across
the Everglades, the purchase gave Disston effective control of
close to one half of Florida. A few military and exploratory
parties had crossed portions of the Everglades and visited Lake
Okeechobee, but no full surveys had been conducted and no
accurate maps existed of Disston's domain.

Governor Bloxham and his colleagues celebrated their
agreement with Disston, which provided them with the cash to
pay off Florida's creditors and thereby freed the Internal Improvement Fund to make good on the promise of acres of land
for miles of track and canals. The transportation companies
raced each other for prime routes and land.

Dissenters argued that Bloxham, in his rush to strike a deal,
had sold the land too cheaply, and, in fact, higher offers had
been rejected in favor of Disston's immediate cash and prior
commitment to the state. Furthermore, critics observed, much
of the land included in the purchase and drainage area was
neither swamp nor submerged, but was piney woods and dry
prairie, a region of saw-toothed palmetto, scrub cattle, and scattered settlers. Given the value of such land for forestry and
agriculture, Disston's purchase price was far too low. The state's
deal also failed to account for homesteaders with legitimate
titles and for squatters with rights earned, they felt, by virtue of
their occupancy.

People living on the palmetto prairie, whose way of life
Disston threatened to change, protested, prompting the state
both to recognize legitimate claims and attempt to silence squatters by selling them their land at one dollar an acre. Having
taken these steps, it then tried to satisfy Disston as well by
crediting the profits to his account, but he objected. He pre-

ferred that the country be settled according to his plan, with people he and his sales agents chose because of their financial means and social standing.

Disston possessed energy, enthusiasm, wealth, and nearly total ignorance of the region he moved to remake. Nor did he attempt to find out about it before starting: Nothing prevented him from exploring the area himself on his hunting and fishing trips, but no evidence exists that he did. Instead, he hastened to meet his obligations. To fulfill his reclamation contract with the state, he established the Okeechobee Land Company to drain what was called the "richest land" in the world—Everglades muck, fourteen-foot-thick deposits of organic soil formed over millennia by the decomposing sawgrass and related sedges and grasses of the marsh—for the production of sugar, coffee, fruit, jute, and indigo. To market the lands he had bought outright, he set up the Disston Land Company. To pay the state, he sold half his purchase for $600,000 to Sir Edward Reed, a British naval architect and civil engineer who owned, among other properties in the state, the Atlantic and Gulf Coast and West India Railroad—once the Florida Railroad, which ran from Fernandina on the northeastern border to Cedar Key on the west coast.

Almost immediately after signing his contracts with the state, Disston started digging. His engineers assembled a dredge at Kissimmee and brought another to Fort Myers on the Gulf coast at the mouth of the Caloosahatchee River. They were to meet in Lake Okeechobee. The plan conceived by Disston's engineers was simple. The prairie and marshland of the Kissimmee basin would be drained into the big lake by means of the channelized river. Water from Okeechobee would be diverted to the Atlantic by way of canals and remade rivers and to the Gulf of Mexico by way of the Caloosahatchee.

Working its way upstream from the Gulf, Disston's dredge deepened the channel of the slow-flowing, hammock-bordered Caloosahatchee River to its source. Crewmen looped ropes around thousand-year-old cypresses and pulled the dredge through tight, narrow bends and shallow water. From the headwaters of the river, the dredgemen blasted through limestone falls—little more than rapids—to Lake Flirt, and then broke a canal through lakes Lettuce, Bonnet, and Hicpochee to Okeechobee. In 1882, an Okeechobee Land Company steamboat made the inaugural run up the remade Caloosahatchee River from Fort Myers to Lake Okeechobee. From there, it continued up the Kissimmee for ninety-two miles. The "historic" journey was a slow, tedious struggle through the rough-cut channels.

At the headwaters of the Kissimmee River, Disston's second dredge cut small canals between Lakes East Tohopekaliga, Tohopekaliga, and Cypress, then joined them to Lake Kissimmee. The sluggish meander of a river wandering south from that lake through the prairie and pinelands was deepened and straightened a little to make it navigable—but only for modest-sized boats.

In April 1883, President Chester A. Arthur brought the press and his friends on a tour of Florida that included a trip to Kissimmee to visit and promote Disston's domain. He was, after all, a major contributor to Arthur's Republican party. Like good tourists, Arthur and company cruised a brief way on the Kissimmee River, which still couldn't handle large steamboats. They fished and viewed the natives—Cracker cowboys and Seminoles—without being quite able to determine which they found more rustic and clownish. The steamboat ran aground. The press praised Disston's reclamation program and his plans for planting fruit trees and other cash crops, like sugarcane and rice.

By 1884, Disston and his associates reported that they had reclaimed more than 2 million acres, and the trustees of the Internal Improvement Fund awarded him half of the total— 1,175,000 acres—as they had agreed. Almost immediately dissenters asserted that several summers of below-normal rainfall had done more to dry out the Kissimmee basin than Disston's canals, and that, in any event, his dredges were too puny to have drained 2 million acres. Although he steadfastly denied the accusations, they were substantially correct, for reasons having as much to do with the vagaries of drainage and of Florida's climate, which often would leave wet land dry one year and the next make all land wet, as with any dishonesty on the part of Disston and his colleagues. A legislative committee reported in 1887 that the actual total the sawmaker had reclaimed more nearly approached 50,000 acres, a judgment Disston disputed. He said he had spent $250,000 to dig forty miles of canals that had dried out his 2 million acres. But in 1888, he agreed to spend another $125,000 to improve his stagnant ditches and to pay an additional twenty-five cents an acre for any more drained land he wanted. Despite the difficulties, Disston's land companies held title to 1,652,000 acres and had unrecognized claims of 347,000 more by 1894, when the dredges stopped work.

* * *

Disston failed to fulfill his most extravagant fantasies for Florida. His dredge bulled and cut its way along the channel of the Ritta River, a dribble of water issuing from the south side of Lake Okeechobee, toward the Shark River and Florida Bay. It spread thirteen miles of spoil along the bank before the limestone ridge cupping the big lake stopped it. Had Disston's Ditch—known for a time as the Thirteen-Mile Canal—been completed, it would have ravaged the Everglades, whose major channel is the Shark River Slough seeping southwestward in a broad, shimmering sheet of shallow water and tall grass. Future drainers turned the ditch southeast where it transformed the tropical Miami River into a canal.

The dredge nibbled another "mosquito ditch" between the headwaters of the Kissimmee and the St. Johns. Following Disston's death, the scheme, like the unfinished canal, was adopted by other ambitious builders who conceived a vast network of waterways that would not only permit continuous steamboat travel from Jacksonville to Fort Myers but also open virtually the whole interior of the peninsula to trade.

Disston's most grandiose scheme involved bringing to fruition a dream that dated back three centuries, to the days of Spanish colonization: a canal across the heart of the peninsula to join the Atlantic Ocean and Gulf of Mexico. The canal would save time, open the interior, and more important, from the shippers' viewpoint, allow craft to bypass the dangerous Straits of Florida where too many men, ships, and millions of dollars' worth of cargo had been already lost to poor navigation, unruly weather, and piracy. Disston's waterway was to run from the Gulf up the dredged Caloosahatchee across Lake Okeechobee to the St. Lucie River and into the Atlantic, but he never completed the Okeechobee-Atlantic connection. Nor did he make any progress toward completing the stretch of Intracoastal Waterway from Jacksonville to Lake Worth that later was to provide a sheltered channel for small craft. His imagination outstripped not only his resources but the equipment and engineering skills of his day. In most cases, the canals his company dug were little better than gashes in the limestone that collected stagnant water where mosquitoes bred and hyacinths flourished. Even the successes caused so much damage and disruption that they frequently required additional work in the future.

The Caloosahatchee River reveals the immediate and long-term effects of Disston's draining and dredging operations. In

1876, the pseudonymous Al Fresco, writing in *Forest and Stream* magazine described the river as "a grand stream. On each bank, rich high hammocks extend back from the river at a distance of one-quarter to one-half mile. Back of the hammocks rich pine land will be found, and beyond this the open prairie country."[3] South Florida naturalist Charles Torrey Simpson related the story of the Caloosahatchee's next fifty years in his memoir *Out of Doors in Florida:*

> I know of no locality in Florida where the hand of vandal man has wrought more dreadful destruction than in and about this once beautiful river, no place in which the peace and holiness of the wilderness have been more completely desecrated. First the Disstons dredged out a canal from Okeechobee into its headwaters which brought down silt and sand that later filled its deep channel. Then the settler came with fire and the ax to destroy its glorious forests; he brought with him lean cattle and the miserable razorback hogs and they ate the herbaceous vegetation and killed out the undergrowth in the forests. The roots which bound the loose, sandy soil together were killed, and the vertical banks, undermined by high water, fell in and filled up the channel. The filling of this has, of course, caused the floods to dig away the banks more and more, in many cases leaving enormous masses of soil which have slid in and lodged along its bottom. . . . A dredge was brought in and for long distances the sand which obstructed the channel was dug out and dumped in hideous and unshapely ricks and masses along the banks and the space between them and the water. But the evil cannot be cured. . . . The river can only be made navigable for shallow boats by constant dredging.[4]

In the 1880s and 1890s, few individuals called the channelization of the Caloosahatchee, or any river, a tragedy. Rather, the drive was for more reclamation and settlement. The desire for profit played the lead in these efforts, but accompanying it, among many developers, was a sense of righteousness, an unwavering faith in the efficacy of their undertakings. They sought to control, as Flagler did, every aspect of development, from the basic town plan to the character and financial resources of colonists. A new society was being ripped out of the Florida "wilderness."

Through the land company he established to handle his

remaining half of the four million acres he'd purchased from the state, Disston promoted his domain throughout the United States and Europe. He also sponsored experimental farms and processing plants, as did Sanford, Plant, and Flagler. His promotional material—with advice on growing vegetables, bananas, citrus, peanuts, rice, indigo, and sugarcane—followed the standard portrait of the state as the closest thing on earth to paradise in terms of its climate and fertility.

Disston established communities at Tarpon Springs, Lake Conway near Orlando, and St. Cloud. Tarpon Springs was a runt of a village on Spring Bayou above Tampa Bay when he decided to make it a resort for his rich friends. The name may have misled him into thinking the place a fisherman's paradise, for the founders of the community in 1876 had apparently mistaken leaping mullet for the larger, unrelated tarpon, which many anglers considered the finest game fish of all. In 1883–84, Disston opened a stage line to Tampa to tie into Plant's new railroad station, and built a resort hotel at Tarpon Springs, which for years remained one of the most fashionable on the Gulf coast. In 1890, the residents of the small town learned that their sand-and-shell roads were loaded with phosphate, and immediately attempted to riot over ownership. By that time, a lust for phosphate had created an epidemic of avarice in north and central Florida, where rich deposits were daily discovered. Some folks were known to salt their fields with phosphate limestone in an attempt to entice unsuspecting, usually northern, speculators to pay exorbitant prices for a few acres of worthless scrub. In Tarpon Springs, citizens verged on shooting each other for prime stretches of road before a diplomatic preacher persuaded them to keep the peace and render unto God the bounty of the land. All agreed; the church gained wealth; the streets became brick.

In 1905, Greek sponge divers made Tarpon Springs the home port for their fleet, abandoning the shallow waters off the Keys where traditional-minded Conchs used long poles to hook the animals from the shallow waters and flats and defended what they considered their territory and prerogatives with violence. They fired on several occasions at the Greek divers, who could wipe out entire beds in short order. Tarpon Springs flourished as the new center of the sponge trade until the 1940s when a red tide—a dense bloom of microorganisms that suffocates marine life—destroyed many of the Gulf sponge beds. Although the industry recovered somewhat a decade later, today Tarpon Springs and its Greek community attract more tourists than sponge buyers. Sponges in the markets are often imported.

On the shores of Lake Conway in central Florida, Disston built a village from scratch. He laid out the town grid and recruited 250 families. For prices ranging from $1.25 to $5.00 an acre, each could purchase farms of twenty, thirty, or eighty acres. He required that each family have a $1,000 grubstake and, in return, provided technical assistance for building, planting, and livestock husbandry. Another planned community—Disston City—never grew beyond its blueprints and today passes as Gulfport on the Pinellas Peninsula surrounded on three sides by St. Petersburg.

Disston's Florida Land and Improvement Company offered farm sites in forty-acre tracts at a cost of $225, payable in full or in ten interest-free, quarterly installments. The company also sold a few large tracts to colonizers with smaller purses and dreams than those of Disston, including in 1884, a group of Scottish investors, who bought sixty thousand acres on the west coast and brought sixty settlers to farm a community they named Sarasota. In 1886, the colony's first manager, Colonel J. Hamilton Gillespie, son of the head of the syndicate, built a four-hole golf course—one of the first in the state. The game became so popular that every first-class resort had to have at least one course. But despite successes such as Sarasota, there weren't enough buyers to keep Disston's empire solvent.

In 1890, Disston began his last major project, organizing the Florida Sugar Manufacturing Company with an initial investment of $1 million. He set to work establishing at St. Cloud, below Kissimmee, a sugar industry to rival and break Louisiana's dominance of domestic production. He hired an accomplished planter, Rufus Rose, to direct white tenant farmers he brought from cane fields in the bayous and Mississippi delta. He had special shoes made to keep the mules from sinking into the muck as they pulled the plows, and had tram tracks laid through fields for the cane cars. He constructed a refinery that produced 1.5 million pounds of sugar in 1895, the operation's peak year.

Using his political connections, Disston arranged for establishment in 1891 of a U.S. Department of Agriculture research station at St. Cloud, whose agronomists introduced some thirty varieties of sugarcane. One of the first USDA agents at the station, Harvey W. Wiley, proclaimed the south shore of Lake

Okeechobee ideally suited for sugar plantations—if the land was properly drained. He recognized that the south Florida climate was mild enough that the cane would reseed; everywhere else in the contiguous states, cuttings had to be set out each year, a laborious process.

The Disston sugar plantation proved short-lived. Planters discovered that reclaimed muckland quickly loses its nutrients and its ability to retain water, making heavy fertilization and irrigation essential. Left in its natural state, it receives fresh organic matter as plants die off and regenerate during the natural cycles of the wet and dry seasons, of flood and fire. The carpet of living and decaying matter also acts as a sponge, absorbing and holding moisture. When the plant cover is removed, the water runs unimpeded through the dry soil, and the dried-out muck literally vanishes in the wind, blown across the peninsula and out to sea. These problems that ruined Disston's model farm have so consistently baffled growers on south Florida's reclaimed land that some people question whether the land should be farmed at all. Fertilizers washed into the lakes, rivers, and the Everglades have created nutrient overloads that threaten native plant communities and the wildlife dependent on them. Pesticides kill fish and fowl. Diverting water for agriculture depletes supplies needed to sustain the Everglades, and their decline, according to experts, has affected the quality of life throughout south Florida, bringing harsh droughts and floods, altering local rain patterns, causing the climate to grow colder and drier.

The national economic depression of 1893 ruined Hamilton Disston. To keep his empire afloat he mortgaged his Florida land to the Columbia Avenue Savings Fund, Safe Deposit, Title and Trust Company of Philadelphia for $2 million. The following year, he laid off his Florida employees because he couldn't pay them. Early in 1896 the trust company called in his loan, knowing he would have to default. At the end of April in a bathtub in his Philadelphia home, he put a pistol to his head and blew his brains out. His heirs let some of the land revert to the state for unpaid taxes and liquidated the Disston Land Company to pay off outstanding debts. For $70,000 in 1901, the United Land Company bought the bankrupt enterprise and gained claims to several hundred thousand acres of Florida real estate. (In contrast, Flagler, during the financial panic of 1907, needed $12 million to continue his Florida adventure, so he went to his

Henry Morrison Flagler at the Knight's Key dock in 1908. The key served as the southern terminus for the Florida East Coast Railway until 1912, when the first train rolled into Key West.

Below, Florida East Coast Railway workers constructing the viaduct for the Long Key bridge on the way to Key West

COURTESY OF THE HENRY M. FLAGLER MUSEUM, PALM BEACH, FLORIDA

COURTESY OF THE HENRY M. FLAGLER MUSEUM, PALM BEACH, FLORIDA

An aerial view of Palm Beach from Lake Worth shows the now-defunct Royal Poinciana *(foreground)* and the original Breakers *(background),* ca. 1903. Below, visitors relax in the courtyard of Flagler's opulent Ponce de Leon Hotel in St. Augustine, 1905.

In the late 1890s, the Tampa Bay Hotel of Henry Plant rivaled Flagler's Ponce de Leon Hotel in St. Augustine. Below, one of the state's busiest ports at the turn of the century, Tampa's harbor still possessed a bleak and underdeveloped aspect. Henry Plant's Tampa Inn sat across his railroad tracks from the docks.

Above, Ybor City on the outskirts of Tampa was the center of cigar manufacturing in the United States and a mainstay of Florida's economy. This photograph of the intersection of Fourteenth Street and Ninth Avenue dates from the turn of the century.

Left, turtlers at Key West display their 350-pound "Big Turtle" on April 1, 1885. Now protected, green turtles are considered one of the world's great delicacies and were hunted relentlessly by turtlers working out of the Keys in the late nineteenth and early twentieth centuries.

The Key West sponge market, ca. 1900. Below, Greek spongers operating out of Tarpon Springs dove for their catch, whereas the spongers from Key West stayed in their boats and hooked the creatures from beds lying in shallow water.

Left, fish being unloaded from a commercial snapper boat at Pensacola around the turn of the century

Below, stevedores transferring bananas from ship to train at Tampa in 1930

Above, a sketch from *Scribner's Monthly*, 1874, shows sportsmen engaged in their favorite activity, shooting wildlife from the deck of a steamship.

Left, this 1874 sketch from *Scribner's Monthly* shows the *Marion* plying the Oklawaha River, one of the most popular excursions for travelers of the period.

Below, the nighttime run up the Oklawaha River from Palatka to Silver Springs was considered to offer one of the most beautiful sights in the country, as the pitch-pine torches placed atop the steamboat's pilot house threw a "strange but clear light" upon the dense vegetation of the shore. This postcard shows the steamer *Hiawatha* of the Hart Line in 1011.

A one-room schoolhouse made of Florida thatch palm, ca. 1890

A "Cracker's home" ca. 1895 on the open palmetto prairie, where travel was often difficult due to sand, dense palmettos, and wetlands

friend J. P. Morgan and requested a loan. Morgan gave Flagler a personal check for $5 million and told him that if he showed it to other bankers he would soon have the full amount. Morgan was right.)

Disston wasn't the first—and surely not the last—developer to work without knowledge or concern for the effects of his machinations on the land and water. He doubtless never even wondered whether his efforts would be anything but positive contributions to a wholesome, ordered society. But his efforts were the first to show the environmental sensitivity of central and south Florida to human invasion. Unfortunately, few people noticed; the majority were more interested in proclaiming his minimal accomplishments proof that the Everglades could be drained, or in the parlance of progress, "reclaimed." They recognized a degree of difficulty but believed themselves capable of anything, given sufficient capital and labor.

Despite the dredged channels and canals, Disston's domain remained largely a blank on maps of Florida development, a place marked by ignorance, occupied by cowmen, hunters, and drifters. Although a way had been opened for steamboats to enter Lake Okeechobee, trains and more extensive dredging were needed to develop fully its vast fisheries and rookeries.

The Disston land deals of 1881 focused attention on the palmetto prairie in the Kissimmee and St. Johns River basins and west of Okeechobee, home of Florida scrub cattle and the cowmen who worked them. Much of the land was unsurveyed and unregistered; nearly all was unfenced. The Seminoles had first herded cattle on the Kissimmee prairies at the beginning of the nineteenth century. White cowmen came to the range in the 1840s as the Army drove the Indians into the Everglades, killed them, or forcibly removed them to the Indian Territory in the West. In succeeding decades, the men and women of the palmetto prairie earned a reputation for ornery independence that persists to this day. They had no use for Disston, the Yankee upstart, and his claim to their region. Although the state accommodated them, by forcing the cowmen to secure title to their spreads, it initiated the demise of the open range.

The cowmen ranched in a fashion the artist Frederic Remington, visiting in the 1890s, found distasteful when compared with that of his beloved westerners. Remington was a guest of the Parker family, owners of the Parker Brothers Ranch in Arcadia and at the time the largest ranchers in the state. The head of the family in the 1880s, Henry Parker, had opened a trading post at Fort Drum, sponsored the first rodeos in the region, and hosted the Fort Drum Frolic, a country party attended by whites, blacks, and Indians. Readding Parker, the founding patriarch, known throughout the region for his habit of using a steamer trunk as a bank, had early on befriended Tom Silas, a former slave and one of the few black ranch owners in the state.

In a *Harper's New Monthly Magazine* article in June 1895, Remington detailed his observations and presented his sketches under the heading "Cracker Cowboys," a term he meant as an insult, although one of the cattlemen with the largest holdings, Jacob Summerlin took pleasure in his title "King of the Crackers." The cattle, which Remington thought "scrawny creatures not fit for a pointer-dog to mess on," roamed unfettered through land that was "flat and sandy, with miles of straight pine timber, each tree an exact duplicate of its neighbor tree, and underneath [the trees grew] the scrub palmettos, the twisted brakes and hammocks, and the gnarled water-oaks festooned with the sad gray Spanish-moss—truly not a country for a high-spirited race or moral giants."

Cowmen fired the prairie from mid-February to the end of March each year to burn back sapling pine, oak, and palmetto and encourage the growth of grass for their cattle. In 1879, timber companies, objecting to the practice because they wanted mature pines, forced the state legislature to limit burning. Ranchers and farmers, however, persisted in their actions, and they were ecologically correct. The prairie was formed and sustained by fire—its plants and animals adapted to the burning. The major birds of the palmetto prairie—the burrowing owl, sandhill crane, and Audubon's caracara—all fed on the charred corpses of insects and snakes. Fire kept the tick population suppressed, which in turn prevented the spread of the diseases they bore among wild and domestic animals. Modern ranch managers continue to selectively burn their now fenced ranges and foresters during the past two decades have begun widely to adopt a policy of letting wildfires burn and setting controlled ones. Across the unique broad, flat palmetto prairie of Florida, it is possible to see a cow two miles away, just as it was a century ago.

The men who herded cattle out of the scrub and wetlands were, to Remington's eyes, as scrawny as their cows, lank, unkempt, and wild. They rode poor mounts, yet they were, he adjudged,

> well paid for their desperate work, and always eat fresh beef or "razorbacks," and deer which they kill in the woods. The heat, the poor grass, their brutality, and the pest of the flies kill their ponies, and, as a rule, they lack dash and are indifferent riders. . . . A strange effect is added by their use of large, fierce cur-dogs, one of which accompanies each cattle-hunter, and is taught to pursue cattle, and to even take them by the nose, which is another instance of their brutality.

In his haste to prove Cracker cowboys a lesser breed than their western counterparts, Remington overlooked or misinterpreted a great deal of information. He talked not to the cowmen but to bankers and storekeepers in Kissimmee who took the cowmen's money but thought them more roguish than civilized. He failed to observe that the dense vegetation where cattle often hid prohibited use of a lariat and made riding in any fashion difficult. Well-trained dogs—usually leopard dogs or crosses with that breed—worked better in the scrub, swamp, and across the open range than a dozen lasso-twirling hands. In a land of often scarce labor, a pack of good herding dogs, with individuals trained to trail, catch, and guard, meant a roundup and drive would succeed rather than fail. Catch dogs grabbed cattle by the nose and held them in place until the hand could tie or brand them. The dogs worked that way until the 1930s when screwworms traveled into the state on Dust Bowl cattle—Herefords brought from Texas to improve native stock, which generally provided inferior beef. The screwworm flies laid eggs in lesions left by catch dogs—and by whips, thorns, limbs, and wild animals—and once hatched, the larvae commenced feeding. They could consume a calf in twenty-four hours. Bears, cats, and deer also fell to the plague (but not because of dogs). The value of the dogs lay in their unsurpassed skill in herding and guarding cattle. Strong and agile, they could throw full-grown bulls to the ground. The dogs were also employed by their masters in a war of annihilation against panthers and wolves.

Remington also forgot to mention the cowboys' distinctive bullwhips, which some handled with enough skill to pop a bird out of the air, kill a rattlesnake, or turn a stampede. The men sometimes used the whips to communicate through a rough code. Remington felt the mosquitoes—as did everyone—but somehow missed the strange, tropical sounds of alligators bellowing, millions of frogs croaking in different keys, the birds, including the limpkin, whose night wail reminded listeners of a person in distress, the constant whir in the heat of insects.

He did, however, notice the lawlessness of the cow towns, the propensity of the hands to drink long and hard. In the early 1870s, the nation's first ride-up saloon, where cowmen could imbibe without dismounting or entering the building, opened in Kissimmee. A decade passed before the West could boast of such establishments.

Into the twentieth century throughout Florida cow country, men paid for their liquor, as they were paid for their cattle and labor, with gold doubloons. Cuba, which was the primary market for cattle, provided the currency of exchange, as it had since 1858. Beginning in the 1880s, railroad, lumber, and turpentine camps, as well as resorts purchased local beef, but Cuba remained the dominant buyer until the 1920s. Prices varied from $6 up to $15 a head, with the entire trade in most years exceeding $1 million.

The herd owners pocketed the greater part of that, and many established family dynasties that continue to control the cattle industry. For example, a physician named Howell Tyson Lykes gave up medicine in order to ranch and export cattle during the years between Reconstruction and the turn of the century. He employed schooners and then steamers and opened offices in Cuba after the Spanish-American War. Today, Lykes Brothers is the largest landowner in Florida, the largest meatpacker, and a major shipping company.

While the most ambitious and lucky ranchers prospered, the hands received low wages that kept them impoverished and living in conditions that only the most blind romantic would admire. Remington had proclaimed that the cowhands were well paid for their labor, but he was wrong. During the four-month herding season, the usually young men earned, at best, $1.50 for long dangerous days—the same as workers on the railroad gangs and in the phosphate mines, meager recompense.[5] By any standard, life on the palmetto prairie was rough and violent. Rousting the feral cattle from the scrub, penning and branding them, sorting them for sale or return to the wild—the traditions of ranching on the peninsula made these difficult and dangerous tasks more hazardous. Unmarked cattle were considered strays unless matched by appearance to a branded mother—and that was such an inexact science that fights often settled the issue. The herds for market were driven by a handful of men and as many as twenty dogs across hundreds of miles of prairie, swamp, and flatwoods to the docks of Punta Rassa or Tampa on the Gulf coast. From there, they were shipped to Cuba or Key West.

Vendettas, wars over cattle and pasture, theft, even bush-whacking, were common. For decades, the ranchers overlooked as a business cost the poaching of their cattle by local Crackers seeking meat for their tables. By the time of the Disston pur-chase, however, the price of beef had risen so high that people had begun rustling cattle for commerce rather than subsistence, and the ranchers around Kissimmee moved with force to stop the practice.

The people of the palmetto prairie were an idiosyncratic lot, at times frightening to visitors and strangers. The oldest families could trace their lineage in the country no farther back than the 1840s, when their forebears had arrived in the wake of troops fighting the Seminoles. More recently had come desert-ers from the Union and Confederate armies, drifting veterans, and fugitives who liked the prairie's and flatwoods' proximity to the Everglades, Big Cypress Swamp, and Ten Thousand Is-lands, where a man could hide from people and the law.

Legends arose around some of these derelicts, just as they had around the brigands who pillaged along the coast in the nineteenth century. The most notorious among them, Ed Wat-son, established a domain of terror in the 1890s up the Chatham River from Chokoloskee, where he ran a sugarcane plantation, shot plume birds, and killed alligators. The stories vary a little but all agree that he was a large man who had fled the Florida/ Georgia border where he had murdered three men. On his plantation he forced into labor fugitive whites and blacks who came to the Ten Thousand Islands to escape retribution for crimes of their own, and when their work was done, he killed and buried them. He was arrested several times for murders in Key West, but skipped bail and retired to the Chatham where he was called with mockery and respect Emperor Watson. In 1910, Watson's foreman murdered and gutted a man and old woman living nearby, and the people of Chokoloskee used the killings to organize a posse that gunned Watson down.

Men like Ed Watson were grotesque parodies of the rela-tively small group of capitalist builders who changed Florida's fortunes in the last three decades of the nineteenth century—

Henry Sanford, Hamilton Disston, Henry Plant, and Henry Flagler primary among them. The man who most bound the quartet was Henry Plant, whose railroad served Sanford's farms and Disston's middle kingdom, whose enthusiasm and salesmanship persuaded Flagler to invest in Florida.

A Connecticut Yankee, Plant had turned southern businessman well before the War Between the States and so firmly established himself that during the conflict his Southern Express Company served as collector of the tariff for the Confederacy, while he sojourned in Europe to avoid too strongly taking sides. After the war, he purchased bankrupt short lines throughout Georgia, South Carolina, and Florida, which he gradually transformed into the Plant System—officially after 1892, the Plant Investment Company. Henry Sanford invested in the Plant System, as did Henry Flagler, who also served as a director before becoming a railroad mogul in his own right.

Plant came to control 600 miles of railroads in Florida; 1,665 throughout the South. His steamboats ran from New York to Havana, Jacksonville, and Sanford; Tampa to New York, New Orleans, Cedar Key, and other ports along the Gulf coast of Florida. He owned the Seminole Hotel in Winter Park, the Ocala House in Ocala, the Hotel Kissimmee, the Hotel Belleview in Clearwater, and the Port Tampa Inn and Tampa Bay Hotel, as well as other inns and hotels at Punta Gorda and Fort Myers. Plant's lone biographer, a quite uncritical gentleman named George Hutchinson Smyth, wrote in 1898—the year before his subject's death—that he "made his own gain and increasing wealth subordinate to the public weal."[6] In an 1895 testimonial, the *Atlanta Constitution* boasted that Plant had "developed the country and revolutionized the face of nature."[7]

Flagler's apologists used nearly identical language to describe their champion. With good reason: The two men operated along parallel lines, creating corporate empires that included trains, steamboats, land companies, agricultural experts, and resource exploitation. They were friends and rivals who divided the peninsula rather than wage economic war against each other.

That territorial division did not prevent them from engaging in rather spirited competition—in luxury hotels. Plant constructed the Tampa Bay Hotel as a direct answer to Flagler's Ponce de Leon in St. Augustine. Plant began construction in July 1888, just seven months after the Ponce had opened to national praise. The five-story Tampa Bay Hotel received its first guests in 1891; and, like Flagler's, it was built in a Moorish architectural style, but of red brick, not cast concrete. The Tampa Bay Hotel cost $2 million to construct and $500,000 to furnish with antiques, sculpture, and paintings from Europe and Asia; the Ponce de Leon had also cost $2.5 million. According to George Hutchinson Smyth, the Tampa Bay Hotel was built to "illustrate its age, the demands of the people, what they enjoy, and what they are willing to pay for."[8] As at Flagler's hotels, one thing they paid for was delivery by train directly to the entrance. (Among the more curious parallels is this: The Tampa Bay Hotel today houses the University of Tampa; the Hotel Ponce de Leon is home to Flagler College.)

When Plant's Moorish palace opened, Tampa was considered ideally positioned to become the state's major city. In a November 17, 1891, article lauding Plant the *New York Daily News* predicted, "Few, if any cities in Florida have a more promising future before them than Tampa." It was a booming harbor handling cattle, phosphate, fish, and produce; a trading post for hunters and trappers; a fishing port; a burgeoning tourist center; and the new home-base for the fast-growing, lucrative cigar industry. Its physical allure owed much to its beautiful bay opening on to the magical waters of the Gulf of Mexico.

Often the reality of the budding city belied its glorious reputation. In pre-Spanish days, the territory of the Calusa—an aggressive nation of hunters, fishermen, and canal and mound builders that dominated southwest Florida—met and overlapped that of the Timucua—farmers from the northwest—at Tampa Bay. Etymologists speculate that Tampa is derived from an old Calusa word, *Tanpa*, which no one can translate. The first Anglo-American settlement on the site had a less poetic name: Fort Brooke, which was established in 1823 during the war of extermination against the Seminole. A settlement of Spanish and Cuban fishermen had stood there since the sixteenth century, but the Calusa and Timucua were gone, having vanished by the time of the American Revolution. In 1867 and again in 1871, yellow fever epidemics raged along the bay, but the little community survived—barely—trading cattle to Cuba, plumes and hides to Yankee brokers. When Plant's South Florida Railroad, completing a 280-mile run from Jacksonville, came to town in 1884, the population totaled no more than eight hundred. The 1890 census counted six thousand.

Soon after his arrival, Plant extended his tracks another ten miles to Port Tampa and constructed a causeway and piers from the train terminal to the deep-water channel he had dredged the year before. Business picked up immediately. Cattle shipments, dominated by Captain James McKay and Dr. Howell Lykes, grew until Tampa challenged Punta Rassa for leadership in the Cuba trade. Techniques for loading the animals onto ships were brutal: Herded to the end of the dock, they were then shoved into the hold, often landing atop each other and breaking legs or even crushing other animals to death.

Tampa Bay formed the heart of the Gulf coast country that visitors in the 1870s found so striking with its white sand beaches, lush plants, and abundant wildlife. Mullet and redfish seemed to fill the water for miles. Sea turtles foraged on aquatic grasses. After Plant deepened the channel and brought in his railroad, his boats and trains began shipping fish out of the port at the rate of fifty thousand pounds a day.

Settlers quickly bought whatever fertile land was available. Farms dating to the seventeenth century were revived and more heavily cultivated than ever before. Pines and hardwood were clear-cut for local consumption and export. By the early twentieth century the thirteen-hundred-acre hammock that had once defined the area north of the Manatee River had been cleared for vegetable farms; and many of those have now become housing developments to serve the complex of cities on Tampa Bay that have never stopped growing.

South of the Manatee River, below Bradenton, Egbert and Pliny Reasoner in 1883 established one of the peninsula's most famous nurseries. Pliny, only nineteen when he arrived, died six years later from yellow fever, but his brother continued the nursery, which remains in the family and has over the years provided fruit trees and root stock to the Soviet Union, China, and various African and South American nations.

West across the bay from Tampa, on the Pinellas Peninsula, another new community began to boom with the coming of a railroad. An exiled Russian nobleman named Piotr Alexeitch Dementieff—which he Anglicized to Peter Demens—fought through a yellow fever epidemic and repeated flooding of his right-of-way to expand a short logging track into the Orange Belt Line, which would reach from Sanford across the rich, central citrus district to the Gulf. The construction delays caused him to forfeit land bonuses from the state, which he had used as collateral for his loans; creditors immobilized his equipment; and workers threatened to lynch him when he failed to meet the payroll. But he escaped every misfortune and finally completed the line from Sanford to an unnamed little village on the Pinellas Peninsula, population thirty. Its founder, John Williams, a transplant from Detroit, wanted to renege on a deal promising the nobleman half his land in exchange for bringing the railway to the hamlet, but Demens forced the issue. In 1892, the community, having grown to a population of four hundred, incorporated itself as St. Petersburg, a name Demens selected to honor his Russian birthplace. Demens received scant else in return, and wandered off to California and obscurity. His Orange Belt Line went bankrupt just before he fled, but, managed by creditors, profited until the freeze of 1894–95. Plant bought the railroad for next to nothing immediately thereafter.

The greatest impetus to Tampa's growth after the arrival of the railroad came from the cigar industry. In 1886, following fires and strikes at their Key West cigar factories, Vincente Martinez Ybor and Ignacio Hoya accepted inducements from Tampa's civic leaders to relocate their businesses. The cigar makers had a habit of such moves: In 1869, Ybor had fled from Havana to Key West to duck the United States tariff on foreign cigars and to escape La Liga, the workers union. Nonetheless, his workers organized nearly as soon as they reached Key West, and over the years the struggle between them and the factory owners became increasingly bitter and violent. So Ybor and Hoya sought to smash the union by moving to Tampa. East of the existing business district, they laid out a factory town and named it Ybor City.

Stetson Kennedy wrote of the new town's earliest days in *Palmetto Country:* "Hardly a person failed to suffer from the ravages of malaria and other diseases which spread because of the polluted drinking water, mosquitoes, and poor sanitary facilities. Plagues of gnats caused temporary blindness, and forced many people to wear goggles."[9] Ybor forestalled a mutiny among his workers by hosting a Christmas picnic on his country estate and improving sanitation and housing conditions in his factory and city. Strikes in Key West in 1889 and again in 1894, during which Spanish laborers were imported as scabs—leading to conflict between the Cuban cigar workers on one side and Key West Anglos and Spaniards on the other—hastened the industry's move to Tampa.

Through the late nineteenth and early twentieth centuries,

cigars were a popular fact of life, a sign of accomplishment and masculinity. So through revolution and war, the Tampa cigar industry expanded, and Florida tobacco farming grew with it. In 1880, ninety acres in north and west Florida were planted in tobacco; after the embargo of Cuban leaf, the total climbed to two thousand. By the turn of the century, in Key West, Tampa, and Jacksonville, 127 factories were producing nearly 200 million cigars annually. Cigar manufacture contributed well over $10 million a year to the state's economy, making it nearly equal to the lumber and naval stores industries combined and larger than phosphate mining.[10]

Plant's efforts focused on diversifying the economy of Tampa, so the city would not become dependent on cigars or cattle or any other single industry. In 1889, he arranged for the federal government to designate the city a port of entry and establish a customs office, which allowed it to expand its Caribbean trade, at the expense of Key West. By then, the Gulf port had already become the dominant transshipment point on the west coast for phosphate, an essential ingredient for fertilizers, baking powder, soap, and glass (today for soft drinks, toothpaste, motor oil, and water softeners, as well). That phosphates caused severe damage to the nation's waterways aroused little concern until the 1960s when environmentalists began demanding their removal from laundry detergents; only a handful of states have agreed, and Florida is not among them.

Recognizing the fervent patriotism of Florida's Cubans, Plant managed to play that island's politics to his advantage during the 1890s. Many of Tampa's three thousand Cubans—along with a like number in Key West and a smaller community in Jacksonville—belonged to the Partido Revolutionario Cubano that José Martí and Tomás Estrada Palma founded in New York in 1891, supporting it with money and weapons. Martí's order to start the revolution in 1895 was rolled inside a cigar and shipped to Cuba, and immediately before an embargo on trade was declared, one of Henry Plant's steamers brought the last shipment of tobacco leaves out of Havana to the Tampa factories.

When war was finally declared against Spain in 1898, Plant lobbied successfully to have Tampa declared the primary staging area for American troops. Despite his arguments about defense of the port and the need for coastal guns, what he wanted was the profit to be made from carrying men and materiel on his railroad. His success spurred other railroad companies to demand camps for their cities: the Florida East Coast Railway for Miami, the Florida Central and Peninsular for Fernandina. The push for military posts glossed over a major disagreement in the state, even among its developers. Newspapers throughout the peninsula initially opposed any war with Spain because their editors and owners—including Plant and Flagler—feared that Cuba would become part of the United States and that Florida would lose any competition with it in tourism, agriculture, and business. Florida's Cubans, on the other hand, fervently favored the revolution and sowed enough fear among the state's Spanish residents that many fled to New York after war was declared. The papers fell in line after they realized that money could be made from war and after the U.S. Congress passed legislation forbidding annexation of Cuba. By war's end, camps in Lakeland, Fernandina, Jacksonville, and Miami, along with the main facility in Tampa, had held 100,000 soldiers; while the Navy had expanded and improved its bases at Pensacola and Key West, where a government-built desalinization plant eased a severe water problem.

The fiasco called the Spanish-American War was fought in the wet season, which guaranteed disease among the troops and displeasure among reporters covering this first "media" war. Rain turned Tampa's streets into quagmires; water shortages, poor sanitation, and disease were problems in every camp. Racial tensions ran high between local whites and black troops; their anger, distrust, and hatred caused violence and near riots in Lakeland and Miami. The heat and humidity and boredom tried everyone. Hearst newspapers' correspondent Richard Harding Davis called Tampa "a squalid, sand-blighted city." Comments about other sites were worse, for good reason. By the end of the war, 379 American troops had died in combat, while 4,784 had expired in the camps of disease, most often typhoid fever from infected drinking water and filthy food and housing. In Miami, malaria was also a problem. The Navy abandoned Key West because of a yellow fever panic (the disease proved to be dengue fever).

The weight of men and goods strained the state's transportation system as well as its cities; nonetheless, as the railroad companies had predicted, the war brought profit—approximately $6.1 million in government expenditures statewide, $4 million of that in Tampa. That city's population, despite the bad press, boomed to 16,000 by 1910. Miami reached nearly 11,000, and Jacksonville climbed to 28,000 to become the state's largest city. Florida's total population had reached 750,000; in the next three decades that total would triple. The pace of growth, even more than the numbers, led to often wanton destruction of land and resources, as newcomers demanded more of less. On the plus side, according to David Fairchild, many veterans of the Spanish-American War returned from the tropics with a taste for new fruit and vegetables and thereby helped expand America's limited palate and encourage cultivation in Florida.[11] But that seems scant reward.

The year after the Spanish-American War ended, 1899, the eighty-year-old Henry Plant died, and his son Morton assumed control of the business, doing what Flagler had once hoped his son would do. In 1902, Morton sold the Plant Investment Company to the Atlantic Coast Line Railroad. With land, steamboats, trains, and 2,250 miles of track from Richmond to Tampa, the railroad became a major power in Florida. By that time, the Seaboard Air Line Railroad also offered extensive service throughout the south and north and central Florida to Tampa. The railway had entered the state by acquiring, as Plant had, bankrupt short lines. In 1924, the company, under S. Davies Warfield, crossed the peninsula from the west coast to Palm Beach by way of Lake Okeechobee. For the first time, a traveler could traverse the lower peninsula by train, rather than travel around the south end by boat or on the rails to Jacksonville and then south. From Palm Beach, the Seaboard Air Line ran to Miami, creating the first competition for Flagler's railroad, too late, though, to profit from the real estate boom that had rocked that portion of the peninsula.

FIVE

A Scarred and Barren Land

Natural resources are the prize: logging, turpentining, and min-
ing lay bare the state. The commissary and convict-lease systems
impose a grotesque slavery on workers. Personal and institu-
tional violence are the norm; no refuge in the jook.

Looking back on his four decades on the peninsula, naturalist
Charles Torrey Simpson observed in 1923, with more sorrow
than humor: "The only attraction belonging to the state that we
do not ruin is the climate, and if it were possible to can and
export it we would do so until Florida would be as bleak and
desolate as Labrador. . . . What natural beauty will we have left
for another generation? What right have we to waste and destroy everything nature has lavishly bestowed on the earth?"[1] In
1945, Thomas Barbour, a Harvard University paleontologist
and naturalist raised on the banks of the Indian River, warned
that Florida "must cease to be purely a region to be exploited
and flung aside, having been sucked dry, or a recreation area
visited by people who care only for a good time, who feel no
sense of responsibility, and have no desire to aid and improve
the land of their temporary enjoyment. It must cease being
treated as a *colony*" (emphasis added).[2] In a 1988 radio commentary, Leroy Collins, governor from 1955 through 1961 and one
of the state's elder statesmen, sounded the same theme, saying
that if residents and visitors alike did not stop abusing its environment, they would soon find nothing left of Florida's natural
beauty.

109

* * *

Florida lacked gold, as sixteenth-century Spanish adventurers discovered to their disappointment, but it possessed in abundance trees and phosphate. For those treasures, corporate and private investors raced from the waning days of Reconstruction through the Depression, when the forests were largely exhausted and phosphate mines and limestone quarries had been gouged out of the earth, leaving thousands of acres of open pits. Like a negative image, exploitation of these resources paralleled development of Florida as a winter resort promoters called "paradise."

The most abundant tree in the state and the one investors most sought was the pine, especially the longleaf and slash varieties. The so-called virgin or first-growth trees could reach four feet or more in diameter and rise to heights of over one hundred feet. The longleaf and sometimes the Dade County slash are frequently called yellow pine, but the milled wood one now finds in lumberyards is a pale descendant of the original growth. The current lumberyard pine comes from farmed stock that lacks heartwood, the dense, hard core of accreted dead cells that combines beauty with strength and resistance to decay and termites that made yellow pine the favored material of builders.

The first-growth forests occupied distinct soil types. Longleaf pine dominated the sandhills in central and north Florida. Dade County pine grew from nearly bare rock, and was lord of the coastal ridge and lowlands. Sand pine made its home on the most nutrient-poor, fast-draining soil in the peninsula, and its poverty and peculiarities protected it from exploitation until developers discovered it was easy land on which to build a subdivision or shopping mall. Pond pine, loblolly, and other varieties of slash pine were mixed with their more numerous relatives in a sea of pine that accounted for three quarters of the state's 25 million to 30 million forested acres.

As the vast pine forests of the American South fell during the opening decades of this century, few people offered laments. The trees suffered, rather, from aesthetic disapproval and a belief that they were good only insofar as, once cut, they served human needs. Sidney Lanier observed that " 'piney-woods' has come to be a phrase conveying a certain idea of inferiority."[3] Many people found them oppressive in their seeming uniformity, and a dense understory of palmetto, wire grass, and vines often contributed to their mystery while hindering passage through their expanse.

Yet pines had their advocates, like Lanier, who discoursed on the difference between trees of the highlands and those of the lowlands. He said:

> As for hill-pines, they stand upon the corrugations of the earth's brow. They represent pain, spasms, paroxysms, desperations. The pines of the plain have higher meanings if lower sites; theirs is the unwrinkled forehead of a tranquil globe, they signify the mystery of that repose that comes only from tested power and seasoned strength—a grandeur of tranquillity which is as much greater than the grandeur of cataclysms as Chaucer is greater than Byron, as Beethoven is greater than Berlioz, as Lee's manhood is greater than Napoleon's.[4]

Charles Torrey Simpson felt as strongly about the Dade County pine. In *Out of Doors in Florida,* he wrote:

> There is a nameless charm in the flatwoods, there is enchantment for the real lover of nature in their very sameness. One feels a sense of their infinity as the forest stretches away into space beyond the limits of vision; they convey to the mind a feeling of boundless freedom. . . . I am at peace with the earth, the forest, the sky, the entire world. As I lie in the long, soft grass I feel that I do not care to go back to the dull, sordid routine of every day life again.[5]

Pines were sought for lumber and for their sap, which was distilled into turpentine and rosin, known collectively as naval stores. The Civil War ruined both industries, but as demand increased in the northern United States and in Europe during Reconstruction, logging recommenced on a large scale, and companies sought through whatever means possible—including construction of railroads and canals—to gain title to timberland.

In the Panhandle and parts of north Florida, logs—called "sticks"—were bartered for goods. Where there were no railroads, lumbermen had to haul timber to navigable rivers. Often the path lay through flatwoods, which for at least part of the year were supersaturated with water, or across loose sand that swallowed wagon wheels. Trimmed trees were skidded, one at a time, from the woods to the river or railroad siding. The log, which might run one hundred feet in length, hung under the axle of a two-wheeled cart drawn by teams of up to eight oxen, which were more surefooted and less bothered by mosquitoes than horses. The wheels were seven to twelve feet in diameter so they could pass through the most inundated terrain. (When possible, carts were yoked together to form trains.) Into the twentieth century, skidding carts coexisted with more advanced forms of transportation—first trams pulled by mules or oxen and later by small steam engines across hastily laid tracks that underwent their own transformation from wood to steel, both of which were abandoned after the trees were gone.

Skidding itself was a traditional method of log removal. In Florida live-oakers had employed it for at least a century prior to the Civil War. Because the wood was too dense to float and therefore had to be carried to ports overland, felled trees were rough-milled where they fell, the live-oakers taking only what they could use and leaving the rest to rot. The federal government's first major set-aside of public lands in Florida occurred early in the nineteenth century when it established live-oak reservations to assure adequate supplies for the U.S. Navy. Europe's maritime nations had already effectively deforested themselves and stripped the North American colonies of white oak to build their ships of commerce and war; live oak was next, and poaching became a severe problem in Florida and the American coastal south.

A popular scam involved persuading poor residents to claim "squatters rights" to live-oak hammocks, which were public land, and to sell the timber to a lumberman who would then sell it back to the government. The live-oaker could earn a $1,500 profit in less than a month![6] The practice abated in the 1860s when ironclad steamboats began to replace sailing vessels, a transition speeded by war-induced timber shortages. By that time most suitable live oaks in Florida were gone; the rest soon fell to citrus growers and men seeking ties for railroads.

Through the nineteenth and well into the twentieth century, demand for forest products on the world market was insatiable: including wood for construction and fuel; and turpentine and rosin for varnish, soap, paint thinner, glue, pharmaceuticals, and plastics. Lumber trains and sawmills seemed to share every spring with a spa; piles of sawdust lined the rights-of-way of newly laid tracks.

The sawmills, like logging camps, were temporary structures. Into the present century the large circular saws ran on steam, necessitating location of the mills near a constant supply of water. Sawdust and scraps fed the burners. Workers communicated in sign language because the noise in the mills made speech inaudible. In labor-poor areas, which included most of the state, the loggers and mill hands were transients, wanderers on the lam from a past or themselves. The operators—independents or agents for large companies—were, like the hands, most frequently male, with notable exceptions. In its December 13, 1884, issue, *Scientific American* reprinted a letter to the *Northwestern Lumberman* from Mrs. Harriett Smith, who, at age fifty-three, operated a sawmill near Tuckertown with, by her admission, an iron hand. She bossed even her second husband, insisting that men were incapable of running a sawmill properly, because they worked only part of each day and failed to keep the machinery in proper repair. She wrote:

> I have always managed my own business, and I expect to while I live. I awake in the morning and plan the day's work while the men are asleep, and at the breakfast table I give every one his orders, including my husband, who never objects to my doing the thinking for the family. My first advice to men who contemplate going into the sawmill business is—don't do it, for not one in 20 of you has the ability to succeed.[7]

The loggers struck observers as a potentially dangerous group. John Muir found them the most threatening people he met on his trip through the South during Reconstruction. While tramping along the Caloosahatchee River around 1900, Charles Torrey Simpson met a "Tennessee hillbilly" named Bill Stallins who had made his way north to south along the west coast, engaging in nearly every type of work to be found on the peninsula, fishing out of Pensacola, cutting cedar near Cedar Key, sponging in Key West, and collecting oysters along the southwest coast. Simpson said:

> One finds such men almost anywhere in Florida; derelicts who have been crossed in love, who have failed in the vortex of city life, who have lost their families or perhaps committed some misdemeanor and left their country for their country's good. They mostly live alone, in miserable shacks in out of the way places, sometimes in part eking out a poor living by trucking, hunting, trapping, or working for others. Their

housekeeping is usually of the most atrocious kind and the
cooking is often equally vile.[8]

The landscape of the logged-out forests rivaled the bleak-
ness of Bill Stallins's house. "The civilization of the pine is that
of the timber-cutter and the turpentine-distiller," said Sidney
Lanier in 1874; "to-day [sic] they set up their shanties and 'stills,'
quickly they cut down or exhaust the trees, to-morrow [sic] they
are gone, leaving a desolate and lonesome land."[9] Destruction
of north Florida hammocks and pinelands, as well as its wildlife,
doubtless contributed heavily to Flagler's decision to direct his
resorts beachward and then to build to the undeveloped shores
of Lake Worth.

While the tourists and new settlers fled south, the major
ports of north Florida and the Panhandle prospered from wood.
With its access by steamboat up the St. Johns to the interior and
its deep-water channel across the bar at the river's mouth, Jacksonville commanded the lumber and naval stores trade and became Florida's foremost city in banking, commerce, and
transportation in the 1890s. Well into the twentieth century, it
dominated the state economically and politically. Today, the
Jacksonville region remains, with the Panhandle, the center of
the peninsula's lumber industry, although the emphasis now is
on pulp for paper and boxes, and slats for packing crates.

Completion of the Pensacola and Atlantic Railroad to the
east bank of the Apalachicola River, where it tied into existing
lines out of Georgia and Jacksonville, opened the Panhandle's
vast forests to large-scale commercial logging early in the 1880s.
Much of that land went to the railroad, which claimed from the
state for its 160-mile effort nearly 3.9 million acres and settled
for 2.8 million—an astounding sum when one considers that
Flagler accepted from the state roughly 210,000 acres, less than
one tenth of the 2.6 million due him for his 522 miles of track.
The squatters and would-be homesteaders in Florida opposed
the gift to the Pensacola and Atlantic Railroad on the grounds
that the land was best divided into 160-acre homesteads and
turned into productive farms. As long as there were forests for
timber companies to claim, however, the people were ignored.

In 1882, with work crews pushing tracks deep into the
pines, eleven sawmills were operating in Pensacola. By 1889, the
Panhandle port had a fleet of seventeen steam-powered tug-
boats servicing the freighters that came in for lumber. In 1896,

a channel was dredged for larger boats. Between 1890 and 1913, the railroad hauled some two million carloads of primarily long-leaf pine to the harbor. Ships carried out at least twenty billion feet of lumber, most of it bound for western Europe. The freighters also left their ballast along the waterfront, thereby providing the city with Swedish granite, Italian blue stone, French tile, and muck dredged from the River Thames.[10] War in Europe in 1914 brought an abrupt bust to the port's lumber-fueled economy, but while the boom lasted, Pensacola flour-ished, becoming in size the third largest city in the state behind Key West and Jacksonville.

Like Pensacola, Fernandina depended almost solely on re-source exploitation for its prosperity. Situated on the northwest edge of Amelia Island, which buffers the St. Marys River from the Atlantic, Fernandina first achieved notoriety when Florida served as a loyalist base during the War of Independence, a refuge for fleeing Tories and a launching pad for raids into the rebellious Colonies. Lying just across the border from Georgia, it later became the favored port of smugglers bringing slaves into the United States in defiance of the Embargo Acts of 1807 and 1808. And as the eastern terminus of the Florida Railroad, it was the major antebellum port on the Atlantic coast.

In the decades following the war, as Jacksonville to the south and Savannah to the north grew, its economic base be-came narrowly focused on timber, fishing, and phosphate. The lumber and naval stores businesses did well until the 1930s, when the last of the first-growth longleaf pine was disappearing, and the switch from sawmills to pulp mills had begun. Fernan-dina is now part of its neighboring beach community and bears its name—Fernandina Beach—yet it remains an example of "old" north Florida, a city of pulp mills and fishing boats trying to save some of its beaches from developers looking for un-spoiled sand on which to build condominiums.

In 1900, Flagler built one of his last hotels, the Continental, at Fernandina as a summer resort, a Palm Beach for rich south-erners, he thought. The place was a bust, a failure he blamed on a general lack of wealthy and sophisticated people in the South.[11] But the problem was less a lack of wealth than south-erners' desire to take their money elsewhere—and perhaps to patronize the establishments of people who did not hold them in contempt. When the hotel burned in 1919, it was not rebuilt.

Few species of trees escaped the saws of the loggers. On the peninsula north and east of Cedar Key, through the Suwannee River watershed, lay extensive stands of cedar. Through most of the nineteenth century, these went for use in the manufacture of pencils and cigar boxes. (The grandfather of Coconut Grove shipbuilder and conservationist Ralph Middleton Munroe owned the pencil factory in Massachusetts where Henry David Thoreau served an unhappy apprenticeship.) By 1896, when a hurricane destroyed the physical port, the first-growth cedar forests were stripped bare, and today, Cedar Key is a fishing village and resort community, with a state museum devoted to the days when resources were treated as limitless.

Cypresses, many of them thousands of years old, went for shingles, for shipping crates, barrels, decks, greenhouses, and paneling. During the booming 1920s, "pecky" cypresses—old trees whose wood had been pitted by rot and centuries of exposure to the elements—became popular as "antique" interior trim. In north and central Florida, narrow-gauge tracks were run into swamps so loggers could cut the cypresses, some up to a dozen feet in diameter, and haul them out. The trees showed their age in girth while seldom growing above 150 feet. The largest strands of cypress, which contained some of the oldest trees in North America, remained inaccessible in the expansive and wet Big Cypress Swamp until the late 1940s.

Along the coasts—south of Cedar Key on the west and Mosquito Lagoon on the east—loggers took out miles of red mangroves for their tannin and fine-grained wood, which furniture makers prized. The trees, with spindly, spiderlike prop roots bowing around them, defined and created the shore. But resort owners preferred beaches of white sand and loggers wanted the sap and wood. Often those cutting the mangroves were contract workers, overloading their leaky boats with timber for mills in Key West or Tampa. In the Keys and south Florida, a common cottage industry was the manufacture of charcoal from mangrove and the associated buttonwood.

The Florida real estate boom of the 1920s brought such a high demand for wood of all grades and types that local supplies proved insufficient and lumber had to be imported. By 1942, in all of south Florida, only 10 percent of the mature or first-growth timber remained uncut or unburned.[12] Some 30 percent of the clear-cut pinelands were no longer capable of producing trees because of soil depletion, drainage, and repeated assaults by ax and fire.

* * *

Logging was surgically clean compared with turpentining—the process of bleeding and distilling sap from pine. An absolute, institutionalized brutality defined the turpentine camps, where contempt for life was the norm and people were simply disposable commodities. The physically destructive nature of the work and the horrors of life in the camp combined the worst elements of chattel slavery and economic peonage. The laborers felt they had drawn assignment to hell. For years prisoners were forced to box the trees, collect the sap, and refine it into turpentine and rosin in the crude stills.

The convict-lease system began in 1877 as a reform and economy measure in Florida and other southern states, which, bankrupt by war, could not afford to maintain prisons. Also, as white males regained control of state government at the end of Reconstruction, they sought legal means to lock their black neighbors back into servitude. One particularly effective way of doing so was passage of vagrancy laws, which permitted arbitrary arrest and conviction of anyone who seemed unable to pay his or her bills or produce a certain amount of money or even proper identification on demand. People moving from one town to another were subject to prosecution, as were those who walked off a job site in search of better employ. John Powell, a convict camp captain, wrote in his account of his experiences, "In the early days it was possible to send a negro to prison on almost any pretext, but difficult to get a white man there, unless he committed some very heinous crime."[13] Fully 95 percent of the prisoners in the late 1870s and early 1880s were black. By the 1890s, the proportion of white convicts had risen to nearly a third, with most of them being, according to Powell, " 'cracker' outlaws," lower-class whites guilty of felonies like murder and grand larceny, or simply of being too poor and illiterate to defend themselves from false charges. Only the most heinous of crimes could land people of means in the camps.

Powell's account, although clearly an attempt to assert his own humanity and righteousness in service to a grotesque system, provides a fascinating look at Florida society and mores from the underbelly. Groups of prisoners were leased to private employers. Until 1915, when the state limited its leasing to black men, crews included men and women, whites and blacks. Public officials generally ignored cries of abuse and torture in the camps, even after Powell, his brother, and brother-in-law were indicted in 1879 for cruelty to prisoners. The case was dismissed when one of the lead witnesses misidentified Powell in court.

In the turpentine camps, work was performed at a trot from dawn to dusk. Each man was expected to box—cut a square and affix a collector into which sap would run—sixty to ninety trees a day. Armed guards watched over the prisoners, who at night were chained into their beds and by day were manacled. Convicts who collapsed during work were seldom given any but the most rudimentary treatment: There were no doctors in the woods. Punishment for anything a guard or captain considered offensive ranged from floggings to consignment to a sweat-box—a lightless, unventilated trap. Camp captains and guards employed a torture method called "watering" in which water was forced through a tube into a prisoner's stomach. Some convicts had permanently distended thumbs from being hung just off the ground by rope tied to their thumbs. Food—pork fat, corn, beans, and often no more than sweet potatoes—provided scant nourishment. Women in the camps were at the mercy of guards, trustees, and every other male around. Every prisoner suffered from malnutrition, filth, vermin, and abuse—whether working in a turpentine camp, on a farm, in a phosphate mine, or on a railroad. The convict-lease system was common throughout the South, but Florida's was particularly inhumane, as witnessed in the title it earned for the peninsula—the American Siberia.

Prisoners weren't entirely passive. Escape attempts were everyday occurrences, but despite assistance from friendly citizens, few were strong and swift enough to elude the foxhounds the guards used to run them to ground. Powell reports that prisoners sometimes fed powdered glass to the dogs and informants, but he goes on to boast that only on the rarest occasion did a fugitive succeed in leaving no trace for man or beast to follow. The more desperate attempted suicide and self-mutilation to avoid work among the pines, but unless they managed to kill themselves or died of infection, they were patched up in a haphazard fashion and sent back to work.

The convict-lease system flourished in Florida until 1923, longer than in any state other than Alabama, where it was abolished five years later. The Florida system met its demise only because state leaders could no longer ignore public outrage—from the nation. William Warren Rogers related the story in his introduction to Powell's book:

In December 1921, Martin Tabert, a twenty-two-year-old North Dakotan who was exploring the South was arrested for hopping a freight train in Tallahassee. Unable to pay his fine, Tabert was sentenced to sixty days in the Leon County jail and then leased to a lumber company. He was sent to a camp at Clara in Dixie County and died there in February 1922, flogged to death by a whipping boss. The young man's parents were informed that he had died of "fever and other complications," and more than a year passed before the real facts were revealed by a fellow convict who had witnessed the torture.[14]

The *New York World* blazoned the story across its pages; the whipping boss was indicted for second-degree murder, convicted, granted a new trial, and acquitted two years later. But as a result of the case, the state abolished the leasing system and replaced it with a new prison at Raiford and work farms throughout the state. Although convicts worked on public road projects under the supervision of state prison officials, floggings were outlawed—but the sweatbox continued in use. Stetson Kennedy in his *Palmetto Country* said of one notorious prison: "Until 1939 the county and city 'Blue Jay' prison farms at Jacksonville employed a novel method of plowing. Trios of Negro women prisoners were harnessed to the plows, which were also guided by Negro women."[15]

Despite the change in form, criminal justice in Florida has remained discriminatory against blacks and poor people. The state's chief contribution to American jurisprudence came not through legislation but through the court appeals of prisoners, the most famous being that of Clarence Gideon. The poor white drifter and hard-luck gambler was arrested in 1961 for stealing change from a poolroom cigarette machine and jukebox. Denied counsel, the indigent Gideon was convicted and while serving his sentence launched a series of appeals that ended with the 1963 U.S. Supreme Court ruling that anyone facing felony charges was entitled to legal representation, regardless of his or her ability to pay.

In 1890, state officials, having concluded that turpentining was too difficult for prisoners, began to award convict leases to farmers and railroad and mining companies, where conditions were marginally better. The men and women who took their place among the pines were free in name only, and even their children continued in peonage, owing their physical, if not spiritual, being to the company store.

By 1909, Florida produced half the country's supply of naval stores, and as late as 1941, the industry was among the largest in the state, employing fourteen thousand people to produce 20 percent of the world's turpentine and rosin. Most of the workers were black; the supervisors and owners, white. The blacks were paid maybe $1.00 a day for men; $2.50 to $3.00 a week for women.

Turpentine hands were recruited from throughout the South, often by their fellow blacks. The most famous of these agents was Henry N. "Father" Abraham, a native of South Carolina who went to work in a turpentine camp in Lawtey, Florida. While there, he became a hoodoo doctor and used the prestige and influence that position accorded him in rural southern communities to recruit workers, receiving payment from the company for each person he brought to camp. For a fee, he healed the sick, removed and cast spells, predicted winning *bolita* numbers. He earned enough from his practice to buy two hundred acres of land, on which he built homes for a dozen black tenant farmers and their families. He became a successful strawberry grower, a wealthy and world-famous hoodoo doctor before his death in 1937. He was one of the few lucky ones. In many ways a decent, generous man, Father Abraham profited from a cruel business and then escaped while continuing to trade on ignorance and superstition.

Fear, greed, and brutality ruled the life of workers and employers. The owner of a turpentine camp, Stetson Kennedy said, "carries a revolver, sleeps with two double-barreled shotguns by his bed, and keeps another shotgun and automatic rifle near the front door." His workers lived in shacks he owned and shopped at the commissary he owned. The store's manager boasted to Kennedy: "We makes a gross profit of sixty percent and a net profit of twenty percent. You know that's pretty good—it takes a good slice offen salaries. We don't hardly have to pay no salaries."[16] They certainly paid no benefits; when the social security system was established, naval stores companies successfully lobbied to have their industry declared agricultural and their workers exempted from coverage. Pay was based on the number of trees a person worked, and once debits were deducted only a deficit remained.

During World War II, surging demand brought about the

use of sulfuric acid to increase sap flow by 50 percent from slash pine. However, the new technique, which proved ineffective on longleaf pine, exhausted trees more quickly than previous attempts to stimulate sap production. After the war, demand for naval stores declined with development of new petroleum-based solvents and various synthetics, such as plastic.

Coincident with the growth of the lumber and naval stores industries was the discovery in the 1880s and early 1890s of unimagined wealth in the sandy soils of north and central Florida. Dr. C. A. Simmons is generally credited with discovering phosphate on his land in Alachua County—home of Gainesville and the Santa Fe River—in 1883, the same year Henry Plant's dredge *Alabama* scraped it from the bottom of Tampa Bay. Simmons lacked the capital to commence large-scale mining, and no one thought of taking appreciable quantities from the bay, so the discoveries were filed away until 1887 when a phosphate company moved into the Peace River region, muddied the water, and tried to disguise what it was doing by announcing that it was extracting tannic acid from palmettos.[17] A year later, a Philadelphian named T. S. Moorehead began mining near the palmetto-prairie cow town of Arcadia, and the following year the Dunnellon Phosphate Company began extracting hard-rock phosphate from sites near the Withlacoochee River.

Dunnellon was the brainchild of Albertus Vogt, a transplant from North Carolina who, broke and near starvation, discovered phosphate on his hardscrabble homestead and recruited investors to provide start-up money for his and his brother's mining company. With wealth came praise: He was described as "a man of handsome physique, fine education, and brilliant mind."[18] He earned the honorific "colonel," although he enjoyed more being called the "Duke of Dunnellon." To the folks along the Withlacoochee and around Ocala, he certainly lived like royalty, with thoroughbred horses he stabled in a converted church and fifty hounds he housed on an island in the river and fed fresh beef. He traveled to Silver Springs, which a land company was converting into a resort and tourist attraction, and threw gold pieces into the pellucid water to see how it magnified their image. He sold his share of the company, went broke in 1904, married his brother's widow—thereby becoming rich again—and died broke in 1915. At most, he may have been worth

$200,000, which made him wealthy by the standards of rural Florida; Henry Flagler at the time was drawing about $2 million a year from his Standard Oil holdings.

Vogt was one of the more colorful characters to come out of the first phosphate boom. By 1895, four hundred companies were operating throughout central Florida. Real estate prices soared and towns popped into existence. By 1900, though, only fifty companies remained, and that number diminished over the years as the industry consolidated. One of the early failures was a company Napoleon Bonaparte Broward started and closed in 1890 because he couldn't overcome the problems of transportation and labor that affected nearly every business in the state. His experience, however, further soured him against railroad companies because he confronted directly their discriminatory rate structure, in which rebates were granted favored customers and those out of favor paid the difference.

Despite its various setbacks, phosphate became a major economic and environmental force in Florida. Virtually all the major ports—Pensacola, Tampa, Jacksonville—had their channels deepened to accommodate ships carrying the mineral. Mining pits left the land scarred. Processing drew down vast reserves of water that led eventually to the drying up of several large springs east of Tampa. It also polluted land, water, and air with toxic by-products that last for centuries. Although countless numbers of fossils of extinct birds and mammals—the rich heritage of Florida's prehistory—were crushed or washed away, the phosphate mines remained important paleontological sites, and researchers often raced to recover important fossils before work commenced.

Phosphate mining was hard, gruesome work. Life in the mining towns was worse. Like their counterparts in the woods, miners worked dawn to dusk, with blacks doing the heaviest labor. Until 1905, when water cannons came into use, miners used picks, shovels, and mules to scrape and tear hard-rock phosphate from the ground; and for the river rock, they employed dredges, which, during the dry season, they pulled and winched through low water. Accidents were commonplace, although for many years reports carried only the names of injured whites, who were generally supervisors. Blacks went unnamed. They were paid dismally as well—around $1.00 a day a year in 1892; $1.50 in 1909. That rose to around $3.25 in 1919 but only after a violent strike, in the aftermath of which the mine owners broke the integrated union. The mine owners lost a union vote in 1939, and in 1955 lost in a major drive to bust the union. By then the industry was highly mechanized and the work force predominantly white, reflecting a demographic shift that paralleled technological changes in mining and refining.

The company town/commissary system lasted until the late 1930s and early 1940s, with only a slight diminution through the years of overt violence against workers. In the frenzied early years of mining, the towns resembled gold-rush communities, complete with prostitutes, gamblers, outlaws, and jooks. Men fought with any weapon they could find. People were lynched, tarred and feathered, drawn and quartered. According to some reports, blacks recruited from Georgia and Alabama to work the mines initially "ran amuck" in an orgy of lawlessness.[19] Making the mix more volatile were local Crackers who wanted nothing to do with the mines or the people working them, and convict gangs who were leased to work the sites. As late as 1925, cowmen engaged in a pitched battle with sheriff's deputies and mine operators over a phosphate company's fencing of ten thousand acres in Polk County. The battles today are in the courtroom over environmental issues and severance taxes, over who among the institutions involved—the state and multinational corporations controlling the business—should pay to remove the heaps of toxic waste material and to turn the open pits into land suitable for recreation or habitation.

Jook joints, hoodoo, old-time-holy-roller-Bible-thumping religion, fatback and grits, family gatherings, dances, vigilante justice and injustice, contempt and resentment toward the company and its agents that controlled life—these bound blacks and whites in the labor force. Their culture and society shaped modern Florida as surely as the flash and glitter of resorts and the fragrance of orange blossoms. Through luck and perseverance some people achieved wealth if not fortune, but for day laborers life was little more than constant struggle. Law and justice were fantasies—guns, knives, ice picks, axes, shovels, were turned into weapons of offense and defense. For many laborers, escaping the hell of work meant a trip on Saturday night to the local "jook," or honky-tonk, perhaps Florida's most distinctive contribution to American culture. *Jook,* pronounced as in "took," has no known etymology, but it does have a rich lore. "As Southern as jazz, fried chicken, corn bread, channel cats, chewing tobacco, and lynching," Stetson Kennedy observed in *Pal-

metto Country, "the jook has universal appeal which has carried it far beyond the Mason-Dixon Line. Also like jazz, it is a Negro contribution to Americana. Fittingly enough Florida, 'the Nation's Playground,' is home of the jook." The jukebox that defined a generation of middle-class diners is a sophisticated version of the old record-player or "jook organ," also called a "piccolo" by blacks. "The major role of the jook," Kennedy said, "is catering to the great masses of common folk who can ill afford to pay admission, cover, or minimum charges."[20]

There were black jooks and Cracker jooks. Although one race entered the domain of the other at its peril, the establishments were strikingly similar. There were jooks that fronted for whorehouses, and those that exploited minors. You could gamble in a jook, meet a lover or friend, fight someone you hated as easily as someone who looked at you or your woman or man with a leer or simply a smile. You could dance across the sawdust-covered, beer-washed floor, eat some ribs or sandwiches of varying degrees of flavor and safety. You could die in a jook, or survive to visit another day.

Yet the internecine conflicts that sometimes took place within the jooks paled beside the racial violence that often flared in periods of economic stress, with an assist from politicians and business leaders eager to enhance their power. During the war against Spain, white troops attacked blacks in Miami. Black troops—most of them veterans from the Indian wars in the American West—ran violently into the prejudice and discrimination that pervaded life throughout the South (and, if one be honest, the country). In Lakeland, black troopers killed a white barber during an argument over his refusal to serve them. In Tampa, black cavalrymen fought with saloonkeepers and lawmen who harassed them. In Key West, black soldiers battled white residents, while white sailors tangled with local blacks.

Black and white workers shared a desire for decent wages for their labor, but their attempts to organize ran into stiff resistance, and the anti-labor union forces usually won because they used race to divide the workers. The same tactic was employed to shatter the Populist uprisings of the 1880s and 1890s, a period when the possibility of alliance between blacks and poor whites who had been forced into tenancy threatened to become real. The Farmers' Alliance took shape through the old plantation country of north Florida and the Panhandle in 1886 and in 1890 joined with the national party convention in Ocala to issue a Populist political platform, calling for a graduated income tax, minting of silver currency, governmental regulation of transportation and communication, recovery of lands from railroad companies and speculators, and a cessation of trading in agricultural futures. The program was guaranteed to offend Florida railroad magnates, timber lords, phosphate miners, and the conventional Democratic politicians who served them.

By the time Napoleon Bonaparte Broward was elected governor in 1905, Florida populism had lost all but its nominal radicalism, Broward's preference being to dispossess and exile all American blacks. Within a decade, southern populism had turned racist, anti-Semitic, anti-Catholic, and rabidly, blindingly Protestant and patriotic toward the United States and Dixie. Sidney Catts, who embodied all these characteristics and became governor of Florida on a platform of paranoid hate in 1917, was also violently opposed to the minimal conservation laws enacted to protect fast-diminishing marine stocks, as well as to rights for blacks and women. Paradoxically, he fought corporations and supported the integrated phosphate workers union in its 1919 strike against mine owners. A staunch prohibitionist, Catts billed himself the Cracker Messiah, champion of the common man.

The bigotry that Catts symbolized burst into violence in the central Florida town of Ocoee in 1920, when members of the Ku Klux Klan assaulted a black orange grove owner named Mose Norman, who had voted in defiance of their threats. Defending himself, Norman killed two of his assailants, triggering a rampage of white bigots through Ocoee, Orlando, Apopka, and Winter Garden, which left thirty-five blacks dead and homes and churches burned. The riots demonstrated forcefully the convoluted logic of racism, which had found its most curious verbal expression in the debate over the Nineteenth Amendment to the United States Constitution the previous year. Florida's representatives, legislators, and governor opposed granting women the vote. U.S. Senator Duncan U. Fletcher complained the amendment would allow two million black women to vote and generally threaten the hegemony of white males, while Congressman Frank Clark insisted that it would assist a "socialist Negro-radical element" in its drive to depose the "lawful" government of white men.

Racism became most institutionalized and depersonalized in the cities. Zora Neale Hurston in her autobiography revealed that not until she went to school in Jacksonville in 1910 did she feel that "I was a little colored girl. . . . I was no longer among white people whose homes I could barge into with a sure sense of welcome."[21] In Palm Beach, blacks were servants with no chance to become more. They pedaled Afromobiles, cleaned up after the wealthy, waited on them, and every Saturday night entertained them with the "cakewalk," a particularly demeaning but popular dance performed for a cake. Off-duty blacks were segregated from guests and white workers, while to entertain friends at her marble mansion, Mary Lily Kenan Flagler would adopt a southern black accent to sing black songs. Such were the times, and bits and pieces of them linger disturbingly thirty years after the major push for civil rights began. Although for legal reasons Palm Beach dropped its most overt forms of discrimination against blacks, it required identification cards for its mainly black workers and servants as late as the 1980s. In Tampa, at the turn of the century, the blacks living in a ghetto called the Scrub spoke a dialect consisting of English and Spanish, with bits of Italian, slang, and African tribal dialects thrown in. In Miami, blacks occupied Overtown, Liberty City, and the "Black Grove," a neighborhood inland from the wealth of white Coconut Grove.

These were parallel cities most Anglos never entered—except for bootleg liquor, drugs, gambling, music, and prostitutes. Many began to believe nothing else existed in the black neighborhoods. In Florida, as throughout the South, a wall of color divided society, decreeing separate schools and public facilities, declaring where people could ride on a bus or be served a meal, drink water, or go to the bathroom. Blacks were denied access to "public" beaches and pools unless they were specifically designated for their use, and few were. It was a struggle to break out of the ranks of wage labor on the docks and construction sites, of domestic servitude in the homes and resorts of the rich. Bereft as a group of political and economic power, Florida's blacks received a pittance for education compared with that appropriated for whites, which was itself inadequate.

Despite discrimination, some blacks did achieve economic success and influence. In the small beach resort of Daytona, Mary Bethune established early in the century a school for blacks that became the respected Bethune-Cookman College. Mary Bethune possessed such stature as an educator that she could counsel presidents on civil rights—but not officials in her home state. Along the upper and middle St. Johns, in south Florida, and the Keys there were blacks who were accomplished woodsmen, hunters, fishermen, and guides equal to any white or Indian. These were people living in thinly populated regions where they were known for what they were as individuals rather than members of a group.

Among the poor in isolated regions, miscegenation occurred with more frequency than polite society cared to recognize, but children of mixed parentage were ostracized by both races. In the backcountry near Ponce de Leon Springs in the Panhandle, an extended clan disparagingly called Dominickers lived. The clan traced its origin to the first years of the Civil War when a plantation owner died and his wife married one of their slaves. Of their five children, three married whites and two married blacks As the clan grew, its members began to intermarry, until, by the 1920s, it was large enough to have a well-established identity. Shunned by whites and prohibited from attending their schools, the Dominickers in turn avoided the black community.[22] Interracial marriage was illegal in all southern states, and even in contemporary Florida, the huge Department of Health and Rehabilitative Services, which administers welfare and child-care programs, possesses on its forms and in its computers no category for children of mixed blood. Social workers must designate them as either black or white, based on the mother's race or the dominant group in the neighborhood in which the parents live.

Blacks were the most visible victims of discrimination, but they were not alone. Florida's first United States senator and one of its largest slaveholders, David Yulee, was Jewish, but for the first half of this century, Jews were excluded, as a matter of policy, from a number of Miami Beach hotels, from Fort Lauderdale, Boca Raton, and Palm Beach, and anti-Semitism persists in various ways throughout the state. In south Florida, half a dozen synagogues were desecrated in the first six months of 1988 alone.

No group was free of bias. Cuban cigar workers—many of whom were black or mulatto—resented their Spanish counterparts, because they were ethnically different, nonunion strikebreakers, and higher paid. Cuban workers also harbored resentment toward Italians who entered the trade as scabs in 1901. The Italians migrated to Tampa after fleeing vicious anti-

Italian riots in New Orleans. The Florida Gulf port, although far from free of prejudice, was more open than most other cities—South or North.

Anglo and Cuban Floridians were locked in a complex relationship. The cigar industry for three decades or more around the turn of the century was the state's largest in terms of profit and payroll. In the last decades of the nineteenth century, Cubans dominated Key West's political and cultural life, achieving wide acceptance if not full integration into Anglo society. Cigar makers dominated the Tampa economy for nearly fifty years. In the twentieth century, as American capitalists and their political puppets came to fear Marxism, a favorite complaint among conservative Anglo Floridians was that Cuban workers were too socialistic and radical—a view the Spanish factory owners shared. The Anglo-American medical establishment violently opposed the socialized medicine plans—forerunners of medical insurance and health maintenance organizations—established by the cigar workers' union. On the other hand, many Cubans snubbed Crackers as filthy barbarians who would work for virtually nothing in the Ybor City cigar factories—an odd reversal of the usual lament that Crackers would not work for anything. At the same time, Cuban women seem to have perceived Anglo men from the middle and upper classes as less chauvinistic and more sensitive toward their needs than Latin males.[23]

In 1910, Tampa newspaper publisher and mayor D. B. McKay recruited Crackers from the countryside to enter the city as vigilantes to attack striking cigar workers who wanted recognition of the American Federation of Labor's International Cigarmakers' Union as their bargaining agent. Shootings and lynchings marked the strike, which was broken, although the union later received recognition. In 1920, another violent strike wracked the city, as manufacturers sought to shatter the union and ban readers from the shop. Introduced in Cuba in the 1860s as a way to propagandize against unionization, the readers had come in sixty years to be seen as sources of radicalism and discontent. They literally read throughout the day to the workers from books and pamphlets the owners perceived as incendiary. After ten months, the union was forced to its knees and the readers abolished.

The readers returned in 1926, with the provision that owners would approve the books and articles they read. The texts were bilingual—English and Spanish, but predominantly the latter—and until that time the workers had selected what they wanted to hear. According to Stetson Kennedy in *Palmetto Country*, those selections regularly included such revolutionary works as *Don Quixote*, *Les Misérables*, reports of Garibaldi's fight for Italian unity and independence, and works by Maxim Gorky and Sigismondo Malatesta. They also read from works by Karl Marx and Leo Tolstoy, as well as from leftist periodicals.[24] The readers by virtue of their education and position in the factories often became spokesmen for the workers. In 1933, the owners finally kept the readers out despite a prolonged and bitter strike. Radios were placed in the factories to pacify but not educate the beaten workers.

SIX

Life on the Wet Frontier

*For relict bands of Indians, backwoodsmen, strays, and tourists
the hunt's the goal, for subsistence, profit, pleasure, science.
Florida becomes a place of "shameful slaughter." Birds of the
air, fish of the sea, and creatures between suffer.*

With Crackers, Conchs, Spaniards, Afro-Americans, Cubans,
Minorcans, Seminole, West Indians, as well as Swedes, Poles,
and a smattering of Asians, Florida's ethnic mix at the turn of
the century possessed a flavor and texture that stratified into
the sort of economic and class distinctions rampant throughout
industrializing America. Old ways of life eroded under the on-
slaught of the changing economy. Everywhere the transformation came through violence against animals, the land, and
people—whether immigrants locked in urban sweatshops or natives driven onto barren reservations where they were supposed
to adopt Christianity and European culture but too often settled
for alcoholism and decay because there was nothing else.

The last decades of the nineteenth century marked the
culmination of white America's war of extermination against
the Indian nations of the West. Tactics, both deliberate and un-
witting, involved the slaughter of food sources—bison and
antelope—massacre of women, children, and the elderly,
negotiation of treaties that were then betrayed, forceable removal of tribes from their homeland, biological destruction
through the introduction of smallpox, and murder of prisoners.
These horrors were developed in prolonged war against eastern

130

tribes during the eighteenth and nineteenth centuries; on the Great Plains and in the southwestern desert, they were perfected.

The federal government's policy toward Native Americans attained a macabre surreality in Florida. When Sidney Lanier visited St. Augustine in the mid-1870s, he observed and wrote about Cheyenne, Kiowa, Comanche, Caddo, and Arapaho exiles in old Fort Marion. After publication of his book, the Indians became popular tourist attractions. In 1886, Geronimo and his Chiricahua followers were sent from the arid Arizona mountains to the damp heat of St. Augustine, where more than one hundred died from consumption—the disease wealthy white northeasterners sought relief from in that city. Some three decades earlier, Florida Indians had been exiled to the Oklahoma Territory to suffer under the extremes of an alien climate.

The Florida campaign ended a decade before the Civil War began—without a formal treaty—with remnant clans of Seminole and Miccosukee, numbering no more than three hundred, isolated along the Kissimmee River to the vicinity of Lake Okeechobee and into the Everglades and Big Cypress Swamp. The state and its corporate supporters, along with profit-seeking individuals, considered the entire region worthless until they discovered muck under the sawgrass, cypress in the swamp, pine in the flatwoods, and thousands of tons of fish in the Big Water.

From their villages in the Everglades and Big Cypress, the Indians, nonetheless, became an economic force on the south Florida mainland in the years between the end of Reconstruction and the arrival of the railroad. Many residents and visitors respected and admired their integrity and their skill as hunters, guides, and suppliers of natural resources.

In a land defined by water, the Indians no longer could establish the large villages consisting of several clans working communal fields or cattle herds that once had marked their culture. Instead, they located their settlements on the larger hammocks, or tree islands, of their swampy homes. The sites they selected were large enough usually to support garden plots for an extended family or two. Meat came not from herding cattle but from hunting and fishing. Rather than traveling by horse or foot, the Indians carved cypress dugout canoes noted for their shallow draft, their seaworthiness, and their beauty.

The Seminole abandoned the traditional walled lodges necessary in cool climates and adopted the open-sided, palm-thatched chickee. Built with a raised floor, it allowed every breeze to pass through and across its occupants while keeping them high and dry. Chickees weren't mobile, like tepees, but the Indians constructed them quickly, with few materials, and some scholars have suspected the design originated in the exigencies of the white man's war of extermination when it was necessary to see the enemy first or die. More likely, it was an adaptation of a design that bands in the region had developed to suit the climate and terrain.

Moving south, the Indians threw off their traditional fur and tanned-hide garments in favor of loose-fitting, brightly colored cotton clothes. The distinctive rainbow-ribboned Seminole shirts and skirts that picture books like to show represent a refinement the sewing machine made possible late in the last century. Today, blue jeans and cotton shirts are prevalent daily garb.

For the most part, the Indians avoided whites. In the years of the War Between the States and Reconstruction, the Indians traded for dry goods and ammunition primarily along the west coast, visiting settlements only to trade for other essentials.

In conducting their business the Indians followed a standard, unvarying pattern that allowed them to keep track of their sales and purchases, as well as watch over even the most trusted storekeeper. The Indians would sell their furs, hides, plumes, venison, bird eggs, or whatever for silver coins—no scrip or gold—then pay separately for each item they desired.[1]

In good seasons, Seminole hunters sold a thousand or more dollars' worth of furs or hides a week, although more frequently the total came to several hundred. In addition, they bought liquor from those merchants who would sell it to them—not all did—and adjourned for a night of drinking, leaving one man sober and their weapons at the shop. (The Indians held no monopoly on spree drinking, a ritual among blacks and whites of all economic and social classes. Only the forms differed.)

Stores devoted to the Indian trade were the first viable commercial enterprises in several locales on the east and west coasts—especially Everglades City, Chokoloskee Island, Okeechobee City (Tantie initially), Miami, and Fort Lauderdale. The first of these to conduct a substantial business was William Brickell's store on the Miami River, which he opened in 1872 in partnership with Julia Tuttle's father, Ephraim Sturtevant. The partnership dissolved after a year and Sturtevant moved across the Miami River while Brickell continued his prosperous Indian trade. After the Florida East Coast Railway came to town, William Burdine opened a dry goods store that conducted business with the Indians and grew into a major department store; Isidor Cohen opened a trading post, as did the Girtman family—fugitives from the 1894–95 freeze that had destroyed their Orlando orange grove.

In 1893, Frank Stranahan moved to the New River to manage a rarely used stagecoach station and ferry crossing. He soon bought the operation and opened a trading post dedicated to serving the Seminole. Flagler has traditionally received credit for founding Fort Lauderdale because he built a company town for his workers at the site of the way station and crossing, but arguably Frank Stranahan and his store gave the place its start. In 1906, Stranahan relocated his business close to the railway, which provided for easier shipment and receipt of goods, but his store remained a major Indian trading center until he sold it in 1912. By then he was a rich man, in no small measure owing to his early dealings with the Seminole, and he remained a friend of the tribe until, despondent over the devastated economy, he drowned himself in the New River in 1929.

His wife, Ivy, continued to work with the Indians until her death at age ninety in 1971. Mrs. Stranahan had taught men and women in the tribe how to operate the White sewing machine, which her husband sold. A staunch member of the Audubon Society, Mrs. Stranahan persuaded her husband to stop buying plumes from the Indians, after the first laws against that trade were passed in 1900 to protect the vanishing wading birds from which they came. His policy made him unique among Florida traders.

On the southwest coast in the village of Everglade (now Everglades City) a German immigrant named George Storter opened a trading post in 1892. The little settlement on the north boundary of the Ten Thousand Islands was a popular retreat for hunters and fishermen, and so the Storter family added the Rod and Gun Club to their businesses. (The club exists today and is being renovated, although its legend as a lodge surpasses the reality.) Barron Collier, who in 1921 began piecing together his one-million-acre empire in southwest Florida, visited the club in its early years and later made the small town his county seat. Everglades City, however, proved too out of the way and too prone to hurricane damage, so he switched the county offices north to Naples.

In the 1880s, Bill Brown, a British émigré, began driving an ox cart from Fort Myers into the Big Cypress to trade with the Indians. Within a few years Brown and his wife Jane took their children to Immokalee and then established deep in the Big Cypress Swamp a trading center at a place called the Boat Landing. Like Mrs. Stranahan, Mrs. Brown taught the Indians how to use a sewing machine, while learning from them the medicinal and nutritional value of local plants. On holidays, the Browns hosted barbecues that attracted Indians and whites from throughout the Big Cypress. Their son Frank sampled nearly every line of work the territory offered, passing from plume hunting to Audubon warden as the trade became illegal and bird sanctuaries were established in south Florida. Later, he served as the first resident supervisor of the Big Cypress Indian reservation, before turning to ranching and guiding hunting parties into the swamp.

The trade in furs, plumes, and hides received scant documentation, in part, no doubt, because few participants thought it important to leave records. There was, for a time, no sense that the game would run out or that conditions were changing *that* much. The records that do exist, however, raise interesting points about the relations between merchants and their customers. Historian Harry Kersey in his study of the Indian trade cites evidence that, despite the wide variance in prices they gave for furs and hides, store owners maintained a steady rate of payment to Seminole and Miccosukee hunters. Apparently, they felt that was the only way to assure the trust and continued patronage of the Indians who understood little, and cared less, about the economics of white business. The traders made up any losses from overpayment by overcharging the Indians for the goods they bought with the money paid them for their trade items. In most cases the merchants maintained a healthy profit margin. The traders also served as important points of cross-cultural fertilization by introducing manufactured goods.

The Indians traded plumes to a much lesser extent than white hunters did. The Indians did not live in the vicinity of the rookeries and were not inclined to make special journeys there. Nor did they possess the modern boats and weapons of the white hunters, who often received their equipment from buyers eager for as many plumes as quickly as possible.

At the turn of the century, Indians on their way into a city to trade often visited with the white settlers they had befriended, supplying them on occasion with fresh food. They also traveled to the southeast coast to scavenge wrecks. In the flatwoods, along the margin of the Everglades, white squatters at times adopted Indian dugouts and chickees in recognition of their superior suitability to the climate and terrain, but, for the most part, the Indians zealously guarded the Everglades by encouraging the notion that it was a trackless wilderness. But the soil was too rich, the game too plentiful, for them to succeed.

Throughout the period of the Seminole trade—1870 to 1930—the state and federal governments pursued their traditional policy of selling the land out from under the Indians—to ranchers and timber companies, to Hamilton Disston and other developers of model farms and communities. The train to Miami in 1896 and the Everglades dredges a decade later further narrowed the options and territory of the Indians. Purveyors of rotgut whiskey, carnival shills who wanted some authentic "wild Indians" for their ticky-tack tourist camps, and well-intentioned but misinformed missionaries and government officials who wanted in the names of justice and Christ to move them from their chickees into cinder block houses—all had equally pernicious effects. By the 1930s, the tribes were shut off from a way of life they had developed as a means of survival and once again dispossessed. Loggers were stripping from the Big Cypress Swamp the huge old trees that Indian craftsmen needed for their dugouts and that, more importantly, sheltered animals. Drainage was destroying the Everglades across which they had poled their canoes to hunt and establish new hammock farms. Although exempt from game laws, they found it increasingly difficult to support themselves from stocks white men depleted by overhunting for recreation and profit. Their income from trade in wildlife had fallen from as much as $25,000 to less than $400 a year. One bright spot was reestablishment of the cattle industry among one branch of the Seminole, but that was thin consolation for the suffering.

Controversy and questions accompany any analysis of the plume, fur, and hide trades, which thrived throughout south Florida. While it is certain that many species of birds were decimated, with some shot into extinction, it is not clear how many were killed and by whom, and similar questions arise with respect to the trapping of otter and to the trade in alligator hides. At the same time, the near terminal decline of crocodiles, turtles, shellfish, and several species of fish is clearly attributable to habitat destruction and to overexploitation by Anglo-American companies and their employees.

By the mid-1880s, the Indians and a handful of whites had been in south Florida for forty years without driving any creature to extinction. They knew where and when to find game and fish, to plant fruits and vegetables, how to build a house that would remain comfortable in the hottest weather. At the least, they had more primitive rifles and a greater need to conserve ammunition and trap only what they could preserve and carry. Though their dugouts were stable, worthy, often large craft, hauling quantities of hides as great as those generated by white hunters—who used wagons, coastal schooners, and later powerboats—was not possible.

Historian Harry Kersey, an expert on the Seminole trade, while stating that Indians dominated the alligator hide trade between 1880 and World War I when more than three million of the reptiles were killed and skinned, maintains that they did not hunt to excess. Yet when demand increased for otter pelts and certain plumes, the Indians hunted heavily. They also led hunting parties into the Everglades and Big Cypress Swamp after already vanishing birds such as the ivory-billed woodpecker and Carolina parakeet, and in quest of larger game—deer, bear, panthers. Billy Bowlegs III, the nephew of one of the last Seminole war leaders, Billy Bowlegs, was renowned as a guide from the 1880s through the 1940s—he died in 1965, aged 103. Flagler, Plant, and other wealthy tourists frequently employed him.

Billy Bowlegs III wasn't alone. The initial survey for the Everglades National Park, conducted during the 1930s, clearly states that both white and Indian trappers and hunters were indiscriminate in their killing. Without doubt, white commercial hunters shot out the great wading bird rookeries on both coasts and throughout the Everglades, with sportsmen and collectors contributing heavily to the slaughter. White bounty hunters and ranchers extinguished the last of Florida's wolves by late in the nineteenth century and soon thereafter wiped out the Carolina parakeet. The census of species hunted to the edge of extinction during the period between 1870 and 1930 is staggering.

Plume birds provide the most colorful and notorious example. By the mid-1880s, rookeries along the west coast, including the famous Maximo rookery on Tampa Bay near the tip of the Pinellas Peninsula, were cleaned out by hunters. Reddish egrets were all but extinct. Flamingos once had nested as far north as the Manatee River and along the shore of Florida Bay, but by the turn of the century they no longer nested in Florida. White ibis, roseate spoonbills, pelicans, and herons and egrets of every hue and size were gone. Many hunters thought survivors had fled to rookeries inland or farther south: They couldn't conceive that the birds would not come back. A similar situation existed on the east coast above Lake Worth. So thorough was the destruction of plume birds that within several generations collective memory of the rookeries was as dead as the birds themselves.

Commercial hunters moved south, along the west coast to loop and twist through the Ten Thousand Islands, around Cape Sable and the settlement named Flamingo into Florida Bay, and past the southeast tip of the peninsula to the Keys. Or they could, like Lake Worth pioneer Charles Pierce and French collector and taxidermist Jean Le Chevelier in 1885, sail from Miami, to the bird-rich Keys, Dry Tortugas, and Florida Bay. Pierce, Le Chevelier, and their companions shot hundreds of each of some forty-two species.[2] They passed, as well, huge quahog clam beds, with one clam being as large, Pierce said, as his companion Guy Bradley's foot.

Le Chevelier appears so often in accounts of plume hunting that in retrospect he assumes symbolic proportions. In the flesh, he was clearly a schemer, a scientific collector of specimens and eggs, a plume hunter, and a man who dreamed of developing a permanent settlement in southwest Florida as a hunting and logging base. When Pierce met him, he was living in Miami, but he was more a roamer than a resident anywhere. According to a Florida law of 1879, which prohibited aliens from killing plume birds, Le Chevelier operated illegally, but no one arrested or prosecuted him. He died in 1895, a free and wealthy man.

Conservation laws meant nothing. In 1891, the Florida legislature voted protection for egrets and other wading birds, but this stopped no one. William T. Hornaday, writing for the New York Zoological Society in 1913, estimated that bird populations in Florida declined 77 percent between 1881 and 1898 from hunting alone.[3] In 1900, the federal government prohibited interstate commerce in birds protected by state laws. The rookeries continued to vanish.

In 1901, William Dutcher, who subsequently became presi-

dent of the National Audubon Society, successfully lobbied for
passage of a new law protecting nongame birds. Because the
state legislature did not appropriate money for enforcement,
the society hired Pierce's former shipmate Guy Bradley to guard
the Cape Sable rookeries. Bradley's father had become a Flagler
land agent and moved his family to Flamingo when it appeared
the railroad to Key West would leave the mainland at Cape Sable
and cross Florida Bay. The Bradley family stayed in the area
after that route was rejected. As the first game warden in south
Florida, Bradley made his rounds armed only with a .32-caliber
pistol, a weapon his friends considered inadequate against men
with rifles and shotguns. In 1905, a poacher named Walter
Smith murdered him. Smith was arrested in Key West but freed
when no one who witnessed his crime would testify against him.

Bradley was the first official casualty in the campaign to save
the nearly vanished plume birds; in 1908, Audubon warden
Columbus G. McLeod became the second when he was gunned
down by poachers at Charlotte Harbor. The federal government
established the Key West National Wildlife Refuge that year to
protect herons and other wading birds, but it took two more
years and a brilliant public relations and lobbying campaign by
Dutcher and a Florida Quaker named T. Gilbert Pearson—
working for the Audubon Society—to rattle the plume buyers.
Pearson's scheme was simple: He went to New York State, the
home of the $17-million-a-year United States millinery industry.
The sweatshops employed twenty thousand people in New York
City putting plumes and sometimes whole birds onto women's
hats. Industry representatives claimed that egrets weren't killed
for their plumes, but that shed feathers were plucked from the
ground and shipped to New York. Bigger lies have succeeded,
but this one failed, and the New York State legislature in 1910
passed the Audubon Plumage Act outlawing the trade. The
slaughter continued, as hunters found higher prices in Havana
for plumes that could be shipped from there to Paris and London. The hats were then legally imported and sold in the United
States.

Three great rookeries on the shores of Lake Okeechobee
were effaced within two years after passage of the Audubon
Plumage Act. Finally, federal legislation outlawed the importation of the plume-adorned hats and at the same time protected
migratory birds through a treaty with Canada. The law worked
because of an assist from changing fashion. By 1917, prostitutes

had adopted feathered hats as part of their uniform and no respectable lady wanted to be confused with them.

But the birds were nearly gone. Once they filled the skies with sound and color, a mobile, cacophonous rainbow! They nested so thickly on the ground that collectors and hunters clubbed or kicked a path through them. Travelers went nowhere on the peninsula without remarking upon the avian life, and once the birds were gone, the visitors asked, "How can anyone say the air is alive?"

Perhaps the largest rookery ever found in North America, harboring one million birds at the headwaters of the Shark River on the peninsula's southwest coast, was obliterated in the 1880s and 1890s. The great plume birds gathered and nested in such rookeries, often located on barrier islands, small keys, or in the mangroves of the Ten Thousand Islands—the rich littoral regions where fish and shrimp spawned, where clams and oysters prospered. The hunt occurred during the spring mating and nesting season, when the birds were in full plumage. Clever hunters, using .22-caliber rifles because the sound of the gun was not loud enough to spook the flocks, massacred thousands of birds in a few days.

Ornithologist W.E.D. Scott described a large rookery he found in Charlotte Harbor soon after hunters had abandoned it:

> A few Herons were to be seen from time to time flying to the island. . . . The trees were full of nests, some of which still contained eggs, and hundreds of broken eggs strewed the ground everywhere. Fish Crows and both kinds of Buzzards [black and turkey vultures] were present in great numbers and were rapidly destroying the remaining eggs. I found a huge pile of dead, half decayed birds, lying on the ground which had apparently been killed for a day or two. All of them had the "plumes" taken with a patch of skin from the back, and some had the wings cut off; otherwise they were uninjured. I counted over two hundred birds treated this way.[4]

At every rookery the same depressing landscape remained after the hunters left—the dead birds scalped or skinned, their carcasses left to crows and vultures, the young starved or starving to death, consumed by raccoons and other predators, as were the eggs. They were islands of the doomed and dead. From the common egret, the hunters wanted only what they called the aigrettes (from the French for egret), the fifty fine plumes that grow from between its shoulders and extend beyond its tail during the mating season; from others they might want head or wing feathers or the entire skin. They had no intention of consuming the flesh or carrying more than they could easily sell.

Of the popular species, the roseate spoonbill was nearly extirpated between 1879 and 1889; the reddish egret—most valued in its white phase—was down to one reported pair by 1890. So thorough was the ruin of flamingos—widely used symbols of fun in the sun in Florida—that during the booming 1920s promoters imported them from the Bahamas, and some experts even today claim they never nested on the peninsula. The great white heron dwindled to perhaps two hundred, many of whom died in a 1935 hurricane; the snowy egret was difficult to find; the American egret and white ibis vanishing. Whatever could be shot was shot. Raptors fell too: The short-tailed hawk was nearly lost; the swallow-tailed and Everglade kites made rare.

To conservationists, the state of wildlife in Florida was deplorable. The New York Zoological Society's president William Hornaday wrote in 1913:

> From a zoological point of view Florida is in bad shape. A great many of her people who shoot are desperately lawless and uncontrollable, and the state is not financially able to support a force of wardens sufficiently strong to enforce the laws, even as they are. It looks as if the slaughter would go on until nothing of bird life remains.[5]

Like its bird protection legislation, the state's efforts to regulate hunting and fishing during the first decades of the century were pathetic. Underfunded and understaffed conservation agencies were established in 1913, abolished in 1915 and not reestablished until 1927, after great additional damage was done. Through its various agencies the state conservation board by 1935 had imposed hunting restrictions and bag limits and sent one hundred wardens into the field to enforce them. At the same time, three million acres (8 percent of the state) were set aside as wildlife refuges, where hunting was prohibited to give animal populations a chance to recover from years of abuse. Oyster beds were seeded in Apalachicola Bay and other depleted sites and leased to fishermen. Hatcheries for shad, bass, and bream were established along with a freshwater license system and strict limits on the size and quantity of most catches. In a significant move, the legislature voted that people using a cane or bamboo pole without a reel needed no license to fish in their home county. Most of those taking advantage of the exemption were poor residents who relied on fish for subsistence, and they caught primarily bream and catfish.

Although in the backcountry, people living in relative isolation from the rising cities continued to ignore the regulations when necessary and convenient, the actions helped a number of species rebound in the short term, most spectacularly the wading birds, which reached a population estimated at two million in 1940. (Rapid urbanization during the past two decades has caused a 90-percent reduction in their numbers, leading many people to fear more for their survival now than at any time in the past.)

Every form of wildlife had its optimum season. Plume hunting and egg collecting were confined to the spring. In summer, when water levels were high in the Everglades and swamps, the hunters took alligators by the tens of thousands; and in the winter they trapped mammals.

Next to birds, alligators provided the most lucrative and abundant source of income for Florida hunters, who between 1880 and 1894 killed at least 2.5 million of the big reptiles. Hundreds of thousands more were lost when nests were raided to satisfy national demand for baby alligators. Working at night when they could use a light that would reflect off the eyes of alligators floating just beneath the surface of the water—allowing their identification from a distance—hunters would club or shoot the reptiles, remove the smooth skin of their bellies and their teeth for necklaces and bracelets, then leave the carcasses to scavengers and decay. The exceptions were small gators—called hornbacks or roundhides—which were skinned in their entirety and used as decorations on various bags. The hunters also would "grunt up," or call, alligators, making them easy prey for a club or rifle shot.

As with plumes, prices for alligator hides and teeth varied according to quality, size, and market demand. As a rule, however, a prime "green," or uncured, hide fetched in the neighborhood of eighty to ninety cents a running foot; teeth brought five dollars a pound. Although demand for Florida alligators declined around 1898, the killing continued past 1916, when the first law was passed to protect them, and increased in the 1950s and 1960s to fill demand for alligator purses, shoes, and belts. Even many conservationists who favored protection of birds and other creatures had found it difficult early in the twentieth century to imagine that the huge reptile was threatened. Others, however, had recognized the danger not only to the alligator but to wildlife in general. Gator holes had served as storage ponds for water and havens for snakes, mammals, and birds; gator nests built next to the holes provided high ground on which plants could grow and animals escape floods in the rainy season.

To people who knew the region, crocodiles were also in severe danger. Senseless killing for pleasure and fear, and poaching for profit, took increasingly great tolls on remnant alligator and crocodile populations until the early 1970s when new federal government statutes outlawing the manufacture and sale of products made from their hides took effect. With protection, alligator populations rebounded so vigorously that the state reinstituted legalized hunting in the fall of 1988, hoping to cull mature animals living in close proximity to people. Either alligators were less numerous than predicted or hunters more incompetent because the quotas went unmet. Crocodiles have not flourished even with legal protection. Confined to the mangrove swamps of Florida Bay, they are victims of south Florida's canals, which in altering the flow of fresh water through the Everglades have caused an increase in salinity and reduction of life in the coastal zone the crocodiles call home.

Federal and state endangered species acts of the past two decades have offered some relief to declining species of other animals as well, including in Florida, the manatee, southern bald eagle, various raptors, wading and perching birds, snakes, and turtles. But decades of overhunting and continued destruction of their habitat have left their survival in question. All some wildlife enthusiasts hope for is stabilization of small breeding populations that would effectively occupy natural zoos. The Everglades mink has perished; the otter hangs on; bears and panthers are rare; the key deer falls under the wheels of cars and trucks.

Demand ran high for nearly every bit of Florida exotica. Plant sellers stripped the Everglades region of orchids, ferns, and bromeliads. The seizure of plants accelerated in the years following World War II as demand for houseplants and nursery stock increased, leading to the extirpation of several species from Royal Palm Hammock, the oldest section of the Everglades National Park.[6]

Throughout the Everglades and Florida Keys, scientific and commercial collectors pursued the brightly colored *Liguus* and *Osyshyla* tree snails, which varied in pattern and coloration from hammock to hammock. Charles Torrey Simpson so prized the distinctive creatures that into his eighties he scaled trees and braved swarms of mosquitoes in a quest for perfect specimens. Snails became active and were easiest to find after rains. Hunters would take snails by the bucketful from a hammock, then torch the vegetation. The fires, as botanist John Small observed, frequently consumed the thin soil of a hammock, down to the rock. Since the snails would not breed in burned-out areas, this meant the extinction of that hammock's unique species, a desirable result for traders because the harder a type of snail was to find on the market, the more precious were the few examples of it.

From everywhere on the peninsula, grasshoppers, spiders, butterflies, and snakes were shipped to collectors and pet shops around the world. The edible, growing part of the sabal palm, where fronds meet trunk, was cut out and sold as "heart of palm." Harvesting the heart kills the tree, and finally the practice was outlawed to protect the Florida state tree, although it continues in rural areas. (Heart of palm from other countries and from nursery-raised trees is available in most food stores.) Moss was ripped from trees for use in stuffing harnesses, mattresses, and carriage and car seats. Moss picking dated back to the days of Spanish conquest, but its pervasiveness by the end of the nineteenth century was greater than at any time before. The peninsula's land tortoise—called the gopher tortoise—was taken from its dry pinelands and shipped to Key West for sale with sea turtles, or turned on the spot into soup. The gopher tortoise, although now protected most of the year, is hunted in season and crushed, year round, under the wheels of motor vehicles. It has suffered most, however, from destruction of the high pinelands.

By the turn of the century, naturalists saw that the sea turtles that nested all along south Florida's Gulf and Atlantic coasts were in trouble from extensive human depredation. Settlers commonly substituted turtle eggs for those of chickens, and the giants themselves—the greens, loggerheads, Atlantic ridleys, leatherbacks, and hawksbills—were taken for food and tortoiseshell combs, brush handles, shoehorns, and other accessories for the well-heeled man or woman. Turtle kraals dotted the shallow water of the Keys and both coasts.

The late naturalist Archie Carr assessed the value of the green turtle in his seminal work *The Windward Road:*

> It was only the green turtle that could take the place of spoiled kegs of beef and send a ship on for a second year of wandering or marauding. All early activity in the New World tropics—exploration, colonization, buccaneering, and even maneuverings of naval squadrons—was in some way or degree dependent on the turtle. . . . It had all the qualities it needed for a role in history. It was big, abundant, available, savory, sustaining, and remarkably tenacious of life. It was almost unique in being a marine herbivore—an air-breathing vertebrate which grazed submarine beds of seed plants as the bison grazed the plains and which, like them, congregated in tremendous bands. It was easy to catch with simple equipment because its pastures lay under clear shallow water; and, moreover, each June it came ashore wherever there was sand, and you had only to walk the beach and turn on their backs as many as you could use.[7]

They made delectable soup. They also possessed a curious trait: Herbivorous in open water, they became carnivorous when kept in kraals and so the longer they were kept confined, the less nutritious and tasty their flesh became. (The turtles had to be kept alive until just before cooking because the meat spoiled quickly.)

The decline in stocks of sea turtles was precipitous. In 1610, mariners reported that turtles around Bermuda were so thick that one could simply pluck them from the water after bashing them with iron bars.[8] Heavy commercial hunting dates to the post–Civil War years, particularly the late 1880s and 1890s when nets replaced harpoons as the weapon of choice. At Key West, the center of the trade for Florida and the Caribbean, turtlers landed 468,256 pounds of turtles in 1890, three quarters of them greens. In 1895, the haul was 410,000 pounds. That year turtling died in the Gulf of Mexico around Tampa and in the bay itself, because of overhunting by fleets operating primarily out of Cedar Key. In 1896, the total at Key West reached 520,000 pounds; it rose to 634,616 the following year. Then everything crashed because of overfishing and the taking of eggs for food. In 1898, turtlers could manage only 72,220 pounds, and by 1937, they were down to 10,000. A brief recovery in 1947 saw 60,536 pounds landed at Key West. Although the dwindling catch spoke to all who would listen, the turtles were relentlessly persecuted until 1971, when they were accorded some protection as an endangered species. But the sea turtles have yet to recover to any great degree. Nesting grounds vanish as men and alien plants like casuarina invade beaches. Throughout the Caribbean, adult greens are killed for canning as soup, a sought-after gourmet item. And commercial shrimp fishermen, many of whom fight regulations and changes in design that would limit the number of turtles incidentally drawn into their nets, compound the slaughter.

If counting birds seemed unnecessary because of their numbers and density, taking a census of sea life was inconceivable. The New World from the time of its discovery by western Europeans was considered a place with limitless supplies of fish. If populations vanished from one area, they simply had become wise to the ways of their pursuers and moved on. Even today, in the face of the absolute depletion of many species and the continuous marketing of what were previously known as trash fish—those no one would care to keep, much less eat—many people, especially fishermen, refuse to think that limits exist and have been surpassed. And where supplies do exist, they may prove toxic because of pollution: Oysters and clams suffer this fate regularly. In the Keys, the queen conch, the defining creature and symbol, is absolutely protected. Throughout the Caribbean, so few conchs remain that costly and difficult aquaculture seems the only hope for their long-term survival; yet the export of conch to restaurants and food stores in the United States and abroad continues. Too much money is at stake for poor islands to forbid it. Shrimpers still work from Gulf and Atlantic coast ports, but their catches don't match historic levels, and most shrimp on the market these days comes from farms, including those being built in the mangrove coasts of Central and South America. The crawfish—the Florida spiny lobster—is protected from human predation in those portions of its Biscayne Bay breeding grounds now under supervision of the National Park Service, while bag and size limits apply outside those waters during the eight-month season for capturing them. Anecdotal evidence suggests that the quantity and quality of the harvest follow a downward curve, but so little is known about the creatures that it is possible to argue whether their numbers are declining. (It is certain that most commercial lobstermen in Florida trap the bulk of their take in the first two months of the season; some even stop trying after that and turn their attention to stone crabs.)

Among fish the declines are remarkable, especially in the past twenty years. Red drum was until recently a popular game fish, but then it became known far and wide as redfish and was taken commercially—for Cajun-style blackened redfish—in such numbers throughout its range that in 1987 it received absolute protection in Florida waters (but not those of Louisiana and other Gulf states) so the population could recover. The once common red snapper has become an expensive fish at markets and restaurants. In recent years, demand for shark fins in Asian markets and restaurants has led fishermen to pursue those ancient predators, which they once avoided, slicing the fins from those they catch and then throwing the shark, dead or alive, back to sea. Even the noble game fish—barracuda, tarpon, and bonefish—that made Florida waters famous have begun to decline because of sports fishing and destruction of mangrove forests along the coasts.

Those last three were renowned fighters long before Ernest Hemingway ever knotted hook to line and let fly. Archie Carr wrote of the experience:

> If it was not something to eat but adrenaline in the blood you were after, you only had to drag a line for a barracuda in the channel or commune with the Bahia Honda tarpon or creep about the marl flats till you saw the tilted shadows of a bonefish, foraging in their primitive peace; and if you made a proper approach, you might hook one of these. After that your life would not be quite the same.[9]

Responsible guides and charter captains now try to persuade clients to throw large fish back alive, especially since taxidermists can make lifelike fiberglass replicas of trophy-sized fish, but many of their clients prefer to keep and have stuffed the carcass.

In fresh water, few deny that the largemouth bass has seen far better days. In 1925, fishermen took from Lake Okeechobee and other lakes bass weighing up to twenty pounds; today, few lunkers weigh in at over ten pounds. By 1935, commercial exploitation of the peninsula's black bass had so depleted stocks that the legislature banned their sale. Hatcheries were established at the same time to restock lakes and rivers with bass, bream, and shad; the alternative was to turn the waterways over to gar and other trash fish. Stocks began to improve through the management programs, but improvement did not represent a return to previous levels, and evidence now suggests that bass in south Florida and other densely populated areas of the state are polluted with heavy metals.

The evidence from earlier times shows such a glut of marine life in Florida waters that it staggered the senses of those who first saw it. William Bartram in the eighteenth century found alligators filling channels in the lower St. Johns so densely he believed he could cross the river on their heads. On the same river, Bartram found twenty-pound bass, and the St. Johns was no exception. Charles Torrey Simpson and others, a century after Bartram's journey, reported mullet so thick off both coasts that they seemed to leave no spot of water showing.

From the seventeenth century on, rough, palmetto-thatched shacks were built on stilts in shallow coastal waters. There, men would stay during the run of mullet and other fish, fall into spring. Many of these fishermen came in ships out of Havana or they were Floridians, often people with mixed blood, born to fishing and the isolated camps, using every means at their disposal to take their quarry. They dynamited fish, poisoned them with sawdust or toxic berries (a tactic learned from the Indians). They deployed huge seines, gill and drift nets that swept the seas, lakes, and rivers clean. In addition to the stilt villages, fishermen worked from ships, plying deeper waters.

The expansion of railroads, the increasing use of steamboats, and the construction during that period of ice factories made transshipment of the catch more certain, and commercial fishermen took advantage of every improvement that raised profits. In the 1930s, techniques for freezing fish encouraged the catching and shipment of even more. For oysters, clams, crabs, and crawfish, canneries were established in towns on the Atlantic and Gulf. The size of the mollusks was extraordinary— five-pound quahogs from the southwest coast beds were the rule. Stone crabs were harvested so heavily that their exportation from Florida waters was prohibited and crabbers were al-

lowed to take only the large claw—the part of the crustacean that
is eaten—and the crab returned to the water (a process that is
more noble in theory than practice since only about 20 percent
of the declawed crabs survive).

In 1880, just over two thousand fishermen worked the
state's waters for profit. Less than a decade later, the legislature
established the Florida Fish Commission to oversee their activities in hope of controlling wholesale slaughter. In 1900, the
total catch—primarily of mullet, snapper, mackerel, grouper,
and bream (the only freshwater fish in the lot)—was 38 million
pounds. By 1905, Broward was calling for laws to protect the
declining oyster beds and fisheries, but, as with birds and game,
enforcement was feeble in the face of organized assault. But the
Shell Fish Commission in 1913 and the revitalized Game and
Fresh Water Fish Commission a dozen years later fought to
stanch heavy harvesting of declining stocks by increasing numbers of fishermen. In 1938, something on the order of seventy-
five thousand commercial fishermen caught 125 million pounds,
and three years later increased that to 137 million. In 1960,
Florida's commercial fishermen hauled in 182.5 million pounds;
in 1965, 200 million; 1969, 161.2 million; 1986, 100.7 million—
despite more sophisticated shipborne technology and aircraft
surveillance. Prices and therefore profits have generally increased in recent years; the stocks inexorably have declined.

Plying fresh water and salt water, the state's one million
sports fishermen and charter boat captains spend $2 billion a
year contributing to the falling stocks, while striving to affix
blame solely on the commercial boatmen. They neglect to mention that there is no difference between ten men taking 10,000
pounds of fish each and two thousand men catching 50 pounds
each.

One of the most grotesque and unnecessary episodes in this
record of "shameful slaughter," as naturalists called it, occurred
in the first decades of the century under state sponsorship. The
destruction had its origins in the appearance of Texas tick fever
in Florida in the second decade of this century, borne in by ticks
imported on cattle from infected herds in western and southeastern states. To combat the virus, the state mandated that
ranchers dip their cattle in tanks filled with an arsenic solution
every fourteen days, which, in addition to killing the ticks, damaged both cattle and the environment. Rain hitting the backs of

recently treated cattle concentrated the arsenic solution on their bellies, causing their hides to crack when the dip dried. Sometimes, it was easier to kill cattle on the range than to round them up for biweekly treatment. The cost of the program drove many marginal ranchers out of business. The environment also suffered, as arsenic washed into the water supply, and the poison's residue, which coated the dipping vats, proved hazardous to animals and people who sought to play in or drink water collecting there.

Arrested in the 1920s after a battle that lasted seven years in Orange County, a little less elsewhere, tick fever erupted again in 1935. The carriers were tropical ticks that apparently feasted on deer blood, and a campaign was launched to exterminate the Florida whitetail throughout cattle country. Conservationists and sportsmen protested vigorously and organized a Deer Protective Organization, which in 1937 obtained an injunction against the slaughter. Georgia and other states responded with a quarantine of all Florida livestock and dogs, and an appeals court overturned the injunction. Blind to the notion that other creatures carried ticks and convinced on the basis of no evidence that 54 percent of the native deer were infected, state officials ordered them shot on sight—all of them.

Throughout cattle country, state-sponsored gunmen pursued the animals with dogs, on horseback, by car, and boat. They used planes to locate herds. They fire-hunted, a technique employed for centuries by Indian, white, and black hunters to bring home game for food. Initially, they followed tradition and used shavings of lighter pine—the heartwood chipped from stumps of downed trees—placed in pans fitted to their shoulders, but they switched in the 1940s to battery-operated miner's headlamps and powerful flashlights. Shining the light into the deer's eyes, they would immobilize it, then shoot it.

The state paid the hunters eighty dollars a month, provisioned them, and added a bounty for each kill, based on ears they turned over to officials. In south Florida the hunters, who often lived in the field for weeks at a stretch in crude and filthy camps, sold the meat to local butchers along the Tamiami Trail who marketed it—illegally—to buyers from Miami and Miami Beach. For poor country men and boys in the Depression years, the deer slaughter was a boon, bringing cash to families that could find no other work.

In central Florida the deer were shot out. In south Florida

they had some allies, including the terrain. They hid in the recesses of Fakahatchee Strand and Big Cypress—deep in swamps neither the hunters nor their dogs cared to penetrate. The animals also found refuge with the Indians. The Seminole on the Big Cypress Reservation flatly refused to allow the state's assassins to kill deer on their land. Deer provided them with food; the murder appeared wasteful. The governor howled at U.S. Interior Secretary Harold Ickes, demanding permission for the slaughter to sweep across Indian lands. In 1940, Ickes sided with the Seminole, but in 1942, a bill sponsored by then Senator Claude Pepper authorized the U.S. Department of Agriculture to continue the assault.

Hunters and environmentalists finally succeeded in placing stories about the destruction in enough national publications that the state's leaders became embarrassed. Bad press, after all, discouraged tourism, their lifeblood. By the early 1950s, the program was officially over, and the state moved to introduce white-tailed deer from Wisconsin into south and central Florida. Although a close cousin of the native swamp deer, the northern whitetails died quickly in the heat and humidity, among the mosquitoes and flies of the swamp for which they weren't bred. In excess of $3 million were spent on the campaign, which suppressed the deer population only as long as it continued. Afterward, the herds regained size and strength for several decades, before increased hunting, which coincided with south Florida's human population growth, began to take its toll. The state massacre did succeed, however, in gutting fox and gray squirrel communities, especially in Big Cypress.

Deer and even scrub cattle still mingle with razorbacks in the Everglades and Big Cypress, but many south Florida hunters leave the region during deer season for the Panhandle, out of state, or, increasingly, private preserves. The decline in stocks has become so pronounced that hunting in south Florida is often no more than an outing in the swamp.

SEVEN

"Water Will Run Downhill"

The campaign against the Everglades leads to scandal and disaster. Lake Okeechobee strikes back and then is locked up.

Hugh L. Willoughby, ex-lieutenant commanding the Rhode Island Naval Reserve, stood, a gleaming clean Winchester in his hands, under the coconut palm, the bold adventurer back from the wilds. A broad-brimmed hat shaded him from the sun, while elevating the temperature of his head a few degrees above comfortable; spotless boots revealed nothing of where he'd been. An unsheathed knife hung between his pants and belt. A canoe lay beached at his feet. Bearded, self-satisfied, he posed: conqueror of the Everglades. He had dug not one ditch since setting forth in 1896 to cross Pa-hay-okee, the "Grassy Water," as the Indians called the Everglades, from the Harney River in the Ten Thousand Islands northeast to Miami, a diagonal through the heart of the sawgrass—a vast marsh and wet prairie no white man had seen to describe, though wandering Indians occupied some of the hammocks seasonally and white hunters passed through, scouting for game, feeding their curiosity. "It may seem strange, in our days of Arctic and African exploration," Willoughby said, "for the general public to learn that in our very midst, we have a tract of land one hundred and thirty miles long and seventy miles wide that is as much unknown to the white man as the heart of Africa."[1]

In his honest recognition that humans already knew the region he set out to explore, Willoughby manifested a generosity uncommon among many of his fellow adventurers who regularly disparaged or ignored the knowledge of indigenous peoples. The Indians, whom he admired for their integrity and charm, called him Willie Bee and appear in turn to have appreciated his adoption of the dugout for preliminary excursions. Although he recognized the value of that craft's design and of using poles for propulsion in traversing the Everglades, he decided on custom-built canoes for his expedition because he felt more comfortable with them. It was a familiarity born of years of use and experience.

He also manifested a distinctive and, for the time, rare respect for local white outdoorsmen, choosing as his guide and scout Ed Brewer, a native Virginian who had lived in south Florida for years and often spent "six-months at a time" in the Everglades. A hunter and trapper, Brewer was considered dangerous by many members of Miami's winter community, who claimed that he sold liquor to the Indians and warned Willoughby to avoid him. But the adventurer trusted his instincts, and wrote, "In our solitary companionship, far from the reach of any law but that of our own making, I always found him brave and industrious, constantly denying himself, deceiving me as to his appetite when our supplies ran low."[2]

Like many a Florida traveler, Willie Bee fell for the look and feel of it all, the aura of a biological and botanical wonderland, and he mourned its passing even while facing it with a progressive's stoicism, avowing that the destruction was for the common good. Thus, on viewing Flagler's Royal Palm Hotel rising from the leveled Indian mound at Fort Dallas, he could say: "In all Florida, I have never seen a more beautiful spot than where this deep, narrow river [the Miami] suddenly opens into Biscayne Bay between those tall graceful coconut trees, that seem to stand as sentinels guarding the secrets of its source, the mysterious Everglades. . . . The romance and poetry must be suppressed for the sterner, material welfare of our fellow man."[3] Yet he railed against the purchase and settlement by whites of an Everglade key formerly occupied by Indians. The new owners destroyed the Indian village and razed the hammock for a vegetable farm near an "unsightly wooden shanty." The change occurred in little more than a year, between Willoughby's visit to the village while preparing for his Everglades crossing and his stop at the island upon its completion. Every sizable patch of high, dry land was snatched up and plowed, even if all around was tall grass and water.

The Everglade key wasn't named or defined as a geological and botanical entity until John Kunkel Small of the New York Botanical Society did so in the second decade of the present century. Small compiled most of the lists of plants found in south Florida's hardwood hammocks. By that time, the works of man had already endangered the largest and most beautiful of them, and he worked against the clock of progress. But that's the story of Florida's development—people who occupied the land as they found it were pushed aside and dispossessed in the drive for "material welfare."

Other explorers had traversed parts of the Everglades before Willoughby and Brewer poled and dragged their canoes across it—or at least peered into it long enough to make up stories. Those who saw marveled at the way the water had carved the limestone not smooth but ragged, leaving twisted knots rising above the surface, and at the grass, sedges, and rushes that made the region a vast grassy water. Small springs bubbling through the surface of the rock proved that the fresh water men called sweet flowed below as well as above the ground, passing through its subterranean channels even into Biscayne Bay.

Buckingham Smith of St. Augustine, who translated the narratives of the early Spanish explorers and bequeathed his estate to aid black Floridians, reconnoitered the area to determine the feasibility of draining or somehow converting it to practical use. He reported in 1848:

> The appearance of the interior of the Everglades is unlike that of any region of which I have ever heard, and certainly it is in some respects the most remarkable on this continent. Imagine a vast lake of fresh water extending in every direction from shore to shore beyond the reach of human vision ordinarily unruffled by a ripple on its surface, studded with thousands of islands of various sizes, from one-fourth of an acre to hundreds of acres in area, and which are generally covered with dense thickets of shrubbery and vines. . . . The surrounding waters, except in places that at first seem like channel ways (but which are not), are covered with the tall sawgrass, shooting up its straight and slender stem from the shallow bottom of the lake to the height of 10 feet above the surface and covering all but a few rods around from your view. The water is pure and limpid and almost imperceptibly moves, not in partial currents, but, as it seems, in a mass, silently and slowly to the southward.[4]

One would expect, after such an elegiac description, that Smith would recommend leaving the Everglades to those who would enjoy it for what it was. But progress demanded a different conclusion and Smith declared that although poets and romantics might find Pa-hay-okee (which he transliterated without the hyphens) inspirational, it was, in its present state, totally worthless to "civilized" man.

In 1882 and again in 1883, the *New Orleans Times-Democrat* sponsored expeditions into areas around Lake Okeechobee to explore the strange lands Hamilton Disston planned to reclaim. The intrepid travelers produced more fluff than stuff and contributed virtually nothing to the knowledge of the region, although they presumably helped sell a few papers.

In 1892, James Ingraham conducted his survey for Henry Plant of a rail line from Tampa to Fort Myers and then across the upper Everglades to Biscayne Bay by way of Lake Okeechobee. His expedition provided a case study in strategic blunders, beginning with the choice of craft—heavy rowboats ill-suited to the task. The men refused to eat food the Indians relied on as dietary staples—the Everglades terrapin, alligator tails, and fish—and relied instead on their rations. Even when their provisions began to give out and they faced hunger, Ingraham and his men did not attempt to catch fish. One can only attribute their actions to fatigue and panic when faced with a strange country. A Seminole found them exhausted and lost and, taking pity, guided them the last few miles to the Miami River and Fort Dallas, where Julia Tuttle received them. Because they had averaged three miles a day on a one-hundred-mile journey the Indians regularly completed in four days in their dugouts, the rumor spread that the Seminole and Miccosukee knew secret channels through the sawgrass but would never lead white men through them. Not surprisingly, Ingraham reported to Plant that the upper Everglades, the tall, dense sawgrass marshes rimming Lake Okeechobee to the south and east, could not easily be crossed by rail but could be drained for agriculture—and he hoped to do it. After joining Flagler's Florida East Coast Railway, he tried, in partnership with Hamilton Disston's former engineer, Rufus Rose, and with Flagler's financial backing, to drain and farm the land, but for economic and political reasons, his plans failed.

Willoughby was interested in the crossing, and after studying Ingraham's aborted expedition, he determined whenever possible to follow the Indians' lead. He learned enough to pole his canoe and employ a guide familiar with the region, however much the more settled, law-abiding citizens of the coast despised him. He worried that the Indians would discover his presence in what he believed to be their sanctum sanctorum and take action against him—a bit of sensitivity toward native feelings generally lacking among many of his cohorts, even those claiming to be their friends. After sailing around the coast from Biscayne Bay, stopping to shoot crocodiles for a museum and repair his nose after an accident that nearly severed it, Willoughby, with Brewer, cut his way through mangroves into the Harney River and began to pole into the sawgrass marsh that defines the true Everglades. A paddle wheel Willoughby designed to measure mileage worked well but no better—to his surprise—than his guide Brewer's innate sense of distance. They picked a channel through the sawgrass, following leads—narrow open channels of relatively deep water cut by alligators or perhaps dugouts—wherever possible because poling through dense stands was physically exhausting and sometimes impossible. The fine-toothed edges of the sedge slashed limbs and canoes. Willoughby and Brewer camped on the tree islands, which varied in size and firmness, from moist beds of willow barely rising above the water to solid ground, which often held remnants of Indian camps.

Limpkins shrieked through the night while frogs sounded. Deer appeared regularly although Willoughby couldn't fathom what they were doing in the sawgrass and water. However, the mosquitoes that had plagued the explorers along the mangrove border diminished as they pressed inland, though they continued to sleep under nets. In fact, the heart of the Everglades proved the opposite of a miasmic swamp. They traveled the Shark River Slough, which Willoughby found "a country of pure water" flowing steadily southwestward in a broad sheet. The air was "wholesome, pure, and free from disease germs."[5] In spots he and Brewer had to drag and push their canoes, but in the main they floated.

Within a dozen years of Willie Bee's crossing, the dredges had begun their grinding waltz through the sawgrass. Sent out by Florida's bold and dogged governor, Napoleon Bonaparte Broward, the dredgemen traveled with less awareness of the area than even the earliest explorers had. Son of a Florida planter of French heritage—whence his name—and a New Hampshire Yankee, Napoleon Bonaparte nonetheless fancied himself a Cracker (a claim that helped him win votes from disaffected Floridians but earned the disapproval of his aunts, who refused to attend his gubernatorial inauguration on the grounds that he had betrayed his class). His family had fled their farm near Jacksonville during the Civil War and afterward, without slaves, faltered in their attempts to revive the property. Parcels were auctioned by the state for back taxes. Following the death of their mother in 1869 and father a year later, Napoleon and his brother Montcalm tried to work the land but spent more time fishing and hunting than plowing. Relatives took the orphaned brothers in, as they had their three sisters, and later Napoleon became a riverman, a steamboat pilot and owner, working out of Jacksonville. As river traffic declined, Broward tried phosphate mining—then a new enterprise—tug boating and salvage, all to no avail. Later, as a filibuster, running guns and men to Cuba on his steam-powered tug, *Three Friends,* he became a hero to Cuban revolutionaries and to many Floridians, especially after the federal government indicted him for his activities—charges rendered invalid when the United States declared war on Spain.

Even before becoming governor in 1905, Broward dominated state politics while embodying the contradictions that tore at its seams. He had served variously as sheriff of Duval County, state legislator, and leader of the "straight-out," or populist, faction of the Democratic party. Broward achieved within his lifetime something of the status of a Florida folk hero, with his talk of the common man and bluster against transportation monopolies—especially Flagler's. But he opposed William Jennings Bryan's plan to nationalize the trains and even more thoroughly disapproved of his liberality on racial issues, opining that all blacks—some 40 percent of the state's population, but mostly disenfranchised—should be exiled to Africa or some other distant shore, never to mingle again with whites. He demanded an end to child labor and more humane treatment for prisoners, but he didn't close down the convict-lease system or improve the brutal working conditions in turpentine camps. Those people were predominantly black. Seeing in automobiles a way to break the power of railroads, he encouraged driving by building roads, and he promulgated traffic rules and mandatory car registration. He supported conservation laws for fish, oysters, game, and forests, but not for alligators, whose decline was exacerbating droughts in the open range and swamps.

Broward stands most prominently as the person who commenced the drainage of the Everglades. "Water," he liked to declare, "will run downhill," and so he and his fellow pseudopopulists decided they could drain the Everglades by destroying their hub—Okeechobee—and thereby provide homesteads for small farmers. Their plan and claims oozed deception and self-interest from the start. Broward could not and would not move with the full power of his authority against corporations that had come to claim most of the state's prime acres, just as they came to hold much of the reclaimed land. The former steamboater was interested first in his own prestige and power, second in bolstering the depressed shipping industry by digging navigable canals from Lake Okeechobee to both coasts and thereby presenting an alternative to the railroads.

South Florida was thus sacrificed to relieve pressure from lower-class whites in north and central Florida who were demanding farms, to open the interior to steamboats, and to bring that potentially rich section of the peninsula under the control of the government in Tallahassee. As early as 1848, Buckingham Smith had predicted that drainage would encourage formation of a new state consisting of what he called south and east Florida, "dissevering the unnatural connection now existing between them and middle and west Florida, sections totally dissimilar in pursuits, interests, and habits."[6] Broward and his allies rejected that scenario fifty years later and imposed their own.

The first engagement in the reclamation campaign took place in 1900 when William Jennings Bryan's cousin William Jennings became governor of Florida and moved to end the land giveaways to the railroads. The Internal Improvement Fund at that time had fewer acres on hand than it had promised, so some adjustment was necessary. Jennings also acted in response to a consensus among Floridians that corporations had run roughshod over the state and its resources—taking everything and leaving nothing in return. The Everglades—especially the four million acres of it that the federal government still held—represented the only virgin land left on the peninsula, and everyone wanted it—railroad and canal companies, lumber companies, politicians—to curry favor, power, and profit. The state thought the "Grassy Water" its due under the 1851 Swamp Lands Act.[7]

A disaster born of human incompetence inspired the first calls for government reclamation of the Everglades. In March 1903 floods in south Florida wiped out farmers working inadequately drained fields, and Jennings seized the opportunity to demand more dikes and canals to tame forever the wetlands. He wanted the United States Congress to pay for the work, but President Theodore Roosevelt opted instead to sign over 2,862,080 acres of federally held land to the state, and the rush was on. Jennings, after turning the governorship over to Broward, worked as special counsel to the Internal Improvement Fund to resolve land disputes with corporations and clear the legal way for the drainage crusade.

Defying opponents who called his scheme folly, a waste of taxpayers' money, and a violation of the law, Broward began his campaign, changing plans and direction to suit political, not hydrological or geological, realities. He first intended to carve a canal for twenty-two miles from Lake Okeechobee to the headwaters of the St. Lucie River, which entered the Atlantic Ocean at Stuart, a village between Palm Beach and Fort Pierce. Then the dredge would cut from the St. Lucie through eight miles of marsh and sawgrass to the headwaters of the St. Johns, thereby providing an inland Atlantic-to-Gulf link by way of Okeechobee and the Caloosahatchee River. That was Disston's unfinished scheme, and Broward boldly claimed it would open six million acres of land to homesteaders. It would also bring increased traffic to his home port, Jacksonville, and solidify its position as the state's economic capital. But Broward changed his mind, because Stuart and environs were bastions of political opposition, and thus unworthy destinations for the canal.[8]

Instead, he would dig first from the south shore of Lake Okeechobee through the New River to Fort Lauderdale, the home of political allies. The engineer on Ingraham's 1892 expedition, John Newman, became head of the project. In 1906, the dredge *Everglades* started digging up the New River from the coast, and in 1907 the *Okeechobee* dredged its way out of the lake. These machines were awkward, lumbering, steam-powered monsters, difficult to operate, more impressive in appearance than in function. They were pulled and pushed through the winding, frequently shallow and narrow channels on the way upriver. The crew of the *Okeechobee* blasted through dense forest and limestone to provide room for the steam-powered shovel to operate: It was slow, dangerous work, requiring the men to fight through muck, sawgrass, and swamps for scant pay and no other rewards.

In the tradition of Florida politics, Broward launched his campaign without funds to finance it. In 1905, he rammed through the legislature a constitutional amendment establishing a Board of Drainage Commissioners with power to "build canals, drains, levees, ditches, and reservoirs, to establish drainage districts, and to levy an annual tax not exceeding 10 cents an acre."[9] The commissioners—the same officials who comprised the Internal Improvement Fund board—established a district around Lake Okeechobee and set a five-cents-an-acre tax, which was promptly challenged in court. The landholders—nonresident corporations owned just over 4 million acres in the district; farmers, ranchers, and village dwellers, 185,020—won an injunction blocking collection of the levy. In 1906, voters around the state rejected the Drainage Act amendment to the constitution, but the dredges were already at work. The following year, Broward pushed another act through the legislature—in clear defiance of the wishes of the people—and established by law rather than constitutional amendment his drainage commission. With an able assist from Jennings, Broward and his fellow Internal Improvement Fund board members also settled outstanding land claims by persuading the railroad companies to accept fewer acres in recompense than they were technically due, the alternative being years of litigation and, perhaps, no land at all. (Flagler's claims were excepted because he was building for Key West and had not provided a full statement of the acreage owed his Florida East Coast Railway.)

Broward's assault on unsurveyed land and water was an environmental disaster, an engineering nightmare, and a political fiasco. The land was supposed to support small farms, but that was before Broward's drainage scheme went awry and the state had to sell off huge parcels to keep the dredges running. Buyers of Broward's submerged acres subdivided their domains and marketed prime Everglades lots to people around the country, with the promise of fields so ripe with blooms and fruit and vegetables that the farmers would think they had gone to heaven—until they started counting the profit and realized they were rich on earth. The biggest buyer was a con artist named Richard Bolles, who agreed in 1908 to purchase 500,000 acres south and east of Lake Okeechobee for $1 million. By the time he was finished promoting and selling his land, Bolles had sullied for decades the Florida real estate industry.

Bolles was a man waiting for scandal to break him, a huckster with all the credentials of a first-rate investment genius. Son of a New York physician, he gained a seat on the New York Stock Exchange at age twenty-three, made a fortune, and departed for the West where he made several additional millions selling ranches in Oregon and Colorado. The Everglades were a logical next step for someone who wanted real estate with instant allure a continent away from his previous conquests, in case a dissatisfied customer was gunning for him. To sell his first 180,000 acres piecemeal, he organized the Florida Fruit Lands Company and prepared a national sales push.

When Broward left office in 1909–Florida governors could not succeed themselves, so he ran for the U.S. Senate and won, but died before assuming the seat–only fifteen miles of canals had been dug. Defying popular opinion, his successor, Albert Gilchrist, continued the reclamation campaign, relying on the dubious scientific surveys of James Wright, a U.S. Department of Agriculture engineer who falsely claimed that all water in the Everglades came from Lake Okeechobee; he ignored the importance of rain. If the lake's water level were lowered, he reasoned, the 'Glades would dry up. Wright, who left the Agriculture Department after a scandal erupted over his inaccurate report and amid charges of a conflict of interest, officially joined the state drainage effort in 1910. He was assigned to oversee the work of the Furst-Clark Construction Company of Baltimore, which had contracted to dig 184 miles of canals–the Miami, North and South New River, and Hillsboro. Within a year, the West Palm Beach Canal was added to the scheme. (Wright subsequently joined Furst-Clark.) The canals drained some land, but also overflowed in places during the rainy season because they were too narrow and shallow–not even up to the inadequate standards of the engineers who designed them–to hold the water rushing into them. Homes and fields were ruined.

By that time, the largest of the land companies–Bolles's Florida Fruit Lands Company, the Everglades Land Sales Company, and Florida Everglade Company, among them–had posted salesmen around the world where they vied for settlers with agents of the railroads and developers from elsewhere in the state. Profits from sales were easier and quicker than from farming the thick muck. Bolles's salesmen proclaimed the east Everglades between the coast and Lake Okeechobee a "tropical paradise," the "Promised Land," the "poor man's paradise," the "land of destiny," the "magnet whose climate and agriculture will bring the human flood," and "richer than the Nile Valley." They loudly bruited forester John Gifford's assertion that a ten-acre tropical farm would support a family in comfort. Northern buyers came in droves. Advertising fliers, low monthly payments, and lotteries for prime sites and prizes were integral to the sales campaign. Bolles even threw into his package town lots in what is today Fort Lauderdale but was then a no-man's-land, the site of a proposed model community he called Progresso.

Prospective buyers traveled from Fort Myers and Fort Lauderdale aboard Bolles's steamboats—*Wanderlust* and *Queen of the Everglades*—to his hotel on Lake Okeechobee at Ritta, where they were shown a carefully cultivated model farm. Within a year, their lies began to catch him and other purveyors of Everglades land. The *Washington Times* (no relation to the current paper of that name) ran an exposé on October 15, 1911, accusing everyone involved in the drainage program of deception, collusion, and fraud.[10]

A month later, disaffected buyers brought a civil suit against Bolles in Kansas City to void their sales contracts. The complaint charged that he had purchased his first block of 180,000 acres for $360,000 and sold it in pieces for $2.88 million, without making promised improvements. Farm sites were unsurveyed and often undrained. Reclaimed land near the canals was prone to flooding in summer and rapid depletion of nutrients during the winter growing season, when irrigation became essential. The insects in the rainy season were so thick settlers could barely breathe, and the snakes, scorpions, frogs, ants, snails, and palmetto bugs swarmed in the millions. The suit was settled in 1913 when Bolles agreed not to collect additional payments until the drainage was completed and to improve the land at his expense. Few buyers stuck around until then, but those who did benefited from their Progresso lots, as the press of new settlers to coastal communities drove up prices of homesites. Congress investigated and the courts began to hear criminal cases arising from the Everglades land business—a scandal wrapped in a farce disguising a disaster.

In 1912, Governor Gilchrist sought to prove the nasty northern press wrong in its accusations of collusion between the state and real estate men by sponsoring a trip from the Gulf to the Atlantic through Lake Okeechobee. A chartered train, "the Hurry-Up Limited," provided free passage for fifty reporters from Chicago, Gilchrist meeting them at Jacksonville for a ride to Fort Myers. There the merry crew embarked on a steamboat up the channelized Caloosahatchee River to Bolles's hotel at Ritta and a tropical feast. The next day, they came to the North New River Canal where Gilchrist mixed Gulf and Atlantic water from two coconuts and proclaimed the cross-state waterway open. The reporters even took a slow trip on a shallow-draft boat down the North New River Canal to Fort Lauderdale, but they were too enthralled with the "mysterious" Everglades and sated from the entertainment to notice the deficiencies of the waterway. They filed glowing accounts, and for a while it appeared that the public relations campaign had blunted the criticism. But shortly thereafter, consumers decided the issue on their own by launching a boycott of Everglades land that they were convinced was being sold "by the quart."

In 1913, the state organized the Everglades Drainage District and began taxing landowners according to their proximity to the canals and the benefits they expected to derive from the drainage program. The move didn't clean up the mess, and that same year the first criminal indictments—distinct from the civil suit against Bolles—were returned in Kansas City against Dr. E. C. Chambers of the Chambers Land Company, charging that he had paid $10 an acre for fifty thousand acres, which he then sold as prime farmland for $50 to $65 an acre, knowing that it was submerged and unfit for agriculture. His trial on mail fraud began in 1914 and drew then Governor Park Trammell and former governor Gilchrist for the defense of Chambers and the state.

In Kansas City, Trammell claimed the drainage would be completed. Arguing that the Everglades was not unusually damp, Gilchrist asked the prosecutor, "You have floods in Kansas City, don't you?"[11] The officials' testimony was no more credible to the jury than that of certain unschooled farmers, who barely knew how to plow and plant. According to historians Alfred and Kathryn Hanna:

> August C. Butts, an Everglades farmer, testified that the only time a frost was not a frost in the Everglades was when it was a hard freeze, and then proceeded to unfold some startling chemical revelations. When asked by the defense if there was

nitrogen as well as H_2O in the rain water in Florida, Butts replied that he had never seen any H_2O in the water, that he was doubtful about the presence of letters and figures of any kind there, but he was positive about nitrogen.[12]

The defense made a mockery of Butts, but failed to gain acquittal for Chambers, who was convicted, ordered to pay a $6,000 fine, and sentenced to two years in jail, not a day of which he served. His convicted codefendants, who received lesser sentences, also avoided serving them.

In December 1913, a grand jury in reform-minded Kansas City indicted Bolles for mail fraud, only to have the charges dismissed the following spring. In 1915, he was again indicted, but fought extradition until his death on a Florida East Coast Railway train near Palm Beach in 1917, at age seventy-four.

Finally neither failure nor near total bankruptcy of the state halted the drainage; and the longer it continued, the more it became clear that corporate farming relying on migrant labor would rule the reclaimed land. Dreamers and small farmers were invited to look elsewhere because they could afford neither the special tractors and plows with oversized tires needed to work the muck nor the irrigation systems required to nourish crops on land that had to be diked and ditched to keep it dry and tillable.

In 1916, state officials launched a second major assault on the Everglades, this time not to create farmland but to lay a road, dubbed the Tamiami Trail, from Miami west to the Gulf of Mexico and up that coast to Tampa.

The WPA Guide of 1939 described the process of construction:

> Surveyors and men clearing the right-of-way worked breast-deep in the swamps. After them came drillers, attacking the hard rock under the muck; more than 90 miles were drilled and blasted. Ox carts were used to haul dynamite; when these bogged down, men shouldered the explosives and floundered through the water. Giant dredges followed, throwing up the loose rock to provide a base for the road.[13]

Following the initial construction through Dade County, progress slowed, as the west coast counties proved unable to raise funds for their portions of the project. The advertising

magnate Barron Collier finally paid for laying the grade out of
Dade to his million-acre domain on the Gulf; then, in 1923, the
State Road Department took over and officially opened the road
to traffic on April 25, 1928. The Tamiami Trail and canal effec-
tively dammed the natural sheet flow of water through the Ever-
glades to the southern end of the peninsula. A later highway,
"Alligator Alley," to the north, linking Fort Lauderdale and Fort
Myers, further blocked the flow.

The impact of the $13-million Tamiami Trail on all aspects
of life in south Florida was immeasurable. The trip from coast
to coast was shortened from a sea-and-train journey through the
Keys that took days to a motorcar drive across the peninsula that
took a few hours. The Trail quickly came to play host to tourist
traps—restaurants, frog farms, airboat rides into the Everglades, Indian villages. It opened small inland areas—around
Ochopee, especially—to agriculture and the Big Cypress and
Everglades to hunters, bird-watchers, and collectors of plants
and snails not wanting to explore the area by dugout or foot.
Moonshiners located new sites for their stills and smugglers
found the road a marvelous place to load onto trucks for shipment around the country contraband brought by air from the
Caribbean or by boat from the Ten Thousand Islands through
Big Cypress Swamp. From the 1960s to the early 1980s, much
of the nation's drug traffic followed that route, contributing a
new episode to the legend of the wild Everglades.

The Tamiami Trail quickly became known as well as a death
trap for every type of wildlife in the region, whose corpses littered it each morning. For many years, the most popular tale of
wildlife vengeance involved the motorist who, while repairing a
flat tire, ran his fingers around the inside of his tire and received
a fatal scratch from the rattlesnake fang embedded there. The
story passed through the decades, crisscrossing the peninsula,
enduring far beyond the time a driver could hit a rattler on the
road. But compared with its present state, especially near Miami,
conditions on the Tamiami Trail during its first several decades
were more bucolic than hectic. Now its identity is nearly forgotten on the east coast where it is better known as Calle Ocho,
Southwest Eighth Street, and Highway 41. Driving is dangerous
when traffic is light, a flirtation with instant death at peak hours
and on weekends as people move toward the ugly, poorly built
strip shopping centers and ticky-tack subdivisions that spill into
the east Everglades from Miami.

Looking at the rapid development of the peninsula today,

it is sometimes hard to imagine the effect a canal, road, or airport, even a rail line, must have had on the land. The construction itself more often resembled a military campaign, complete with explosives and hundreds of mercenaries. The tools of the north, designed for temperate plants and soils, could not deal with the dense tropical growth and underlying limestone any better than the early vegetable farmers could figure how to maintain fertility in Everglades muck. Unfazed, the developers proceeded, often blindly, while adapting machinery to their purpose. On Miami Beach, for instance, Carl Fisher, who was devoting the millions earned from his invention of automobile headlamps to the task of converting a soggy, tropical sand key into a world-class resort, introduced a metal drum lined with machete blades and drawn by a tractor for clearing palmetto, which generally defies even the blades of bulldozers. To traverse swamps and wetlands, Floridians created hybrid vehicles—swamp buggies and airboats. The buggies, although now customized "all-terrain" or "off-track" vehicles, were Model Ts with balloon tires that waddled across the wet prairies and marshes. The airboats, invented in the 1920s, were flat-bottomed craft with an airplane engine and propeller mounted above the stern to send them skimming across the shallow water, flattening the grass before them. As a consequence of such ingenuity, Florida today is crisscrossed and scarred, carved and sliced every way, with few areas beyond at least the sound of some form of motorized transportation.

Land clearance was so haphazard and ruinous that John Kunkel Small began predicting that south Florida would one day join the family of the world's great deserts, whose latitudes it shared. The rains, he thought, would stop coming as the marshes and the swamps that fed them dried out, and the soil would burn up or blow away so that no new vegetation could take root.

A surprising early victory for natural preservation of the fragile environment came in 1916, with an assist from James Ingraham. Flagler's Model Land Company, in 1910, cut a fifteen-mile road from the growing agricultural town of Homestead to Paradise Key, the site of one of the most distinctive hammocks in the Everglades, beloved by botanists and birders. The author Kirk Munroe and his wife Mary led a group of people protesting the road on the grounds that it exposed the key to the type of agricultural development that had ruined so many other hammocks in the area. Mary Munroe, president of the Florida Federation of Women's Clubs, discussed her worries with Ingraham, who conveyed them to the Flaglers. Mary Lily Flagler agreed to donate 960 acres of the key and surrounding area to match a like number deeded by the state legislature. In 1916, the 1,920-acre tract became the Royal Palm State Park, and five years later the state added another 2,080 acres to it. Compared with even the smallest parcels being practically given away to developers, those acres amounted to a pittance, but compared with the nothing that had existed, they represented a major victory.

In 1922, the men and women who had fought for Royal Palm State Park in the Everglades, together with other like-minded Floridians, formed the Florida Society of Natural History to lobby for an Everglades National Park, a campaign that became more organized and vocal when Miami landscape architect Ernest Coe took up the cause. In 1928, he and plant explorer David Fairchild organized the Tropical Everglades National Park Association. Coe's drive and Fairchild's considerable prestige and influence in Washington, D.C., eventually won the day, although the park was not dedicated until late in 1947.

By 1920, the effects of the drainage were unpleasantly clear. Charles Torrey Simpson, who watched how the project harmed his beloved Everglades, said in his book *In Lower Florida Wilds:*

> One of the results of partial drainage is that along . . . [the] east border numerous low, timbered "islands," which were formerly quite wet, have been now changed to dry land. A considerable part of the foundation of these groves is peat and in dry times it is liable to fire, and once begun it is well-nigh impossible to extinguish it. . . . So it happens that while the draining of the Everglades makes it possible for forests to spring up and flourish in some places it is the cause of their destruction in others.[14]

In 1919 and again in 1925, the state passed legislation making it illegal for people to start a fire within the Everglades Drainage District because the sawgrass and muck burned out of control.

For all their inadequacies, the canals succeeded in lowering the level of Lake Okeechobee from 21.0 to 16.5 feet above sea level. The Big Water no longer spilled over its southern shores as readily as in the past and in dry years—1912–20, for example—people could believe they had conquered the Everglades.

They misread the situation. During the wet summers of 1922 and 1924, Lake Okeechobee washed over its banks and inundated fields. By then the North New River Canal was so full of silt it was unnavigable and not capable of draining excess water from the area. Subsidence of the reclaimed land exacerbated the problem. In some areas, more than four feet of soil had vanished into air in less than a decade—oxidized, burned, blown away! The loss was great enough to reverse the normal sheet flow of water from Lake Okeechobee south into the Everglades. As the soil vanished from reclaimed lands, water flowed north toward the lake. Only outside the agricultural district did it resume its normal course.

The state pressed onward. It struggled through the twenties to cut the St. Lucie Canal through rock and a meandering river to the Atlantic in the belief the large waterway would more dramatically drop the water level in Lake Okeechobee. To forestall flooding until the canal opened, the state constructed a mud levee—five to nine feet high and forty feet wide—around the south rim of the lake. Between 1907 and 1929, 79 million cubic yards of dirt and rock were excavated for 440 miles of canals; 100,000 acres were declared reclaimed. A mournful prediction Simpson had made in 1920 seemed about to come true. He had lamented:

> There is something very distressing in the gradual destruction of the wilds, the destruction of the forests, the draining of the swamps and lowlands, the transforming of the prairies with their wonderful wealth of bloom and beauty, and in its place the coming of civilized man with all his unsightly constructions, his struggles for power, his vulgarity and pretensions. Soon this vast, lonely, beautiful waste will be reclaimed and tamed; soon it will be furrowed by canals and highways and spanned by steel rails. . . . Gaily dressed picnickers or church-goers will replace the flaming and scarlet ibis, the ethereal egret and the white flowers of the crinums and arrowheads, the rainbow bedecked garments of the Seminole. In place of the cries of wild birds there will be heard the whistle of the locomotive and the honk of the automobile.[15]

Bolles and his contemporary land sharks were high-rolling con artists in a gallery of rogues and toughs that made the Lake Okeechobee region a liquid version of the palmetto prairie, as wild as the legendary Wild West. Cowmen on the north end of the lake regularly battled with loggers and catfishermen in the fields and towns. During the tick eradication program of the 1920s, the ranchers added government agents to their list of enemies, and soon put hunters, hikers, moss pickers, and frog giggers there as well. On the south and west shores of Lake Okeechobee, Crackers and white settlers turned on black workers brought in to tend crops and fields because the whites wouldn't stoop to the work. Their actions were a sad reprise of the attacks on Henry Sanford's workers three decades earlier. From the east coast, anglers railed against the commercial fishermen, charging correctly that they killed game fish—especially largemouth bass. The commercial fishermen countered, as they do today, that they are feeding people not hiding behind money and privilege. There were bootleggers and moonshiners, roving outlaws sufficient to put most people ill-at-ease. Simpson recalled that he "often could not buy food or even get the opportunity of lying on the floors of outhouses," because people feared lone travelers who looked like tramps, which he often did while exploring and collecting specimen plants and snails.[16]

For all the miscreants and wanderers, there were decent people, like physician Anna A. Darrow, "Doc Anner" to her patients, who arrived in 1911 from Chicago with her husband and traveled around the lake for years treating Indians, whites, and blacks. By horseback, carriage, car, and boat she made her calls, whatever the hour or circumstances of her patients, many of whom paid in kind when they were able to pay at all. The people she served were fortunate; in most rural areas doctors were rare, home remedies the only treatment. Crackers, blacks, and Indians had different, but sometimes overlapping, herbal medicines, customs, myths, and superstitions—a few of which worked. Most black and white communities had at least one woman who served as midwife, nurse, and medical expert of first and last resort, with the same person frequently serving both races. Hoodoo doctors similarly would not discriminate. Indian medicine men, schooled through study and practice, enjoyed respect not only from their tribes but also from settlers in the backcountry who learned from them when given the opportunity.

The Congregational Board of Home Missions and various solo churchmen campaigned to Christianize the wild people of Lake Okeechobee. The board's steamboat *Evangel No. 1*, fresh from its maiden run in 1909 in the Keys, where its crew tried to impress the way of the scripture on Flagler's Overseas Railroad workers, finally sailed up the Caloosahatchee to the Big Water and entered local legend as the "Gospel Navy." In 1920, a Baptist preacher from Alabama, Edward Dunklin, marched to the lake and started preaching to anyone who stopped to listen. He became known to whites as the "sinner hunter"; to the Seminole as "Jesus Man"; and to blacks as "Li'l Bro' Dunklin." The local newspapers named him "Gospel Peddler," but his nicknames found more appeal than his message against drinking, fighting, and fornicating. Dunklin's services, like those of many intinerant preachers, were most valuable as social events, bringing together, under the aegis, if not the reality, of kindness and peace, people ordinarily too scattered and disparate to communicate.[17]

Even by Florida standards, the lives of these settlers were rude and hard. Houses were often little more than thatched palmetto or tarpaper shacks with uncovered windows and crude doors, flimsy, hot and dirty, considerably worse than the homes built of salvage one could find along the east coast and Keys, the more substantial frame or log homes of north Florida, or even more firmly constructed palm structures. The reliance on thatch palms for roofing and walls was so great in some areas that the native plant became nearly extinct. The architecture reflected the transient nature of much of the population—men there to log or fish in season or as long as they could stand the job before moving on—and from the lack of adequate transportation. Bringing material for building solid homes by steamboats that had to navigate the narrow, shallow canals or ply the twisting Kissimmee or Caloosahatchee was time-consuming and expensive. Few new settlers could pay the price.

The catfishermen discovered the lake around 1905 and commenced hauling tons of the bottom feeders—some weighing more than thirty pounds—from the shallow water. Trotlines—long lines with individually baited hooks—traps, and cast nets were employed, but seines ranging from 500 to 1,000 yards long were preferred because of the amount of fish they could bring in on each walk. The crews were "soldiers of fortune and refugees from justice who found safety and a livelihood in this isolated wilderness," as well as "honest, hardworking men and youths who set about laying the foundations for both fortune and prominence in the days to come."[18]

In the winter of 1913–14, the lake hosted fifty catfish camps.

"A camp," according to Lawrence Will in his *Cracker History of Okeechobee,* "was nothing but a long narrow shack built of palmetto thatch on a frame of cypress poles, or maybe it might be tarpaper tacked on 2 × 4's. Offshore a bit, or even far out in the lake, would be the skinning bench, a platform perched on spindly piles, roofed with cabbage leaves or furs. Sometimes a camp was a houseboat, with a covered porch on which the cats were skinned."[19]

A typical camp housed sixteen or more men—four dragging the long seines and the remainder tending trotlines and skinning the fish; one cooked. The lake was so shallow for most of its extent that the crews simply waded far offshore to work their seines. Boats would go to the skinning benches to pick up the fish and haul them to shore for shipment, by steamboat until after about 1915, then by train. Accomplished skinners, according to Will, cleaned three hundred fish an hour. The men were paid by the fish—three cents for cats, one cent for anything else—and averaged $35 to $50 a week, plus room and board in the rustic camp, for the eight-month season. Shippers bought catfish from the camp owners for five cents a pound, and sold them for twenty-five cents a pound to canneries and factories for processing and sale. At the height of the fisheries, between 1915 and 1925, more than 150,000 pounds of catfish left Okeechobee weekly—5 million a year—bringing to those involved $1 million or more annually. The largest catfisherman, Tom Bass, employed seventy men and owned forty-five boats and eight refrigerated railroad cars. The industry's demise bankrupted him and his commercial empire, which had come to include shipping and construction.

The prosperity of the catfisheries coincided with expansion of rail service to the lake. By 1929, the tracks encircled Okeechobee and the trains bore vegetables and timber as their primary cargoes, the fisheries having died.

As early as 1925, Cracker historian Will said, it was clear that "too many seines, no closed season, and the lowering of the lake [through drainage] combined to make the catfish scarce."[20] The decline spurred sport fishermen to redouble their effort to force a reluctant legislature to outlaw seining in fresh water. The Palm Beach paper had led the campaign, but its success failed to help its chief target, since the bill declared Lake Okeechobee and Lake George on the St. Johns "not fresh water," so seining could continue. In 1950, the Game and Freshwater Fish Commission began to regulate catfishing in the big lakes and finally prohibited seining, thirty years too late to make a difference. Now, of course, catfish are trapped or farmed; large ones are uncommon.

Faced with the collapse of their industry and lured by the potential of higher profits for less arduous effort, catfishermen sometimes switched to other occupations around the lake or drifted south and west to the Keys or the Ten Thousand Islands where they could make big money smuggling contraband of every sort.

One of the first people to buck the lunacy of the con artists and state officials was Thomas E. Will, a populist and past secretary of the American Forestry Association, who, for his efforts, became known as the John the Baptist of the Everglades. Will was also a former president of Kansas State University, having replaced the father of plant explorer David Fairchild in that post after a bitter political fight between the populists and traditional Republicans. In 1913, Will purchased New Okeelanta on the south shore of Lake Okeechobee and devoted the next ten years to an ultimately futile attempt to build a utopian community based on cooperative labor and joint ownership of the town and all its utilities. A lack of adequate transportation for shipment of produce hindered his effort, as did the political and economic climate of the times.

Little communities kept springing up like weeds, many less ambitious in conception than New Okeelanta though no less difficult to sustain—South Bay, Belle Glade, Chosen, Pahokee, Canal Point. In 1915, Moore Haven, at the junction of the dredged Caloosahatchee River and Lake Okeechobee, became the first settlement in the Everglades that merited the title of town. It served as a way station on the so-called Cross-Florida Waterway, the route completed in the late 1920s, roughly as Hamilton Disston had imagined, following the St. Lucie Canal from the Atlantic to a channel across Lake Okeechobee to the Caloosahatchee Canal and River to the Gulf. (The new route supplanted the inadequate waterway, with its North New River Canal link, which Governor Gilchrist had christened eight years before.) Like many other Florida communities, Moore Haven began in the dreams of one man—James A. Moore of Seattle, who moved to the lake and started the South Florida Lands Company. When after two years his venture failed, he sold out to Clarence M. Busch, an Atlantic City, New Jersey, developer, and his partners, John J. O'Brien and George Q. Horwitz. In disgust over Busch's dishonest real estate dealings—selling at a premium land that lacked the promised improvements—his partners took thirty-six hundred acres as their equity and set up the DeSoto Stock Farms Company. Horwitz died, and his widow, Marian, became O'Brien's partner and, soon, his wife. During World War I, before women were allowed to vote, she served as mayor of Moore Haven, an otherwise not enlightened town in a backward area.

The O'Briens' attempt to establish a community of British émigrés northwest of Moore Haven failed. Crackers resented the English for their dress, customs, and condescension, the O'Briens for their Catholicism and superior airs. They also opposed the O'Briens' use of black farm workers—the first employed on the lake—so vehemently that Mrs. O'Brien organized "vigilance" committees to protect the laborers from attack.[21]

The violence and bigotry didn't keep other farmers from bringing in blacks to work side by side with white workers in harvesting the crops. The use of migrant labor increased through the middle 1920s as sugarcane became the primary cash crop of the lake region. By the 1940s, government-run migrant camps had become models of oppression. As they were taken over by growers, they came to represent the worst of the company town—poor, dirty, crime- and alcohol-ridden places where people often lived without hope. Growers charged for shacks or trailers or vermin-infested bunks in a barracks prices higher than those being charged for comfortable city apartments. Food costs at the company store added to a debt that mounted daily and left the workers in thrall. The efforts of labor unions, the Florida Christian Migrant Ministry, and other groups to help the people in the camps achieve some dignity and education through organization or social programs did little more than alleviate the suffering of a few individuals. The system remained.

Hamilton Disston had started commercial sugarcane production near St. Cloud, and when he went belly-up financially, a syndicate of Cuban planters bought the enterprise, then abandoned it after failing to solve the technical problems associated with sugar growing in Florida. No successful plantations were established until 1915 when the Southern States Land and Timber Company, which had bought two million acres around the lake in 1902, began extensive plantings of cane near Canal Point and at Indiantown.[22] Within three years, high sugar prices brought on by war-induced shortages had drawn more companies into the area. The U.S. Department of Agriculture and the state opened experiment stations on the shores of the lake to explore the unique properties of the muckland and assist farmers in plant selection and cultivation.

The Florida Sugar and Food Products Company started in 1920. Next, the Moore Haven Sugar Corporation tried planting and kept at it for three years, finally halting operations in 1925 after winter drought and summer flooding spoiled successive crops. During 1925–30, the Southern Sugar Company planted extensively around Clewiston; the Depression ruined it. Charles Stewart Mott of General Motors and Clarence Bitting bought the bankrupt company and renamed it the United States Sugar Company, which expanded until it produced 90 percent of Florida's cane and became one of its biggest exploiters of migrant labor. Lake Okeechobee had become the land of the corporate farm.

Around the southern rim of the now diked lake are miles on miles of the flattest land to be found, all in sugarcane that is burned, then harvested each winter, as the refineries spew their distinctive white smoke into a sky made wider by the flat earth. The ground has subsided, sinking well below the surface of confining levees, and is kept dry through a network of canals and pumping stations, which force much of the fertilizer-enriched wastewater back into the lake. In fifty years, eight or more feet have vanished to wind, rain, and fire, and some experts predict the fields will be played out by the turn of the century, if the federal government hasn't ended the sugar subsidy first. Then the acres will be appraised at their Depression-era worth— nearly nothing—until developers move in with subdivisions, shopping malls, perhaps a regional jetport to serve the six million people living in the southern part of the state.

Broward's campaign to drain the Everglades became an article of faith for Florida politicians for more than half a century and arguably remains so to this day despite well-publicized pronouncements to the contrary. Not even scandals could halt the dredges for long. Along the upper St. Johns—a beautiful marsh and cabbage-palm dominated land—drainage for agriculture and development proceeds at a distressing pace, leaving one to

recognize that the Everglades are protected only because celebrated and a national park. Canals carve the east coast inland
from Fort Pierce and spurt through southwest Florida where
new citrus groves replace those ruined during the harsh freezes
of the mid-1980s. Every Floridian with a memory longer than
two decades has a tale to tell of how the place was—sometimes
as far back as yesterday.

It took no longer than two decades to play out the catfish,
to rip out the timber, to start building roads, to bring the paradise peddlers into court, and finally to have the whole state go
bust after an orgy of real estate buying surpassing people's
wildest imaginings. By the 1930s, drainage, development, and
advances in transportation had molded the peninsula as it is
known today, and the growing human population altered the
landscape on a more massive scale than nineteenth-century
dreamers had conceived, relying no longer on trains and steamboats but on cars, trucks, buses, tractors, and planes.

EIGHT

Fool's Gold

Florida real estate creates a national frenzy. Speculators buy, sell, and buy a paradise of sand and dreams. The boom falters; hurricanes batter the Gold Coast. The state falls into depression.

If railroads opened the peninsula to development, automobiles transformed it, exposing more land to more people in the years following World War I than only the most fanciful promoters had considered possible. The car provided rapid personal mobility and created demand for roads to what previously had been nowhere. In the 1920s, the all-powerful railroads and ascendant automobiles drove Florida into a period of unprecedented growth culminating in a buying frenzy that left the nation's bankers breathless and the state bankrupt three years before the nation as a whole plunged into the Great Depression. People holding contracts on property could do nothing but watch as their fortunes in sand turned to fool's gold. To the naturalists, the collapse of the real estate market was a disaster that came too late. Reviewing the madness of those boom days, Charles Torrey Simpson wondered whether "the world is better off because we have destroyed the wilds and filled the land with countless human beings."[1] Another emergent form of transportation, the airplane, while contributing to the booming 1920s, would have its greatest effect in the decades to come when it would combine with the omnipresent automobile to make American tourism a mass phenomenon unbounded by distance or time that threatened to crush Simpson's beloved Florida under the weight of sheer numbers.

Resort life prospered through the first decades of the twentieth century, defying in its richest enclaves the worst of the Depression. Though that economic disaster forced Flagler's Florida East Coast Railway into receivership, the Palm Beach he created continued to epitomize for many Americans the highest and most raucous expression of resort living. In the years following Flagler's death, two unlikely men—a gadabout turned architect and an aesthete bastard son of a sewing machine maker—brought to Palm Beach a new look and style that soon extended their influence throughout southeast Florida.

The transformation commenced in 1917 when Paris Singer built a cottage there that he called Chinese Villa and painted orange, green, yellow, and blue, with a stuffed alligator perched on the ridge pole.[2] Singer, one of sewing machine tycoon Isaac Merritt Singer's seventeen illegitimate children and a former lover of dancer Isadora Duncan, also began appearing around town in the garb of a dandy artiste—baggy pants, Riviera shirt, a Basque beret, and purple espadrilles. That he was rich, tall, and blond—the essential, if illegitimate, Anglo-Saxon male— made him acceptable, albeit a little naughty, and his peers soon adopted his choice of colors and clothes. Abetting Singer's aesthetic enterprises was Addison Mizner, an international resort sport who had encamped on the shores of Lake Worth with a pet monkey and discovered himself to be an architect.

Wanting to do his part for the Allies during the Great War, Singer donated 160 acres for a convalescent home in Palm Beach—the Everglades Club—which he commissioned Mizner to design. After receiving only thirty-three requests for beds in response to 300,000 inquiries mailed to veterans around the nation, Singer decided to convert his rest home into a true club. Thus, a bastion of Palm Beach exclusivity was born of an attempt at charity. Mizner became the architect of choice for people seeking to build distinctive, $1-million Palm Beach homes, despite his tendency to forget an essential element—say, a kitchen, staircase, or front door on even his most expensive projects.

Singer went bust with the Florida real estate market and died in debt. Mizner fared no better in the long run. During the 1920s, he designed more than $50 million worth of Palm Beach mansions while laying out a resort city of his own called Boca Raton. Whatever his deficiencies, the hotel he designed there remains a model of elegance, a well-kept example of his distinc-

tive adaptations of Mediterranean design; and his other buildings bespeak an architectural vision missing from too many of
the imitative, Band-Aid– and pink-colored structures that continue to spring up to house and serve white, middle-class people. The ethnic and racial discrimination that permeated much
of south Florida's development was codified in a number of
cities from Palm Beach to Miami Beach, including Mizner's Boca
Raton, which excluded Jews and blacks.

General T. Coleman Du Pont became one of the chief financial backers of Addison and his brother Wilson Mizner at
Boca Raton. Addison designed a flashy hotel and club while
Wilson promoted the new town and planned to put electric
gondolas, manned by token gondoliers, in its canals. When, in
1926, their claims became too hyperbolic for Du Pont's taste and
his sense of foreboding became too great to ignore, he withdrew
his support from the Mizners, sending them and Boca Raton
into financial ruin and earning for himself the title "Daddy of the
Bust."

The Cracker houses built on stilts of pine or cypress heartwood, with a breezeway down the middle and wraparound
porch; Seminole chickees; and the amalgamated Mediterranean
style of Mizner marked the peninsula's most distinctive architecture. In the 1930s and 1940s, Art Deco—or Tropical Deco—
rose from the sand of Miami Beach to join them, and since then
a few other styles have appeared, including the playful postmod
ernist designs of Arquitectonica, the Miami-based firm of husband and wife, Bernardo Fort-Brescia and Laurinda Spear. But
it was Mizner who built multilevel courtyards, removed the
heavy wrought-iron from the Hispanic home, exposed the raft-
ers in his rooms, and added tiled pools and mosaics to interiors
and exteriors. He established factories to make the tile, ceram-
ics, and furniture he required. Mizner also elaborated on
Singer's recognition that the bright, cloud-festooned sky, the
flat terrain, the ocean, and lush vegetation of south Florida
demanded facades painted in bold pastels that the sunlight in-
tensified. At its best, the design pops from the landscape without
abusing it or the senses.

The WPA Guide, with the sort of humor that hurts, described the wealthy northerners who made Florida their winter
home during the first decades of this century as Yankee "con-
quistadores," a designation even the locals making their yearly
nut off that seasonal business approved. The foremost expres-

sion of the winter residents' imperialism occurred not in Palm Beach but in Miami, on the shores of Biscayne Bay, where International Harvester magnate James Deering migrated after being ordered to guard his health. He built a Renaissance palace to make the princes he emulated drool with envy. He called the place Vizcaya, a $15-million baroque mansion of stuccoed concrete, trimmed in coral, and roofed with tiles that had once covered an entire Cuban village. Balconies off each second-story bedroom overlooked the central courtyard; a swimming pool lay half indoors, half outdoors. Deering decorated the interior with imported tiles, Renaissance art, and adornments from any Italian palace he could raid. Formal gardens, fountains, and canals where gondolas cruised defined the grounds. The mangrove shore lining Biscayne Bay was cleared and filled with sand to create a sweeping view and promenade from the palace to the water. Construction of the 160-acre estate proceeded through the teens and took nearly as many years as the bachelor millionaire was able to live in his palace. After his death, the grounds were subdivided to make room for a hospital and other facilities. Dade County eventually opened the house and the remaining ten acres as a public museum.

James Deering's brother Charles had earlier built an estate on the shores of Biscayne Bay where he had established an arboretum for tropical trees, an aviary for herons and egrets, and a collection of succulents planted by botanist John Small, the irascible defender of south Florida's tropical hammocks. Charles Deering also maintained one of the most distinctive mangrove forests on the bay, which he laced with canals. He supported a collecting boat, *Barbee,* regularly taking it on expeditions to the Keys and around the tip of the peninsula, with Small, Charles Torrey Simpson, and other naturalists as his guests.

Across the bay from the Deerings, Carl Fisher worked to turn his reconfigured sand key into a first-class resort. The owner of the Indianapolis Speedway had already brought the Dixie Highway, U.S. 1, to Miami Beach so travelers could come directly by car across the wooden bridge John Collins had constructed from Miami. But the island had not matched the instant success of Miami, and Fisher was grasping for promotional gimmicks. In 1915, with Miami Beach incorporated as a city, Fisher offered free lots and later sewers, sidewalks, and schools to anyone who would build a home on his island; there were few

takers. Finally, he decided to portray Miami Beach as a high-
fashion, luxury resort and sell his land for a premium. To catch
people's attention, he commenced turning the island into an
adult playground where the banal met the bizarre, importing
not only the usual gondolas for his canals but also a pair of
elephants he named Rosie and Carl after his wife and himself.
The gimmicks worked, and people began to heed his pitch.

Miami was not alone in its expansion. Port facilities and
harbors were enlarged at Pensacola, Jacksonville, and Tampa, as
well as Miami, to accommodate steamships. The work in Miami
transformed the port into a center for cruise ships, and today it
is the largest in the world for those floating resorts. At Jacksonville, dredges deepened the channel across the bar where the St.
Johns River met the Atlantic and then extended it upriver to the
city's port and beyond to provide passage for barges and ships
to Sanford on Lake Monroe. Sedimentation has forced constant
maintenance of this and every other barge channel and canal in
the state. By the mid-1920s, business leaders in Jacksonville
were lobbying heavily for a Gulf–Atlantic Ship Canal that would
bring traffic across the peninsula directly to their port. In 1927,
the federal Rivers and Harbors Act authorized a survey, which
designated a route bisecting the state from Palatka across the
Central Highlands near Ocala to the small Gulf fishing village
of Yankeetown. Business leaders of Florida's largest and most
politically important city had served notice that they supported
any large public works project that would advance their interests
regardless of its consequences for the rest of the state.

Tampans pioneered new ways of creating land and of traveling by car. Early in the century, two entrepreneurs, Alfred
Reuben Swann and Eugene Holtsinger, created a beachfront by
filling mud flats and wetlands on Tampa Bay. They built a road
named, appropriately, Bayshore Boulevard (Miami has a Bayshore Drive) and platted a subdivision for the rich, which sold
out almost immediately. In 1919 in DeSoto Park, Tampa, a
group of less well-to-do motorists formed the first Tin Can
Tourist Camp, a forerunner of the roadside campground for
recreational vehicles and trailer-tents. Tin Can Tourist Camps
sprang up around every major city in Florida and along most of
the highways and byways during the 1920s, and flourished until
the motel supplanted them. With a mixed economy of shipping,
mining, ranching, shipbuilding, and tourism, Tampa expanded
rapidly, achieving along the way notoriety as a center of violent

conservatism for its racial bigotry and antiunionism.

From the famous industrialists of the period—the Deerings, Vanderbilts, Edison, Ford, Firestone, and their peers—to lesser but not always less wealthy lights, Florida was the southern terminus, a place for winter mansions. All one had to do was pick the coastal town for settlement—the established communities of Palm Beach, Miami, the upstart Miami Beach, on the east; Tampa, St. Petersburg, Fort Myers, Clearwater, on the west; Winter Park and Orlando in the middle. The process of building luxury homes along every shore and of linking bodies of water with canals that small boats could navigate accelerated through the boom years of the 1920s and continued through Depression and resurgence, with the more ambitious builders creating their own lakes and shorefront. When, in the late 1960s, the state attempted to gain some control over the waterfront builders in order to protect the land and underlying aquifer, it was beaten in the U.S. Supreme Court, which ruled the lakes private property unless they had been surveyed as navigable bodies of water in the nineteenth century. Few fell into that category because officials had been too lazy, too cheap, and too eager to dispose of the state's land to bother with charting remote and difficult-to-reach areas.

Along the coasts, fill and drainage were carried out under an 1856 state law allowing construction out to the navigable channel of a body of water. Theoretically, whole estuaries could be filled, including thousands of shallow acres of Biscayne Bay. Fortunately, it was a costly and time-consuming process that was disallowed when technology made it easier. In 1957, the legislature passed the Bulkhead Act reaffirming state ownership of land lying below the mean high-water mark and requiring permits for dredging and filling operations. Yet approval was seldom denied during the following two decades, and the creation of new shores accelerated. Forests of mangroves that once had wrapped around the peninsula from the Indian River to Cedar Key were flattened; sand pumped from the ocean, Gulf, and bay bottoms buried their remains. Approximately 40 percent of the state's wetlands had fallen to agriculture and construction by World War II; today, the total has reached 75 percent. Thus, man had altered more than a third of the state's land!

Demands for preservation rose to meet the destruction. In Miami, conservationists warned that the seawalls would cause more damage in the event of a storm by failing to break properly and absorb the flood tide. Although they had no scientific explanations for their belief, they sensed that the canals and walls were harming the bay. Miami's sewer lines dumped untreated effluents into canals, streams, rivers, and Biscayne Bay itself. Sediment and fresh water racing down the Miami River, which essentially became a canal after the dynamiting of its rapids in 1909, hastened the ruin of the bay. Coral reefs began to suffer; turtle and manatee grass died; the place acquired an identifiable and unpleasant odor. No official in the state seemed to care that pollution of its waters became illegal in 1913 as part of a toothless statute written to appease conservationists and tourism officials without harming builders, businesses, or communities. If fishing declined in a specific area, the boats moved on to another—to please their passengers and keep the fish houses packed. By forcing rainwater to run off the land rather than seep into it, the canals prevented proper recharge of the freshwater aquifer underlying Miami, which, when combined with depletion of that supply through wells, allowed salt water to flow inland; wells became unusable along the coast. Miami's experiences were echoed along Tampa Bay, Pensacola Bay, Jacksonville, Charlotte Harbor—wherever man met the state's waters.

In the heady years of the early 1920s, the dream of Florida mattered far more than its realities. Buoyed by victory in the War to End All War, flush with optimism and money, people climbed into their cars and puttered down the open roads toward America's near tropics, away from congested cities with their foul air, general filth, and cold. Trains and boats bore additional thousands to Tampa, Miami, Fort Myers, Jacksonville, Orlando. No place escaped the boom of the 1920s, though no place experienced it more profoundly than the lower east coast of the peninsula.

The "boom" was a collective national lust for Florida land, an orgy of town building, hucksterism, construction, and destruction. Florida possessed whatever a person sought—a healing climate, year-round recreation, abundant fertile ground. In 1920, the average midwestern farm yielded $20 to $50 an acre while mango groves in Dade County brought in $2,000 an acre ($10,000 in 1987 for the exotic carambola). Tales of fortunes in celery and strawberries, citrus, tomatoes, and avocados spread through the nation. No scandal could stanch the flow of people.

Seemingly insignificant developments contributed to the

boom in ways difficult to measure. Screens became available to keep bugs out while the windows stayed open to breezes and cool night air. Yellow fever vaccines ended fear of that debilitating disease. First ice factories and then refrigerators made it possible not only for fishermen, hunters, and especially growers to minimize spoilage in shipment of their produce but also for individuals to keep food fresh. Air-conditioning was used in movie theaters in the 1920s and gradually enlarged its domain. Within two decades after the Second World War, it had become a fixture in nearly every Florida home. It was during those Roaring Twenties that professional baseball teams started traveling each spring to train in Florida in what sportswriters came to call the Grapefruit League.

Some 2.5 million people entered the state during 1925, and many of them stayed. Throughout the peninsula—especially along its coasts—housing shortages were so severe that the chambers of commerce discussed building temporary shelters. People rented rooms, porches, couches, and bought whatever was available for whatever price for fear they would lose out on a bargain. "Binder boys" played on that, working the streets and storefronts, finding property they would buy for a minimal down payment and promise of a larger installment in a month, then immediately sell for an immense profit. It became commonplace for property to change hands two or more times in a day, and many local residents joined the fray, buying and selling paper that may or may not have represented real property and had value only as long as someone kept buying.

Thousands of new subdivisions were platted around the state, and by the height of the frenzy, 1925, northern banks were publicly warning their customers not to invest in Florida real estate, although altruism played no role in their concern: They were worried about the extraordinary level of withdrawals. At the same time, northern papers carried special sections promoting Florida subdivisions, still a common practice. The State Roads Department, which had developed its first comprehensive plan in 1919, struggled to keep pace with demand, spending $18 million a year on construction. Between 1924 and 1928, mileage tripled from 748 to 2,242.

Railroad construction increased dramatically after a ten-year pause marked only by completion of Flagler's Overseas Railroad. By 1927, the state held six thousand miles of track. The Florida East Coast Railway double-tracked from Jacksonville to Miami during the height of the boom, a costly operation that hastened its decline into bankruptcy. But for all their construction, the railways lacked sufficient equipment to handle all of the freight coming into the peninsula. Yards became snarled, as full cars heading south blocked sidings full of empty cars heading north.

The Clyde Steamship Line, which had assumed control of traffic on the St. Johns River, began carrying passengers from New York to Miami and the Atlantic Coastline ran steamers from there to Havana. To meet demands for building materials in the peninsula, sailing vessels were hauled from drydocks to join the new generation of steam-powered freighters. In an ironic twist, the state was importing lumber from the Pacific Northwest, South America, and Canada, while ripping out its own remaining forests as fast as possible for internal use and export.

A dramatic shift in tax policy at the state level also drove the boom. In 1925, under Governor John Martin, the state amended its constitution to abolish inheritance and income taxes, a move that had the desired effect of attracting elderly and wealthy émigrés. Recognizing the profit in good publicity, the state's newspapers joined in an undeclared but no less real agreement to suppress or downplay bad news, while accentuating the positive, meaning growth. Miami, which had advertised itself since 1915, and other cities and developers ratcheted their promotional campaigns to ever greater levels of outrageousness. They offered visitors and new residents a paradise never imagined on heaven or earth, where sun and blue skies vied with palm trees and ocean breezes to drive all troubles away.

Few places in peninsular Florida escaped the collective madness of the boom. Landowners in those areas that were spared—the old plantation belt of north Florida and the Panhandle—did not consider themselves fortunate, as they watched acres of swamp and sand become fortunes overnight.

In Tampa, D. P. Davis, miming Carl Fisher, turned Grassy Island and Depot Key—two partially submerged atolls—into solid islands he named for himself and subdivided into homesites landscaped with the ubiquitous casuarina and other subtropical plants. In the first three hours of business on October 4, 1924, he sold three hundred lots for $1,683,582; by the time he closed the books that evening, he'd sold $18 million worth of real estate. Flush with his millions, Davis moved to St. Augustine, where he hoped to repeat his Gulf coast success, but the bust of 1926 overtook him, and he died broke, an all too common condition in those days.

St. Petersburg developers filled their bayfront for housing and for a landscaped, bench-lined system of parks and promenades. The city's leaders built with an eye toward permanent settlers and winter visitors who would return annually for the sun and recreation. Few of their peers in Florida were as concerned with public amenities.

In November 1924, George S. Gandy opened a fourteen-mile bridge from Tampa to St. Petersburg for automobiles and streetcars. The bridge, which he'd begun planning from the first days of his arrival in St. Petersburg in 1903, made the Gulf coast beaches of the Pinellas Peninsula more accessible to Tampa residents and set off a merry rush of construction in both cities. Gandy completed the project without spending a cent of his own or the government's money, relying instead on hucksters to sell stock to the public. The population of St. Petersburg grew from 14,000 to just over 50,000 between 1920 and 1925. Tampa's doubled in the decade to just over 100,000.

In Sarasota, the pattern repeated itself, only there it was clearly condensed into two years, 1924–26. "[The] population doubled and housing construction was unable to keep up with the demand," said the authors of the WPA Guide. "Large tourist hotels and business buildings were erected, recreational facilities expanded, a 4,000-foot harbor channel was dredged, and a causeway was built across the bay to connect with the islands, which were cleared and landscaped."[3]

Amid the lakes and highlands around Orlando, citrus cultivation expanded rapidly into the hammocks and pinelands, consuming tens of thousands of acres. The small community that pottery manufacturer George Eugene Sebring had designed after the mythical Greek city of Heliopolis and named for himself in 1912 hired an official greeter in 1924. The city of Sebring survived the crash, remaining a citrus center and home of America's most famous Grand Prix automobile endurance race, until Disney World landed to its north and growth began to roar down the highways toward it, business strip after fast-food strip along the road, tracts of homes and trailer parks swarming behind.

From Palm Beach to Miami, the pace of development and land sales left residents aghast, agape, and sometimes rolling in money. Flagler's workers' town, West Palm Beach, grew from

1,700 in 1910 to 8,000 in 1920 to 30,000 five years later, with
100,000 additional people visiting the city during the height of
the boom. Miami's population nearly quadrupled from just
under 30,000 to more than 110,000, as it became the second
largest city in the state. Following Mizner, architects elaborated
a style called Florida-Mediterranean, which combined real and
imagined Italian, Spanish, and Moorish elements.

Many of the graded acres were insect-infested, with thin
sandy soil, sun- and wind-battered year round—hardly places to
build a home. Charles Deering sold his estate, Buena Vista, in
1925 and moved south of the city into the unspoiled pinelands
and hammocks of Cutler Ridge, which vanished four decades
later. David Fairchild recalled the destruction of Buena Vista in
his 1938 autobiography:

> [T]he magnificent *Ficus nitida* tree, the wonder of the Miami
> region, was torn to pieces and dragged out by tractors as the
> entire place was turned into a ghastly waste of suburban lots
> which to this day have not been sold. This wrecked land is
> a tragic memorial of those crazy mad days in which the trees
> of the "hammocks" went down, destroyed by an army of
> road builders, carpenters and cement mixers.[4]

Land in the flatwoods, west on the Atlantic Coastal Ridge
behind the hammocks that lined the coast, sold at the crest of
the boom for $25,000 an acre while a front foot of prime down-
town commercial space fetched $20,000 in Miami. A tale is told
that the owners of a building on Flagler Street in the heart of
the city rejected a $6-million offer for a building they had pur-
chased for $350,000 in 1919. Early in the 1920s, the trustees of
the Flagler estate rejected an offer of $10 million for the Royal
Palm Hotel, a decision they came to rue when in 1930 the ter-
mite-infested hulk was condemned and demolished. New construction reached $100 million a year, and total valuations rose
from $63.8 million in 1921 to $421 million five years later. By
1925, deposits in Miami banks had reached $1 billion—most of
it from real estate or illegal whiskey. The city and surrounding
communities paved 420 miles of road.

The voices of the booming community were the financiers,
pitchmen, and builders—Carl Fisher on Miami Beach with elephants, $350,000 Roman baths, and the "bathing beauties" that

titillated and scandalized the nation; George Merrick with a
$3-million annual advertising budget for Coral Gables; Glenn
Curtiss and James Bright with the Hialeah horse-racing track
and the extravagant Opa-Locka torn out of *The Arabian Nights;*
the Mizner brothers with their motorized gondolas and pom-
posity at Boca Raton; Charles Green Rodes with his instant
waterfronts in Fort Lauderdale; and, Joseph W. Young with
Hollywood, a $40-million city north of Miami engineered by
General G. W. Goethals, fresh from ramming the canal through
the Isthmus of Panama.

Whenever possible, builders employed celebrities, even
presidents of the nation, to promote their property. Heavy-
weight boxer Gene Tunney extolled the virtues of south Florida.
President Warren G. Harding came to play golf, with Carl
Fisher's elephant Rosie serving as caddy. Photographs of national politicians fishing or golfing became common fare for
newspapers and newsreels. Royalty was displayed under the
palms; the wealthy were urged to invest not just in homes but
in whole cities. Far from abating, the practice has continued into
the present, with celebrities frequenting popular and exclusive
coastal communities from staid Palm Beach to offbeat Key West
and receiving the adulation of the media and civic leaders.

Carl Fisher's promotional activities paid off so spectacularly
during the boom that rumors were constantly being spread
about his intentions to build here, there, and beyond. Mini-
booms resulted, although Fisher steadfastly denied the rumors
and ran newspaper advertisements saying so. He was having
more fun promoting Miami Beach. He imported flamingos and
claimed he would make them breed at his resort—a promise the
birds wouldn't let him keep. He purchased Charles Deering's
aviary to enliven the island made barren by construction, but the
birds flew to the mainland as soon as they were released and
didn't return. He ordered fifteen identical speedboats constructed and sponsored a race on Biscayne Bay that became a
fiasco as wind and waves thwarted drivers accustomed to cars,
not boats. The sands sprouted hotels—some fifty-six by the time
of the Florida real-estate crash of 1926—faster than the exotic
tropical vegetation—the palms and casuarina, royal poincianas
and hibiscus, the bougainvillea and coral trees—turned the bare
island green. Christian ministers in Miami railed against the
one-piece bathing suit Fisher's first wife wore while learning to
swim and became apoplectic when he advertised his hotels with

a bevy of bathing beauties. He created a polo field to attract people who might otherwise travel to more ritzy Palm Beach.

Between Miami Beach and the mainland, Fisher constructed the one-half-by-one-quarter-mile Star Island for his yacht club and luxury homes by dredging more sand from Biscayne Bay. Palm and Hibiscus islands followed. Fisher's islands were off the new Dade County causeway, which opened in 1920 and connected Miami to the south end of Miami Beach. The developer and impresario had arrived with a fortune estimated at $50 million and by 1926 had increased that to $500 million. When he died, largely forgotten, in 1939, he left an estate valued at less than $50,000.

John Collins, who had planted avocados and coconuts on Miami Beach when it was still a sand key and then enlisted Carl Fisher's money and energy to develop it, sold his wooden bridge to the north of the new causeway to investors who, following Fisher's lead, built a series of Venetian Islands they linked by causeway, toll road, and drawbridge to Miami and Miami Beach. The Venetian Causeway, county-owned and in poor repair in 1989, is old enough to be a landmark in an area where change is often all that is permanent. Newer causeways bracket it to the north and to the south, leaving it as the scenic, and neglected, route between cities. But if Dade County officials have their way, the causeway will be torn apart in the 1990s, the drawbridges that are symbolic of an older and more relaxed Florida replaced by structures that hump across the open water of Biscayne Bay, allowing boats to pass beneath them.

While Carl Fisher's elephant Rosie defecated on Miami Beach and the beauty queens gamboled with celebrities in the Roman baths, George Merrick planned to erect a new town in pinelands where his father, Solomon, the minister of the Coconut Grove Congregational Church, had established the family home and a thriving citrus grove. Merrick, who had lived in south Florida since childhood—his longevity in the region made him a rarity among its developers—was married to Eunice Peacock, the granddaughter of Charles and Isabella, who had emigrated from London to not-yet-christened Coconut Grove in 1875. Charles and Isabella built of salvaged wood the bay's first guesthouse, the Peacock Inn; and Isabella—called Aunt Bella—became known as "the mother of Coconut Grove" ("mother" being an honorific as loosely applied in south Florida as "colonel" was throughout the Confederacy) because of her hospitality and generosity. The unrelated Munroes—Kirk and Ralph—held court there, along with other winter residents the locals called "swells" because they rode in on the surf. The swells dubbed all the white locals Crackers, so things evened out until George Merrick decided to build in the pinelands—prime Cracker country. The denizens of Coconut Grove couldn't figure it out because to them Biscayne Bay was the be-all and end-all of Florida.

Merrick envisioned what he called a "City Beautiful," a south Florida adaptation of Mediterranean civilization. "At heart," said Avon Park resident and novelist Rex Beach, who wrote a brochure extolling Merrick and his planned city, "he was a writer, a poet, an artist, but fate with curious perversity decreed that he should write in wood and steel and stone and paint his pictures upon a canvas of spacious fields, cool groves and smiling water ways." Unlike most other Florida developers, Merrick was a man of modest finances, but what he lacked in money, he possessed in aptitude for city planning and marketing. Using his father's grove as a base, he eventually accumulated ten thousand acres. He began mapping out a city in all its particulars, down to the style and color of buildings—determined not to begin construction until his blueprints were complete. His was to be, in his own words—through Beach, "a 'balanced city,' planned to provide for people of all classes and every income, and even the most modest houses are as carefully thought out and as charmingly executed as the finest."[5] Coral Gables—named for the house his father had built in his grove—was to hold 100,000 people and cost $100 million to develop. With its emphasis on balance and harmony, it was a breath of freshness in an area that shunned almost everyone but wealthy Anglo-Saxon Protestants.

Nearly as soon as he opened his land office, Merrick sold $150 million worth of lots and plowed $100 million back into the town, digging forty miles of winding canals that the ubiquitous gondolas plied, erecting the $10-million Biltmore Hotel, and placing a block-long building holding apartments and studios at the grand entrance off the Tamiami Trail coming out of Miami. Little villages within Merrick's city evoked places he'd never seen—China, the French countryside, the Netherlands, and he decreed that the houses there should match the distinctive styles of those nations. He built fountains and golf courses, which were considered essential to all new developments, and

landscaped the streets and lots. To provide intellectual stimula-
tion and culture, he gave $5 million and 160 acres of land to
establish the University of Miami, which, despite several fine
departments and scholars, has failed to achieve the academic
preeminence Merrick envisioned, although its has raised foot-
ball and partying to a level approaching religion.

Merrick's skill at marketing approached his talent for urban
design. In an old limestone quarry, above an artesian well, he
constructed a free-form Venetian Pool where, from a float, William Jennings Bryan pitched the new town for $100,000 a year
and blocks of real estate. Merrick brought prospective buyers in
by bus to examine the town, hear "the Great Commoner," and
eat a free lunch. Understanding that the unique qualities of the
south Florida landscape are sometimes best appreciated from
above, the also arranged for people to tour the site by airplane
and dirigible. On the cusp of the real estate bust of 1926, he laid
out bridle paths and imported foxes for hunting. The foxes
flourished along the canals and golf courses, living off mangos
and other fruit, as well as small game, and still roam the city's
residential areas. Guests at the grandiose Biltmore Hotel could
play golf on the adjacent course; swim or view water shows in
the largest outdoor pool in the nation; or ride the gondolas or
shuttle bus to a private, coconut-shaded Biscayne Bay beach.
The more adventuresome enjoyed free guest privileges at Merrick's fishing camp on Key Largo—fishing being among the most
popular and profitable tourist attractions in the region. Photog-
raphers would wait at the charter docks to portray the conquering anglers with their sailfish, swordfish, tarpons, and decks full
of everything else that hit bait and died.

Merrick's aesthetic sensibility led to creation of one of the
most attractive communities in south Florida, but it failed to
bring him lasting wealth. Initially, bankers would not back him
because he lacked his own capital and they lacked faith and taste.
After the bust, overextended, he went broke, like nearly all his
competitors, and his plans and city languished through the Depression before beginning again to grow. Significantly, most of
that expansion has occurred according to Merrick's initial plan
Today, numbering some 40,000 rather than 100,000 residents,
the city stands out as a pocket of green in a sprawling, pastel-
and-gray suburban mass. It is, however, removed from its
founder's vision of a city where artisan and professional mingle,
where people of every class live. The citizens of Coral Gables are

predominantly upper-middle-class to wealthy, with a smattering of the solidly middle-class. Blue-collar workers are in short supply; the few poor are shoved into isolated corners of the city and ignored by officials in the hope they will leave.

Not to be outdone in the creation of beauty, but unwilling and unable to do so itself, the growing city of Miami used an obscure Florida law to annex the village of Coconut Grove one summer during the peak of the boom. Flagler had coveted the community on the bay that had shunned him as something of an unsophisticated, new-money land-grabber, and the Munroes and other of its winter residents had maintained a vocal opposition to the lunacy of the boom, frequently in conflict with their neighbors as well. But the city moved while most of the "swells" were gone and outvoted those residents who remained, thus seizing legally the picturesque settlement.

Glenn Curtiss and James Bright had more money and fame than George Merrick, but less taste and aesthetic integrity. They platted a town named Hialeah around the shallow, flood-prone canals of the east Everglades. They dedicated their town to horse racing and jai alai, the Basque court game Curtiss imported from Cuba to entertain and, like the horses, encourage gambling. A giant Seminole Indian cutout at the main entrance to Hialeah pointed prospective buyers toward the bare sand lots of the unbuilt town. Curtiss and Bright took their profit and applied their experience to creating another subdivision they named Miami Springs.

Bright, an old Missouri rancher, persuaded one Joe Smoot to build Hialeah Park in 1924 and sponsored the first horse races there in 1925, when gambling was illegal. The track operated in 1926, then was forced to close for two years after church groups protested. It reopened through subterfuge and operated that way until gambling became legal in 1931. Smoot and Bright stationed black swans, Seminole Indians, and imported flamingos in the track's infield and decked the grounds with royal palms. Hialeah Park became known as one of the most distinctive racetracks in the nation, although in recent years newer tracks in south Florida have challenged its importance to horse racing, if not its charm.

Bright did more than hawk sand and run racetracks: He bred the first Florida thoroughbreds on his ranch near Davie and persuaded Carl Rose to start raising racehorses near the central Florida town of Ocala, which subsequently achieved renown for its stock. Bright also worked diligently to improve Florida ranching by crossbreeding Brahmans with scrub cattle and Holsteins and importing South American Parra grass for the fenced-in range. He also helped reestablish the Seminole in the cattle business; and in honor of his efforts, the Seminole reservation northwest of Lake Okeechobee was named for him.

Curtiss made some $35 million building motorcycles and airplanes for the Army Air Force in World War I, and lost nearly all of it in south Florida sand. After Hialeah, Curtiss decided to build a town that embodied the look and spirit of illustrations he had seen in a copy of the *Arabian Nights* and came up with Opa-Locka, a shortening of the old Indian name for the site near Miami, "Opatishawockalocka," which he couldn't pronounce. To promote Opa-Locka, he employed men dressed as Saracens and mounted on Arabian horses to chase veiled women through the streets of his city. But the buildings and houses he adorned with minarets, domes, and assorted other pseudo-Moorish accoutrements were as flimsy as Merrick's were solid and the town never prospered. It became largely a black city, despite initial codes enshrining segregation as official policy.

In Hollywood, a hop above Miami and notch below Fort Lauderdale, Joseph Young's crew boss, G. W. Goethals, threw fifteen hundred trucks and tractors at the trees and palmettos and scraped out streets and building lots at a rate of two blocks a day. Young bused prospective buyers to the site of his new town when it was no more than a flat, sandy expanse, devoid of any structures, and many of the women fainted upon seeing the barren land.[6] Young spent $20 million on his town, a luxury hotel, and on Port Everglades, which over the years became a major regional harbor, as he had dreamed. He dug canals to create waterfront housing, though not as many as Fort Lauderdale came to boast.

In that old military base, way station, and trading post, Charles Rodes invented finger islands: man-made, geometrical peninsulas reaching into the canals and waterways, through the center of which ran a road. Homesites radiated from the road to line the sides and tip of the finger and give every house a boat anchorage. Gondolas traveled through the canals, as did the dugouts of Seminole Indians coming to trade and the powerboats of residents and charter captains. In Melbourne, Tampa, and elsewhere, finger islands became the rage to meet the demand for private beaches and piers.

Throughout south Florida, the new canals created hundreds of miles of waterfront property, and few buyers bothered to imagine the rivers and streams that had meandered through the wetlands. Only those living near the shoreline noticed that their wells were becoming saline. South Florida was the Venice of North America, an exotic vacationland of water, sun, and warmth where everyone spoke English. And the skies were not cloudy all day, a point emphasized in the Gulf coast city of St. Petersburg, where the newspaper began to offer itself free on any day the sun didn't make at least a token appearance.

Around the state, practices for erecting new subdivisions varied little: Zoning laws were weak or nonexistent, except in planned communities like Coral Gables or Sebring. Wherever a speculator had land he could place his community, often little more than a cluster of houses. Roads were marked off, lots platted, houses built, if there were buyers and backers. Many sites were left empty after financing began to fail in 1926. For years others consisted of isolated homes, served by wells and privies (later septic tanks).

For doggedness and chutzpah, few developers surpassed W. J. "Fingy" Conners, a pugilist, investor, visionary, and expletive-spitting labor leader. Conners shipped out on a Great Lakes steamer at the age of thirteen and landed eventually on the Buffalo docks where he became, by virtue of shrewdness, bombast, courage, and force, the head of the stevedores, a position that brought him enough wealth that by 1902 he was a visitor at the posh Royal Poinciana in Palm Beach, the labor lion lying down with the capitalist bears, Henry Flagler and friends. According to historians Alfred and Kathryn Hanna, Conners, while lounging at Palm Beach, became the model for Jiggs in the popular cartoon strip *Bringing Up Father*. He also developed a fascination for Florida land and in 1917 sought to establish his own petit duchy with the purchase of four thousand acres on the south side of the West Palm Beach Canal for what he claimed would be the biggest farm in the state. After failing to produce crops as promised, he bought the Southern States Land and Timber Corporation's experimental farm and renamed it Connersville. Failing again to profit from his investments, he bought the town of Okeechobee from the Florida East Coast Railway in 1924 and added it to his twelve thousand acres.

At the time, a traveler or baron-to-be could reach Okeechobee by boat, by train, or by horse. Conners petitioned the state

Left, Frederic Remington portrayed Florida's Cracker cowboys in the August 1895 issue of *Harper's Monthly* as a scrawny, unkempt lot. This typical hand is accompanied by his leopard dog. Right, near Leesburg around the turn of the century, a country woman believed to be named Mrs. Morton bagged this alligator.

In the late nineteenth century, Florida was frequently called a "paradise for devotees of the rod and gun." These hunters in Central Florida display their deer; on the ground to the right lies a sandhill crane killed for camp meat.

Travelers picking citrus at Bartow, Florida, ca. 1900

Below, the flat white sand at Ormond Beach was an internationally renowned racecourse at the turn of the century, a place for auto makers and drivers to attempt to set new records for speed. Bottom, the nation's first "Tin Can Tourist" camp was founded at De Soto Park in Tampa in 1922.

Over the decades the boats have changed but the sport has remained the same—fishing This party boat worked out of St. Andrews Bay in 1961.

During the late nineteenth century, the Seminole Indians kept the small settlements of South Florida alive through their hunting, trapping, and trading. This man paddles and poles a dugout crafted from a single cypress.

Convicts leased to private companies by the state worked at bringing in turpentine under conditions worse than those of the most inhumane plantation until the 1920s. Turpentining was considered the most arduous work in the state, whether undertaken by convict or "free" workers held in economic bondage.

The Dunnellon Phosphate Company's section-one pit in October 1906

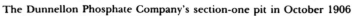

The International Minerals and Chemical Company phosphate mine, ca. 1960

A lumber camp in northwest Florida at the turn of the century. The large-wheeled oxcarts were used to haul pine out of the woods to the rail line.

By the time of this photograph, 1929, few first-growth longleaf pine forests like this one remained in the state.

A three-thousand-year-old cypress cut by the Burton Swartz Cypress Company in Perry, 1936

Fruit packing was a prosperous cottage industry in the 1890s.

The freeze of 1895 devastated the Florida citrus industry.

Floyd's fruit stand in Miami in 1922. Roadside stands continue to sell and ship citrus.

An orange-packing and -processing house in Avon Park, 1924

to license his construction of a road from the east coast to Okeechobee City. He wasted more than $1 million trying to build across the wet prairies and hammocks before hiring a professional engineer to complete the task. Using marl and limestone dredged from the West Palm Beach and St. Lucie canals to make a solid road bed, construction crews completed the road in July 1924. At Okeechobee City, three thousand people turned out for the opening ceremony to hail "the Great Developer," whom they placed in the class of Henry Plant and Henry Flagler—a nice bit of hyperbole. That first day, three thousand motorists paid $1.50 apiece to ride Conners's toll road; for the next few years, he earned an average of $2,000 a day. He also tried to promote Okeechobee City as "the Chicago of the South," a ploy that brought few buyers. Conners died in 1929, and a year later the state bought his road.

The boom's rewards were spread unevenly through Florida society. In cities like Miami the tremendous escalation in property values placed inordinant financial pressure on many long-time residents, who found their taxes increased tenfold to one hundredfold nearly overnight. Unable to pay, they were forced to sell or lose their homes at a government auction. Poverty increased; the economic health of black sections of Miami, Tampa, and Jacksonville worsened as the disparity in wealth grew and more people were forced off the land to seek employment. Fast money from land, construction, smuggling, and enterprises associated with tourism—gambling, prostitution, and jook joints—made south Florida a place noted as much for its sinfulness as for its climate and natural beauty. By boat and airplane, smugglers brought liquor, drugs, and illegal immigrants from Cuba and Caribbean islands to work in the sweatshops, mansions, and resort hotels. Today's drug runners surpass their forebears in firepower and quality of transportation, but not in boldness or violence. In 1926, the murder rate in Miami stood at 1 killing for every 908 citizens—higher than any contemporary figure for the area. Illegal wagers were placed on greyhound and horse races, on jai alai, in casinos, at cock and dog fights, and on a game brought from China by way of Cuba called *bolita*. The numbers game spawned minor industries among fortune-tellers and entrail readers. Lawlessness and fear of crime reached such a pitch in Miami that the Ku Klux Klan offered to police the city; the mayor declined.

* * *

No precise explanation exists for the bust of 1925–26. As early as 1925, investors had begun to cool on Florida real estate, sensing that prices had spiraled to such a height that they had to collapse and that the claims of developers exceeded propriety and possibility. Flimsy buildings and outright fraud in land sales had triggered investigations by lawyers and the Better Business Bureau. Throughout Florida, bankers began to refuse new loans and called in outstanding notes rather than refinancing them. A dip in the bull stock market reinforced their hard-line policies. Fire in the Breakers Hotel in Palm Beach deepened in investors—known as much for superstition as reason—a sense of foreboding.

On January 10, 1926, the *Prinz Valdemar*, a Danish training ship, which had been converted into a floating hotel to alleviate the housing shortage in Miami, toppled at the entrance to the city's newly expanded channel. Old sailors and salvage experts like Ralph Munroe advised blowing the wreck up immediately if it couldn't be refloated, but for inexplicable reasons it lay blocking passage for two months while freighters bringing goods and supplies waited offshore. The steamer *Lakevort* faltered and ran aground in the outer channel, further complicating sea transport. When the dredges of the U.S. Army Corps of Engineers finally began to dig a temporary channel around the *Prinz Valdemar*, they too were grounded. Finally, the ship was refloated and towed into the Miami harbor where it became an aquarium and monument to incompetence—or worse. Some critics speculated that the Florida East Coast Railway blocked salvage of the *Prinz Valdemar* in order to enhance its own economic position.

Despite delays, work proceeded on the Dade County courthouse, located in a hammock where turkey vultures had roosted for centuries. (The vultures would return after its completion in 1927, as they do every winter, flapping down upon its ziggurat-style roof and circling in the sky over downtown Miami.) Despite the outward signs of continued growth, people were cashing in their lots and leaving, or simply never showing up to complete deals. Overextended banks around the state began to fail, and even solid ones sagged under the crumbling load of binders and mortgages. Land prices tumbled from tens of thousands to thousands, from thousands to hundreds.

On September 18–19, 1926, the first major hurricane since 1906 smashed out of the Caribbean into Miami and burst across Lake Okeechobee with winds estimated at 130 to 150 miles an hour. Most of the area's residents had never experienced the fury of a big storm. The hurricane struck on the night of the eighteenth—these were the years before names were applied to anthropomorphize the fury—shattering buildings, blocking roads with downed trees and sheered roofs, knocking out power and communications. During the morning of the nineteenth, the eye passed over Miami, leading the uninitiated to believe the storm was finished. But a hurricane with its cyclonic winds strikes twice, the second time, after the eye, or center, passes, from the opposite direction of its initial assault, often with greater fury. The returning winds and rain caught the celebrants unawares. By that night the city lay in ruins, and the Everglades and Okeechobee had absorbed equally devastating blows.

The dead numbered more than 370; the injured, 6,000. Cheaply constructed homes and buildings—more than five thousand in all—lay in ruins. Boats, blown off their moorings, littered beaches and lawns, rested against trees. Damage was estimated at $76 million, and 18,000 people were homeless throughout southeastern Florida. The waterworks were down, and disease threatened the survivors. Miami and most of Miami Beach looked like targets of a bombing raid, with buildings gutted and crumbling. Of the new communities, only Coral Gables passed the test: Its houses stood through the worst of the hurricane because Merrick had demanded they be built properly.

Scientific and religious explanations were offered for the devastation of the storm. Some people speculated that the filling of Biscayne Bay to create causeways and artificial islands had closed off a natural channel for the sea surge that accompanies hurricanes and often is as destructive as the wind and rain. A fundamentalist preacher in New York, John Roach Straton, voiced the view of the religious Right around the country when he said: "And yonder is beautiful Florida. How beautiful. But how she did depart from God's way! She turned after the worship of Mammon. Race track gamblers were welcomed. The Sunday sermons were forgotten in the mad rush for gold. But God did not forget them. It is to be hoped that Florida will return to God, and it seems now that she will."[7]

The governor of Florida, John Martin, and mayor of Miami, Edward Romfh, were loath to admit the severity of the damage on the grounds it would be bad for business. They balked at a Red Cross drive to raise disaster-assistance funds and supplies and publicly minimized the problems of the area, even while its people struggled to cope. Although rebuilt with relative speed, Miami and Miami Beach could not recover the momentum of the boom.

In the aftermath of the storm and the failure of the canals to handle its floodwaters, officials installed pumping stations to speed the flow of fresh water to the sea. They worked, in a way, until overloaded by heavy rains, and then water backed up and overflowed the silted-in ditches, as it had in the past.

Just short of two years later, on September 16, 1928, another hurricane struck the Florida coast, smashing into Palm Beach that evening, then racing for Lake Okeechobee. The swank resort and its workers' town, West Palm Beach, suffered $10 million in damages as homes, offices, and roads were wiped out, but the storm's full fury struck inland. Winds raging at over 100 miles an hour created a storm surge that drove the big lake—swollen from two months of heavy rain—over and through the already discredited earthen dike on its south shore. In the first hour of the hurricane's assault the water level in the Everglades rose four to eight feet. The new farm towns of Belle Glade and South Bay were washed away. Houses provided no refuge as wind, rain, and flood tides tore them off their foundations. The official death toll stood at just over eighteen hundred but later unofficial estimates placed the total as high as twenty-four hundred, the injured accounting for several thousand more. No Florida hurricane on record has taken so many lives. Fully two thirds of the victims were black farm workers, many of whom could not be identified. Because health workers feared epidemics, the corpses were stacked on funeral pyres and burned. The flood tide drowned hundreds of alligators and, after receding, stranded thousands of fish on high ground. President Herbert Hoover toured the area and promised to build a levee no storm could breach.

The tragic irony is that Indians had foretold that Lake Okeechobee would spill over its rim once again to feed the Everglades. But no officials paid heed to the warnings—if they even heard them. Later, after the storms, the story would spread that the Indians could predict hurricanes by watching the way the sawgrass bloomed. Scientists speculated that atmospheric changes preceding a hurricane made the pollen from sawgrass visible for several days before the blow. Whether predictable or not, the disaster underscored the incapacity of the new drainage systems to deal with normal natural occurrences, for hurricanes regularly visit Florida, with rarely a year passing in which some area is not struck.

These two storms doubtless contributed to the decision of thousands of investors—bankers, home buyers, and future farmers—to seek paradise elsewhere.

The citrus industry, recovering from the outbreak of citrus canker that had led to a quarantine and destruction of infected trees between 1915 and 1925, suffered a more severe setback in April 1929. Scientists discovered Mediterranean fruit flies on a grapefruit tree at the U.S. Agriculture Department garden near Orlando, and subsequent surveys proved the insects had infected local groves. Pesticides, fire, and the National Guard were thrown into a war against the scourge that cost $6.7 million and lasted more than a year.

An occasional house or cluster of homes would sprout from the fallow land during the next several decades, but not until the mass migrations following the Second World War would heavy construction equipment return en masse to these sites. In his memoir, *Stop-time*, Frank Conroy described a failed subdivision from the 1920s where his family built a home in the 1940s. "Inaccessible without city transportation," he said, "without city water, sewage, or electricity, without stores or gas stations, without, in most instances, a single soul living on the premises, the speculators' subdivisions weren't even worth cannibalizing. Like neat surgical scars on the surface of the earth they were left, empty, under the hot Florida sun."[8]

NINE

Tropical Sandbar

Florida rises and falls through the ages, changing shape with the global tides to become a sedimentologist's dream. Ancient animals flocked from north and south for warmth and food. Humans appeared early and stayed, creating unique societies. Remnants of their lost world tantalize, but give few answers.

At the turn of the century state officials established geological and biological surveys to catalog Florida's dwindling resources and help business devise ways to exploit them profitably. In the process, the scientists assembled a portrait of a profuse and complex land born of the sea, supporting a broad range of life, including unique human cultures, and subject to vicious assault by natural forces.

Lying between latitudes 24° and 31° 30' north and longitudes 80° and 87° 30' west, with water on three sides and the warm Gulf Stream racing through its southern straits, whipping around its tip, and nearly kissing its eastern shore, the peninsula is the manifest portion of the Floridan Plateau, a thumb-shaped chunk of rock dividing the Atlantic Ocean from the Gulf of Mexico. Geologists have recently determined that the plateau, which extends under south Georgia, belonged more than 250 million years ago to what is now Africa, when that continent was joined to North America in the super landmass called Pangaea. During the schism occurring tens of millions of years later that created the Atlantic Ocean, Florida and south Georgia stayed behind to form one of the most geologically stable regions of North America.

The Floridan Plateau and its emergent land, which resembles in profile a broad sandbar, are creations of water—the shells and bones of its creatures, as well as its chemicals and minerals. Piled up over millennia by oceanic currents, these precipitates compacted and, when exposed to air, hardened to form overlapping layers of highly porous rock—primarily limestone and dolomite—that collected more detritus and grew through periodic inundations and dryings out. Some 50 million years ago, the peninsula was an island south of North America; 40 million years later, there was nothing. During succeeding epochs, fluctuating sea levels created and obliterated peninsulas shorter and squatter than the present one. The cycles grew more frequent during the Pleistocene (2 million to 10,000 years ago), the Ice Age, when each glacial advance exposed nearly all of the Floridan Plateau and each withdrawal reflooded successively smaller portions of it. The ocean's oscillations cut eight identifiable terraces or beaches into the limestone—at 270, 215, 170, 100, 70, 42, 25, and 10 feet above today's sea level—which are identifiable at various locations around the state.

Marine geologists believe that, after a long decline at the start of the Holocene (recent) epoch, sea levels have increased some thirteen feet in the past four thousand years.* During the last fifty years, the sea has been rising at the rate of one foot a century, which many scientists attribute to a general warming of the earth from the so-called greenhouse effect, created by CO_2 emissions from the industrial age's use of fossil fuels that prevent heat from escaping the atmosphere. Higher sea levels, coastal flooding, and changed climatic patterns that will bring desertification to once fertile lands are a few of the consequences of this global warming. Should the most dire predictions prove true, Florida's major cities will vanish under the advancing tides.

As a creation of the climate and the ocean, rather than of the sort of geological collisions that build mountains, Florida is a land of subtle gradations more than dramatic contrasts. Of its 58,560 square miles, 4,298 are lakes, rivers, springs, and canals. Before heavy development began a century ago, wetlands covered as much as 60 percent of its surface; now they occupy 15

---

*For many years it was an article of faith that the east coast of the peninsula was actively rising and the west was dipping into the Gulf, but recent observations have called that assumption into question.

to 20 percent. Florida boasts 1,350 linear miles of coastline, a total second only to Alaska among the states. Its five broad topographical regions are the Central Highlands, the Tallahassee Hills, Western Highlands, Marianna Lowlands, and Coastal Lowlands, each of which contains various ridges, hills, plateaus, depressions, and valleys. No elevation in Florida reaches even four hundred feet in height.

The coastal plains wrap around the entire state and comprise most of the area south of Lake Okeechobee, known broadly as the Everglades region. At their southern extremity the lowlands fade into the shallow water of Florida Bay. Running down the east coast, like a spine, between the shore and inland plains is a rock formation called the Atlantic Coastal Ridge, a line of ancient barrier islands and sandbars rising twenty to forty feet above sea level. The high ground of the ridge supports the major cities of Florida's Atlantic coast, which are growing at such a rate that the entire 320 miles and its adjacent lowlands will be urbanized by the turn of the century. Demographers predict a similar fate for a parallel 200-mile urban strip on the west coast lowlands from Marco Island to St. Petersburg, with a third corridor crossing northeastward for 138 miles from Tampa to Daytona Beach across the Central Highlands.

Flanking the lowlands offshore from the peninsula are barrier islands—4,510 of them are larger than ten acres and thousands more are too small to count. Florida's most famous chains of islands are the Keys' and the Ten Thousand Islands with Marco at their head, while individual islands of renown include the sand keys of Miami Beach and Key Biscayne; Merritt, the site of Cape Canaveral and the Kennedy Space Flight Center; and Sanibel and Captiva. Their beaches replenished daily by Gulf currents, the last two islands for years represented paradise to shell collectors from around the world. With the 150-mile Florida Reef, the Keys form the "Coral Reef Zone," the site of some of North America's most spectacular underwater treasures. The reef is not an unbroken wall; rather, it is a collection of complex ecosystems harboring more than two hundred species of fish and fifty of the magnificent reef builders, the corals themselves, which look like rocks or plants but are animals called filter feeders that form colonies in warm, shallow tropical water: Among them are star, brain, elkhorn, staghorn, rose, finger, and the related sea fans and sea whips. The reef also harbors countless shipwrecks dating to the days of the Spanish

Florida Topography

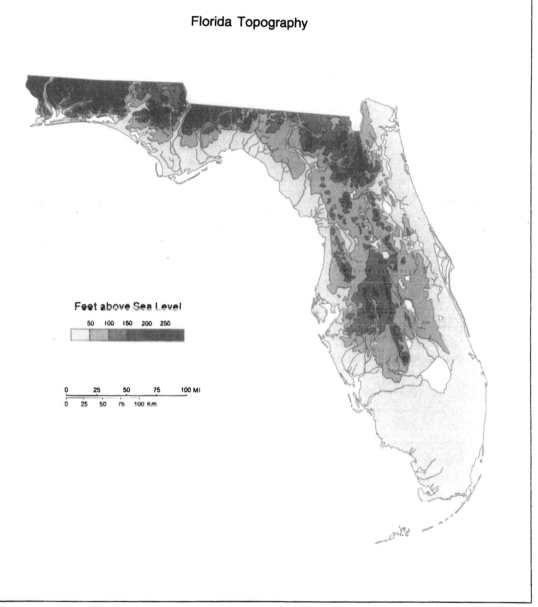

Feet above Sea Level

50 100 150 200 250

0   25   50   75   100 Mi
0   25   50   75   100 Km

Water Resources Atlas of Florida, Institute of Science and Public Affairs State University

treasure fleets of the sixteenth and seventeenth centuries and attracting divers eager for gold.

In south Florida the coastal plain rises less than 100 feet from Florida Bay to a point northwest of Lake Okeechobee where it meets the Central Highlands. Stretching down the peninsula from the Georgia line in a broad rectangle that narrows at its southern extremity to resemble a pointing finger, the highlands are bounded on the east by the St. Johns River and on the west by the Gulf coastal lowlands. The highlands are more diverse and less steep than their name implies, ranging in height from 40 feet above sea level in the lowest valleys to 290 feet at the summit of Iron Mountain, the site of Bok Tower, in the Lake Wales Ridge, whose sandy, well-drained soils support many of the state's most productive citrus groves. The majority of Florida's eight thousand lakes and many of its springs are found in the undulating terrain of the Central Highlands.

The Tallahassee Hills run for 100 miles from the west edge of the Central Highlands along the Georgia border. Nearly a uniform 25 miles wide, the rolling hills reach their peak in a plain some 300 feet above sea level. Rivers draining from Georgia cut through a region noted for its mix of temperate and subtropical foliage, its rich farmland, and its vast pine forests (now largely tree farms for pulp mills). Since the 1890s, miners have taken Fuller's earth from the hills for use in degreasing wools and in the manufacture of petroleum products.

West of the Tallahassee Hills lie the Marianna Lowlands and west of them rise the Western Highlands, which contain, at 344 feet above sea level, the state's highest point. The Marianna Lowlands are actually eroded highlands, which climb out of the coastal plain to a height of some 245 feet.

The beds of porous rock that give shape to Florida's surface form underground reservoirs that may hold well over one quadrillion gallons of water—20 percent of the total in all five Great Lakes.[1] The largest of these subterranean reserves, underlying the whole of Florida and portions of neighboring states, is the Floridan Aquifer, a predominantly artesian body of water covering 82,000 square miles. The chief repository for this aquifer is a formation of limestone called the Ocala Uplift that was laid down in the late Eocene, 40 million to 50 million years ago, and rises from a depth of 1,200 feet under the Keys to 115 feet above sea level in central Florida, where it is mined extensively for the manufacture of cinder blocks and cement. Through much of central and west Florida, a honeycomb of subterranean passageways joins the Ocala with other rock beds to expand the size of the aquifer and create the classic karst topography of the region, which is defined by an abundance of sinkholes, springs, caverns, caves, and natural bridges born of the collapse of limestone caused by fluctuations in water levels. Many of the region's lakes originated in sinks, and the process continues, with the most notable recent case being that of a large hole that opened in Winter Park in 1981 and is now called Lake Rose.

Coarse sand and clay washed down over the millennia from neighboring Georgia and Alabama cover the limestone of central and west Florida with a clastic veneer. Where the veneer is loose, water easily drains into the aquifer, but where the clay is dense and impermeable, nothing enters or leaves. Water trapped between those impermeable layers becomes pressurized when fresh supplies enter the aquifer from other locations and rushes away from the incoming source through fissures in the limestone. The water boils to the surface through such openings at rates ranging from more than one billion gallons a day to just a few score. The majority of Florida's estimated 320 springs, which are among its most stunning natural features, result from this artesian flow. Releasing water of translucent clarity at constant temperatures through all seasons, the springs have always attracted wildlife and humans to their banks.

Like a French pastry, five surficial or intermediate aquifers, contained in interleaved layers of limestone, overlay the Floridan Aquifer in various parts of the state where it lies deep beneath the surface. Because Floridians draw 90 percent of their drinking water from these subterranean sources, their integrity is vital to the state's future. When researchers updated the Florida Geological Survey's catalog of the springs of Florida in the 1970s, they found water rushing from the Floridan Aquifer through those boils free of residues from the pesticide DDT, which had been heavily used for thirty years to control mosquitoes, and of other man-made pollutants. A decade later, two common pesticides—Temik and EDB—were detected in drinking-water wells in central Florida, and later organic solvents were observed seeping into the aquifer from Alachua County. It became clear that Florida, like other parts of the nation, faced a serious threat to its groundwater, and the legislature took the tentative first step of requiring that state hydrologists monitor water quality in the aquifers; but it failed to arrest the flow of pollutants from homes and businesses. Disposal wells, where sewage and industrial waste are injected thousands of feet into the brackish water of the aquifer, are gaining popularity, but they are founded on the dubious assumption that the pollutants will never mix with potable water lying nearer the surface.

The gravest immediate threat to Florida's groundwater comes from the rapid depletion of supplies and simultaneous development of areas crucial to their recharge. In Atlantic and Gulf coastal regions, salt water fills the aquifer when fresh water is not replaced. Inland, as the levels fall, wells must be sunk ever deeper, which increases the risk of their drawing only brackish, unpotable water. In the Miami area, saltwater intrusion along the coast between 1907 and 1940, when the Everglades were being drained, forced officials to relocate wells inland. Unrestrained population growth during the past four decades has so depleted the Biscayne Aquifer that salt water has flowed far enough to again threaten the municipal wells. In parts of the Panhandle, the water table has declined more than 60 feet in three decades; in Jacksonville, the drop has been 20 feet; in Sarasota, 19 feet.

Phosphate mining in west-central Florida, especially in the region of Polk and Hillsborough counties called Bone Valley because of its vast deposits of fossils, has lowered the aquifer 40 to 60 feet, causing several springs to stop flowing. In central Florida, around Orlando, urbanization and agricultural expansion have dropped levels more than 55 feet since 1920, causing sinkholes to form more frequently than at any time in recorded history. Humans alone are responsible for the decreases, and water managers know that without fundamental shifts in consumption and development patterns, the situation will worsen, threatening severe disruption and forced rationing in hard-pressed metropolitan areas along the coasts and perhaps inland around Orlando.

Springs and sinks are the most graphic links between Florida's aquifers and the surface waters that resupply them. In addition to its nearly eight thousand lakes ranging in size from 1 to 436,000 acres, the state contains seventeen hundred streams running from .5 to 500 miles.[2] Four of the state's five largest rivers cut through the Panhandle and Big Bend, where it turns into the peninsula: the Apalachicola and Suwannee, which begin in Georgia, and the Choctawatchee and Escambia, originating in Alabama. Together, they drain 38,000 square miles into the Gulf of Mexico. The Apalachicola and the Choctawatchee are alluvial rivers, bearing silt and organic debris from the Appalachian Mountains and fields of Georgia and Alabama, material that helps make Panhandle farmland the most fertile in Florida. The state's third-ranked river, and the largest flowing solely within its borders, the St. Johns, drains 9,168 square miles of east and central Florida. Springs feed all of these rivers and form the source of many smaller ones, called runs.

The St. Johns and other peninsular rivers have their sources in vast expanses of marshes and swamps, not snow-covered mountains, and generally meander, at a pace slower than a crawl, in and out of their channels, across banks that barely exist. Where the Miami and other southeastern rivers and creeks flowing from the Everglades crossed the Atlantic Coastal Ridge, there were rapids, not white water but fast riffs prized for their uniqueness and beauty in the flat land, until the dynamite of developers blew them away early in this century.

For several millennia before the south Florida water drainage project was completed, the Kissimmee River, running south to the St. Johns's north, bent and twisted for 98 miles to feed an inland sea that sloshed into a vast expanse of freshwater marsh and wet prairie and continued flowing in a broad sheet to the end of the peninsula. Although the terminology can be confusing, this entire 13,000-square-mile watershed is called by some geographers the Everglades. Defined by water, flatness, and a superabundance of life, the region is generally divided into a complex mosaic of twelve natural communities: scrub, consisting primarily of scrub oak, saw palmetto, and sand pine; cabbage palm hammocks; pine flatwoods and palmetto prairies; hardwood swamp forests; prairie grasslands; the coastal sand dunes, featuring in succession beyond the beach, sea oats, palmetto, sand pine, and other salt- and drought-tolerant trees and shrubs; cypress swamps; marl prairies; freshwater marshes; Everglades marshes, sloughs, and rock islands, or keys; hardwood hammocks; and mangrove forests and coastal marshes. The classifications reflect the essential observation that elevation, often of only a few feet, defines communities. Subtle shifts find grandiose expression, as sawgrass gives way to shrubs rising into a dense forest of gumbo-limbo, mahogany, royal palm.

The farther south one moves, the more the plants take on

a tropical flavor, especially in the hammocks. Early in this century, John K. Small cataloged 500 of these pockets of hardwood along the Atlantic Coastal Ridge and on the rock islands of the Everglades, including the five-mile-long Brickell Hammock where Miami now rises. Today, there are 125 hammocks in Everglades National Park and 50 outside it, many of them greatly diminished in size. Trees of West Indian origin include gumbo-limbo, also called "the sunburn tree" because of its red trunk that peels and "the living fence" because of its habit of taking root wherever it falls; poisonwood, a relative of poison ivy but far more of an irritant; manchineel, another toxic plant; coco plum; torchwood; paradise tree; fiddlewood; snakewood; buttonwood; mahogany; ironwood; pigeon plum, which Indians ate; blolly; papaw (wild papaya); mastic; and mangrove. Eight types of palm mix in the canopy while the understory of the hammock consists of ferns and grasses.

A half century ago, Charles Torrey Simpson wrote of his feelings on entering the climax forest of south Florida:

> Leaving the trail I worked my way out into the dense, tangled growth, and as I sat down at the foot of a great tree and gazed around and upward it seemed as though the spirit of the forest took possession of me. . . . Not the slightest sound disturbed me; in fact one of the charms of the great forest is its stillness. I sat and fairly drank in the wonderful silence and loneliness of the hammock. In such a place one must be alone to enjoy the full beauty and sweetness of it all. . . . I bared my life, my all to the Great Power of the Universe, call it Nature, God, Jehovah, Allah, Brahma or whatever you will, and reverently worshipped.[3]

Pa-hay-okee, the "Grassy Water" or, as historian Marjory Stoneman Douglas named it in 1947, the "River of Grass," originated some six thousand years ago, when the climate of the peninsula turned warm and centuries of heavy rains washed the salt out of Lake Okeechobee's water. The sawgrass, botanically the sedge *Cladium jamaicensis,* represents 70 percent of the plant life in the shallow marshes and deeper sloughs that make up the true Everglades. In the upper Everglades and along the sloughs where water was relatively abundant throughout the year, the sawgrass grew to heights of fourteen feet and added constantly, as it died and decayed, to a bed of rich muck that reached a depth of more than a dozen feet in some areas. In the seasonally dry lower 'Glades, the grass struggled to grow a few feet from nearly bare rock. The Shark River Slough, the primary channel of the grassy water, flowed southwestward for ninety miles from Lake Okeechobee, its width ranging up to forty miles, its depth varying from three feet or more at the height of the summer rains to nearly nothing except in its deeper channels and leads in dry times. The Everglades's other major slough, Taylor, whose headwaters are now a lock on a canal, lies to the east and drains south into Florida Bay. In the millennia before the canals and levees reshaped their upper reaches, these marshes and sloughs covered more than a third of the total of six million acres of wetlands lying south of Lake Okeechobee. (At least 30 percent of it has been drained and filled.)

Completing this vast mosaic are wet prairies and swamps. Deriving their name from their gooey limestone and clay soil, the marl prairies lie to the east and to much of the west of the Everglades marshes and are themselves laced with lesser sloughs. Generally lower water levels, the absence of organic soils, and a different mix of grasses and sedges distinguish the marl prairies. Tree islands and the larger Everglades keys form the high ground in both the marshes and prairies.

To the west and north of the grassy water lies the twenty-four-hundred-acre Big Cypress Swamp, a region at once foreboding and enticing. The bald cypresses stand largest in the vicinity of deep water, which perforce fills the lowest ground so that the topography of the land, viewed from above, has a peculiarly inverted aspect. The trees themselves are festooned with bromeliads and orchids, accompanied by royal palm. The deep water harbors a startling array of wildlife and fish through every season. Surrounding these domes and strands are vast plains of dwarf trees that for centuries have eked sustenance from the infertile marl covering the area. They are popularly called pond cypress and believed distinct from the larger bald cypress, but these trees are stunted because of insufficient nutrients and water, not different genes.

Water flows in a sheet through all parts of the Everglades south of Lake Okeechobee, although historically it was more abundant in the upper than in the lower 'Glades, for during its long, slow journey 82 percent was sucked up by plants and evaporated by the sun, never to reach the coast. (During the summer, water temperatures in the sloughs reach 95 degrees

Fahrenheit—that of a warm, life-giving broth.) Clear, sweet water creeping south on a grade of less than two inches a mile slipped through coastal prairies and mangrove forests into the 850-square-mile mud flats of Florida Bay, Whitewater Bay, and the Gulf, often forming into rivers—the Shark, Harney, Lostmans, Turner, primary among them. Water also flowed southeast between the Everglades keys and in times of high water spilled through transverse glades that cut through the coastal ridge in most of present Broward, Dade, and southern Palm Beach counties. Draining the Everglades to the east were the Miami, New, Little, Hillsborough, and St. Lucie rivers, Arch and Snapper creeks.

Biologically, Florida's mangrove forests are among its most intriguing communities; they are also its most inhospitable to humans because of the lack of solid footing under their dense tangle of roots and their swarms of mosquitoes. The forests, which once extended as far north as Cedar Key on the Gulf and New Smyrna Beach on the Atlantic coast and are now largely confined to the Everglades National Park, form a buffer zone between salt water and fresh water, land and sea, that makes them a rich breeding and feeding ground for birds and fish. They are also vital to south Florida's $2-billion-a-year saltwater fishing industry. Despite their productivity, the mangroves are among the state's most limited botanical communities, supporting only about thirteen varieties of plant. The salt marsh, which mingles with them along the coast, consists of twenty-three species, compared with more than a hundred in a freshwater marsh.

The animal life of the mangrove forest is dependent upon a proper blend of fresh water and salt water, which the roots of the trees and the mud beds around them help maintain by serving as a kind of filtration system, absorbing and minimizing pulses of water with too much or too little salt. Efficient as they are, the mangroves cannot compensate for a lack of fresh water flowing off the mainland, and consequently, because south Florida's drainage has interrupted the sheet flow of the Everglades, water in the forests along the edge of Florida Bay has become too saline for fish and insects that once dwelt and bred there. Baby ospreys and other fish-eaters starve in their nests for want of food. Paradoxically, the lowered freshwater levels, by allowing salt water to push far upstream along coastal waterways, have encouraged mangroves to spread inland, supplanting the cypress as the primary tree of the river swamp.

* * *

The red mangrove and many other tropical plants flourishing on the peninsula show Florida to be a bridge between the torrid and temperate zones of North America and, thus, in popular lore, to be "subtropical" (a term meaning only that geographically the state lies near the Tropic of Cancer). In central Florida, where the zones overlap, cold-sensitive plants grow at risk from sudden frosts and more temperate vegetation begins to suffer from too much warmth. Throughout the peninsula, flowers and crops, such as tomatoes, commonly raised during the summer in more northern latitudes, are cultivated fall through spring, when the temperature drops low enough for them to blossom and set fruit.

Except in the northern tier of the state, where winter cold fronts bring steady precipitation, most of the peninsula receives the majority of its water from summer showers and storms. Statewide, an average of 54 inches of rain falls annually, with significant local variations. The Keys average 40 inches a year, compared with 66 inches in the western Panhandle, 51 in Orlando, 50 in Tampa, and 55 in Jacksonville. In Miami, the average annual rainfall is nearly 60 inches, while on Miami Beach 47 is normal. It is common for rain to fall in one block and not in an adjacent one or for a sudden, drenching shower to pour from a cloudless sky. What residents look for in the rainy season—roughly late May through October—is the afternoon thunderstorm that breaks the heat and humidity. These cloud bursts can send the temperature crashing 10 to 20 degrees, bringing a perceptible chill to the air, though the temperature seldom drops below 70.

Much of the summer rainfall is recycled, as moisture returns to the atmosphere through evapotranspiration—either through plants (transpiration) or directly from water in lakes, rivers, and wetlands (evaporation). A line that snakes from Cedar Key across the peninsula to Daytona Beach was designated by Garald Parker, when he was the state's chief water expert in the 1940s, as the Florida Hydrological Divide. The region lying south of that line, holding 78 percent of the state's population and accounting for 75 percent of its annual water consumption, is totally dependent upon rain for its supply. Yet, because 44 percent of the state's annual rainfall occurs in this region, more water is being drawn from the aquifers than is being replaced, and continued population growth worsens the situation.[4]

Climatologists have argued that drainage around Lake Okeechobee and along the coastal ridge in southeast Florida has made less water available for transport back to the atmosphere, resulting in locally diminished precipitation, which further dries out the region. Since, without rain, the land south of the 29th parallel eventually becomes dry prairie at best, desert at worst, the issue is a significant and troubling one that state leaders have, nonetheless, refused to address because it challenges the water control apparatus of the region and because the changes are imperceptible when viewed from the vantage point of electoral politics when what matters is what occurs between elections.

The long tradition of building on low-lying land subject to inundation during periods of high rain has led to repeated disasters and spurred the drainage projects that have done so much environmental harm. The only way to avoid the damage is not to build on the wetlands, but such a policy would have serious implications in low-lying areas of south and central Florida, where a rapidly expanding population has repeatedly confronted the mainstay of the region's weather—the deluge. The National Weather Service reports that few places in Florida escape cloudbursts that produce 3 or more inches of rain in a two-hour period or 10 inches in a day. Localized storms often drop extraordinary amounts of rain—23.3 inches fell on Key West in one day in November 1980; 22 inches in Fernandina Beach in November 1969—but the most torrential downpours generally are associated with hurricanes or tropical storms, which hit some part of the state about twice a year and are essential to the life cycles of many areas.

In southeast Florida, tropical cyclones contribute 10 to 15 percent of the annual rainfall, while in the Panhandle, the total reaches toward 30 percent. Although rainfall averages from 6 to 8 inches during a hurricane, in 1950, one dumped 38.7 inches on Yankeetown, a small village south of Cedar Key, the largest twenty-four-hour total ever recorded in North America. A two-day tropical storm poured 35 inches on Trenton, Florida, 30 of which fell in one day. In 1947, 6 inches fell in one hour in Hialeah, while, at the opposite extreme, a 1941 storm with 123-mile-an-hour winds dropped a mere third of an inch of rain on Miami.

Running June through November, the hurricane season usually peaks during September and October. The National Hurricane Center in Coral Gables calculates that Key West and Miami stand a one-in-seven chance in any given year of experiencing hurricane-force winds. Palm Beach and Pensacola are next at one-in-ten; indeed, in recent years the Panhandle, along with Louisiana and Texas, has received an abundance of storms. Defying the odds, no major hurricane has bulled across the densely populated lower east and west coasts or the burgeoning midsection of the peninsula for nearly thirty years, leading to annual speculation that a killer will strike.

The last major storm to hit central Florida, Hurricane Donna in 1960, flattened Everglades City; caused extensive flooding, property loss, and power outages in and around Tampa and Orlando; and left people dead, dazed, and homeless, as it swept along the southwest coast and crossed the middle of the peninsula. The population has increased since then by a factor of four, and the vast majority of those residents have never experienced a full-blown hurricane. Many new glass-and-steel buildings may not be able to withstand sustained winds in the range of 120 miles an hour without considerable damage. Subdivisions that are packed on floodplains and drained wetlands would be swamped. For coastal communities, the storm surge of a large hurricane—high tides driven by the wind—could be as destructive as the storm itself.

Hurricanes can substantially alter natural communities. Many of south Florida's tropical plants, insects, and snails have been borne to its shores from their Caribbean homes on driftwood. Winds have swept birds before them from the islands and even Africa. During this century, storms have brought the great white heron and stretches of mangrove coast in the southeast and southwest to near extinction, as plants and animals already suffering from the effects of human activities have been unable to rebound.

Few tropical cyclones arise in November, which marks the transition between the peninsula's wet and dry seasons—six months of low rainfall, abundant sunshine, and generally moderate temperatures. Houses frequently lack adequate heaters, especially in south Florida, where open windows are the norm during the winter. A blast of freezing air, which can reach as far south as the Keys, can wipe out thousands of tropical plants and animals, fruit and vegetable crops. Yet the cold dissipates quickly: Jacksonville has experienced only five days in the past three quarters of a century when the daily high temperature was below freezing.

Mean annual temperatures rise from the high 60s in north

Florida to the upper 70s in the Keys, with southeast Florida just
a few degrees below that. Seasonally, the mean in winter for the
entire state is 58 degrees: the low to mid-50s in the north, low
60s in the middle, and mid-60s to 70 in the south. In the summer, the mean temperature hovers around a deceptive 81 degrees, with highs and lows around 90 and 74. Although the
coasts, because of prevailing winds, are generally a shade cooler
than the interior by day, they remain warmer at night because
of radiant heat from the sea.

Many visitors and residents complain loudly and colorfully
about the humidity, which they find unbearable when combined
with the heat of summer. The National Weather Service has
created a Temperature-Humidity Index, which hits 79 at the
beginning of June and sits every afternoon through September
between 79 and 81. According to the weather service, a reading
of 79 means "all people will feel uncomfortable; as the index
passes 80, discomfort becomes more pronounced."[5] Presumably no one could live in Florida during the summer months
before air-conditioning became nearly universal in the 1960s
and 1970s—nonsense, of course. One learns to move more
slowly in the heat of the day, to seek shade and breezes, and
hope for the customary cooling thunderstorm. On the other
hand, air-conditioning is essential for the sort of high-rise, of-
fice-oriented, man-made attraction Florida has become. It al-
lows people to defy patterns of life the tropical climate otherwise
decrees.

Enamored of Florida's delightful climate, paleontologists
early in this century spoke of the peninsula as the "Ice Age
winter resort" for North America, a haven for beasts fleeing the
advancing glaciers. While that view strikes experts today as an-
thropomorphically simplistic, it nonetheless conveys a sense of
the congregations of animals that gathered on the peninsula
from all latitudes throughout that epoch.

During the four major glacial periods of the Pleistocene, the
exposed Floridan Plateau was dominated by dry grasslands interspersed with hardwood forests and bogs, which supported
not only fugitives from the north but also species from the more
arid regions of western North America and tropical animals
foraging northward. From South America came giant ground
sloths and armadillos, capybaras, and the tapirs, llamas, peccar-
ies, and camels—northern species that had migrated south and

were returning to their ancestral latitudes. Tropical carnivores roaming into the peninsula included the now extinct hog-nosed skunk and spectacled bear and several species of cats that are recognizable today—margays, jaguarundis, ocelots, and jaguars, with anecdotal evidence suggesting that ocelots and jaguars remained indigenous into the nineteenth century and that jaguarundis may live today in isolated parts of north Florida.

Nontropical sabercats (popularly called saber-toothed tigers), the related scimitarcat (whose fossil remains in eastern North America have been found only in Florida), giant felines, dire wolves, and hyenoid dogs joined the hunt and fell into extinction at the end of the Pleistocene. Predators that survived into recent times were the omnivorous black bear, the gray wolf *(Canis lupus)*, the red wolf *(Canis rufus)*, the bobcat *(Lynx rufus)*, and the panther *(Felis concolor)*, which migrated from western North America and evolved into a distinctive subspecies. The bobcat has continued to flourish while the panther struggles to survive, with experts estimating that no more than forty remain in the wild. Eyewitness reports from the eighteenth century describe a wolf that was black with white markings and may have represented either a distinct subspecies or a cross between the red and gray wolves. We will never know. Florida's wolves were shot and poisoned into extinction by the first decade of this century. The red wolf, which once ranged throughout the Gulf coast of Florida, Louisiana, northeast Texas, and other areas of the South, no longer exists in the wild, although captive breeding programs are designed to bring it back, but not in Florida.

The peninsula was a hunter's paradise. Mammoths lived there, as did several species of prehistoric horse; the giant, long-horned bison *(Bison antiquus)* and its successor *Bison bison*. These "buffalo," which roamed the Great Plains in herds of up to a million well into the nineteenth century, also grazed through the forests and meadows of eastern North America until white hunters killed the last one near the end of the eighteenth century. Among the array of mice, rabbits, deer, and antelope were the glyptodonts—beshelled mammals—and more reptiles, amphibians, fish, insects, and birds than paleontologists have been able to classify.

Although archaeologists disagree over the precise date, sometime between 20,000 and 15,000 B.P. ("before present," as the scientists count time) humans first settled the peninsula.

Wielding stone weapons and accompanied by dogs, these Paleo-Indians quickly established themselves among the peninsula's foremost predators. They also gathered grains and nuts to supplement their diet. To whom these people were related and whence they came are mysteries, for recent DNA mapping of their brain tissue, some of which was found near Melbourne and at Little Salt Spring and dated to 7,000 years B.P., has shown them to be ethnically different from any other contemporary group in North America.*

Throughout the Pleistocene and into the Holocene epochs, the mix of plants and animals shifted with changes in the earth's climate and sea levels. The steppelike grasslands that rose during the ice ages of the Pleistocene gave way to marshes, glades, and swamps during the interglacial periods, when the peninsula diminished in size and became warmer and moister. Animals would migrate in search of more hospitable areas, adapt, or die. By most solid estimates, Florida in the Holocene has hosted 90 species of mammals—including at least 6 now extinct—400 species and subspecies of birds, at least 4 of which are extirpated; more reptiles and insects than one cares to count; and 700 species of fish, 100 of which are edible. Those represent a minority of all animals that have dwelt on the peninsula.

The most dramatic changes in animal demographics have come through the deaths of entire families of animals. These mass extinctions have swept the earth with such frequency that they appear to be a part of the natural life cycle of species. Shunning that perspective, some scientists have sought explanations in the stars and developed elaborate models to blame the passing away of the dinosaurs sixty-five million years ago and other mass dyings on asteroid attacks or equally dire cosmic phenomena. Other paleontologists have provided solid, if less astronomically spectacular, evidence that dramatic shifts in climate are directly tied to the extinctions; and Florida's fossils support their view. There have been eight such catastrophes during the past nine million years, which have brought an end

---

*The archaeological excavations at Little Salt Spring on the southwest coast, Melbourne on the east, and Harney Flats near Tampa, have yielded important material, but the work has proceeded slowly and sometimes the sites, like those at Melbourne and Harney Flats, have been lost to developments or highways. Administrators at the University of Miami have allowed Little Salt Spring, which it owns, to go largely unexamined by refusing to support excavations of what represents the most significant Paleo-Indian campground yet discovered in North America. Archaeologists believe that other ancient camps may lie offshore in the Gulf of Mexico, but the search for them is limited by a lack of funds and of sophisticated remote-sensing equipment that could locate them through water and mud.

to 220 genera of mammals—far more than have evolved in the same time period.

The largest of these mammalian extinctions occurred at the end of the Pleistocene, between 15,000 and 10,000 years B.P., during which time glaciers reached their farthest advance south and began their long retreat, thawing the world's deepest freeze. The rising ocean washed over the edges of the fully exposed Floridan Plateau, and rain fell so heavily it lay on the low ground for months at a time. Everywhere vegetation changed to meet new conditions, and the animals suffered. Mammoths, *Bison antiquus*, the last of the ancient horses of the family Equidae, the dire wolf, sabercats, scimitarcats, and glyptodonts—all were among the several scores of species that perished. Others fled the peninsula and North America, never to return.

In the 1940s, some experts posited that Paleo-Indians killed off the large grazing animals that vanished during this period, and their argument continues to have some currency among opponents of human hunting and of recent environmental legislation. While the Paleo-hunters may have pushed some animals over a brink to which changes in climate and forage had driven them, they possessed neither the numbers nor the weaponry to eradicate them. Other species, including the giant predators such as the dire wolf and sabercat, appear to have reached an evolutionary dead end, as the earth warmed and size no longer was advantageous.

In the east, the austere yet beautiful Florida scrub stands as a unique, isolated remnant of a plant community once stretching from southern California across the southwest, Texas, northern Mexico, and into Florida. The climatic changes that made the world warmer and moister some nine thousand years ago isolated the scrub from its western counterparts and confined it to the sand ridges of the coast and the interior, where water races through the soil nearly as fast as it lands to create a dry environment in a moist land. For this same reason, scrub provides some of the most important aquifer recharge areas in the peninsula.

Scrub is a fire in waiting. It appears as a several-hundred to several-thousand-acre pocket in the mass of larger pinewoods, like a poor neighbor occupying the less desirable draws and slopes and having fewer belongings. On average, sand pines grow for twenty to forty years, then combust. In the Ocala National Forest, which was established in 1910 as the Big Scrub and still contains the largest pockets of the community, ten

thousand acres once burned in an hour! Scrub depends on that
fire to break open the sand pine cones that renew it. Until recent
years rangers tried to prevent fires in the forest, but now, recognizing fire's essential role in its ecology, they seek only contain-
ment of the flames.

The cycles of changing climate continued for the first four
millennia of the Holocene Epoch. Then, around 6,000 years ago
the conditions again warmed, and Florida began to blossom
with the flora and fauna common into the historic period. React-
ing to the climatic upheaval and what appears a simultaneous
decline in ruminants, the people of the peninsula established
semipermanent villages along the rivers and lagoons to capture
fish and turtles and to harvest shellfish and mollusks, which
came to dominate their diets. Villagers would relocate in response to conflict, pestilence, or a loss of their food supply.
Although they continued to use spears thrown with the aid of an
atlatl as their primary weapon and maintained other cultural
affinities with their ancient forebears, the makers of these settlements differed enough in their way of life from the Paleo-hunters that archaeologists call them the Archaic people. They
fashioned tools, weapons, and adornments from local shells and
from stones, for which they traded extensively with groups
beyond Florida.

Sifting through the fragmentary remnants of the Archaic
period, archaeologists have identified several major cultural
changes, which, over the course of three millennia, contributed
to the emergence of new societies. Around 4,000 years ago
(2000 B.C.), the Archaic people of Georgia and Florida began
making pottery—eight centuries before other groups in North
America. Within five hundred years, the Indians were carving
vessels from the soft-stone steatite imported from Alabama and
Georgia and producing more-elaborate vessels, which archaeologists have designated Orange fire-tempered ceramic (not because citrus grew in the peninsula—it did not—but for the
county in which the pots were first discovered).

Around 1000 B.C., people in southeastern North America
began cultivating corn and squash to supplement what they
gathered, and they also developed a new type of ceramic vessel
for cooking and storage. During this Transitional period, the
peninsula's expanding population spread into previously unsettled areas, and regional differences began to emerge. Examining

pottery styles and other fragmentary evidence, archaeologists have concluded that by 500 B.C. a group of people dwelling along the lower St. Johns River and its tributaries had distinguished themselves from others in Florida. Soon, these St. Johns people were joined by those of the Deptford culture, which extended along the Gulf coast from Tampa Bay to Alabama and whose members stamped a design of checks and grooves on their pottery with a wooden paddle. In south Florida, several other groups began to create their own nonhorticultural societies.

All of these tribes depended on shellfish as their dietary staple, and throughout peninsular Florida, the discarded shells and other detritus of their lives rose over the centuries to significant heights—thirty or forty feet above sea level—forming rich high ground upon which hammocks grew after the people left. These middens initially served not only as garbage dumps but also as burial mounds, holding the remains of people whose flesh had apparently been boiled or stripped away, perhaps by vultures and other carrion eaters, before they were interred. Whatever the sequence, nineteenth- and early-twentieth-century grave robbers and archaeologists convinced themselves that the Paleo-Indians of Florida and their heirs were cannibals, as the first Spanish explorers four hundred years before had charged. (This persistent story arises more from Christian bias against "heathen savages" than from fact.)

Over nearly a millennium, the Deptford people around Tampa Bay created a new style of village design, which featured prominent mounds, constructed not of trash but of soil hauled from the surrounding countryside. So pronounced was this development around A.D. 500 that archaeologists have designated it the Weeden Island culture, after the place where the first sites were examined, and accorded it special significance in the history of pre-Columbian Florida. The Weeden Island culture stretched at its height from Tampa Bay through the Panhandle and parts of central Florida into Georgia and Alabama.

The precise nature of the socioeconomic changes occurring at the start of the Weeden Island period remains a mystery, but apparently for the first time, Florida's Indians established large villages that functioned as independent political entities or capitals of a circumscribed territory. Headmen or religious/political leaders occupied houses placed on the man-made mounds. Potters created totemic animals, which some archaeologists believe represented the guiding spirit of the leader's clan and both imbued him with and embodied his power. As authority became more centralized, the funerals of village leaders became more elaborate and costly in terms of human life. Individuals were apparently sacrificed upon the death of the headman—whether his slaves, servants, relatives, wives, or captives is impossible to determine—and buried with him inside his house. The new headman then either built another mound or erected his home on top of the tomb.

Mounds may also have served as sites for religious ceremonies and as easily defensible forts—their purpose being as open to speculation as is that of Stonehenge, the standing stones of Avebury and Carnac, and the stone circles of Europe and North America. Abundant evidence exists that the early people of Florida worshiped the sun and moon, so it is conceivable that some of the mounds, like many ancient temples and rings, were tied into astronomical observations and religious rites that were an integral part of daily life.

Invading groups from the powerful Mississippian culture of the southeast repeatedly overran Georgia and north Florida between A.D. 800 and 1000 and finally absorbed the indigenous Weeden Island people. The conquerers introduced a more sophisticated form of agriculture than the simple slash-and-burn method in use at the time, and firmly established a new society in the valley of the Apalachicola River, which archaeologists refer to as the Fort Walton culture, after the Panhandle site where they first unearthed its artifacts. Fort Walton people patterned their villages on the Mississippian model, constructing large mounds around a central plaza laced with canals and roads. Their society was organized into rigid classes—nobles, from which the cacique, or chief, was drawn; priests; warriors/hunters; commoners; and slaves, or captives. Inheritance was probably matrilineal, and although the precise status of women is unknown, there is evidence that they could become chiefs. Expanding populations and the resultant declines in arable land and game may have spawned the social stratification by making it necessary for groups to defend and extend their territories.

Through cultural evolution, trade, and conquest, the people of Florida formed the tribes and confederations that Spanish adventurers encountered in the sixteenth century. In the Panhandle the heirs of the Fort Walton people became known as the Apalachee, a resented and powerful tribe that controlled the

busy trade routes into Florida from the upper Gulf coast and
Mississippi valley. The Timucua confederation of fifteen separate and sometimes warring groups occupied the northern third
of the peninsula, with a western branch consisting of the Potano,
Yustaga, Ocale, Utina, and Osochi, and an eastern division dominated by the Saturiwa, Acuera, and Freshwater groups. An agricultural people on the north side of Tampa Bay, the Tocobaga
fell alternately under the sway of the Timucua and the Calusa,
whose territory ran down the southwest coast to Cape Sable and
inland to Lake Okeechobee. The Tekesta occupied the southeastern coast of the peninsula from Florida Bay to Biscayne Bay,
with the Jeaga, Ais, and assorted smaller tribes north and west
of them.

At the time of Ponce de León's landing in 1513, the population of these people stood at approximately 100,000: 48,000 in
the Timucua confederation, including Tocobaga; 20,000
Calusa, 5,000 Tekesta; 2,000 Ais and Jeaga; and 25,000 Apalachee.[6] A band related to the Choctaw of the Mississippi valley
lived around Pensacola Bay, but they, like other scattered
groups, usually lived under the influence of more powerful nations. Alliances shifted constantly as caciques and their followers vied among themselves for food and captives. The Indians
had no qualms about enlisting the Spaniards and, later, French
and English as allies in their raids against neighboring villages,
a practice the Europeans were to exploit fully for their own ends.

The only extant portraits of Florida's natives come from
Jacques Le Moyne, the artist commissioned to record the history
of the French colony established on the St. Johns River in 1564
and obliterated the following year by Spanish forces. Some years
later, Le Moyne, who had survived the massacre, composed
from memory forty-two water colors of the Indians, which exist
today only through the engravings of Theodore de Bry, who
prepared them for publication in England in 1591 as the *Narrative of Le Moyne surnamed DeMorgues*. (De Bry appears to have lost
the original paintings, although one was found near Paris in
1901.) Although flawed by an insistence on creating idealized
human forms, the drawings, along with the artist's brief text,
present a remarkable record of the Timucua nation and several
of its people. The sequence reveals their dress and adornments,
their ball game—like a combination of stickball, lacrosse, and
soccer—played with such violence between warriors of neighboring villages that some of the participants died; their kings
and queens; a smattering of their worship of sun and moon;

their celebratory rituals; their villages; and their weapons and style of combat.

Like Florida's other northern tribes, the Timucua lived in dome-shaped, palm-thatched huts surrounding the cacique's house, which was built on a mound with avenues radiating from it. A fence of vertical logs enclosed the village in a partial spiral that provided only one opening, which although easily defensible from direct assault became a gateway to death when attackers first fired flaming arrows into the thatched homes and then ambushed the survivors as they fled. The eastern Timucuans occupied coastal villages for nine months, moving during the winter to inland hunting camps. They produced two crops of maize a year on communal fields and raised pumpkins and beans on individual garden plots. Wild nuts—acorns, walnuts, and pine nuts—persimmons, plums, and berries supplemented the Timucuan diet seasonally. The menu included fish, deer, buffalo, dog, turkey, manatee, shellfish, turtle, alligator tail, and whale blubber from those that occasionally beached on the coast. (The southern tribes ate nearly all of these foods, although they consumed more seafood and apparently no farm produce. They used pine nuts and coontie, instead of maize, to make bread.)

Twice yearly Timucuan villagers delivered their corn harvest to their cacique, who managed the public food supply. In times of plenty, people took whatever they needed from the storehouse; however, during the winter or when supplies were short in other seasons because of crop failure, the cacique rationed food according to social position and need. He also served as war leader, mediated intratribal disputes, and presided over marriages. Under duress or when defeated in battle, he would pay tribute to another cacique, plotting vengeance as he counted out the maize kernels and hostages.

Below the cacique in the stratified Timucuan society were elders, shamans, warriors, women, children, and transvestites (Le Moyne calls them hermaphrodites, a term referring to their preference for women's garb and ways). The women wore skirts of moss woven so finely it looked like blue-green silk, and beads and no tops; the men, G-strings and perhaps a tail of woven grass, along with beads and metal belts. Men and women pierced their ears and adorned them with painted fish bladders. Caciques and other leading men wore plumes in their hair, at least for visitors and ceremonial occasions. Noblemen and women were tattooed on their upper thighs and arms with a plant-based dye that made them sick for weeks after the ritual. Little is known about regional variations in dress and decoration, although it appears that flimsy grass or moss coverings were common through most of the peninsula. Furs provided warmth and among some northern tribes were the material of choice for daily garb. The Tocobaga around Tampa Bay tattooed themselves, according to the customs of the Timucua; Calusa rulers dyed their skin.

The world of the Timucua and the other Florida tribes was one of ceremony and mystery, in which the limbs and scalps of fallen enemies were returned to the victors' village and suspended from high poles arranged in a circle. "Then the men and women sit down in a circle," Le Moyne wrote, "where their sorcerer, holding a small image, begins to curse the enemy, uttering a thousand imprecations in a low voice. While the sorcerer is repeating his curses, three men kneel opposite him. One of them pounds on a flat stone; two others rattle pumpkins filled with small stones or seeds and accompany the sorcerer's words with a chant."[7]

Each vernal equinox, the tribe hung from a post in the center of its ritual circle the herb-filled hide of the largest deer killed that year. It remained there until the following spring, as an offering of thanks and prayer to the sun for the hunt and harvest. Le Moyne portrayed without much explanation the sacrifice of the first-born child of each woman in the village, saying he witnessed the ritual once, when a mother offered her infant to the cacique, and six warriors killed it while the women of the tribe comforted her in her sorrow. Among the southern tribes, according to some reports, first-born infants were sacrificed only on the death of a chief, and whether this was the habit of the Timucua remains a mystery.

Florida's Indians danced through the night or until exhaustion overtook them. During these ceremonies, men, women, and children scratched and cut themselves as a means of purification. At various healing rites and on other occasions, according to Le Moyne, they would smoke tobacco, which they cultivated for such purposes. Warriors apparently also used tobacco to cut their hunger and increase their endurance while on the hunt, but after a century of contact with Europeans they abused the leaf for its narcotic effect alone.

Consumption of cassine, the black drink brewed from the

plant *Ilex vomitoria,* was an essential part of every ritual and public meeting. The powerful purgative was believed to cleanse and purify the warriors, giving them strength and clear minds for the hunt, for battle, or for religious observance. The drink was ubiquitous among southeastern tribes and remains a part of the traditional green corn dance of the Seminole, Miccosukee, Creek, and related nations. Some white pioneers adopted it in the belief it would make them as strong as the Indians. Women and children could not consume cassine, although whether the prohibition applied to women chiefs, no one can say with certainty.

Le Moyne's drawings tantalize as much as inform. He portrayed four staff-bearing men carrying a litter holding the queen-to-be of the tribe, the future wife of the cacique, an attractive young woman, tattooed, beatific. Flutists marched before; fan wavers walked alongside; pearl-bestrewn, fruit-laden maidens behind; with a rear guard of warriors. Chiefs and principal men, at least, appear to have had multiple mates, with the first wife holding primacy among the others, but Le Moyne is silent on that and, therefore, on the status of the woman he portrays—was she the first wife or the latest? Where was her home? Sometimes, beautiful virgins of noble birth kidnapped from neighboring villages were married to the cacique and accorded semidivine status. On other occasions, the headman selected as his bride the most attractive daughter of one of his tribe's principal families. Joseph Campbell in *The Way of the Animal Powers* suggests that the society in De Bry's engravings of Le Moyne's watercolors is reminiscent of Polynesia and Southeast Asia more than of North America.[8] The bits and pieces of the language that have survived remain unclassified, as do the ethnic affinities of the Timucua and those of the more southern Florida tribes.

The most unique and sophisticated Indian society in Florida was that of the Calusa, who are numbered among the few groups in the world to have established a highly organized society in permanent towns that was not supported at least in part by agriculture. From their home territory on the southwest coast, the Calusa often exercised hegemony over the neighboring Tekesta, Ais, Jeaga, and Guacata of the Lake Okeechobee region and gave definition to what archaeologists have called the Everglades Tradition.

For centuries, the people of the southwest had traveled and traded extensively throughout the Caribbean and along the coasts of Florida in huge cypress dugouts that held forty or more men. They transported plants, animals, raw materials, and tools; they may also have carried home the idea of mounds for homes and common buildings from the Weeden Island people of north Florida, for around A.D. 500 they began placing their homes and tombs on man-made elevations to keep them free from inundation in their wet land. (The mounds exceeded in height the forty- to fifty-foot kitchen middens.) The Calusa dug canals to provide passage into the villages for their dugouts, graded causeways, and established turtle kraals and fishponds. The largest Calusa towns were on the barrier islands of Marco, Sanibel, and Captiva, and at Canal Point on the edge of Lake Okeechobee, which they called Mayaimi. Examined and pillaged during the drainage campaigns of the 1920s and 1930s, this fortified inland town appears to have served as a trade center for the Calusa and their eastern neighbors. Reports from the early Spanish period suggest that an average village held thirty to forty people, but some town sites show evidence of a larger population, at least seasonally. (The neighboring Tekesta had a major village at Key Largo on the southeast coast.)

The dwellings of the Everglades people reflected their adaptation to their environment. Whereas north and central Florida Indians built enclosed huts, the Calusa erected chickees—the open-sided structures with thatched-palm roofs raised by stilts and earthworks above flooding by tides and rains. Because chickees offered no protection against the dense swarms of mosquitoes common along the southwest coast, some people have suggested that the Calusa employed smudge pots or smeared fish oil on themselves to ward off the insects, but, like tribal people in the tropics today, all of Florida's natives probably learned to live and suffer with them.

Calusa culture found its highest expression in carved wooden figurines of animals and totemic, half-human and half-animal creatures, as well as masks of clan spirits—wolves, deer, otters, beavers, cats, turtles, bats, bears, and birds. The masks were adorned with moveable ears and along with the statuary were painted in a rich array of colors. Calusa craftsmen also carved elaborate wooden—and sometimes sandstone—plaques with portraits of animals, insects, and even the thigh bone of a human. These works reveal a culture tied closely to the observable, natural world that must, nonetheless, have been a place of power and spirits, taboos, and totems.

By far the richest sites of Florida's early people were located in the southern part of the peninsula; and the most important among them were explored or destroyed by the 1930s. The most spectacular of these was the ruin of the Calusa settlement at Marco Island, which yielded some of the oldest and best-preserved carved objects found in the Americas, but not before they were nearly lost. Excavating Marco at the turn of the century, Smithsonian Institution archaeologist Frank Cushing watched in horror as the bright dye on the beautiful artifacts he had uncovered faded as soon as they were exposed to air. He reacted quickly enough to preserve the wood by sealing the treasures in trunks, although the color was lost. The most famous is a small figure of a kneeling panther-woman—her head and upper body feline, her posture and lower body distinctly human.

TEN

Fatal Fantasies

Ponce de León claims La Florida for Spain. Conquistadors seek gold and find death. Menéndez erects a colony on the corpses of French and Indians. Eventually, no natives remain.

Juan Ponce de León, the Spanish explorer, landed somewhere between the West Indies and Mexico on April 3, 1513, and called the place La Florida, because it was the Easter season, *Pascua florida,* and the land he'd coasted for several days appeared lush with trees and flowers. There's a chance he pulled to shore near St. Augustine, as various historians and tourism directors have claimed for years, but there's a higher probability he kissed and speared the dunes near Cape Canaveral. Latitude was measured with difficulty, especially in open water; longitude was a fantasy in the absence of workable clocks and accurate devices for determining ship speed. Cartographers based their charts and maps on hearsay, faith, conviction, and the rough sketches of navigators. The results were often surreal. Ponce, after naming his harbor Florida, claimed for the Spanish crown every contiguous parcel of land, without more than a vague notion of what that included—virtually all of North America, Spain later argued. Ponce was searching under charter with the king, who had named him *adelantado,* or territorial governor, for an island the Caribs called Bimini, a place of pearls, gold, silver, and a fountain with the ability to restore an old man's vigor and vitality. Some reports held the water responsible; others said beautiful nymphs living near the spring rekindled the potency of aged warriors.*

From his first landfall Ponce sailed south along the coast to explore what he believed was an island. He found the Gulf Stream; Biscayne Bay; the Keys, which he named Los Martires because they looked from afar like suffering men; the Marquesas; and the Tortugas, where his crew took their fill of green turtles, birds, and monk seals. Ponce and his crew approached the alien land with a mixture of awe and bombast, certain they could defeat any monster they might see and not quite willing to meet it. But they were unable to contain the natives of the southwest coast who assaulted them with bone- and shell-tipped spears and armor-piercing arrows. Spanish chroniclers claimed that the Indians attacked without provocation, and it is possible that, having learned from Caribbean tribes with whom they traded of the brutality of these metal-clad whites, they wished not to deal with them at all. Before his Florida voyage, Ponce had served for four years as governor of Puerto Rico, a post awarded him for his butchery in suppressing the native populations of that colony and of Hispanola.

The ferocity of the natives convinced Ponce that he had not found bucolic Bimini, and he retreated east to renew his search. He found the island that bears that name now but didn't meet the specifications then and proceeded to the Bahamas. There, the Indians told him the land he had dubbed La Florida they called Cautio, because its inhabitants covered their genitals with woven palm fronds.

Ponce ignored Florida until 1521 when, while smashing a rebellion among the indigenous peoples of Dominica and Guadeloupe, he heard reports of slavers encroaching on its shores. After completing his bloody campaign, the sixty-one-year-old warrior organized an expedition to settle his territory and claim its natives for his own profit. Ponce landed on the southwest coast at what is now Estero Bay, among the same Calusa who had attacked him eight years earlier. No one can say whether the Indians recognized his pennant—a red lion rampant—or whether they simply knew to confront men who came in big, sail-draped ships, but as soon as he touched shore, they at-

---

*It is fashionable in some quarters to claim that Ponce's search for the Fountain of Youth has no basis in fact and therefore is unreal. Such reasoning arises from modern skepticism and overlooks the reality of the sixteenth century, when mermaids lived and sea monsters patrolled the Spanish Main, like pirates. Invalids and sick people actively sought the healing waters of spas and baths.

tacked. Fearless before the Spanish crossbows and arquebuses, the Calusa continued their assault until an arrow cut through the old slaver's armor and his troops withdrew with their fallen leader to their ship. They immediately raised sail for Cuba, where Ponce died of his wounds.

History has treated Ponce no more kindly than did the Indians he sought to conquer. A veteran of Columbus's second voyage who lost the governorship of Puerto Rico when the explorer's son Don Diego asserted his prior claim to the island, Ponce was not even the first to discover the land he wasn't seeking. Supporters of John and Sebastian Cabot argued that those navigators coasted the peninsula in 1497; while the French claimed late in the sixteenth century that they possessed legal rights to settle the territory because Breton and Basque fishermen had begun traveling there decades prior to the Cabots' cruise or Ponce's landing. The French spoke truthfully, although the rules of discovery and possession legitimized the counterclaims of Spain.

Ponce's greatest contribution to the Spanish empire has received little notice. In marking the Gulf Stream, he helped chart a new course home, through the Bahama Channel, for the treasure fleets from Mexico, which in turn led to development of Havana as the major port of the Caribbean. From the Cuban capital, troops and ships could watch the Straits of Florida for pirates and bad weather, moving to protect the ships or salvage cargo, as needed.

Ponce's death left a vacuum into which fortune hunters fresh from campaigns in Central and South America moved. They wanted to plunder—gold, silver, precious stones, and pearls—and to enslave the people to replace those dying in mines and fields throughout the Spanish colonies.

In 1527, Pánfilo de Narváez received a royal patent to conquer and colonize the uncharted territory between the Rio de las Palmas in eastern Mexico and the Florida peninsula. A vain and brutal man devoid of loyalty to anyone but himself, Narváez was celebrated as the butcher of Cuba's natives and the man who, sent to arrest the rebellious Cortés in Mexico, became his ally and henchman.

Narváez set sail that June with five ships, 600 colonists and troops, and assorted supplies. At Santo Domingo, 140 men deserted, after deciding the benefits of that colony were greater than the potential riches of the unknown territory. A hurricane near Cuba later sunk one vessel, killing 60 men, and scattered the remaining four ships. After regrouping, the fleet reached Florida in April 1528, landing just before Easter on the shores of Tampa Bay, which the Spanish called Espiritu Santo. From his first landing, Narváez sought to brutalize and intimidate every Indian he encountered, seizing all who crossed his path and demanding of them maize or precious metals. At Tampa Bay, he found corpses interred in cases salvaged from a Spanish ship and covered with deer hides. The commissary on the expedition declared the practice pagan and ordered the cases smashed, desecrating the dead. In an effort to rid themselves of their brutal visitors, the Indians told Narváez that their northern neighbors, the Apalachee, possessed gold.

Early in May, the adventurer decided to advance overland against the Apalachee and sent his ships along the Gulf coast to Panuco (probably on Pensacola Bay) to await a rendezvous. Alvar Núñez Cabeza de Vaca, appointed treasurer of Rio de las Palmas by the Spanish king and thus one of the expedition's senior officials, objected to the plan:

> I said it appeared to me that under no circumstances ought we to leave the vessels until they were in a secure and peopled harbor; that we should observe the pilots were not confident and did not agree in any particular, neither did they know where we were; that, more than this, the horses were in no condition to serve us in such exigencies as might occur. Above all, that we were going without being able to communicate with the Indians by use of speech and without an interpreter, and we could but poorly understand ourselves with them, or learn what we desired to know of the land; that we were about entering a country of which we had no account, and had no knowledge of its character, of what there was in it, or by what people inhabited, neither did we know in what part of it we were; and beside all this, we had not food to sustain us in wandering we knew not whither.[1]

Narváez ignored the advice and ordered the ships off, after dispatching one for Havana to protect himself from criticism by Spanish officials should his expedition fail. He wanted the dissenting Cabeza de Vaca to leave as well, but the treasurer decided to stay so he could not be accused later of cowardice.

Narváez started his march north from Tampa Bay with three hundred men, forty of them mounted, with foot soldiers carrying "two pounds of biscuit and half a pound of bacon." They traveled for fifteen days without seeing an Indian, living, when their rations gave out, on cabbage palm hearts. After crossing the Withlacoochee River, the Spaniards seized a group of Timucua as hostages and followed them to their village where they pillaged the maize supply.

Wherever he traveled in the country of the Timucua, Apalachee, and smaller tribes, Narváez demanded food and allegiance to the pope and king or death. In the vicinity of the Suwannee River, Indians playing reed flutes first welcomed the troops and offered them maize, then, offended by their guests' avarice, attacked. Withdrawing, the Spaniards seized hostages to serve as guides through "a country very difficult to travel and wonderful to look upon. In it are vast forests, the trees astonishingly high."

Hungry and exhausted, the would-be conquistadors approached the village of Apalachen in the Panhandle, a community of forty thatch huts surrounded by snag-choked lakes and dense forest. The Spaniards attacked, seizing the women and children who tried to defend their village in the absence of their warriors. When the Apalachee men returned, they traded their cacique for the other hostages and then started a series of raids to regain their town and leader.

In his chronicle of the expedition, Cabeza de Vaca reported that after twenty-five days in Apalachen,

> in view of the poverty of the land, the unfavorable accounts of the population and everything else we heard, the Indians making continual war upon us, wounding our people and horses at the places where they went to drink, shooting from the lakes with such safety to themselves that we could not retaliate . . . , we determined to leave that place and go in quest of the sea, and the town of Aute [a village to the north that the Indians said held gold].

First, Narváez and his troops had to fight their way clear of the town they had despoiled. It was not easy. The Apalachee, like all Florida Indians, were accomplished archers and fighters. "They go naked, are large of body, and appear at a distance like giants," Cabeza de Vaca said. "They are of admirable proportions, very spare and of great activity and strength. The bows they use are as thick as the arm, of eleven or twelve palms in length, which they will discharge at two hundred paces with so great precision that they miss nothing."*

The conquerers found Aute, at the headwaters of the St. Marks River, abandoned and burned by its forewarned occupants, though the fields held ripe beans, maize, and pumpkins, on which they feasted. Narváez dispatched Cabeza de Vaca down the river to seek the sea and ships that weren't there. Returning to Aute, Cabeza de Vaca was greeted by colleagues sick and badly shot up from an attack the previous night. They staggered down the St. Marks, reaching its mouth with only two thirds of the original three-hundred-man force. Narváez, who knew less of navigation than of travel through alien terrain, ordered ships built. The men converted all their spare armaments, stirrups, spurs, and other iron goods into nails, saws, and axes. They raided Aute daily for maize, ate oysters, and slowly killed off their horses for food while the work progressed. In September, six months after landing, they embarked in five crude boats, caulked with palmetto fiber, rigged with ropes made from horse manes and tails, and sails stitched from their clothes. They killed and ate the remaining horses and shaped the poorly cured hides into leaky, putrid water bags. They loaded their boats so heavily that the gunwales barely rose above the water of what is now called Apalachee Bay.

For thirty days, the Spaniards drifted and clumsily sailed in those boats, touching shore only near Pensacola, where they fought with the Choctaw. They drew fresh water from the mouth of the Mississippi and they subsisted on raw maize. Finally, Narváez declared that every boat had to fend for itself and abandoned the last of his command.

Of the five rough boats, two were lost and three ran aground off the Texas coast, including that of Narváez, which later was swept to sea during a storm, with him aboard. He was not seen again. Cabeza de Vaca survived, along with three others—the final four of Narváez's original force of three hundred men—scattered across the sand, unaware of each other, so pressed for food that several consumed the flesh of their dead

---

*The wood bows remain a mystery. Some observers claim they were seven to eight feet long. Jacques Le Moyne portrays them as recurved—an improbability. My palms are four inches across; so even at that measure the bows would be no more than four feet in length, requiring a strong man to draw them.

comrades.* Different groups of Texas coastal Indians rescued
the four and held them for eight years until Cabeza de Vaca led
their successful escape to Mexico. On his return to Spain, he
achieved celebrity for his account of his suffering and courage.
It is apparent from Cabeza de Vaca's reticence about Florida
itself that he exaggerated his hardships in order to discourage
adventurers from seeking a patent to conquer that territory,
which he wanted for himself.

The king accorded that honor to Hernando de Soto, naming him governor of Cuba and adelantado of Florida, which title
he could pass to his heirs. Pizarro's foremost captain in the
destruction of Incan civilization and a man renowned for his
courage and tenacity, the thirty-six-year-old De Soto assumed
he would succeed with ease where the self-serving Narváez had
failed. Although Cabeza de Vaca refused a request from the new
adelantado to accompany his expedition, he advised his relatives
to liquidate their estates and sail for the riches of the new land.
Spain's noblest sons gathered around De Soto's banner, and a
group from neighboring Portugal joined them, including one
"gentleman of Elvas," who recorded the captain's last campaign.

With seven ships holding six hundred men, assorted horses,
dogs, hogs, provisions, and weapons, as well as his wife and
those of other senior officials, De Soto left Spain in 1538 for
Cuba, by then a rich and fertile colony. It was also a land rife
with fresh rumors, attributed to captive Indians, of gold in
Florida. Such was the greed of the adventurers that few bothered to seek more specifics, which they wouldn't in any event
have received. Florida's Indians always told their invaders about
towns of vast riches somewhere north or west, and one can only
assume they did so to move the violent newcomers out of their
own territory and against their enemies.

In May 1539, Hernando de Soto sailed from Havana for
Florida, with his six hundred men and nine vessels and landed
at that same Tampa Bay that had brought such ill fortune to
Narváez.† The expedition found a village of eight palmetto-
thatched houses, with the cacique's occupying a mound "for

---

*This and a handful of other reports of shipwreck survivors eating their fallen mates
represent the only authenticated accounts of cannibalism in Florida, although several
Spanish chroniclers repeat charges that the natives ate their own dead as well as that
of their captives.
†At one time, historians believed the site of his landing was Charlotte Harbor, but they
have come to agree on Tampa Bay and now trace his wanderings from there.

defense" at one end and the temple at the other. The occupants had fled inland to the flatwoods, leaving food and pearls unguarded, and De Soto's men took both. The gentleman of Elvas reported that soon after landing, "when Balthasar de Gallegos came into the open field, he discovered ten or eleven Indians, among whom was a Christian, naked and sun-burnt, his arms tattooed after their manner, and he in no respect differing from them."[2]

He was Juan Ortiz, a member of Narváez's expedition who had returned to Havana after the troops disembarked and then joined a search party sent by the lost conquistador's wife. The Indians at Tampa Bay captured him and staked him over a fire for slow roasting. The cacique's daughter interceded on his behalf, claiming, according to Ortiz's account, that the presence of a Christian would bring honor to the tribe. Her father, Ucita, relented and after Ortiz was healed–mythologizers say by the physical and spiritual love of the daughter–assigned him the task of guarding the temple at night from scavengers. One night a wolf hauled off the body of the child of one of the principal men of the village, and although Ortiz tracked and mortally wounded the creature, he was unable to recover the corpse by morning, a failure that nearly brought his death. But, after finding first the child's body and then the dead wolf, the cacique and his principal men decided to spare the Christian again. (The gentleman of Elvas reported this story in 1557, fifty-nine years before Captain John Smith told of his rescue by Pocahontas in Virginia, and the suspicion exists in many quarters that the English captain borrowed freely from the adventures of Juan Ortiz.)

For three years, Ortiz lived among his captors, becoming something more than a slave if less than a leading man. His fortunes changed when a rival cacique forced Ucita to flee his town and the defeated leader decided to sacrifice Ortiz to the angry gods. Ucita's daughter again saved the Christian, who may or may not have been her lover (the gentleman of Elvas was reticent on such matters), warning him that he was to be burned and setting him on the path to the village of a rival cacique, Mococo, who harbored him for nine years until De Soto came. Mococo then sent Ortiz back to his own kind, doubtless thinking some protection or advantage might accrue to his people. The cacique provided De Soto with a person Narváez only dreamed of having–an interpreter familiar with the people and their language. Ortiz knew little geography, however, telling De Soto he had not traveled more than ten leagues from Mococo's village, a bit of ignorance that didn't keep him from repeating rumors of a rich country to the north where Paracoxi ruled, collecting tribute from Indians as far south as the country of the Calusa.

Hearing the news, De Soto marched his force in November 1539 up the coast and inland to Apalachen, where they stayed until May in a state of constant conflict with the tribespeople. From Apalachen, De Soto sent troops west across the Panhandle and dispatched a party to Havana for provisions, agreeing to meet them at Pensacola Bay at the end of 1540, a rendezvous he failed to keep.

Despite the obvious botanical and biological wealth of the land and a hefty supply of pearls from the oysters that covered the coast, the Spaniards continued their feverish search for gold, interrogating each Indian they caught, seizing on every report of rich cities somewhere north or west. Often they kept the captives as slaves to pound maize and make bread for senior officers. Food was always in short supply because the Spaniards were incompetent and lazy hunters. The gentleman of Elvas reported:

> The Indians never lacked meat. With arrows they get an abundance of deer, turkeys, rabbits, and other wild animals, being very skillful in killing game, which the Christians were not; and even if they had been, there was not the opportunity for it, they being on the march the greater part of their time; nor did they, besides, ever dare to straggle off. Such was the craving for meat, that when the six hundred men who followed Soto arrived at a town, and found there twenty or thirty dogs, he who could get sight of one and kill him [did so].

De Soto died from fever in June 1542 on the banks of the Mississippi, a man still questing for gold, and his troops committed his body to the river. (The interpreter Juan Ortiz also died during the expedition.) In 1543, 330 members of his original force, along with 100 Indian slaves, floated out of the mouth of the Mississippi and sailed down the Gulf to Mexico, with a loss of 10 more men along the way.

Everywhere he traveled, De Soto pillaged the fields, leaving the Indians nothing. He and his troops also spread death through battles and, more insidiously, infection of the natives with diseases to which they had no immunity.

The Indians fought De Soto at every turn, firing fish-bone-, shell-, and flint-tipped cane arrows that split on impact with armor and sent slivers through its gaps. But for all their courage, the Indians could only badger the Spaniards, who overwhelmed them in pitched battles. All they gained, if the legends are true, was a new dog to mix with their native breeds and razorback hogs, which provided meat to many generations of Indians and settlers.

After De Soto's surviving subalterns reported the presence of a rich, if wild, country, other adventurers followed. In 1546, Father Luis Cancer de Barbastro, a Dominican priest renowned for pacifying the hostile Indians of Guatemala, secured permission to approach Florida's natives. A leading proponent of the view that abuses by the military were making the conversion of indigenous peoples impossible, Cancer planned to land in a part of Florida that the conquistadors had not visited; but his pilot steered him and his five companions—three priests, a lay brother, and an Indian woman who was to serve as interpreter—to Tampa Bay, which Narváez and De Soto had already despoiled. The Tocobaga attacked the landing party, killing one priest and the lay brother, while the woman, christened Magdalena, returned to her people. Ignoring the pleas of his remaining colleagues and a Spaniard the Indians had held captive since De Soto's incursion seven years earlier, Cancer decided to meet the Indians alone and martyr himself.

The bishop of Cuba and other Church leaders agitated for new expeditions to convert Florida's Indians and bring women from there to Cuba to service the troops and replenish the island's native population. Unofficial raids by military detachments from Havana occurred regularly throughout the sixteenth century, with the Spaniards claiming that they were rescuing shipwreck victims and punishing the heathens who had lured their vessels to ruin on the Florida Reef with false beacon fires. The tribes of south Florida were indeed salvors, taking from wrecked galleons tools, weapons, food, and liquor. The gold and silver possessed no intrinsic value although some of the tribes on the peninsula refashioned coins into ornaments. Reports persisted for many years that the cacique Carlos—a name the Spaniards applied to several generations of Calusa leaders that may have been a variant of Calos, the Indians' name for themselves—stored his treasure in a deep pit and kept scores of Spanish slaves for sacrifice and other unnatural acts.* As far as the Spaniards were concerned, all of the most hideous tales of survivors were true, and the Indians had to be both punished and saved. What the horror stories never explained is why shipwreck victims not only were spared but also adopted into the tribe.

A decade after Cancer's martyrdom, Tristan de Luna, a former associate of De Soto and veteran of Coronado's quest for the seven cities of gold, sailed from Cuba with five hundred soldiers and one thousand colonists for the upper Gulf coast. He planned to plant settlements in the country De Soto had sacked, including the territory of the Coosa in present-day Alabama. De Soto's fight with that tribe was the bloodiest of his march; his legacy to them was disease. Finding the Coosa ruined by epidemics and bereft of riches, De Luna's followers became demoralized and mutinous. In April 1561 at Pensacola Bay, on orders from the king, Tristan relinquished his command to Angel de Villafane, who was charged with settling Santa Elena on the east coast, but by then the game was hopeless. The majority of the remaining colonists, reluctant to face additional hardship for scant reward, deserted, and at Santa Elena, a storm prevented the remainder, including De Villafane, from dropping anchor. They sailed home in failure.

For a few years, while it sent its forces elsewhere in the search of precious metals to restock its treasury, Spain left Florida to the Indians. Their scavenging of wrecks continued to arouse fear and loathing but not sufficient passion to launch a major campaign when, despite the influx of the riches of Central and South America, the Spanish government was often hardpressed for funds to maintain itself and its empire. Colonial governors paid taxes reluctantly; travel was slow and risky. Merchant ships were instructed to travel under escort through the Straits of Florida and along the Atlantic coast on the Gulf Stream until clear of the Bahama Channel and into open water. But because their galleons were awkward, waddling craft, hard

---

*There are reports that Carlos named himself after learning that Charles was the name of the greatest leader in Europe, the king of Spain, but these appear to have their origin in jingoism.

to manage except with a stiff wind filling their sails, captains usually took advantage of fair weather without waiting for the pod to form before they proceeded. In the absence of serious threats from pirates, their violations of the rules were tolerated. Sailing as they did in the fall to catch the prevailing winds, seamen feared most the hurricanes, waterspouts, and squalls common to that season, because they knew that bad weather claimed more victims than all the pirates on the sea.

Spain's interest in Florida quickened in 1562 after officials learned that Jean Ribault, a devout French Calvinist, had sailed two small boats, bearing 150 people, into the St. Johns River (San Juan, to Spaniards), which he called the River of May, after the month in which they landed. Ribault, who traveled under the sponsorship of Gaspar de Coligny, a Huguenot like himself and admiral of France, called the land "the fairest, fruitfullest, and pleasantest of all the world."[3] The Huguenots traded with the followers of the Timucua cacique Saturiwa for several days, then coasted north to Port Royal where Ribault left a 28-man garrison to hold the region for the king of France. The commander returned to their homeland for supplies with the promise he would reappear in six months.

Unsuited to life alone in a strange land, his men contented themselves with begging food from the Indians around the post they had named Fort Charles and visiting new tribes in order to take advantage of their generosity. They hauled their booty back to the fort, but fire destroyed most of it and the Indians, offended that the Frenchmen produced no food for themselves and offered no gifts in return for what they received, refused to share any more of their harvest. Winter was approaching, there would be no more corn until the following summer. Famine, homesickness, and disgust at a plight unbecoming French gentlemen drove the rude colonists into quarrels that led to mutiny.[4] Finally, the garrison, though unschooled in shipbuilding and navigation, set to work constructing boats, using pine sap for pitch and moss for caulking. On the long trip to France, their craft became becalmed and their rations gave out. The survivors consumed the flesh of their dead comrades to relieve their hunger, and, upon arriving back in Europe, claimed the natives were cannibals, repeating the charges of Narváez's men two decades earlier.

Civil war in France and the fall from grace of Ribault's sponsor drove the colonizer to England where he published an account of his voyage of "discovery" and attempted to persuade Queen Elizabeth to back another venture. When she procrastinated, he tried to return to France, and she ordered him thrown into jail for a year, to keep anyone from gaining an advantage in North America. Coligny, restored to power in France, sent René de Laudonnière to establish a new colony in Florida on the banks of the River of May. The three ships he commanded bore three hundred men and four women—a combination of idealistic Huguenots out to establish the kingdom of God, of artisans, tradesmen, and soldiers, among whom was the artist Jacques Le Moyne. The party included no farmers and no hunters; they would rely on their military power, the Lord, and the goodwill of the Indians.

Saturiwa and his people greeted the French colonists as they sailed up the St. Johns five miles, and Laudonniere wrote home, "The place is so pleasant that those which are melancholic would be inforced [sic] to change their humour."[5] Although initially displeased when he saw that the white men planned to build a fort in his domain, Saturiwa agreed to assist in its construction after Laudonnière pledged to send his arquebusiers on a raid against his southern neighbors.

After completing Fort Caroline, Laudonnière reached out to the cacique he had pledged to help Saturiwa defeat, Utina, who, living inland, was closer, the French believed, to treasure. Laudonnière's troops assisted Utina in two bloody raids against his rival the Potanou, but they found neither gold nor silver.*

The Utina and Saturiwa soon realized that the French at Fort Caroline were freeloaders, taking food in exchange for little. Their arquebuses were frightening and effective in war, but not worth the price of allegiance, especially with winter drawing near. Offended by Laudonnière's assistance to his enemy, Saturiwa cut off the free supplies of maize, fish, and meat he had been providing. The French turned to Utina, assuming they would call in chits due for their services. When refused food because they had already seriously depleted supplies, they kidnapped the cacique and alienated his people. After a battle, the French exchanged their hostage for maize, which the aroused warriors then prevented them from carrying out of the village. The French freeloaders withdrew, bereft of hostage and provi-

---

*In the absence of precise identifiers, archaeologists refer to the cacique and villages of the Timucua by the same name.

sions, trapped by their own duplicity in the poverty of their fort.

Indecisive and ill, Laudonnière attempted to ration supplies to a troop he could no longer command. A group mutinied, stole two boats, and went in search of Spanish ships to plunder. They seized one vessel, before losing one themselves to a Spanish patrol, which hauled it back to Havana. The surviving mutineers returned to Fort Caroline, but the raid had alerted the Spaniards to an intruder in La Florida, and so the faltering colony became the target of a retaliatory strike it had no way to thwart.

Saturiwa finally agreed to trade fish, but not maize, to the desperate colonists for knives, axes, hoes, and clothes. The French beat the fish bones into powder to make bread and watched for sails that might signal their rescue.

John Hawkins, the slave-trading English brigand and hero, entered the mouth of the St. Johns to take on fresh water and traded the famished colonists a ship to carry them back to France in exchange for the bulk of their firearms and ammunition. As they prepared to depart, Jean Ribault appeared with seven ships and more people—five hundred troops and artisans; seventy women, wives of colonists and prostitutes—and relieved the incompetent Laudonnière of his command.

The respite from tribulation was brief. Having learned of the French colony, Philip II named his captain general of the guard of the treasure fleet, Pedro Menéndez de Avilés, adelantado of Florida—which to the Spaniards meant the region from Labrador to Mexico—with a patent to smash Fort Caroline, settle and exploit the country for Spain, guard the Bahama Channel against pirates, and Christianize the natives. By all accounts, Menéndez, whose brother served as admiral of the fleet, was a courageous, shrewd, pious, ruthless officer and something of a pirate himself. He departed from Spain in June 1565 with an armada befitting a crusade—nineteen ships, one thousand people, and all the provisions required for conquest and colonization.

After leaving his colonists at Puerto Rico, Menéndez reached the mouth of the St. Johns River in September with five ships and eight hundred troops. He immediately attacked Ribault's fleet, which fled, and then withdrew down the coast rather than attack Fort Caroline. The harbor he chose for anchorage was the site of an Indian village that became the Spanish town of St. Augustine. Echoing the French, whose words he could not have known, Menéndez's biographer Bartolome Barrientos said, "We entered and viewed the country thereabout, which is the fairest, fruitfullest and pleasantest of all the world."[6]

While Menéndez's men threw up fortifications, Ribault sailed from the St. Johns with 600 men, leaving Fort Caroline and its 240 inhabitants in the care of Laudonnière and 27 soldiers, only 10 of whom had weapons. After failing to trap Menéndez anchored inside the sandbar at St. Augustine, Ribault's flotilla was swept down the coast by a squall and wrecked.

Menéndez took advantage of his rival's misfortune to launch an overland attack. At dawn on September 20, after a four-day forced march, his 500-man force swept through Fort Caroline, killing 138 and sparing only 56 women and children, whom he kept as hostages. By most accounts, Menéndez hanged his male prisoners and ordered placed over them a sign saying, I DO THIS, NOT AS TO FRENCHMEN, BUT AS TO LUTHERANS. The artist Jacques Le Moyne, Laudonnière, Ribault's son, and some 50 to 60 others escaped the slaughter and managed several days later to board the remaining ships and flee homeward.

Menéndez renamed the fort San Mateo and left 300 of his troops there while he returned to St. Augustine, where Indian runners arrived with word of a French corpse to the south at Mantanzas Inlet. Marching down the beach with 50 men, the adelantado encountered 208 of Ribault's troops and demanded that they put themselves at his mercy. Famished in an alien country with no means of escape, they consented, and Menéndez had them ferried across the inlet in groups of 10, then fed and bound. After all were under control, he commanded Catholics among the captives to step forward, and 12 Bretons did so. Then he weeded out 4 carpenters and caulkers he planned to enslave because he needed their skills. His troops herded the remaining captives into the dunes where, upon reaching a line Menéndez had drawn in the sand, they beheaded them.

Hearing several days later of another group of Frenchmen on the coast, he again sallied forth from St. Augustine and found Ribault with 320 men, 150 of whom, including the French commander, placed themselves at his mercy, unaware of the fate of their comrades. Menéndez promised safe passage to his rival leader, then had him and his followers ferried 10 at a time across the same Mantanzas Inlet. He culled out the fifer, drummer, trumpeter, and 2 young pages, and then ordered his troops to slaughter the rest behind the dunes because they were infidels. In French accounts, Ribault's head was quartered and the pieces impaled on posts around the fort at St. Augustine.

The 170 soldiers and sailors who refused the adelantado's offer of mercy fled to the vicinity of Cape Canaveral where Menéndez captured 150 and, for inexplicable reasons, returned them, alive, to Europe. The last 20 vanished without a trace.

The massacres outraged France, which nonetheless did no more officially than lodge a protest and claim it had a right to North America because of prior visits by its fishermen. Philip II countered that the Huguenots had merely received their just reward. It was the usual diplomatic nonsense compounded by enmity between son-in-law, Philip II, and mother-in-law, Catherine de' Medici, ruling France while the heir, her son, Charles IX, grew up.

Vengeance came from the sword of French adventurer Dominique de Gourgues. As a young mercenary, he had been captured by Spain and chained on a slave galley on the Mediterranean until the Turks seized the ship and pressed him into their servitude. After the Knights of Malta freed him, he became a pirate and slaver, traveling to Africa and Brazil, killing Spaniards wherever he found them. In 1567, he launched an expeditionary force he'd financed himself against Menéndez, landing with one hundred arquebusiers and eighty sailors in northeast Florida and forging an alliance with Saturiwa. The Spaniards had alienated the Timucua and every other nation in Florida by molesting and kidnapping their children, raping their women, stealing food, enslaving captives. Led cross-country by his Indian allies, De Gourgues surprised the fort and slaughtered all but a handful of its inhabitants, whom he captured and hanged under the sign I DO THIS, NOT AS TO SPANIARDS, BUT AS TO TRAITORS, ROBBERS, AND MURDERERS. The Timucua dismantled the empty fort, and the French sailed home, leaving their allies at the mercy of the Spaniards who remained at St. Augustine, intent at last on settling Florida. Queen Elizabeth of England first honored the avenger of Ribault and his colonists, then King Charles IX of France reluctantly did the same—such were the politics of the age.

Recognizing that Florida abounded in the natural resources Spain desperately needed, especially timber, for which the deforested nation was dependent on Germany, Menéndez moved quickly after establishing St. Augustine and suppressing the French to extend his influence. He established garrisons at Santa Lucia (St. Lucie), San Mateo (again), Port Royal (South Carolina), Tampa Bay, Biscayne Bay, and eventually the shores of the Chesapeake Bay. He also acted to convert the Indians, first using his soldiers and then bringing in Jesuit priests, who reaped only discord. The Ais rejected and overwhelmed the mission at Santa Lucia; the Tocobaga killed one of the priests sent into their country and drove his two colleagues away. Menéndez's soldiers of God did send a group of Tekesta to Spain for schooling in Catholicism, but the tribesmen soon forced closure of the Biscayne Bay mission. In 1572, after six years of disappointment, the Jesuits withdrew from the peninsula, and by appointment of Philip II, the Franciscans took charge.

The adelantado focused much of his energy on winning and betraying the confidence of Carlos, cacique of the Calusa. Menéndez hoped not only to establish relations with the tribe of salvors and reclaim their gold and silver for support of his colony but also to gain news of his son, who had disappeared with his ship a decade before. Menéndez had heard from other survivors that Carlos held a dozen Spanish captives, so he clung to some hope.

The meeting of Carlos and Menéndez at Charlotte Harbor figured in many a popular fantasy—the ruthless Spaniard facing the tall, graceful, painted, egret-plumed Indian; the rigid Inquisitor laying his palms in those of a man he considered a sensualist. Menéndez presented Carlos a shirt, breeches, and a hat, garb that perhaps amused the cacique, who would have baked in the tropical heat had he worn them. Ship's fare was offered—honey and bread. After giving Menéndez a silver ingot and gold coins, Carlos stated through an interpreter that he'd received insufficient food—meaning that to the Indians the gifts they were offered were hardly evidence of friendship and respect—so Menéndez took him aboard his flagship for a feast and afterward refused to let the cacique disembark until he promised to release his captives, many of whom were integrated into the tribe, with husbands, wives, and children. Of the eleven Carlos freed, three women opted to remain with the Calusa. The adelantado offered more gifts, and Carlos reciprocated with an invitation to a feast where, according to the freed Spaniards, he planned to murder his guest.

With an armed escort and a band, Menéndez went to the Calusa village. His troops traded feverishly with the Indians, swapping knives, machetes, axes, for gold and silver, believing the natives were dupes for accepting the trades. The Calusa felt the same: They could use the tools, not the ingots. Menéndez held himself above the fray to prove to Carlos he was a superior man, and at the feast, he sought to underscore the point by delivering a speech in Calusa to a woman he took for the queen, only to learn she was sister of the chief. He demanded to meet the wife of Carlos and when the beautiful young woman appeared, he repeated his words. Carlos offered his sister, who, according to all sources, was unattractive, to Menéndez to be his wife, explaining when the adelantado hesitated that if he refused the gift, he would have a war with the Calusa. Menéndez had been married since his youth and was, as well, a staunch Catholic. His brother-in-law and biographer, Gonzalo Solís de Merás, was a member of the expedition, so nothing he did would go unreported. But wanting money more than virtue, Menéndez accepted Carlos's sister.

A priest baptized her Doña Antonia, and Menéndez slept with her and made her, to the Indian mind, his wife. He made himself a bigamist, too, but none of his biographers addressed the issue. Menéndez demanded that Carlos have a cross erected in the village, and the cacique obeyed, while refusing to smash the clan masks and figures the Spaniards called idols. Menéndez then sailed for Havana with his new bride and her retainers, determined to have her instructed in Catholicism that she might return and convert her people.

From Havana, Menéndez traveled to the east coast to suppress mutiny among his colonists and rebellion among the Indians at Santa Lucia. Upon his return to Havana, he avoided Doña Antonia, who waited in a convent, telling her when she confronted him that a man returning from sea could not sleep with his wife for eight days. Doña Antonia sneaked into his bed, but he rejected her, assuming a few worthless gifts would appease her. Menéndez returned her to her brother and told him it was time for the Calusa to convert, but Carlos bought another nine-month delay by agreeing to send his heir and two other members of the tribe to Havana for indoctrination. The heir returned as Don Felipe, a Catholic, and Doña Antonia sailed again for Havana, determined to become pregnant with Menéndez's child to secure the alliance of the Calusa and Spain. Her husband again rejected her.

On his last visit to Charlotte Harbor, to the village he'd named San Antonio, Menéndez brought the woman he'd spurned and a Jesuit priest to establish a mission guarded by soldiers. After they disembarked, Menéndez sailed to Tampa Bay and befriended the Calusa's enemies, the Tocobaga, in a clear violation of the trust Carlos and his sister had placed in him.

When Carlos protested, the priest and soldiers arranged his assassination and the installation as cacique of Don Felipe, who, they assumed, would be their puppet. The young man promptly married his sister in defiance of the priest, who then had him murdered. After the distraught Calusa torched their village and fled into the Everglades, the Spaniards returned to Cuba.

Menéndez left Florida in 1572 and died two years later while preparing to lead the Spanish Armada against England. His fleet numbered 260 vessels—twice the number of the Invincible Armada of 1588 that the British fleet under Sir Francis Drake destroyed, bringing an end to Spanish hegemony in the New World. That defeat came three years after Drake, on his way home from a piratical voyage through the Spanish Main, sacked and burned St. Augustine, then a struggling village of three hundred. In the aftermath of Drake's raid, Franciscan priests and Spanish military experts criticized the placement of St. Augustine, saying it was too far north to protect the treasure fleet, but nothing was done to establish a new capital on the east coast.

Following the departure of Menéndez, the Jesuits abandoned the last of their missions in south Florida, and their successors, the Franciscans, concentrated their efforts on the two major northern tribes—the Timucua and Apalachee—as well as on the Guale of the Georgia coast. By the middle of the seventeenth century, they had established thirteen missions among the Apalachee, eleven among the Timucua, and eight among the Guale. The missions were outposts of the Spanish state and the Catholic Church, where priests exercised absolute authority in the name of God, pope, and king, with the bishop thrown between. Claiming a divine right to treat the Indians as they desired, they brooked no interference from military or civilian officials. In theory, the missions existed to Christianize the Indians, but in practice, they were permanent work farms devoted to cultivation of cash crops and to trade in fur, hides, and other natural resources. The Indians were converted from seminomadic, free people, to virtual slaves of the priests, captives of the mission subject to arbitrary whipping for failure to work or pray and paid nothing for their goods and labor. The missionaries further undermined the Indians' social order by beating caciques in the presence of their people and suppressing most traditional religious and cultural activities.

With no sanitation, filth built up, fields played out, and the people, no longer allowed to move freely to more productive sites, as was their custom, and weakened by the abuse of the priests, fell prey to disease. The missions became death camps. The population plummeted from 100,000 at the time of Ponce's landing to no more than 25,000 in 1656. By 1674—eighteen years later—the height of what white historians like to call the golden age of missions in Florida, the indigenous population had fallen to 10,766, with most of them living in Apalachee.[7]

The Indians struck back by rebelling, running away, and illegally trading their goods outside the mission. Major uprisings among the Apalachee in 1647 and the Timucua and Apalachee in 1656 led to thousands of Indian deaths and to an investigation but no reform of the system. Moderately more successful in easing the oppression of the Church were the acts of subterfuge that fueled escape and the black market. Taking advantage of a constant food shortage among soldiers and colonists, the Indians traded corn and meat for tools and weapons, including firearms they were forbidden by Spanish law from bearing. The Apalachee and southern tribes also traded directly with Havana and with the British colonists north of Florida, who provided them with guns, ammunition, and whiskey, with which to badger the Spaniards and ruin themselves.[8]

The firearms and firewater offered no protection against the epidemics of yellow fever, typhus, measles, and smallpox—all introduced by Europeans—that decimated Florida's natives in the seventeenth century. Tens of thousands of people perished; entire villages vanished. A major outbreak of smallpox killed 50 percent of the population between 1614 and 1617. "The great heap of bones which gave Key West its name, from 'Cayo Hueso' or 'Bone Key,' " wrote Marjory Stoneman Douglas in the *Everglades*, "was not so much evidence of a battlefield, as has been claimed, but proof of the death by disease of a whole village or villages."[9] In 1649, 1659, 1670, and 1672, epidemics struck again. After the last assault, the Indians living in the rich highlands of central Florida amounted to a few hundred—no more. Chaos reigned in the villages, with rival factions promoted by priests and military officers struggling for control.

Combined with the decline of the Spanish empire, which made supply ships rare, the disasters brought severe shortages of goods and labor. Fields went unplanted and even game became scarce in the mission country of north and central Florida because of both overhunting and disease. Parasites, including ticks, brought to Florida on Spanish cattle infected deer and bison herds, which, lacking immunity to the infections they bore, perished.

Thinly populated and poorly defended, Florida by the late seventeenth century had become a bloody playground for rogues seeking booty and slaves. The depredations of the brigands operating out of Biscayne Bay and the Keys had so aroused the southeastern tribes that they attacked on sight any British, Dutch, or French sailor—all of whom they called Nickaleers—stranded on the peninsula's shores. The Spaniards, who were tolerated only because they were present to inflict physical punishment and grant favors, encouraged the assaults as a means of keeping out people they felt threatened their colony. In 1668, British buccaneer Robert Searles, also known as Davis, stole two Spanish ships in the Caribbean and plundered St. Augustine, killing fifty people. Four years later, reeling from the raid and feeling threatened by the growth of the British colonies to the north, the hard-pressed empire started building the coquina Castillo de San Marcos that stands today as a tourist attraction and stone reminder of that era. In 1675, acting as proxies for British traders, Yuchi and Yamasee Indians of Georgia and the Carolinas swept through the north Florida missions and into the southern part of the peninsula, seizing people and cattle. In 1680, white Carolinans sold their former allies, the Yuchi, into slavery in their home colony and in the Caribbean. A few years later, the Carolinans redirected their Yamasee allies against the mission-bound Timucua.

The rapid proliferation of European colonies in North America and the Caribbean during the opening decades of the eighteenth century increased the already high demand for labor and virgin agricultural land. English colonists began to join their Indian mercenaries in bolder and larger slave raids into Florida, justifying them in the name of European nationalism when possible, conducting them clandestinely when not.

In 1702, James Moore, the conniving governor of Carolina, led a party of English colonists, Lower Creek, and Yamasee into Florida where they burned and looted homes, seized Indians and blacks, sacked St. Augustine, and besieged the Castillo de San Marcos for a month before reports of an approaching Spanish fleet forced their retreat. Moore impoverished the colony of Carolina in the process of decimating the Timucua nation. Discredited, he rehabilitated himself in 1703 by ransacking the Apalachee missions, slaughtering and seizing more than 5,700 people. Lower Creeks attacked again the following year, and the Spanish withdrew from the barren, war-scarred Apalachee missions with the last 300 members of the tribe.

All the tribes of Florida were being pressed toward extinction. By 1708, 334 Timucua remained. The Ais and Tekesta numbered no more than several hundred, and the Jeaga were so diminished that the remnant Calusa absorbed them. The loss of ranches and missions combined with the growing number of refugees in St. Augustine to worsen the already chronic food shortages and force the colonists on occasion to consume their dogs, cats, and horses.

Despite its travails, the capital survived as a poor but active multiracial community where of necessity black, Indian, and white intermarried and raised their mixed-blood children. By the mid-eighteenth century, 27 percent of the children baptized in the town were black, mulatto, or black and Indian; 3 percent were mestizos born generally to Indian women and white men. Scholars today believe that the total was actually higher but that, in keeping with Indian customs, the children were registered in the mother's village, not in St. Augustine.[10] In addition to the Spaniards, a small English community resided in the city through most of the seventeenth century.

Attempting to shore up its defenses, Spain, in 1699, had finally established a permanent settlement on Pensacola Bay in what was called West Florida, which extended into present-day Alabama and Georgia. Short of labor, the colonists employed convicts who burned buildings nearly as fast as they erected them. During the first three decades of the eighteenth century, troops from the nearby French settlement at Mobile harried the Spanish town, seizing it during periods of conflict in Europe, only to lose it through negotiation or reconquest.

As the situation grew more chaotic and the savagery of the colonists more extreme, the Yamasee leader Brim organized an uprising to drive all whites from southeastern North America. "Brim," said the ethnographer Charles Fairbanks in his 1956 report for the Indian Claims Commission of the United States, "was probably one of the most brilliant Georgians, white or red, of whom we have any record."[11] On Good Friday, 1715, Brim, whose wife and daughter-in-law were Apalachee, led his warriors against plantations in Carolina while the Upper and Lower Creeks attacked all whites in their homelands. Simultaneously assaults were launched against locations in Florida. The revolt faltered and collapsed when the Carolinans, through luck, managed to prevent the Cherokee nation from joining the battle. Brim led his followers to Florida where Spanish authorities had begun welcoming runaway slaves and Indians betrayed by their English allies.

The Southeast became a region of shifting alliances as the Indians sought to play French, English, and Spanish troops against one another while the Europeans did the same with the Indians. Brim was a master of the diplomatic game, but his efforts bought time, not security, and he became a forgotten man after his people were obliterated. In 1728 and 1740, white Carolina and Lower Creek forces conducted raids against the Yamasee, remnant Florida Indians, and the last of the Guale who had migrated toward St. Augustine with the collapse of the missions in southeastern Georgia.

Spain tried to strengthen Florida's northern and southern borders from the raiders, sending its troops to build Fort San Francisco de Pupa and Fort Picolata on the St. Johns, but it could barely keep them garrisoned. The English brigands from the north simply marched around them.

A tribe that wasn't a tribe but whose people had been tribal settled into a fortified village one mile north of St. Augustine to the consternation of the English in the Carolinas and the new colony James Oglethorpe had started at Savannah with the forced labor of convicts. Called Fort Moosa by the Spanish and Fort Mose by the English, the moat-encircled redoubt was peopled by runaways from the British colonies who had been granted their freedom when they reached Florida. Between 1738 and 1763, the fort was a thriving community of one hundred people and a beacon to blacks held in bondage.[12]

In 1739, Oglethorpe marched against St. Augustine to avenge, he claimed, one smuggler named Jenkins whose ear the Spaniards had removed after catching him at work nine years earlier. Oglethorpe's rationalization for his assault ranks as one of the more absurd in history; his real purpose was to enslave runaway Africans and Indians, to annex new territory, and to steal whatever goods and food he could find. He took the two St. Johns River outposts and then sailed for Fort Moosa and St. Augustine with sixteen hundred men. The fort was abandoned, but he seized thirty horses and prepared to attack the Spanish capital. His siege failed after St. Augustine's defenders launched a sneak counterattack on Georgia troops camped at Fort Moosa and Spanish warships arrived from Havana. Oglethorpe assaulted the city again in 1742 and was repulsed, after which he contented himself with raids through proxies.

With the north effectively out of their control, but St. Augustine secure, Spanish officials in Havana refocused their attention on south Florida. In 1743, a party of Jesuits landed at Upper Matecumbe Key to Christianize the remnant Tekesta, Calusa, Ais (called the Santaluces), and subtribes. The Indians said they would renounce their customs—including sacrifice of the first-born child and polygamy—in exchange for free food and alcohol from the Spaniards. Shortly after the priests built their mission, a smallpox epidemic ripped through the Indians camped there, and many of the surviving warriors, according to the report of the Jesuit priest, Father José Maria Monaco, drank themselves to death. A few futile years later, the priest abandoned his mission, and Spanish troops razed the fort to keep it out of the hands of Britain or brigands. The disease-plagued Indians perished.

Spain officially withdrew from La Florida after signing the Treaty of Paris in 1763, the formal declaration ending the Seven Years' War that reconfigured the boundaries of Europe's North American colonies. From France, England took Canada while Spain received the Louisiana Territory. Spain traded Florida for Havana, which England had seized as a bargaining chip near the end of the conflict.

Spanish priests and government officials brought with them from Florida the last of the indigenous people—80 Tekesta and 180 Apalachee. The rest were dead or so scattered they no longer constituted independent groups. The belief persists that some Calusa—so-called Spanish Indians—remained in the fastness of the Everglades and gradually merged with the Seminole or Miccosukee—but scant evidence exists for that view. The southern tribes vanished.

* * *

Primarily Florida belonged to a few colonists in St. Augustine and Pensacola, runaway slaves, roving white traders, fishermen, and hunters from Cuba and North America, and immigrant Indians. The majority of the seven thousand people in the territory, these Indians were Creeks who had raided with Oglethorpe and then taken up residence in the unpopulated but rich lands of north and central Florida. Cowkeeper, the chief of the Oconee, a Lower Creek tribe, settled with his followers near the Alachua Savanna, hunting deer and buffalo, then herding cattle abandoned by the Spanish. Other bands of Upper and Lower Creek followed until they occupied a line from Apalachicola to the St. Johns. These were the first Seminole, the most intransigent Indians of the Southeast, outcast, outlaw bands unwilling to submit to any authority but their own, and they counted in their number fugitive slaves noted for their courage and intelligence. They were implacable foes of the Spanish, who began calling them *cimarrón,* a word usually applied to shipwrecked sailors, meaning "wild" or abandoned, which in Muskogee became *seminole* as the liquid *l* took the place of the *ro* sound absent from their tongue.[13]

ELEVEN

A Natural Eye

William Bartram explores British colonial Florida and records the natural state in his Travels. *He views the beginnings of the Seminole nation, marvels at the plants and animals, the pellucid waters.*

The 75-horsepower outboard pushes the workboat upriver at 25 miles an hour for fifteen minutes, then dies. Starts again. Dies. In a stand of hardwoods on the east bank, black vultures roost, their wings spread to dry in first light. There must be a hundred or more waiting. Ospreys cross and recross the river. Several dive for fish, and miss.

"I once saw one go so far under it got too wet to fly. It swam to shore with its wings," says David Girardin. A free-flowing font of such lore, Girardin is operations manager for the St. Johns Water Management District, one of five regional agencies that guard the flow of the state's fresh water. Marine biologist, canoeist, sailor, "bird freak, amateur botanist, herpetologist, and historian," he works out of district headquarters in Palatka, the bustling steamboat port and health spa for consumptives in the late nineteenth century; in the late twentieth century, a somnambulant "old" Florida town of twenty-five thousand an hour from Jacksonville by car.

Girardin is also one of a relatively rare breed, the Florida native—a "Cracker," to some transplants. Yet lately he has talked of leaving his home state: "I came up here from south Florida because they ruined it. Now they're coming up here and buying all the land to escape the mess they made."[1] In Florida lingo "they" refers to everyone involved in the development of suburban sprawl, which requires bulldozing the countryside. It's an amorphous-specific collective noun that isn't meant to be complimentary. Along the banks of the lower St. Johns, "they" are offering vast sums to descendants of slaves who home-steaded after emancipation on riverbanks no one wanted. Now Jacksonville flows toward them and home builders seek prime waterfront lots; they would tear down the homesteads.

This hot August morning, Girardin is playing tour guide for a run upriver. The boat's fitful engine serves less to impede progress than to focus attention on the shore. To the east is the site where Denys Rolle, Esquire, of London, England, estab-lished a plantation of forty thousand acres in the 1760s. England had just wrested Florida from Spain, and the British crown was pushing land. Rolle planned to raise indigo and in the process reform prostitutes and other miscreants, following Ogle-thorpe's example in Georgia. His plan and community, Rolles-town, fell to disease and dissension in a few years, as summer heat, insects, physical abuse of the workers, and isolation turned adventure to misery. For several decades a power station has occupied Rolle's old bluff, a prime chunk of real estate that rises from the swamps that make up the better portion of the river-bank in this area. The station relays megawatts from a large coal-burning, sulfuric-smoke-belching power plant downriver about fifteen miles. The destination—south Florida.

The outboard coughs back to full speed, and the boat planes south on the calm river, nearly a mile wide and now winding among small, forested islands, the Seven Sisters. Along the banks a few fishermen cast for bass; great blue heron stand motionless as if waiting for something momentous or nothing in particular. Perched on a stump in midriver an anhinga cranes its snake-neck full length to the sun and spreads its wings to dry. (A foul-tasting bird with plumes unfit for hats, the anhinga, or water turkey, escaped the human predation visited on other birds and flourishes through much of the peninsula.) Only the osprey are aloft, preying.

Murphy's Island rises on the east. Past the shore-defining bald cypress, in among the live oak, hickory, pine, tupelo, liquid amber, and sabal palm, is a Timucuan tumulus, one of the few that remain unrazed along the east coast. Girardin used to swim from a natural beach on Murphy's Island until an alligator decided he intruded too much and tried to bite off his arm. Even so, he prefers gators to developers.

Murphy's Island, like every other wooded stretch of land and swamp along the St. Johns, has been logged out at least once in the last 150 years; the thick timber now is second and third growth. Still, Girardin figures it is perhaps the only place in the area that William Bartram, a Quaker naturalist who explored East and West Florida during the British interregnum in the late eighteenth century, could recognize today. For emphasis, he traces the far shoreline of the St. Johns with his hand. Houses, apartments, factories, and power stations appear to occupy every bluff and rise. Although Murphy's and its sister islands have thus far escaped development, Girardin fears it's only a matter of time before *they* manage a road and bridge through and over the swamp—time and money to bypass environmental regulations and engineering problems.

Bartram hunted flowers and often traveled alone through what was considered tough country in that last lull before Florida became an American frontier. He wandered along the historical cusp, a scant decade after Spain pulled out with the last, sick remnant of the indigenous people, when disaffected Indians from the southeastern United States began to forge in the void a new nation. Now the place is cut, plowed, developed, and people attempt to track Bartram to find what was lost, what remains. The Federated Garden Clubs of Florida have placed their plaques along Bartram's trail—or what scholars led by the late Francis Harper have managed to reconstruct of it. The plaques direct attention to the vista, then recount what Bartram saw or did there. That's why David Girardin is on the river early this August morning, fighting with a reluctant motor—to follow William Bartram.

Although it seems an odd place for the study of natural history, one of the stops on Girardin's quest is a Burger King in East Palatka which peddles its fare from a riverfront location. For the diners' added pleasure, a catwalk runs from the parking lot to a bluff overlooking the St. Johns. But there aren't any tables at riverside, and the customers consume their Whoppers and fries in the air-conditioned dining room, away from bugs and heat. Girardin hasn't come for the food, which he will eat only in emergencies, but because an informant in Gainesville has reported that a painting of Bartram landing at the Seminole village at Palatka in 1774 hangs in this franchise: "The artist painted him in blue jeans!"

The portrait may once have been there, but it's gone now. Instead, there's a collection of neo-Romantic paintings showing late-nineteenth-century steamboats plying the river, each with its paddle wheel tucked inside the hull, for protection from snags, hyacinths, and low-hanging tree limbs. That Bartram, among all figures in Florida's patchwork history, could plausibly have hung in East Palatka's Burger King is testimony to his status as a demigod among the state's amateur historians. And if a contemporary artist did actually dress the eighteenth-century naturalist in blue jeans, the uniform of 1960s flower children and radicals, peace marchers and environmental activists, it would have been creative anachronism at its finest. Bartram, one feels, would fit well in jeans: The Seminole, in giving him nearly free run of their territory, named him Puc-Puggy, the Flower Hunter, and for two hundred years fans and critics alike have suggested he inhabited that enlightened, ethereal zone reserved for bodhisattvas.

Bartram provides the clearest, most detailed view of early Florida. At least three times he traveled up and down the St. Johns cataloging its plants and animals, its look and feel. He crossed and recrossed the peninsula from St. Augustine to near the mouth of the Suwannee River, and he journeyed along the Panhandle, from Mobile to Pensacola. The best record of his adventures and findings—and for two centuries the only one publicly known—is contained in one brilliantly quirky volume entitled *Travels through North and South Carolina, Georgia, East & West Florida, the Cherokee Country, the Extensive Territories of the Muco-gules, or Creek Confederacy, and the Country of Chactaws: Containing an Account of the Soil and Natural Productions of those regions, together with observations on the manners of the Indians.*

Bartram's *Travels,* as it is called, first appeared in Philadelphia in 1791, fourteen years after he concluded his twenty-four-hundred-mile, four-year journey through the Southeast. Subscribers to the first and, for 138 years, only American edition included George Washington, John Adams, Thomas Jefferson, and most serious amateur naturalists. That distinguished list notwithstanding, the new country greeted its first major scientific work, from the man who in 1794 was accounted its only living zoologist of international stature, with something approaching a yawn. Critics thought Bartram too rapturous and rhapsodic, too favorable toward the Indians, and perhaps too unbelievable because of the lushness and variety of life he reported. Still, *Travels* spread far enough that John James Audubon some forty years later would accuse Bartram of causing a land boom in Florida. In Audubon's view, that was bad because the climate was unhealthy for solid citizens, the scenery, on the whole, no delight, and the insects intolerable. He may have desired the place for himself, since on his own excursion he reveled in massacring birds along the Keys and in Florida Bay, among other adventures in the name of his art.

Europeans were more appreciative of Bartram's opus. Within ten years at least eight editions appeared: two in London; two, Paris; one, Dublin; one, Amsterdam; one, Berlin; and one, Vienna. They were all pirated from the American edition; Bartram received no royalties. All are now collector's items bringing prices in the thousands of dollars a copy, when and if they come on the market.

Travels was an opening salvo in the Romantic movement in literature and a model for the meditations of later naturalists. Samuel Taylor Coleridge found inspiration for Kubla Kahn's sacred river and "caverns measureless to man" not in Marco Polo's accounts of China, as one might assume, but in William Bartram's accounts of Florida. Coleridge admired the work for being in the school of the "old travellers," and drew on its images frequently, as did his fellow poet and neighbor, William Wordsworth. "Ruth" and the *Preludes* reverberate with images and ideas voiced by Bartram.

Fortunately, in the young United States Henry David Thoreau read Bartram and any number of fledgling naturalists journeyed to the Bartram Botanical Garden at Kingsessing, Pennsylvania, on the banks of the Schuylkill River to study, learn, and sometimes borrow liberally from the man who produced little else besides the *Travels* in his lifetime. Foremost among them were the ornithologist and poet Alexander Wilson and naturalists Thomas Nuttall and Thomas Say, a Bartram nephew. Benjamin Smith Barton, a longtime friend and the first professor of botany at the University of Pennsylvania—a position Bartram was offered and declined—often published Bartram's observations as his own, as did several other experts. His generosity in this regard has caused Bartram never to be credited for many of the plants and animals he discovered.

Valid reasons exist for Bartram's delay in publishing *Travels:* He had sent his field report to his British sponsor, John Fothergill, thinking he would publish it, but the War of Independence raged and then Fothergill died. Joseph Banks, a promi-

nent patron of the natural sciences in England, bought Fothergill's collections, which included Bartram's report and original
drawings of plants and animals, but he sat on them until his
death when they passed to the British Museum. American naturalist Francis Harper rescued the journals in the 1940s and
published them; in the 1960s the drawings were finally printed
in a single volume. Bartram finished the manuscript for *Travels*
in the 1780s and arranged for its publication but the deal fell
through. He could not arrange another subscription until 1791.

Thomas Jefferson, while President, twice asked Bartram to
serve as chief scientist for major explorations of the American
West—the Lewis and Clark Expedition and a survey of the Red
River. Each time the naturalist declined because of age—he was
over sixty—and ill health—he often had trouble with his eyes.

The cause of that strange affliction remains unknown, but
Florida historian Charlotte Porter has speculated that Bartram
suffered from syphilis.[9] Certainly *Travels*, despite its eighteenth-
century reticence on matters sexual, suggests that the unmarried Bartram was no virgin. His descriptions of plants and
Indian women are highly sensual. Nor does he shy from discus-
sing—albeit without graphic details—an orgy he witnessed
among some Seminole and trappers near Palatka. Symptoms of
his recurring eye and related health problems, and the mercury
salt treatments he gave himself, point toward venereal disease
with secondary meningitis. But since the symptoms match other
pathologies as well, one is left guessing.

In fact, on the whole, William Bartram remains an enigma
163 years after his death at eighty-four of cerebral hemorrhage.
His life occurred offstage; even in *Travels* he is a wanderer in the
classical literary tradition, providing only occasional biographical details. He writes sometimes of his depression or sudden
elation and amazement at a beautiful natural scene, but otherwise is invisible, a man willing to watch and present people,
plants, and animals on their own terms. His observations have
served for 200 years as the primary text on the natural life of
Florida.

Born April 20, 1739, he was the seventh child of John and
Ann Bartram, a prosperous Quaker farm couple in Kingsessing.
A tireless traveler and collector who introduced more than 150
new species of plants to England and Europe during the eighteenth century, John founded the first botanical garden in North

America at his home and, with his friend Benjamin Franklin, established the American Philosophical Society in Philadelphia. He provided plants and seeds to Carolus Linnaeus, Alexander Garden, Peter Collinson, Sir Hans Sloan, the Eighth and Ninth Baron Petres, the Second Duke of Richmond, and seemingly every other major collector and botanist of his day.

That was a heady time for the sciences of plants and animals. Linnaeus was working out his binomial classification system. Gardens had burst into vogue in England, bringing a great demand for exotic flowers and shrubs. Trees were needed to reforest the British Isles, which had been denuded to build the ships and accoutrements of empire, and to adorn the royal Kew Gardens. (Many of the majestic hardwoods broken in the sudden storm of the fall of 1987 were gathered by John Bartram.) He and his fellow collectors around the world were in demand; their journeys more often life-threatening adventures than pacific strolls through the forest grubbing saplings and seeds.

In 1765–66, as botanist to King George III, John Bartram traveled to the newly acquired Florida peninsula, with his son William, and followed the St. Johns to near its source. William, called Billy, was twenty-six and already an accomplished painter of animals and plants, but he was a failure at business and, apparently, society. Thinking art an unlucrative pursuit, John had thrust his son into a mercantile career when he was seventeen, and Billy had made a go of it for the next nine years, five as an apprentice in Philadelphia, four in North Carolina on his own. He was miserable and when his father invited him to journey to Florida, he gladly quit his business.

Early in 1766, after his father had completed his mission, Billy decided to remain in Florida, as a planter, a slave owner, and pioneer. John reluctantly agreed to fund him. The Bartrams were Quakers and opposed to human bondage. John had freed his slaves years before; William, toward the end of his life, penned a rousing condemnation of the institution. Yet now he determined to remain on the banks of the St. Johns, and to meet the British crown's requirements for land grants, he had to import slaves for a plantation. The slaves, in the British view, were to beef up literally and figuratively the underpopulated peninsula, making it a productive bastion against Spanish intrigues and a dues-paying member of the empire. Spain's occupancy and Britain's surveys had proven to commercial eyes that the place was best suited for large-scale monocropping, production of naval stores and lumber, and exploitation of wild game for hides.

Billy Bartram couldn't manage his slaves, nor could he raise crops or build a house or clear land with alacrity. A family friend from South Carolina, Henry Laurens, traveled up the St. Johns early in the summer of 1766 and found Billy mired in indecision and ineptitude, intimidated by one of his slaves, ill and low on provisions. By August he had abandoned his plantation near Picolata, twenty-odd miles north of Palatka. Continuing from that time to the present is the misleading portrait from a Laurens letter of "poor Billy Bartram," a sensitive, sickly lad unsuited to the rigors of the world.

At twenty-seven he went to work as a draftsman for the cartographer Gerard De Brahm, who established the line at the Apalachicola River by which Britain divided East and West Florida. They conducted surveys for physician Andrew Turnbull's model plantation at New Smyrna, a 100,000-acre plot that was to produce hemp, indigo, and sugar for the profit of its partners and to become a Utopia for its workers. Turnbull brought as indentured servants a mixed lot of Greeks, Minorcans, Turks, and Italians who were to live and work together in harmony. They landed in 1768 and cleared fields and feuded for a decade, when Turnbull lost a fight with the British governor of Florida and the settlement broke up in recrimination and factionalism, with the Minorcans—the majority—fleeing to freedom in St. Augustine, where they became the best-known fishermen and sailors in Florida. Turnbull and his partners blamed Spanish agents from Havana for agitating among the Catholic Minorcans, but Bernard Romans, who surveyed Florida during the period, said the revolt of the servants arose from abuses perpetrated by the greedy physician.

Sometime in the winter of 1766–67, Billy Bartram was shipwrecked off present-day Daytona Beach. The details, again, are vague, but he made his way to St. Augustine and thence Philadelphia. For the next five years his vita, though sketchy, is the prototype of the struggling American artist forced to conform. He asked his father's friend Peter Collinson to check on positions in London as a draftsman, but none was available. He worked as a day laborer. He tried business again only to flee abruptly for North Carolina when bankruptcy and creditors threatened.

In July 1772, he finally declared his independence, announcing in a letter to his father that a mercantile career brought him too near trivialities and people, and left no time for drawing and observations of nature. Therefore, he planned "to retreat within myself to the only business I was born for, and which I am only good for (if I am entitled to use that phrase for anything)." He was thirty-three and aimed for the wilderness.

John told him to return home forthwith but William had already written British physician, plant collector, and patron of natural scientists John Fothergill for support. With reservations Fothergill, who corresponded with John Bartram and had previously bought drawings by William, agreed. William was to get fifty pounds a year in return for seeds, plants, and specimens. For drawings of birds, snakes, insects, plants, fish, reptiles, and mammals made from life, he would receive extra pay.

Billy journeyed forth March 20, 1773.

"Stokes Landing," David Girardin says, "it's got a shipyard for oceangoing tugs." They push and pull barges up the river as far as Sanford on Lake Monroe, through a channel the U.S. Army Corps of Engineers maintains at great cost to taxpayers and the environment of the river for the profit of a few shipping companies and their political thralls. The landing looks overgrown, abandoned. Nearby was Spalding's Lower Store, a trading post belonging to Panton, Leslie, and Company, which served as Bartram's home base during his two years of travel in Florida.

The morning sun casts the east shore in deep, nearly black shadows and highlights the west woods. There are at least ten shades of green in the dense foliage.

"It's real pretty the way the sabal palm stand out," Girardin says. He throttles the motor down and eases the boat toward shore to settle a debate about a raptor ensconced on the top of a cypress. "Osprey," he decides at last. "You can tell by the black band on the head." But for a few yards it appeared to be a southern bald eagle. Raptors, especially the osprey, eagle, swallow-tailed kite, and peregrine falcon—all native to these woods and waters—nearly perished after the state began spraying DDT for mosquito control in the 1940s. Since the pesticide's banning two decades ago, the osprey have begun to return and the eagle populations started to drift upward, although both birds are officially listed as threatened. Scientists have reintroduced the peregrine, using stock from the American West, and

it has begun slowly catching on in its old territory; the Everglades kite, which comes no farther north than the upper river
marshes, remains just a step above extinction, despite some
encouraging signs.

The boat drifts with the slow current. Thunderheads mass
for their daily assault. "I was hoping we'd see an alligator,"
Girardin says. "They've come back stronger than anybody believed they could, and faster." Come back so strongly that hides
from farmed and legally hunted alligators have begun to slide
back onto people's feet, wrap around their bellies, dangle from
their arms, and the tails have become a delicacy in fancy restaurants and gourmet food stores.

Bartram ran into alligators south of Lake George where
Lake Dexter bulges from the river, near a place called Mud Lake.
Preparing to go fishing for his dinner, he observed bull alliga-
tors bellowing prior to battle and the victor roaring approval.
After the confrontation, Bartram set out:

> But ere I had halfway reached the place I was attacked on all
> sides, several [alligators] endeavoring to overset my canoe.
> My situation now became precarious to the last degree: two
> very large ones attacked me closely, at the same instant,
> rushing up with their heads and part of their bodies above
> the water, roaring terribly and belching floods of water over
> me. They struck their jaws together so close to my ears, as
> almost to stun me, and I expected every moment to be
> dragged out of my boat and instantly devoured, but I applied
> my weapons so effectually about me, though at random that
> I was so successful as to beat them off a little.[3]

He stuck close to shore, caught a stringer of largemouth
bass for dinner and paddled back to camp, alert and afraid.
Another encounter with an alligator, which he shot, convinced
him he would get no sleep that night. Still later he again heard
the alligators roar and, looking, "saw a scene, new and surprising, which at first threw my senses into such a tumult, that it was
some time before I could comprehend what was the matter."

The ruckus rose from a huge assemblage of alligators, and
Bartram knew he was recording a scene beyond the ken of most
humans. He wrote:

> How shall I express myself so as to convey an adequate idea
> of it to the reader, and at the same time avoid raising suspi-

cions of my veracity. Should I say that the river (in this place) from shore to shore, and perhaps near half a mile above and below me, appeared to be one solid bank of fish, of various kinds, pushing through the narrow pass of St. Juan [Johns] into the little lake, on their return down the river, and that the alligators were in such incredible numbers, and so close together from shore to shore, that it would have been easy to have walked across on their heads, had the animals been harmless. What expressions can sufficiently declare the shocking scene that for some minutes continued, whilst this mighty army of fish were forcing the pass? During this attempt, thousands, I may say hundreds of thousands of them were caught and swallowed by the devouring alligators. . . . The horrid noise of their closing jaws, their plunging amidst the broken banks of fish, and rising with their prey some feet upright above the water, the floods of water and blood rushing out of their mouths, and the clouds of vapour issuing from their wide nostrils, were truly frightful. The scene continued at intervals during the night as the fish came to the pass. After this sight, shocking and tremendous as it was, I found myself somewhat easier and more reconciled to my situation, being convinced that their extraordinary assemblage here, was owing to their annual feast of fish, and that they were so well employed in their own element, that I had little occasion to fear their paying me a visit.

Bartram with that passage became the first to report the bellowing of alligators and the bizarre assemblage feasting on a run of fish. Many scientists discounted his observations, and some continue to doubt, though Audubon and others confirmed various of them. In 1854, Major John Eatton Le Conte, who had surveyed East Florida three decades earlier for the United States, testified to Bartram's veracity:

I remember when it was more the custom to ridicule Mr. Bartram, and to doubt the truth of many of his relations. For my own part I must say, that having travelled in his track I have tested his accuracy and can bear testimony to the absolute correctness of all his statements. I travelled through Florida before it was overrun by its present inhabitants, and found everything exactly as he reported . . . even to the locality of small and insignificant plants. Mr. Bartram was a man of unimpeached integrity and veracity, of primeval simplicity of manner and honesty unsuited to these times, when such virtues are not appreciated.[4]

One does not have to abide the myth of poor, sensitive, effete Billy Bartram to recognize in the man a unique consciousness. Charles Wilson Peale captured a sense of it in his portrait of the aged traveler, his friend and neighbor, a gentle man, remote and present. At the start of *Travels*, Bartram professed his animism: "If we bestow but a very little attention to the economy of the animal creation, we shall find manifest examples of premeditation, perseverance, resolution, and consummate artifice, in order to effect their purpose." Plants also exhibited volition and premeditation. All of creation deserved human respect, and Bartram gave it, mourning a rattlesnake, refusing to kill sandhill cranes because, though excellent food, they were so marvelous singing on the wing. As an old man, the Traveler, as he was sometimes known, kept a pet opossum and a crow that often perched on his shoulder or accompanied him to his garden. His pantheism led him to observe and record as few had before him and no one could after.

By the time of his travels, whites had occupied Florida for just over 250 years and left nothing but a largely unexplored, unsurveyed land hosting 20,000 people, one fifth the number of people inhabiting it when Juan Ponce de León first drove his flagstaff into its sand. These inhabitants included the tribes of the emergent Seminole nation, whites and blacks from the American Colonies and Europe, and wandering Choctaw. Fully 13,000 of those citizens were fugitives from the rebellious Colonies—5,000 English loyalists and 8,000 of their slaves.

The majority of the population was clustered along the lower St. Johns and across the northern half of the territory into the Panhandle. The interior of south Florida was largely unknown to whites, who confined their fishing and hunting to the coasts and Keys. The task of settlement begun by the loyalists and Americans, whom solid citizens called rogues, did not begin with a vengeance until the 1820s, sixty years after the first Spanish withdrawal, when slave-driving southerners poured across the border in search of fertile cotton lands.

When Bartram appeared in Florida, he encountered and dutifully described twenty-five- to thirty-pound largemouth bass; ten- to twelve-foot diamondback rattlesnakes, thick as tree limbs; live oaks "twelve to eighteen feet in girth" and rising eighteen or twenty feet before dividing "into three, four, or five great limbs, which continue to grow in nearly an horizontal direction"; wild grape vines up to a foot in diameter; bald cy-

press with trunks "eight, ten, twelve feet in diameter, for forty
and fifty feet straight shaft." Bartram's catalog of his findings
runs for pages in *Travels*—eight are devoted to birds alone—and
his formal census doesn't touch the plants. Seemingly nothing
escaped him. In his 1958 *Naturalists Edition* of *Travels*, the botanist Francis Harper extensively documented Bartram's observations and attributed to him zoological firsts in the description of
three species of snakes, six of frogs, two of lizards, probably six
of mammals, several scores of birds, and two or three of fish, as
well as the gopher tortoise and Florida terrapin.

Bartram was the first to distinguish in writing between the
black vulture and turkey vulture, and he proffered an insightful
discussion of bird migration, the first original contribution by an
American to the field. That was significant at a time when even
reasonable scientists believed sparrows hibernated all winter
under pond ice. Bartram also observed that Florida deer,
horses, bison, and other mammals were smaller than their
northern cousins and correctly attributed the phenomenon to
climate and nutrition. Covering thin soil, the grasslands in
Florida provided poor fodder, and the warm, subtropical
weather, which nurtured parasites and punished large, lumbering creatures, was better suited to smaller animals, especially
among ruminants, than more temperate environs.

Through the years more than a few historians and visitors
have proclaimed that when it comes to flowers there is no feast
in Florida. One can only assume they have arrived in the wrong
season and never read Bartram. During his travels, he observed
nearly every type of vegetative community in the northern two
thirds of the peninsula—from scrub to longleaf pine, hardwood
hammocks to bayheads, swamps to marshes, wet prairie to canebrakes, indigo plantations to feral groves of sour oranges, which
the Indians roasted and ate with honey, often after cutting down
the tree to permit easy harvesting. He seems to have missed the
Everglades only because he didn't venture that far south. In his
wanderings he identified some 400 species of flowers, shrubs,
trees, vines, and mosses—125 of which he had not known.

Bartram's most celebrated floral discovery, the celestial lily
from Lake Dexter, was not identified again until 1931. Failure
to find it before then provided fodder for those seeking to dis-
credit all of his observations and prove that no place could have
produced such abundance—certainly not the cut-over and
drained state they saw. Bartram also identified royal palms along

the banks of the St. Johns, trees that are unsuited to freezing weather and no longer grow there. Charles Torrey Simpson and other early-twentieth-century naturalists accepted his identification and speculated that a freeze in 1835 that devastated foliage throughout north Florida extirpated them. Later, naturalists doubted Bartram, thinking he confused the royal with the sabal or cabbage palm—a most unlikely mistake because the royal has pinnate, the sabal palmate fronds—the former are long, like a feather; the latter broad, like a fan. The royal palm resembles a vegetative classical column; it is a majestic tree that is hard to misidentify.

Bartram's talent lay in his ability to portray the state's fecundity, to set the natural scene through lavish layering of detail and place his diverse specimens in their context. His approach was aesthetic and thematic, far removed from the neutered, data-drenched prose that too often passes for scientific literature today. Yet in their efforts to reconstruct the pre-Ponce flora and fauna, modern botanists and zoologists recognize a valuable guide in Bartram. That he has received less official credit for his finds is as much a result of his failure to apply binomial Latinate names, following Linnaeus, as of any other factor. In his defense, the rules were changing as he wrote: he was caught in the systematization.

Girardin steers the boat in among the young cypress knees at Stokes Landing, looking for remnants of Spalding's Lower Store. In the 1940s, archaeologist John M. Goggin found a few foundation stones and shards of Indian pottery. Little else remained of the center of the white man's fur trade with the Seminole in the 1770s, from which Bartram rode for Alachua Savanna and the Little St. Juan (the Suwannee River) with a band of white traders. He passed through "native wild Indian regions" roughly paralleling small tributaries of the St. Johns. In effect, he witnessed the infancy of the Seminole nation.

In Cuscowilla, a large hammock and the principal settlement of the Cowkeeper, top chief of the Seminole, Bartram received his name, Puc-Puggy, and pledges of protection and friendship. He then went to view what he called "the great ALACHUA SAVANNA." He marveled over his prize:

> The extensive Alachua Savanna is a level, green plain, above fifteen miles over, fifty miles in circumference, and scarcely a tree or bush of any kind to be seen on it. It is encircled with

high, sloping hills, covered with waving forests and fragrant
Orange groves, rising from an exuberantly fertile soil. The
towering Magnolia grandiflora and transcendant Palm, stand
conspicuous amongst them. At the same time are seen innu-
merable droves of cattle; the lordly bull, lowing cow and
sleek capricious heifer. The hills and groves reecho with
their cheerful, social voices. Herds of sprightly deer, squad-
rons of the beautiful, fleet Seminole horse, flocks of turkeys,
civilized communities of the sonorous, watchful crane, mix
together, appearing happy and contented in the enjoyment
of peace; till disturbed and affrighted by the warrior man.

Bartram spent several days "coasting" the savanna with an
old trader and meditating on the "great sink" into which its
water appeared to drain. Later on his return from the Suwannee,
he

passed over part of the great and beautiful Alachua Savanna,
whose exuberant green meadows, with the fertile hills which
immediately encircle it, would if peopled and cultivated after
the manner of the civilized countries of Europe, without
crowding or incommoding families, at a moderate estima-
tion, accommodate in the happiest manner, above one hundred thousand human inhabitants, besides millions of
domestic animals; and I make no doubt this place will at
some future day be one of the most populous and delightful
seats on earth.

Bartram was no prophet, and he lacked the will and resources of a Henry Flagler to bring his vision to fruition. Lying
just south of Gainesville, the Alachua Savanna is now called
Payne's Prairie and is an eighteen-thousand-acre state preserve.
Overlooking the prairie is a triple-decked observation tower of
pressure-treated lumber. On each observation deck is a small
plaque with a quote from Bartram's paean to the savanna.

The basin he so admired was formed some ten thousand
years ago, in the Pleistocene, when underlying limestone dissolved and the terrain settled to form an immense bowl. So the
savanna is a shallow sink, covered with sawgrass, sedges, herbs,
and stray shrubs—vegetation common to Florida marshes and
other wet prairies. At times, debris have clogged the sinkhole,
and the savanna has become a large, shallow lake, as it was late
in the nineteenth century when boats plied its hyacinth-coated

waters. When the plug dissolved, the lake vanished.

Savannas, to endure, must suffer pulses—alternating periods of inundation and drought. Bartram says the Alachua Savanna was covered with a sheet of water in winter that evaporated under the intense summer sun—despite frequent rains—leaving only ponds and streams. Both extremes act to preserve the distinctive mix of grasses and herbs. Floods drown larger trees. Drought brings fire that purges them and burns back the grass, whose ashes form a bed of nutrients to support new growth. Drought also causes concentrations of fish in small areas—ideal feeding holes for birds, bears, cats, alligators, otters, and other fish lovers.

For ten millennia prior to Bartram's visit, animal activities, including those of humans, complemented the natural pulses. Grazing herds of deer, bison, and, later, cattle and horses chewed saplings back to ground level and kept the savanna grass and sedges cropped and fertilized. Indian hunters burned the prairie to drive animals into ambush, so they could attack with spears, bows, and later guns. They were not the only predators. Bartram reported seeing the distinctive black-and-white Florida wolf, which was similar to an Indian leopard dog he encountered on the Suwannee. Panthers, wildcats, and bears prowled the surrounding hills and foraged on the prairie.

When the Florida park service moved in around the middle of this century, the prairie bore the scars of nearly two centuries of predation by white Floridians, who went after land and water as well as animals. Dikes and ditches built into the savanna to claim its muck for agriculture and active fire control programs had blocked the pulses. Inexorably the prairie was turning to forest, its populations of plants and animals dropping. In no way did it match Bartram's dream or description. Wolves and panthers were gone, along with the Seminole, their cattle, and their horses. Bears were rare visitors; sandhill cranes hung on, as did alligators, but one had to search for them.

In recent years, officials and environmentalists have attempted to restore the prairie to its previous glory as a wet savanna. State rangers have begun to open the dikes and flood the land, referring to Bartram's descriptions, which provide the best evidence of the prairie's former state. Fires sparked when the area is dry are allowed to burn their course. In many ways, the Alachua Savanna is thus a man-imagined and managed exhibit of a lost past. Deer flourish, and rangers have attempted to establish a breeding herd of Plains bison. Cattle and horses would probably fare better. Young bison, beleaguered by the omnipresent Florida ticks, almost invariably develop severe anemia. Young and old bison alike suffer in the heat and humidity.

William Bartram understood more of the interconnectedness of plant and animal life, water, and soil than did most of his contemporaries. He trusted his senses and the knowledge of traders and Indians. Sometimes, leaping into ignorance, his imagination erred, but he never backed down from trying. Nowhere is the mix of accurate observation and fancy more apparent than in his descriptions of springs, sinks, and caverns—openings out of and into subterranean Florida.

The Alachua Savanna is a sink pockmarked with sinks. The largest, the Alachua Sink, drains much of the prairie into the Floridan Aquifer. Bartram called the Alachua the Great Sink where, from bordering hills, he saw a honeycomb of cavities:

> [Some are] twenty, thirty and forty yards across, at their superficial rims exactly circular, as if struck with a compass, sloping gradually inwards to a point at bottom, forming an inverted cone, or like the upper wide part of a funnel; the perpendicular depth of them from the common surface is various, some descending twenty feet deep, others almost to the bed of rocks, which forms the foundation or nucleus of the hills, and indeed of the whole country of East Florida.

During the dry season, he noted, the sink's clear water supported alligators, gar, and "unspeakable numbers of fish." Bartram believed those lucky enough to escape gators and gar "descend into the earth, through the wells and cavities or vast perforations of the rocks, and from thence are conducted and carried away, by secret subterranean conduits and gloomy vaults, to other distant lakes and rivers." The water flows that way—not far from the savanna the Santa Fe River disappears into a sink to continue its flow underground before reemerging—but bears no fish.

But throughout *Travels*, Bartram celebrated subterranean waters, springs, caverns, and sinks. He believed that the Suwannee, for the length of its Florida run, was fed only by great springs. (It, in fact, has two river tributaries.) He understood that the springs were fissures in limestone through which aquifer waters roiled to the surface, and he correctly saw the flow of rain and surface water through sinks and springs as essential to their purification and recharge of the aquifer.

Geologists have refined that broad outline in less exciting prose: Of 78 first-magnitude springs in the United States—those discharging 100 cubic feet or more a second—27 are in Florida. (Idaho is next with fourteen.) The state, in fact, has more springs—320, releasing 8 billion gallons of water a day—than any other region of the world, as well as the largest, a submarine spring in the Panhandle that spews forth 2,000 cubic feet a second, 1.3 billion gallons a day.

The Suwannee River receives water from fifty springs, nine of the first magnitude. Bartram visited one of those—Manatee Springs, a winter feeding hole for those graceful sea cows that forlorn sailors once mistook for mermaids. He had paddled early in his journey to Blue Springs on the upper St. Johns, where the endangered manatees still migrate in winter, but to reach that haven they must travel several hundred miles up a river that on weekends is a superhighway for speedboats racing down the east side, up the west.

The St. Johns drinks from fifty-one springs, four of the first magnitude. Twenty miles south of Palatka, Salt Springs are small in terms of water flow, second magnitude at best, but, like the other springs of the lower basin, they are clear, cool—averaging around 70 degrees Fahrenheit year round—and rich enough in naturally occurring chloride to be undrinkable. Most are on the west shore, the base of the Central Highlands, the visible expression of the Ocala Uplift.

Bartram visited Salt Springs, which he named the Six Mile Springs (for what he miscalculated as the length of the run their water makes to Lake George) first with his father in 1766, then alone eight years later. The run's water then and now is pellucid. That's the way of Florida-spring runs—clarity to sand bottom.

One can imagine the scene he sets:

A vast bason [sic] or little lake of crystal waters, half encircled by swelling hills, clad with Orange and odoriferous Illisium groves. The towering Magnolia itself a grove and the exalted Palm, as if conscious of their transcendant glories, tossed about their lofty heads, painting with mutable shades, the green floating fields beneath. The social prattling coot en-

robed in blue, and the squealing water-hen, with wings half
expanded, tripped after each other, over the watery mirror.

He made camp and wandered the surrounding forests, de-
scribing and collecting flowers, cacti, trees. He examined a
stretch of scrub that no longer stands and wondered about the
topography of the place, why the bluffs resembled oceanic
shorelines. He couldn't know what latter-day geologists have
found: that through the eons the ocean has overwhelmed and
then withdrawn from the peninsula, creating multiple, sometimes overlapping shorelines on what is now dry land.
    Finally, Bartram sat so that

> just under my feet was the inchanting [*sic*] and amazing
> crystal fountain, which incessantly threw up, from dark,
> rocky caverns below, tons of water every minute, forming a
> bason [*sic*], capacious enough for large shallops to ride in.
> . . . About twenty yards from the upper edge of the bason,
> and directly opposite the mouth or outlet to the creek, is a
> continual and amazing ebullition, where the waters are
> thrown up in such abundance and amazing force, as to jet
> and swell up two or three feet above the common surface:
> white sand and small particles of shells are thrown up with
> the waters, near to the top, when they diverge from the
> center, subside with the expanding flood, and gently sink
> again, forming a large rim or funnel round about the aper-
> ture or mouth of the fountain, which is a vast perforation
> through a bed of rocks, the ragged points of which are pro-
> jected out on every side. Thus far I know to be a matter of
> real fact, and I have related it as near as I could conceive or
> express myself.

He expected a greeting of disbelief. But there was more to
tell of the grove surrounding the basin, of the scores of fish and
alligators, the stingray, all somehow coexisting. Perhaps, he
thought, because prey detect predator. He watched "whole armies" of fish descend into the boils, then float back into the
basin in an elaborate underwater ballet. He sought to express
the optical qualities of the water:

> This amazing and delightful scene, though real, appears at
> first but as a piece of an excellent painting; there seems no
> medium, you imagine the picture to be within a few inches

of your eyes, and that you may without the least difficulty touch any one of the fish, or put your finger upon the [alligator's] eye, when it really is twenty or thirty feet under water.

The Salt (Six Mile) Springs are today a recreation area in the Ocala National Forest, bound on three sides by a cement wall to prevent erosion and give them the polished feel of a pool, like too many springs today. Limestone no longer protrudes above the surface of the boils. The groves of hardwood fell years before chainsaws were invented. A few fish cruise the margins, but not in vast armies. Waterfowl and alligators are invisible.

Standing on the freshly mowed lawn that slopes down to a sand beach, David Girardin says the Salt Springs are the farthest point upriver blue crabs will migrate. Beyond here, salinity drops to nothing. That explains, he says, why Bartram observed such an astounding mix of saltwater and freshwater fish.

A few campers now fish from their outboard motor boats where the springs widen and pool for their run. Girardin says the fish are healthy and edible south of Jacksonville, though over the years water quality has declined because of the influx of industrial waste from pulp mills—half of the state's total—power plants, and various factories; raw sewage from towns and cities; fertilizers, pesticides, and herbicides from agriculture and suburban lawns. Around Jacksonville, the lower St. Johns can bear no more human filth: Fish are deformed and cancer-riddled, the river bottom saturated with heavy metals, the river itself a receptacle for industrial waste.

As state officials launch a cleanup operation, they are plagued by the grim specter of Lake Apopka. The source of the Oklawaha, the largest tributary to the St. Johns, and the peninsula's fourth largest freshwater lake, covering forty-eight square miles, Apopka once provided the finest largemouth bass fishing to be found in the world. In the 1950s and 1960s, the lake suffocated under tons of nutrients that had run into it over the years from surrounding muck farms. In 1966, one million fish died in Apopka, and the lake has been dead since—a place of trash fish, hyacinths, no diversity of plants and animals. It cannot return on its own, and every remedy, including the proposed draining and cleaning of the lake, as if it were a large bathtub, is expensive to contemplate much less execute. Without the removal of the lucrative muck farms that line its shores, no solution is practical.

During the past fifty years, 62 percent of the floodplain of the St. Johns River, the lush vegetation that so enthralled William Bartram, has been diked, drained, and ditched for farms, groves, and ranches. If normal patterns of development are followed, that agricultural land will soon become covered with suburbs to house the state's booming population. The river suffers, the groundwater suffers, the springs suffer, and so do the wildlife and people. One cannot travel Florida today without bashing into those realities.

Having abandoned the recalcitrant boat for a pickup truck, Girardin drives north from Salt Springs through the Ocala National Forest where maturing forests mix with clear-cut fields, pointing out the vegetation, speculating on what will become of Florida. As he guides the truck across a small bridge crossing a river overhung with thick, moss-laden limbs of live oak and lined with cypress, negative thoughts momentarily slip away. He halts and stares down on the Oklawaha, the river that stopped a canal from rending the peninsula in half. Damaged by a man-made reservoir at its confluence with the St. Johns, the Oklawaha still meanders for much of its seventy-nine miles through a jungle of hardwood. The water is clear here, with a tannin brown hue, and cool, having picked up the Silver Springs Run. Each second 540 to 1,300 cubic feet of water pulse into the run from the springs, plied, as they have been for nearly a century, by glass-bottom boats. They are a tourist mecca and famous; they are transcendent.

Bartram never traveled this way, though in 1823 a warrior seduced by the peninsula did. U.S. Army Lieutenant George McCall said that looking into the pellucid water of the springs was "like looking into the air." Their crystalline beauty enchanted and amazed him. He seemed on top of the bottom though it was forty feet away. Reading McCall, one longs to hear Bartram, the celebrant and poet, scientist and artist, describe the uncultivated Silver Springs.

TWELVE

The Seminole War

Seizing Florida from Spain, Americans wage a war of extermination against its Indians and their black allies. Fear of free slaves and avarice drive the white men.

Dressed as Hamlet, the doubt-wracked Dane, Coacoochee, the Seminole war chief, addressed his white tormentors at Fort Cummings. His subchiefs, Horatio and Richard III, flanked him, while his retinue watched in a grab bag of Shakespearean rags. They'd pulled the costumes from the wagon of a traveling theatrical company they had attacked outside of St. Augustine, murdering the troupe.

It was the fifth of March, 1841; he'd been fighting without rest for four years. After reviewing how the soldiers and their government had deceived him, he addressed an issue beyond their ken:

The land I was upon I loved, my body is made of its sands; the Great Spirit gave me legs to walk over it; hands to aid myself; eyes to see its ponds, rivers, forests, and game; then a head with which I think. The sun, which is warm and bright as my feelings are now, shines to warm us and bring forth our crops, and the moon brings back the spirits of our warriors, our fathers, wives, and children. The white man comes; he grows pale and sick, why cannot we live in peace? I have said I am the enemy to the white man. I could live in peace with them, but they first steal our cattle and horses, cheat us, and

271

take our lands. The white men are as thick as the leaves in
the hammock; they come upon us thicker every year. They
may shoot us, drive our women and children night and day;
they may chain our hands and feet, but the red man's heart
will be always free.[1]

The eloquence of Coacoochee could no better buy an end
to the campaign of extermination and removal than had his
extraordinary prowess in battle. The son of the Miccosukee
chief Philip and the sister of Micanopy, head of the Alachua
Seminole, he had united these two main groups of Florida Indians, but that March, broken, Coacoochee agreed to surrender
within two or three moons. He then began roaming from fort
to fort, collecting free food and whiskey for himself and his
people.

Convinced that Coacoochee intended to delay his formal
surrender until the crops were harvested and his people fed
and rested, when he would resume fighting, Major Thomas
Childs slapped the Indian leader and fifteen of his followers in
irons at Fort Pierce and shipped them all to New Orleans for
exile into Indian Territory. Colonel William J. Worth, the U.S.
Army commander in Florida and the man immortalized in the
nation's richest lake, ordered Coacoochee returned so he
could be used as bait to lure other Indians westward. Manacled
aboard a transport ship anchored two miles off Florida's west
coast, preparing to ask his people to surrender, Coacoochee
addressed his captor:

[The white man] said he was my friend; he abused our
women and children, and told us to go from the land. Still
he gave me his hand in friendship; we took it . . . he had a
snake in the other; his tongue was forked; he lied, and stung
us. I asked but for a small piece of these lands, enough to
plant and to live upon, far south, a spot where I could place
the ashes of my kindred, a spot only sufficient upon which
I could lay my wife and child. This was not granted me. I was
put in prison; I escaped. I have been again taken; you have
brought me back; I am here; I feel the irons in my heart.[2]

After more than two decades of warfare, Worth must have
known that Florida's Indians considered being chained and
manacled physical and spiritual degradation of the worst sort.
They could never accept as a friend a person who approved such

treatment. If he harbored any compassion for his foes, he never expressed it in his deeds. A Quaker by birth, like the pacific William Bartram, Worth was a good and vicious soldier to the end. He continued the long-standing, much condemned practice of seizing Indians under a flag of truce and even added the refinement of luring them into negotiations with food and liquor.

Obeying Worth's command, the thirty-year-old Coacoochee brought in 320 men, women, and children and traveled with them in October 1841 by boat to New Orleans, thence by foot and wagon to Indian Territory, where they were forced into proximity with the Creek, their kinsmen and sworn enemies. In the cold winters, improperly clothed, housed in tents, supported meagerly by a government that, as a matter of policy, cared little for their welfare, they perished, not as free people but as prisoners and exiles.

Four months after Coacoochee's removal, Worth requested of his superiors in Washington, D.C., permission to end hostilities and allow the remaining Seminole to live unmolested in the Everglades and Big Cypress Swamp, arguing that no sane white man wanted that land. Permission refused, the good soldier sent his troops to pursue the Indians by dugout and afoot into the deepest swamps and glades. Under the worthless white flag of truce, Worth engineered the capture of the headman, Halleck, in the spring of 1842, along with 43 warriors, 37 women, and 34 children. As he had done with Coacoochee the previous year, Worth used Halleck as an emissary to induce the last 400 Indians to surrender. Halleck failed in his mission and was shipped with his band to Oklahoma to join the other suffering exiles.

The remaining Indian clans became divided into small groups, living everywhere and nowhere. On August 14, 1842, Worth finally declared an end to the war and left the last undefeated Indians isolated in the south Florida wilderness. Scattered fighting continued for another six months, but as far as the government was concerned the conflict was over. For his performance, Worth was promoted to brigadier general.

The cost to the United States government had finally become too high for the reward—in terms of dollars, men, and materiel. The official number of government dead was 1,466, of whom 328 died in action. The seven-year conflict cost more than $40 million. Various states—primarily Alabama, Georgia, Missouri, Tennessee, and Florida—also lost hundreds of militiamen and several million dollars they barely had, but the winners were still white Americans.

Slave-owning Floridians had secured the territory for themselves, seizing for a fraction of their worth—even when military expenditures were factored in—the fertile soils of the eastern Panhandle and north Florida, the heart of cotton-growing country, as well as the rest of the peninsula. Poor whites could be directed to the less fertile soil of the interior, satisfying their need for land and removing a potential challenge to the privilege of the planters. The federal Armed Occupation Act of 1842 provided 160 acres in "Indian country" for homesteaders who would clear and plant at least 5 acres, and build a home. In two years, 1,312 homesteaders consumed 210,720 acres, with more than a few of them showing up only long enough each year to plant and harvest their crops. By 1845, virtually every piece of Florida lay in someone's name, even if never surveyed. The forts established during the war against the Seminole served as supply depots and later became town sites for the new settlers— thus, Fort Pierce; Fort Lauderdale; Fort Maitland; Fort Dallas, which became Miami; Fort Brooke, Tampa; Fort Bassinger; Fort King, Ocala. Roads built and surveys conducted in prosecution of the war provided additional impetus to settlement of the state.

The war also smashed a thriving culture of Indians and blacks, who lived among them as free people or titular but not hereditary slaves: Their children were free at birth. Many of these blacks—traditionally referred to as Indian Negroes—were runaways from plantations in Georgia, the Carolinas, and later north Florida.

For the United States, the Seminole War encouraged formation of a standing, professional army, as the various state militias, including Florida's, proved incapable of fighting a prolonged war. At the time, Floridians and leaders in other states claimed their citizen-soldiers superior to the United States Army, a band of uncouth, underpaid, abused immigrants and derelicts ruled by officers who thought themselves aristocrats. Despite their claims, the states' volunteer forces were little better. The militiamen went home promptly when their term of service expired, often in mid-campaign, and even while in the field, they barely tolerated the command of professional officers. Florida's militiamen refused to fight unless on horseback, which left them ill-suited for the final years of a conflict that involved slogging through swamps and wet prairies until their feet swelled and lacerations from the sawgrass festered.

In Florida, troops and officers gained experience in Indian warfare and conducted extensive field tests of new weapons, including rockets and repeating rifles. The navy learned amphibious warfare and the army added to its inventory pontoons, invented of necessity for crossing Florida's rivers and swamps.

William Bartram had found the Indians in the vicinity of the Alachua Savanna, along the Suwannee, and near present-day Tallahassee, to be moral and honest people, hunters, herders, garden-plot farmers. Interested in plantations for indigo and sugar and in trade for hides and furs, the British arranged by treaty for the Indians to surrender the east coastal lowlands and take the territory of the highlands and Panhandle—what became cotton country. The Seminole thus came in the 1760s to control the interior and west coast of the peninsula south to the Keys and the Panhandle west nearly to Pensacola. Their access to the sea permitted their trade with Cuba and the Bahamas to flourish, to the annoyance of those British houses seeking commercial monopoly.

An isolated band settled around Charlotte Harbor where its members may have absorbed remnant Calusa, a smattering of Choctaw, and mixed breeds fishing along the coast. At some point, these tribes and people appear to have coalesced into a group known as the "Spanish Indians," led in the 1830s and early 1840s by Chakaika, a giant of a man, standing six and a half feet tall and weighing nearly three hundred pounds. Named by whites because of their language, which combined Spanish and various Indian dialects, this group engineered some of the most daring and bloody raids of the war, including one against Lieutenant Colonel William Harney on the Caloosahatchee River in 1839 and another against Jacob Housman, a wrecker and trader on Indian Key.

Harney came to establish a store to serve Indians theoretically at peace with the white men. After provoking an attack on his camp, he escaped with his life, something few of his men accomplished. Housman, who abused the Indians while taking their goods, fled a raid that resulted in destruction of his key and the death of Dr. Henry Perrine, a pioneering horticulturist sitting out the war on the island in the hope he could soon take possession of his twenty-four-thousand-acre township on the

Florida mainland, between Cape Florida and Cape Sable. The township later fell into the hands of Henry Flagler and now is a mix of urban sprawl, fruit groves, and vegetable fields named for the physician.

The former United States consul in the Yucatan, Perrine wished to establish the cultivation of tropical plants in the United States and lobbied Congress for the south Florida land grant. When the Indians attacked on August 7, 1840, Perrine tried to reason with them and stalled them long enough for his wife and children to duck into a tunnel leading from the house to the turtle kraal and safety in the shallow water under a dock.

After Perrine was murdered and his body and papers burned with his home, Chakaika became the most wanted of chiefs, and Harney finally ambushed him in the Everglades, avenging himself and Perrine. In an act of barbarism, he strung his victim's corpse from a tree and left it to rot, beside those of two other Indians he had hanged. After the raid, Harney crossed the Everglades from east to west, completing his expedition at the river that today bears his name.

The battles of the 1830s and 1840s represented the culmination of nearly fifty years of struggle between Americans and the Seminole for possession of Florida. The opportunistic Spaniards joined the American War of Independence in its closing days, in sufficient time to wrest Florida from a drained England in the Treaty of 1783. After attempting unsuccessfully to revive its discredited mission system, Spain awarded a trade monopoly to the British firm of Panton, Leslie, and Company, a move the Indians approved, for among the partners in that firm was Alexander McGillivray, an Upper Creek leader.

Son of a Scottish father and French-Upper Creek mother, McGillivray was a mico, a major chief, who through his position in the trading company also assumed the role of spokesmen for the Florida Seminole. He despised Georgians and other Americans out to grab Indian lands and tried whenever possible to foment conflict between the United States and Spain, in order to keep them occupied with each other and out of Creek affairs. Accused by his American foes of being a Spanish agent, he was the only force binding the Seminole to the Creek Federation.

His foremost rival in Indian affairs was William Augustus Bowles, a loyalist who married the daughter of a Lower Creek chief named Perryman and moved with her to the Bahamas when Britain surrendered Florida. From his base on the islands, he traded with east coast Seminole for the British firm of Miller, Bonnany, and Company. Agitating among Florida Indians of Lower Creek origin, he sought to break the monopoly of McGillivray's firm and establish a "State of Muskogee," with himself as leader. In 1792, he captured the Panton, Leslie store in St. Marks and was in turn seized under a flag of truce by Spanish forces. He was shipped first to Cuba then to the Philippines, whence he made his way back to Florida and attempted unsuccessfully to reestablish his influence after McGillivray's death in 1793. The turmoil following the loss of two charismatic, powerful leaders produced more independent Indians in Florida, groups bent on converting their geographical separateness from their Creek cousins to the north into political independence.

In 1811, the Americans struck at the Spanish territory. With the not so clandestine backing of the federal government, Georgia adventurer George Mathews seized Amelia Island, Fernandina, and Fort Moosa, and proclaimed an independent republic. The United States government, threatened by the British and Creeks intent on avoiding dispossession and assimilation, dropped their support of Mathews, and the Alachua Seminole counterattacked at the behest of hapless Spanish officials. The Indians needed little persuasion, since white Georgians regularly raided their villages and the settlements of blacks in their midst, stealing people and cattle. Georgia militiamen marched on the Indian villages in 1812 to relieve Mathews but were repulsed. Tennessee volunteers and U.S. Army troops then conducted retaliatory raids against the Seminole early in 1813, destroying homes and food stocks. Mathews's republic failed without strong U.S. support.

In 1814, Andrew Jackson, fresh from the unnecessary Battle of New Orleans, smashed the Creek Federation, sending several thousand Upper Creek refugees (Red Sticks) into Florida where they mingled with the Seminole, infusing them with fresh anti-Americanism. During the next few years, Jackson supported various extralegal campaigns against Florida's Indians and free blacks.

The loyalty of the Indians toward the blacks living among them continues to confound observers. Reports from the time indicate that the blacks were Ashanti, Ibo, Egba, Senegalese— considered the fiercest tribes in Africa. While relying on them heavily as allies, laborers, and interpreters, the Indians shunned intermarriage with them, as they did with all non-Indians (despite the tribal ban, unions between blacks or whites and Indians did occur). The largest black settlement was around a British earthen redoubt built during the War of 1812 called Fort Prospect Bluff on the Apalachicola River, which American whites called "the Negro fort." For fifty miles upstream and downstream of the fort, free blacks and runaways resided after 1814.

In 1816, the United States Army built Fort Scott on the Flint River, a tributary of the Apalachicola on the Georgia-Florida border. In order to provoke a response from the blacks along the river, Andrew Jackson, then Major General of the Army, ordered his subaltern in the southern district, Brigadier General Edmund Pendleton Gaines, to supply the new fort from the Gulf of Mexico by way of the Apalachicola River, in direct violation of international law, since he would be passing through Spanish territory. When the blacks shot at his gunboat, Gaines ordered hot shells fired into Fort Prospect Bluff, which blew up the ammunition storehouse, destroying the fort and 270 of its defenders—men, women, and children. Only 64 people survived.

White Georgians continued to conduct raids across the border to steal slaves and cattle and to loot Indian villages. The Seminole retaliated when possible. In March 1818, Jackson led a force of two thousand marauders, including Coweta Indians, into the Panhandle where he sacked and burned native towns. Among the few Indians he captured rather than killed was a teenager whose name was variously transliterated as Ussa-Yahola (Black Drink Hallo-er), Asse Heholar, Hasse Ola, Assi-ola, and finally Osceola.[3]

Jackson invaded Florida with the backing of President James Monroe and in the face of minority opposition in Congress. The goal, said the President and his general, was to suppress black, Indian, and white agitators, smugglers, and pirates. In 1819, Spain capitulated to the real motive for the assault and agreed to cede Florida to the United States, although the treaty was not formalized for two more years. Thus ended what is often called the First Seminole War though the conflict was of a piece with those that followed.

Named first governor of the new United States territory, Jackson soon grew bored and retired to his Tennessee home and national politics. In 1821, William Duval, an Indian hater and Jackson loyalist, became governor, and Gad Humphreys, a political ally, was named Indian agent. The new rulers of Florida were already agitating for removal of the Indians, many of whom, after Jackson's attacks, had fled to the peninsula's interior, out of the line of white migration. The Americans also pressed even harder for enslavement of the blacks living among the Indians, claiming they were all runaways.

At the time, the five thousand Seminole occupied nearly forty villages, concentrated along the Apalachicola River and through what came to be called Middle Florida to the Suwannee River. In the Central Highlands, their territory extended from the Alachua Savanna south to Tampa Bay, with more isolated villages around Lake Worth and Charlotte Harbor. Geographically and linguistically the Seminole were split broadly into Mikasuki (referred to in this text by the modern spelling Miccosukee), who were Hitchiti speakers, the language of the Lower Creek, and Indians, who spoke Muskogee, the language of the Upper Creek. The Tallahassees, Muskogee speakers, lived in the hill country now known by that name.

Differences among groups are difficult to sort out today, but early in the eighteenth century, Florida's Indians represented many bands that once had belonged to the Creek Federation. The white conquerers for their own convenience came to lump them all together as Seminole; and until the Miccosukee forced their recognition as a tribe in 1962—after their leader Buffalo Tiger arranged acceptance from several foreign governments, including that of Fidel Castro in Cuba—Florida's Indians were known by that name.

The lands the tribes occupied were the most suitable in Florida for plantation farming. Moving to secure the region, United States agents led by James Gadsden, a friend of Andrew Jackson, coerced thirty-two chiefs, including the titular head of the incipient Seminole nation, Neamathla, to sign in 1823 near St. Augustine what became known as the Treaty of Moultrie Creek. The Indians agreed to relinquish their claim to all of Florida except for a four-million-acre reservation in the interior of the peninsula, below a line running from Tampa Bay to the east coast, and a smaller territory for Neamathla and his allies in the Apalachicola basin. According to the American interpretation, the chiefs ceded more than twenty-eight million acres to the United States. The Indians also agreed to turn over runaway slaves and fugitives in their midst and to cease direct trade with Cuba. The terms of the treaty were fixed at twenty years for Indian occupation of the reservation, at the end of which time they could be moved; the monetary value, when all direct payments and rations were figured, amounted to about seventy-eight cents an acre. In a concession to reality, the federal government agreed to extend the reservation borders northward to include agriculturally fertile land, if necessary to ward off starvation. Nowhere did the boundary come closer than twenty miles to the coast.

The migration of white slave-owning planters into Middle Florida from the depleted soils of Virginia, the Carolinas, and Georgia accelerated. They established cotton plantations on the rich alluvial soils and hammock land from Apalachicola to the Suwannee and soon spilled across north Florida. Along the coasts, they created huge sugar plantations, expanding on those already cultivated by settlers from the Spanish and British colonial periods.

Under federal law, farmers could purchase eighty acres at $1.25 an acre if they settled it and filed appropriate notice at the land office. Some were yeomen, others speculators out to fulfill minimum requirements and make a profit. Men receiving both the choice assignments in the government of the new territory and the prime agricultural land were Jackson loyalists.

The rapid settlement demanded a new geopolitical arrangement, for it became difficult for delegates to the territorial legislature to make the alternating trips between Pensacola and St. Augustine, the capitals of West and East Florida respectively. In 1824, Tallahassee, lying midway between the old Spanish settlements, was named capital of the territory and soon became the center, as well, of the thriving plantation culture of Florida. It was a world organized for white males, with only those over twenty-one years of age eligible for the full prerogatives of citizenship, including the right to vote.

Through most of the territorial period, transportation remained difficult, with roads often consisting of no more than logs laid side by side and becoming quagmires after even moderate rain. With federal aid, territorial officials built a twenty-five-foot-wide road through their new capital from St. Augustine to Pensacola, some four hundred miles, at a cost of $20,000. Another road ran from New Smyrna to ten miles north of the tiny settlement called Cowsford that became Jacksonville. Male citizens were required to donate twelve days a year to maintenance of the road, a requirement many ignored or satisfied by sending their slaves. It took ten days to travel round-trip from

St. Augustine to Tallahassee, thirty for the mail to reach Pensacola.

Ellen Call Long, daughter of the fourth territorial governor, Richard Keith Call, recalled the first years of American occupancy in her *Florida Breezes:* "[M]any who had already come to stay left in disgust, proclaiming abroad that Florida was but a sand bank; but others told of cotton fifteen feet high, ten stalks of sugar-cane to the bud, and where the lands had escaped annual burning, were found spontaneous the tender plants of Cuba, in the hiaco plum, orange, mangrove, maguey, and even coffee on the extreme peninsula."[4]

Those who stayed, including Call, dubbed the territory "the Eden of America," while arguing it would be better with the Indians gone and with more certain lines of communication and transportation. A Jacksonian and general of the territorial militia, Call resurrected the dream of Menéndez of a canal across the peninsula—connecting the Suwannee and St. Johns rivers—that would bring business to new settlements and allow ships to bypass the treacherous Straits of Florida. But repeated surveys proved it impractical by the 1830s, and developers had become enamored of railroads, the first of those being a mule-drawn monstrosity running from Tallahassee to St. Marks to haul primarily cotton. This track boasted of being only the third railway built in the country, a sizable achievement, supporters claimed, for a sparsely populated region.

The white males with money and property who exercised power in north Florida believed that by consigning the Indians to the territory's poorest land, they would leave them little option but to move out of the territory in search of better conditions. Instead the Indians either moved off the reservation or refused to enter it in the first place—wisely, because conditions there were atrocious. Drought in 1825, combined with the loss of their old fields and the poorness of reservation soil, brought famine to the Indians. Those who had put themselves in the care of the government received insufficient rations to survive and so began to hunt their former land with the recalcitrants. The whites who had flocked into Middle Florida claimed that the wandering, starving hunters threatened their lives and herds, usually of scrub cattle belonging no more to one man than to another.

In 1826, Indian Agent Gad Humphreys engineered the election of a primary chief for all the Seminole, a move he and other officials believed would unite the Indians and make them more malleable. The whites backed Tuckose Emathla, whom they called John Hicks, a Miccosukee. Humphreys and his colleagues wanted a Miccosukee because they were more numerous and pacific than the Alachua Seminole, who claimed primacy in the nation's affairs because of their longevity in Florida. Although John Hicks lacked power within the world of the Indians, he embodied a chain of command whites could understand and in their eyes was the leader of the Seminole tribe.

The famine and suffering of the Seminole worsened after a hard freeze in 1828, which some observers attributed to deforestation for plantations—an argument echoed 150 years later by scientists examining the effects of logging on Florida's climate. Traders wandered the reservation, selling rotgut liquor to the Indians, thereby stealing their government dole and casting them deeper into poverty.

For their part, the Seminole handed runaways over to their owners only to hear them demand all blacks living among the tribes. Some white traders sold slaves to the Indians, then demanded their return on the grounds that they were fugitives. Racial slurs; derogatory comments about dirty, shiftless, drunken Indians; and physical abuse became commonplace. Because they practiced premarital sex and polygamy, the Indians were adjudged lewd; because they gambled, they were thought cheats; because they were Indian, ugly. The portrait, of course, is the negative of "white" virtues. Yet Bartram and other reliable observers commented consistently on the comeliness, honesty, and morality of the Seminole. Agent Gad Humphreys occasionally defended them and placed the blame for the conflict squarely on greedy whites, but the situation worsened.

In 1832, a new territory was forced upon the Indians at Payne's Landing on the scenic Oklawaha River. James Gadsden, the architect of the Treaty of Moultrie Creek, stage-managed the parlay. He told the Indians present that the government would not continue to feed them on their Florida reservation and that they must move to land in the western Indian Territory they would share with their sworn enemies and kinsmen, the Creek. According to later reports, Gadsden bribed the black interpreter Abraham to misrepresent the treaty in order to get the signatures of the chiefs. Given that Abraham couldn't read and that the treaty was couched in indecipherable ambiguity, whether the adviser was corrupted or simply doubly betrayed along with the

Seminole is an unresolvable question. But clearly, the federal government's agent used whatever tactics he felt necessary to secure the signatures of seven chiefs and eight subchiefs on a document obligating the Seminole to send their leaders to inspect the Creek reservation and pledging removal there of the entire nation, should they approve the country. Under terms of the treaty, the Seminole also were to surrender their four-million-acre Florida reservation for cash and grants totaling $80,000—or two cents an acre. They were to move west over a three-year period, become part of the Creek nation, and draw their annuity from its leaders. They also would give up all fugitive slaves in their midst—another vague demand that could be stretched to include every black person among them.

The chiefs later argued they would never have agreed to such lunacy had they understood it, because they lacked the power to make such absolute decisions. Furthermore, Micanopy, leader of the Alachua Seminole, and several other micos swore they never signed the treaty. They charged that Gadsden had coerced young warriors into forging the marks of their leaders. Objective white observers condemned the treaty as a fraud and a blight on the nation's honor, but they lacked the authority to alter it.

In October 1832, seven chiefs and Abraham traveled to the Creek lands in the Indian Territory of present-day Oklahoma. They disliked what they saw, but government agents at Fort Gibson in the territory forced them to sign a document agreeing on behalf of the Seminole nation to relocate there over the next three years, as specified in the Treaty of Payne's Landing. By some accounts, the agents said the chiefs could not return home until they signed the paper.

The only Florida Indians to ally themselves with the whites were the Apalachicolas, living along the river, who, despite abuse from raiders, served as scouts and spies for American forces fighting the Indians of the peninsula. As a reward for their loyalty to whites and betrayal of their kinsmen, the Apalachicolas were exiled to northeastern Texas between 1832 and 1838.

The Seminole had no plans to move within three years or a lifetime. In 1835, the year set for the migration to begin, a February freeze—perhaps the harshest to hit the peninsula in a century—devastated crops, destroyed orange groves, killed cattle and wildlife, and drove the Seminole to the edge of starvation. Government agents attempted to use the Indians' hardship as leverage for forcing them to abandon their homes. After months of acrimonious debate, during which Osceola emerged as the spiritual leader of the intransigents, U.S. Indian Agent Wiley Thompson forced sixteen chiefs to reaffirm the Treaties of Payne's Landing and Fort Gibson. He struck from the list of chiefs the names of five who refused to do so—Micanopy, Jumper, Holata Mico, Arpeika (whom whites called Sam Jones), and Coa Hadjo. At one conference, according to legend, Osceola, the handsome and bold war leader, slashed the treaty of Fort Gibson while it lay open before General Duncan Clinch, stating that the Indians did not recognize it.

In June, Thompson seized and chained Osceola until he agreed to sign a paper validating the Treaty of Payne's Landing and to bring in his followers to prepare for migration. Seventy-nine came into Fort King and left nearly as soon as Osceola was free. In November, Osceola killed Charley Emathla, a chief who was preparing to move his people to Indian Territory, and the Second Seminole War began. George McCall, a young officer who had marveled at Silver Springs, the beauty of the peninsula, and the honesty of the Indians wrote, "This outbreak of the Seminole, which I predict will prove to be a seven years' war, and cost us fifty millions of dollars, has been brought about either by huge blundering, or by unfair dealings on the part of Government agents."[5] He was correct on all counts.

The Indians tended to attack travelers, homesteads, and plantations near the borders of their reservation or in their homeland around the Alachua Savanna and on the east coast around St. Augustine. By the end of 1835, they had destroyed a number of sugar plantations on the Coastal Lowlands that were among the oldest on the peninsula. Settlers abandoned their homes, leaving the Central Highlands' rivers and the east coast below St. Augustine nearly clear of white people. Ammunition and food were in short supply in other white settlements, as the Indians, who had stockpiled both, roamed the country. Planters in many areas sought to keep the Florida militia under General Richard Keith Call from entering their land, for fear the vigilantes' presence would draw Indians into a ruinous attack, a sentiment revealing the esteem in which the citizen—soldiers of Florida were held.

The U.S. Army's first commander in the war, Duncan Clinch, was more intent on protecting his holdings in north

Florida and southern Georgia than on engaging the Indians. In December 1835, he drew most of his force from Fort King, site of the Indian agency, north to his plantation. On December 28, Osceola gained vengeance against Indian Agent Wiley Thompson, murdering him while he was taking an after-dinner walk and dividing his scalp among the warriors who participated in the assault.

That morning, a force of Seminole had ambushed a regular army troop of 108 men marching from Fort Brooke to Fort King under the direction of Major Francis Dade. Later reports held that the troop's slave-guide, Louis Pacheco, betrayed its movements to the Indians, and he may have for he fled to the protection of his masters' enemy. The Seminole, attacking as the troop entered a stretch of piney woods, killed all but 3 men, although only 1 lived long enough to describe the incident. The Indians carried the soldiers' food and ammunition from the site of the battle, which came to be called the Dade Massacre and is commemorated by a state park. Black fighters came after their Seminole allies had left, killed the wounded, and scalped and looted the dead. Though he had planned the ambush on the column, Osceola did not participate because his allies had sprung the trap before he had killed Wiley Thompson at Fort King, fifty miles north of the Dade Massacre. Nonetheless, he was invoked as the physical leader of the assault by fearful whites.

Florida's territorial leaders issued a summons throughout the south for volunteers to fight the "savages," especially the "Negro-Indians," considered the most brutal and threatening of the lot. As a bonus for their efforts, they were to divide twenty thousand head of Indian cattle and several million acres of land.

Clinch, with his troops ensconced in the slave quarters of his plantation, renamed Fort Drane, dithered over how to attack the Seminole, who cut his supply lines at will. The army possessed inaccurate maps and nearly no firsthand knowledge of the countryside. Incapable of feeding themselves on the march and too incompetent to develop adequate supply lines, they could stay in the field only as long as their rations held—no more than two weeks. They also limited their campaigns to the dry months, avoiding the summer, the "sickly season."

In 1836, Winfield Scott replaced Clinch as commander of the U.S. Army troops in Florida. A proper soldier, author of the army's training and combat manual, Scott stated publicly that white Floridians were paranoid about Indians and as a result panicked at the faintest whisper of attack. Richard Call, leader of the state militia and the new territorial governor, as well as one of the most belligerent Floridians of his day, concurred. A number of white males of the territory then burned Scott in effigy and denounced Call while continuing to demand the removal of the Indians—by the United States government. Finally, dissenters from the war were forced to retreat from public debate. In 1836, 103 company commanders resigned their commissions in the army rather than continue service in Florida. A number of those objected to the disease—mumps, measles, malaria, yellow fever, and cholera were epidemic—and lack of support; others opposed the conflict as unjust.

Florida militiamen rotated through the war zone—thirteen thousand in 1835–36—drawing six dollars a month in pay, going home as soon as their three-month hitch ended. They spent much of their time in the field arguing with regular troops, whom they resented—the officers for their education and privilege; the enlisted men for their humble origins. Each party thought the other incapable of successfully prosecuting the war and set out to prove their case through subversion and outright disobedience.

Winfield Scott attempted to mount a traditional campaign against the Indians and failed, as his horses and men faltered for lack of provisions. The Seminole under Osceola, Alligator, Jumper, Philip, Coacoochee, Arpeika, and Abraham continued to snipe at them from hammocks and swamps then fade away before the troopers, encumbered with supplies and artillery, could form scrimmage lines to retaliate. Frustrated and weary, Scott left Florida before the summer of 1836. Intent on displaying the virtue of citizen-soldiers, Call then led a summer campaign more notable for its bombast than for its military success. He lost six hundred horses to starvation and his men suffered famine because supply lines were nonexistent.

In the fall, Thomas Jesup assumed command of the forces in Florida and soon commenced a war of attrition and betrayal that rates as one of the more disgraceful episodes in the army's dishonorable treatment of Native Americans. Continuing the practice of sowing discord among the Indians, Jesup regularly employed a large force of Apalachicola and Creek spies and scouts, supplementing them, when possible, with warriors from western tribes. He also sent a letter to raise recruits in which he stated, "This is a negro not an Indian War."[6] Jesup, Quartermaster General of the Army before his assignment to Florida, organized supply lines and divided his forces to pursue the Seminole into their territory. Under the command of Alexander Dallas, for whom the fort at the mouth of the Miami River was named, a naval force comprised of a schooner, four steamboats, and four cutters—the largest in the United States at that time— prowled the coastline in an unsuccessful attempt to cut off the Indians' trade with Cuba and the Bahamas.

Jesup achieved his greatest victories through treachery. In March 1837, at Fort Dade, he agreed with three Seminole leaders acting on behalf of Micanopy, the dominant chief of the Alachua, to allow all blacks among them to migrate with them to the Indian Territory. When white slavers objected to the arrangement, Jesup renegotiated with the chiefs to turn over all blacks who had come to live with them during the war—whether fugitives or captives from plantation raids. He also drove off and killed Indian cattle so that those Seminole, honoring the truce, who came to Fort Brooke for removal, would be dependent on the pitiful government dole. Osceola and Arpeika raided the detention camp and led seven hundred men, women, and children back into the interior of the peninsula.

Inadvertently, perhaps, Jesup had begun to divide blacks and Indians through his equivocation and secret deals. By fall, some fugitives returned to their plantations because the constant movement and hunger associated with the conflict had worn them down—body and soul. Jesup offered freedom and protection to any blacks who turned themselves in, then betrayed those who did so, awarding them as booty to his troops and Creek mercenaries in his service. The flow of surrendering blacks immediately dried up. After floundering for several additional months, Jesup began simply to ship all blacks who dropped out of the war west with captive Seminole, as he had originally promised, and within a year he had succeeded in draining a significant percentage of the black warriors from the battlefield. The action outraged white slavers who continued to trade in the people, as if they were futures, and initially dogged the exile troop along its route west. But the courts ruled in favor of the blacks and Indians. Zachary Taylor, who succeeded Jesup in command of the Florida war, continued that policy, earning for himself opprobrium from the more rabid whites.

Pausing only for intermittent truces, which he invariably violated, Jesup pursued the Seminole across Florida, bringing steamboats into battle, building roads and forts, employing new revolvers, rifles, and shotguns, threatening to deploy blood-hounds. He commanded a force of up to nine thousand regular troops and militiamen—the largest in the country—but he could not win by fighting. Early in the fall of 1837, he seized Coacoo-chee, after capturing his father, Philip, and Blue Snake under a flag of truce, in direct violation of every rule of warfare. Then, in October 1837, Joseph Hernandez, a Spanish Floridian and the territory's first representative to the United States Congress, acting on orders from Jesup and as a brigadier general in the state militia, went to meet with Osceola and Coa Hadjo under a flag of truce and imprisoned them.

Osceola, generally recognized as the spiritual and tactical leader of the Seminole, was incarcerated in St. Augustine at Fort Marion and then the Castillo de San Marcos, along with Coacoo-chee and the black John Cowaya, both of whom escaped from the prison by slipping through a fifteen-inch gap in the bars of their cell and sliding down a rope made of sheets. They brought sixteen warriors and two women out of captivity with them, when they fled the old city. Osceola stayed; some say he was suffering from the quinsy and malaria that killed him.

Transferred to Fort Moultrie in Charleston, South Caro-lina, so he could have no contact with the Seminole in Florida or the Indian Territory, Osceola continued in declining health. Shortly before Osceola died on January 31, 1838, he allowed the artist George Catlin to interview him and paint his portrait, which now resides in the Smithsonian Institution. The war leader's family and close followers could not prevent the presid-ing surgeon, Frederick Weedon, from desecrating his corpse by removing his head and taking it to his home in St. Augustine, where he used it to intimidate his children.[7] The skull traveled eventually to the Surgical and Pathological Museum in New York where it vanished during a fire in 1866; Frederick Weedon went unpunished in this life, as did General Jesup.

Osceola, in one of those peculiar twists, became a folk hero, the proud and noble warrior fighting to preserve his homeland from rapacious invaders. Unfortunately, he could no more end the war through martyrdom than through his courage in battle. Today, some twenty towns, three counties, two townships, one borough, two lakes, two mountains, one state park, and one national forest (in Florida) in the United States bear his name.[8]

Publicity generated by the capture of Osceola and a na-tional economic depression combined to bring to Florida more

Migrant workers picking grapefruit early in the 1920s in central Florida

The deep muck soil of the Everglades Agricultural Area around Lake Okeechobee demanded special equipment, like this treaded tractor, roller, and plow used in the 1920s.

Migrant workers' hovel at Belle Glade on the south shore of Lake Okeechobee in 1939

The Miami River and the Miami River Canal, which superseded it, are shown in this January 1912 photograph. The hammock in the foreground is now Miami, which stretches deep into the eastern Everglades.

A dredge works on the Tamiami Canal (ca. 1921), which paralleled the road crossing the Everglades and then running up the west coast to link Miami with Tampa.

Charles Torrey Simpson, John Victor Soar, and Paul Matthaus carry saw cabbage palm out of the hammock near Madeira Bay in south Florida.

PHOTO BY JOHN KUNKEL SMALL, FLORIDA STATE ARCHIVES

Wading birds in the Everglades are threatened by urbanization and declining water levels.

Airboats are the best way to travel through the sawgrass marsh of the Everglades.

bove, the mangrove forest of Cocoplum Beach
ar Miami in September 1925

ght, Hernando de Soto in the Florida forest

FROM NEVIN O. WINTERS, *Florida: The Land of Enchantment*, CA. 1918, FLORIDA STATE ARCHIVES

Theodore de Bry's engraving of French artist Jacques Le Moyne's painting of an Indian raid in the sixteenth century

Artist's reconstruction of the landing of Pedro Menéndez de Avilés on the shore of Biscayne Bay in 1567

Left, Seminole war leader and chief Coacoochee. Right, freedmen and their children outside the slave quarters of the Kingsley Plantation, ca. 1880

Etching from *Harper's New Monthly Magazine* of wreckers from Key West at work in the 1850s

Walt Disney's property in central Florida, photographed in 1967

Disney World just before its opening in 1971

militiamen and adventurers than Jesup could integrate into his
troop, so he turned the defense of north Florida over to the
volunteers and pursued the Indians with his fighting forces,
capturing chiefs, subchiefs, warriors and their families, impris-
oning those he feared would escape, and holding the rest in
detention camps until he could ship them west. Coacoochee and
Arpeika, the aged Miccosukee medicine man, became the dominant war leaders of the intransigents, as those Indians, primarily
Miccosukee and Tallahassee, refusing to leave their homes came
to be known. They fled south toward Lake Okeechobee and
Jesup sent seven columns in pursuit, with one, led by Colonel
Zachary Taylor, driving down the Kissimmee River.

Above Lake Okeechobee on Christmas Day, 1837, Taylor
fought one of the largest battles of the war against Arpeika,
Coacoochee, Alligator, and some 400 warriors. Taylor led just
over 1,000 men, most of them regular troops, but he sent his
Missouri volunteers as the vanguard through a sawgrass prairie the Indians had torched to provide open lines of fire. Seminole riflemen cut the Missourians to pieces, then shot up the
regular infantrymen before giving way to the superior force.
Taylor lost 26 men, with another 112 wounded, while Indian
casualties were 11 and 14, respectively, but because the Seminole withdrew to the lake and then faded into the countryside,
his assault was declared a major victory. The Missourians complained that he had made them sacrificial lambs by sending
them first into combat, while Taylor said they had fled after
the opening volley and been shot from behind. He survived
the controversy; more important from a military standpoint, he
proved that it was possible to take the battle into the last
stronghold of the Indians.

Jesup was wounded in the Battle of Loxahatchee on January
24, 1838, another victory in which the government troops suffered heavier casualties than the Indian forces they defeated. In
his final act as commander of the Florida troops, Jesup parlayed
with the last free Indians, wined them, dined them, and promised they could stay in the interior of south Florida. He wrote
to Washington, D.C., to Secretary of War Joel Poinsett request-
ing approval of his pledge. When it was denied on March 17,
1838, Jesup ordered the Indians camped nearby under terms of
a truce seized. In all more than 500 were captured, including
151 warriors, and shipped to Indian Territory. Soon Jesup
gained reassignment from Florida, having sent 2,900 Seminole
Indians into exile and killed 100 more. Perhaps 1,200 remained

in scattered bands, fighting, attempting to hunt and plant gardens, for their cattle were gone—stolen, driven off, shot—and they had nothing but the land and salvage for survival.

Neither Indian nor black—no man, woman, or child among them—escaped hunger and exhaustion, constant fear that any move might result in capture or death. Mothers taught their children to play in absolute silence. Widows gave their late husbands' guns and ammunition to warriors who would take up the battle, leaving less for hunting, and by all accounts the women were among the most adamantly opposed to migrating from Florida. The fall, winter, and spring campaigns of the white troops prevented the Seminole from planting and harvesting crops, year after year, because those are the growing seasons in Florida.

When Zachary Taylor assumed command of U.S. Army troops in Florida in 1838, the war had already cost more than $9 million, and there was no end in sight. Taylor sought to establish a line from New Smyrna on the east coast to Fort Brooke on the west to divide whites from Indians. Wetlands comprised 60 to 70 percent of the area south of the line; north of it lay rich farmland, rivers, and springs. Planters and speculators poured into every open area, with the population of the territory increasing by twenty thousand between 1830 and 1840. The boundary proved a fiction. Indian raiding parties ranged through the state attacking isolated homes and wagons. Most of the time, they struck not the powerful, monied interests opposing them but poor Crackers in shacks in the pinelands, people who became implacable enemies, as sudden in exacting vengeance as the Indians. Proof that the cycle of violence was unnecessary came from those few whites who, having befriended the Seminole, remained unmolested by them through the hostilities; but far from serving as models, they became pariahs among their countrymen.

War was profitable, and many of the same people who screamed for the total defeat of the Indians were loath for the conflict to end. A government policy of providing free rations to settlers fleeing their homesteads had created semipermanent colonies of refugees around army forts, with many of the people staying for years. Individuals who claimed the Indians had seized their slaves or enticed them to run off would accept government compensation and later attempt to reclaim those same slaves for which they had been paid. In some cases, owners were reimbursed two or three times for the same person. Weary of those abuses and the general whining of the local political leaders, Taylor finally charged that white Floridians were deliberately provoking the Indians by kidnapping blacks and stealing cattle in order to continue the conflict.

The United States military also financed public works that the territory could not otherwise have constructed. Taylor's troops alone built 848 miles of road, established fifty-three posts that became the nuclei for settlements, and constructed 3,643 feet of causeways and bridges.

The political debate over the war was a cacophony of conflicting special interests. Following the lead of Richard Call, many of Florida's whites proclaimed the regular army incapable of bringing the Indians to bay. They repeatedly urged the use of more militiamen, advice Taylor ignored, having learned from bitter experience that the civilians were brave only while on horseback and under all circumstances were indifferent soldiers who would not leave the vicinity of their homes. In the wetlands, horses were an impediment, not an aid. Call's charges and demands became so obstreperous that in 1839, he was relieved of his office as territorial governor by President Martin Van Buren. Florida's delegate to Congress, David Yulee, argued for more troops and more aid so that every Indian could be removed, every black enslaved. Others in Congress saw the war against the Indians as a slave grab and used debate over it to press the case for abolition—an issue they were otherwise prohibited from addressing directly.

In 1839, the Territorial Council of Florida, having heard about the bloodhounds that ran rebels to ground in the Jamaica Maroon Revolt, 1655 to 1739, sent to Cuba for a pack of dogs and their trainers. Jesup had first threatened to bring in the animals; now the Floridians paid $151.72 each for thirty-two dogs, and Taylor agreed to try two of them in south Florida. The bloodhounds, trained to track fugitive slaves, refused to take the trail of Indians, but their presence provoked outrage throughout the United States. Dogs, the argument went, should not be used against free people. The bloodhounds were turned to other tasks, while the Territorial Council sent the U.S. Army the bill for all of them.

Exhausted and frustrated, Taylor resigned his Florida post in 1840. His successor, Walker Armistead, an incompetent officer, allowed the Indian haters among white Floridians and within his command to run rampant. Chief among them was William Harney, for this was the year Chakaika and his Spanish

Indians attacked the lieutenant colonel, burned Indian Key, killed Henry Perrine, and was in turn beaten. On that occasion, Harney disguised himself and his men as Indians, contrary to Armistead's orders, so they could sneak up on the hammock where Chakaika and his band were camped. It was Armistead whom Coacoochee came to meet at Fort Cummings, when, arrayed as Hamlet, he delivered his soliloquy.

Armistead's successor, William Worth, commanded more than five thousand regular troops—the highest number in the territory at any time. All militiamen were out of service by then because they cost more and were less reliable. It was Worth who ordered Coacoochee to lead his people into exile, who seized others under flags of truce, and who perfected the tactic of sending small dugout-borne squads of men to roust Indians from their hammocks in the Everglades and swamp, with Harney becoming the best of his subalterns at the attacks. George McCall, promoted to captain, found the slogging so laborious and painful that he began to think the land he'd once called Eden had turned to hell.

Worth gained his most lasting renown for bringing the war to a close in 1842, with perhaps 300 to 400 Indians still at large. Worth promised the Indians that they could remain south of a line from Charlotte Harbor to the middle of Lake Okeechobee and west of a line from that point to Cape Sable—roughly the Big Cypress Swamp and Everglades, land no white men wanted. Lieutenant William Tecumseh Sherman, who successfully marched through Georgia little more than two decades later and became one of the most feared army leaders in the wars of extermination against the Plains Indians, had come to the territory to serve under Armistead and was there at the end. By then 3,824 Indians and blacks had been shipped to the reservation in the Arkansas Territory.

The truce lasted until 1849, when word spread of the murder of five white men in south Florida and whites fled their farms and plantations. Chief Billy Bowlegs turned over the killers, but cries grew louder for the removal of the last of the Indians. In 1851, after passage of The Swamp Lands Act, the state legislature passed a resolution demanding that action so it could claim every last soggy acre for its profit and benefit. Florida officials commissioned a con artist from Alabama named Luther Blake to bribe the remaining Indians to migrate; he persuaded thirty-six to do so and charged the state $48,000. For their part, white settlers, speculators, and soldiers began to encroach on the demilitarized zone Worth had created and on Indian territory as well.

In 1855, members of an army surveying party led by one Lieutenant George Hartsuff found Billy Bowlegs's hammock garden and ruined his banana plants. They were invaders and hostile, so Billy Bowlegs raided their camp, and the troopers retired to report an attack. Secretary of War for the United States Jefferson Davis issued orders to the commanding general, William Harney, to clean out the Indians, and his troops commenced a hammock-to-hammock search in what became known as the Third Seminole War.

This time the government supplemented its troops with civilian hunters like Jacob Michler who were paid bounties for the living Indians they brought in for removal. The government also paid Chief Billy Bowlegs $6,500 for surrendering, with $1,000 apiece for each of his four subchiefs, $500 for warriors, and $100 for each woman and child. As the Civil War burst over the nation, officials turned their attention elsewhere, leaving one hundred Indians in the remote areas of south Florida, so isolated no one bothered to pursue or find them, although as whites two decades later began to colonize the region some agitated for the removal even of that remnant.

Not until 1934 and 1937 did the Seminole finally sign treaties with the federal government that formally marked the end of the war of removal and fixed the boundaries of their south Florida reservations—Big Cypress, Brighton (on the northwest shore of Lake Okeechobee), Immokalee, and Hollywood. The Miccosukee have a reservation at Forty Mile Bend off the Tamiami Trail and a larger state preserve in the Big Cypress.

Even today the Indians must struggle to pursue their traditional ways. In the Big Cypress National Preserve, the Miccosukee and Seminole retain hunting and timber rights, but the arrangement is tenuous because the area has been so heavily exploited and because of legal disputes over whether Indians have the right to kill protected species even for religious purposes. Tension also exists among the rangers, environmentalists, Miccosukee and Seminole over the Indians' cutting of cypress trees for their construction business, which centers on erecting chickees for private homes and developments in south Florida. The Indians claim that the decline of the environment is not of their making; rather, they are trying to survive on the least productive land in south Florida, an area to which they were driven against their will.

THIRTEEN

A Slave State

Slavery defines society. Prosperous plantation owners lead the state into secession and Civil War. Defeat and partial recon-struction leave the state open for exploitation, while an aberrant key flourishes. The call of the tropics.

In June 1844, the steamer *General Taylor,* on patrol of the Florida coast to interdict Indians trading with Cubans and Bahamians and live-oak pirates dealing with anyone, was diverted to the booming city of Key West to take on board in chains, Jonathan Walker, bound for trial in Pensacola. Floridians—few of whom were natives—charged that the Massachusetts-born Walker was a Yankee provocateur although he had immigrated to the old Panhandle city in 1837 and worked for seven years as a ship-wright and later a railroad contractor. An abolitionist, he none-theless employed black slaves in his railroad work because no other laborers were available, and although he boarded them in his house and treated them like members of the family, he found his conscience unable to abide keeping them in bondage. He moved his family back to Massachusetts, then went to Mobile to pick up a coastal schooner he planned to sail around Florida and back north. During his stop in Pensacola, his former workers pleaded with him to take them to freedom and he agreed to sail them to the Bahamas. A wrecker from Key West hauled them over at gunpoint before they reached Cape Florida, and the *General Taylor* then carried Walker to Pensacola where, sick and malnourished, he was chained to the floor of his cell.

In the North, Walker was a cause célèbre, and abolitionists, including Frederick Douglass and William Lloyd Garrison, raised money for his defense. In Pensacola rabid slavers reviled him while his friends offered succor, among them a local grocer who provided him with food. Tried for "stealing" four of the seven slaves he aided, he was convicted, pilloried for an hour, then branded on the ball of his hand with "S.S.," for "slave stealer." By most accounts few people had the stomach for watching a man branded. Later, the territorial authorities decided to try him for theft of the remaining three slaves, but at the trial in May 1845, the local jury defied the judge and prosecutors, who demanded a stiff penalty, and, citing public sentiment in Walker's favor, fined him a total of forty-five dollars. Financial assistance came from the North and Walker went home to a hero's welcome from abolitionists and fame as the subject of John Greenleaf Whittier's poem "The Man with the Branded Hand."

The central fact of Florida society in the years 1821 to 1865 was human bondage. To the planters, slaves represented not just labor but the sine qua non of an aristocratic way of life. Slaves tended the fields, provided the skilled artisans and unskilled laborers, produced the goods and services that turned the profits and kept the larders full. To work in the field, even if next to slaves, was to be a lesser man, and, throughout the Florida Territory, many young heirs of the new gentry would turn to professions like law if they owned fewer than thirty slaves, which was deemed the minimum number for operating a plantation in proper style. Those with insufficient wealth to partake fully of leisure often pursued it nonetheless and drove themselves into bankruptcy.

The privileged white men and women of Tallahassee traveled between plantations to party and dine, to hunt, and to discuss the pressing affairs of the day—the value of Christian virtue and civilization; life in their summer homes in the mountains of Georgia, Carolina, Tennessee; politics; the threat of slave insurrection; and the need to remove the Indians. They marveled at their own prince, Achille Murat, a nephew of Napoleon, husband of a Virginian, a slave owner, womanizer, flatterer—he represented all to which the planters aspired. Horse racing provided the major spectator and participatory sport for men and women while true gentlemen proved their worth according to the arcane rules of the *code duello*. The Southerners

around Tallahassee were less decadent than their Creole counterparts in Pensacola, an older and more naughty city mixing
Spanish, French, and English elements but no less devoted to
parties and the avoidance of anything resembling physical labor.

A major cost for the leisure of the planter class was the
perpetual fear of an insurrection. The fear found expression not
only in the war of extermination against the Seminole and the
blacks in their midst but also in a tightening of the repressive-
ness of human bondage and racial discrimination, especially as
abolitionism gained strength in the North and in the South
cotton became king. By the 1850s, black people in Florida had
to belong to someone or have a white benefactor to vouch for
their integrity and obedience. Key West passed an ordinance
prohibiting all blacks—slave and free—from walking the streets
after dark. The discrimination against free blacks in Key West
became so oppressive that many left, as did their counterparts
in Pensacola and St. Augustine. Yet at the same time planters
allowed their skilled slaves—the blacksmiths and carpenters—to
hire themselves out to other planters and businessmen, even in
distant cities. The white owner kept 70 percent or more of the
wages.

In hard times, this slave-lease system brought income to
planters while reflecting the labor shortages common throughout the South. Poor whites seldom knew a trade and to engage
in one was to become in their minds and the eyes of upper-class
white society little better than a slave. So blacks not only tended
the fields and the children, they built the houses, the railroads,
the carriages, bridges, furniture.

Within the state, there were, in 1860, 77 plantations of
more than 1,000 acres; 288 with 500 to 1,000 acres; 1,123 farms
over 100 acres; and 4,676 with fewer than 100.[1] Unless kept by
businesses in the city or owned by residents there as household
servants, slaves resided in the country, on the farms and plantations, the largest of which were self-sufficient, except for certain
dried goods, munitions, and luxuries, including liquor, wine,
and fashionable clothes. Cotton ruled the fields, but corn, sweet
potatoes, and garden crops were raised to feed slaves and masters, as were pigs and often cattle. Overseers generally super-
vised the work of the slaves, receiving for their effort a salary,
a cut of the profit, and other perquisites, including personal
servants and concubines. In short, slave society in north Florida
varied little from that in the rest of the South except perhaps in

its profitability. The region proved well suited to cultivation of prized Sea Island cotton, with planters harvesting 600 to 800 pounds per acre in prime soil, compared with 300 pounds in South Carolina.

Cotton production was so lucrative that the seven largest plantation counties—Jackson, Alachua, Marion, Madison, Jefferson, Leon, and Gadsden—contained property valued at $48 million, compared with $73 million for the entire state. In those counties, even the planters with fewer than thirty slaves, the ones without overseers who worked in the fields themselves, led a leisurely existence, with time for hunting and money for some luxuries to adorn their rough-hewn homes.

Most of the cotton was brought by river to ports at St. Marks, Apalachicola, Pensacola, Fernandina, and St. Joseph. Apalachicola and St. Joseph, the former now an "old" Florida town, the latter nonexistent, represent the Panhandle version of "a tale of two cities." At the end of the river whose name it bears, Apalachicola became the territory's earliest boomtown, a cotton port surpassed on the Gulf of Mexico only by New Orleans and Mobile. It was born in scandal, platted on a Spanish grant bought by Forbes and Company. Early settlers either bought Forbes land or simply squatted, believing they had a home, but the Apalachicola Land Company thought otherwise, and in 1835 the U.S. Supreme Court voided the Forbes grant, leaving many residents without clear title to their homes. The Apalachicola Land Company offered to let them repurchase their lots for a premium of $13,000 each, an outlandish price, even for the cotton boomtown.

Dispossessed residents moved to St. Joseph Bay, where they started a new town in 1835. Within a year, St. Joseph threatened the dominance of Apalachicola in the cotton trade, and a railroad from the new city to the Apalachicola River further improved its chances of becoming the major Panhandle port. By 1839, St. Joseph had a population of four thousand and was a flourishing coastal resort and trading center. Early in 1841, yellow fever decimated the city; only five hundred people still lived there in August when a hurricane and tidal surge flooded streets and buildings. Residents abandoned what was left to scavengers and the once thriving port—famous for its bars and prostitutes, its drunks and brawls—became for local preachers a sign of their Lord's punishment of evil.

*   *   *

No misfortune—neither war nor hurricanes nor crop-killing freezes—could slow Florida's growth, which was proceeding at a faster rate than that of every other state and territory in the nation except Texas. The population rose from 34,730 in 1830 to 54,447 in 1840. In 1845, Florida became a state in the Union, along with Iowa, to maintain the peculiar geopolitical balance between slave and free states. In 1850, the population of the new state stood at 87,555; in 1860, 140,500. The number of blacks increased faster in the decades before the Civil War than that of whites, rising from 7,587 in 1830 to 26,526 in 1840, and 61,750 in 1860.[2] Slaves made up 40 to 50 percent of the population statewide, but in the plantation counties of north Florida they often formed a two-to-one majority. Free blacks—only 932 in 1860—were concentrated in the old Spanish towns of St. Augustine and Pensacola and in Key West.

In 1860, 5,152 Floridians legally owned slaves, but with their families they totaled some 25,000 men, women, and children—about 30 percent of the white population. Of those, 47 individuals owned more than 100; 423, more than the 30 that divided planters from yeomen. At the time, slaves brought at least $1,000 on the market, making people the most valuable property of other people. A top blacksmith and a beautiful young woman—to be a concubine—would sell for as much as $3,500. Manacled and chained, the people were marched from auctions in Savanna or Richmond, New Orleans or Annapolis, to Florida.

Between 1808, when the United States outlawed the importation of slaves, and 1861, as many as 250,000 Africans were sold into bondage in the American South, with Florida serving as the point of entry for many of them, legally until 1821, when it became an American territory.[3] The frenzy for human chattel drove buyers less to question the origin of the people they purchased than their appearance and docility, their skills and strength, whether they had shown any tendency toward independence or rebellion. On St. George Island during the last Spanish rule, Zephaniah Kingsley, a white man married to an African princess, imported slaves, trained them on his plantation, and then sold them across the border in Georgia for exorbitant prices. A man of great moral ambiguity, Kingsley lived until 1843, well past the time Florida's American rulers instituted laws prohibiting mulattos and free blacks from inheriting property. Wishing to take care of his wife and children, he had moved them to Haiti, but they still were unable to claim either their Florida holdings of more than three thousand fertile acres and slaves or proceeds from their sale.

During the 1850s, cotton, lumber, turpentine, and an incipient railroad industry, which would lay four hundred miles of track by 1861, brought boom times to plantation Florida. The state floated so many bonds for public works that a number of northern business leaders thought secession little more than a tactic to avoid honoring debt.

The Southern elite demanded of itself a racial purity it perpetually undercut in practice, as slave owners sought sexual pleasure among the people they owned, in effect raising two families—one of "blue-blooded" nonworkers; the other of "dark-blooded" laborers. Race became and remained the dividing line between legitimacy and illegitimacy; virtue and nonvirtue; freedom and slavery. In the piney woods, hardscrabble whites with no hope of economic improvement frequently adopted the racial prejudice of the planters they resented and envied; at least, they were better off than slaves.

Anyone who offered succor to slaves or spoke for an end to human bondage was the enemy; and as abolitionism gained strength in the North and war fever rose, many received worse treatment than did Jonathan Walker, the man with the branded hand. "In East Florida," wrote W. W. Davis in his mammoth 1913 study, *The Civil War and Reconstruction in Florida*, "bands of whippers and thugs operated through the country at this time. They were reported to have secret signs of recognition and pass-words and to be bound together by 'horrid oaths and penalties.' Men were dragged from their beds at night, stripped, blind-folded, taken into the woods and whipped."[4] Calling themselves "regulators," a name they preserved through the war, the proslavery marauders murdered three Calhoun County men believed to hold pro-Union views. Open warfare resulted when the victims' relatives sought vengeance, but suppression of the violence did nothing to calm the situation. Those prominent individuals whom regulators couldn't attack, like Richard Call, a slave owner steadfastly opposed to secession, and District Court Judge William Marvin of Key West, they ignored in an attempt to make them nonpersons.

The massive influx of northerners and Cuban and Haitian immigrants during the past four decades has made Florida seem less a state of the old South than of the Sunbelt, a new place untouched by that brutal conflict between slave and free states. But myths about the Confederacy persist as do its symbols, and people throughout south and central Florida—including the arbiters of public opinion in its major newspapers—point to north Florida as "southern" when they wish to make a point about their own more refined "northern" sensibilities, while those in north Florida reverse and return the compliment. In political terms, the dichotomy serves the purpose of stirring prejudice and bias to undermine discussion of serious social issues, for no area of the state has a monopoly on discrimination. In cultural terms, it reveals how little Floridians know about the history of their adopted state.

In January 1861, sixty-four delegates to a special convention voted for secession from the United States; five representatives from non-slave-holding counties opposed the resolution. East Florida and thinly populated counties in the southwest, around the Caloosahatchee River, for example, hosted the majority of white Union sympathizers during the war years. In the south, some were cattlemen; in cities like Jacksonville, they were real estate dealers, mill owners, merchants—the bourgeoisie. In the backcountry, many poor whites simply tried to avoid service on the grounds that they had families to support and the conflict was a rich man's war.

After the state seceded, Union troops stationed in Pensacola moved quickly to occupy partially completed Fort Pickens on Santa Rosa Island at the head of the bay. Similarly the United States Navy held Fort Jefferson in the Dry Tortugas and Fort Taylor at Key West for the duration, completing work on both installations and using them to launch raids into the state and blockade the coast.

Those setbacks were easily ignored in the first year of the war, when the Confederate Army triumphed on the battlefield. Many Floridians volunteered for service but, following the habit established in the Seminole War, they demanded short enlistments, prompt payment, and assignment to the cavalry—for the romance and prestige—and soon proved themselves a generally undisciplined lot, as fond of drinking and brawling as fighting Yankees.[5] Within the state, their mission was to defend the major ports—Apalachicola, Fernandina, and Jacksonville—and to break the Union blockade at Pensacola, but they failed on all counts, and by 1862, nearly all had been ordered to the Tennessee front, leaving the coasts unprotected.

Also in January, U.S. Marines overran Cedar Key, and in February Union Army troops seized Fernandina before marching on Jacksonville, where the retreating Florida regulators—the irregular home guard—torched sawmills, warehouses, businesses, and hotels to punish Union sympathizers. A month after entering the fire-damaged city, the Union troops also captured St. Augustine, while the regulators devoted themselves to harassing civilians in the interior whom they believed disloyal to the Confederacy.

In April, Union forces occupied Apalachicola, which 80 percent of the population had abandoned for refuge in the Central Highlands and plantation country of Middle Florida. They found that the people, just one year into the war, had been subsisting on fish and oysters from the bay because the Union blockade and Confederate demand for provisions had left them no other food. In May, Pensacola fell to the Union and in the fall Jacksonville was taken and abandoned a second time. In March 1863, the third Northern force to invade Jacksonville included two black regiments sent to foment rebellion on the plantations, a prospect that frightened even the most solid Unionist. A band of regulators under Captain John Dickison blocked their advance at Palatka, and in the subsequent retreat, white federal troopers looted and burned a third of Jacksonville, an atrocity for which the Confederates blamed the black soldiers.

The Union's strategic withdrawals from Jacksonville left its sympathizers in the area open to reprisals from the Confederate regulators, whose leader was Dickison, called "the Dixie Eagle," a dashing figure to some, a cutthroat to others. Dickison, his troop of 150, and other mounted irregular troops carried the state's defense until its formal surrender on May 10, 1865. The vigilantes were celebrated for their military deeds and fearlessness against Yankees, which were real enough, but their primary goal was to keep Florida's 62,000 slaves on the farm through beatings and killings of anyone who showed even the slightest inclination toward insubordination. Although the Rebel intimidators were largely successful, 1,044 escaped slaves managed to join the black Union regiments by war's end (with some 1,300 Florida whites also turning out for the United States), and perhaps that many more became guerrillas.

Blacks fighting in Florida were in army regiments and bands of Union irregulars, operating primarily out of bases on the east coast from 1863 through the armistice. The black raiders, the

historian W. W. Davis said, spurred Southerners "to greater
effort because they realized a servile race was being employed
to subdue them."[6] In 1864, they joined forces with white Union
guerrillas to sack the west Florida towns of Eucheanna, Marianna, and Tampa, in what was their most significant military
victory of the war.

Some of the most intransigent white Union partisans operated out of the Big Bend counties of Taylor and Lafayette, which
ironically became a redoubt for unregenerate Southerners after
the war. The men were so bothersome to Florida officials that
they violated every rule of warfare in attempting to wipe them
out. In 1864, Confederate Lieutenant Henry Capers discovered
an abandoned guerrilla base camp on the Aucilla River, then
decided to destroy cabins and seize women and children resid-
ing along the nearby Econfina and Fenholloway rivers on the
grounds that they represented the families of the nonexistent
men in the deserted camp. He sent his captives to a concentration camp near Tallahassee, an act that roused other Southerners to protest against his distorted logic and mistreatment of
noncombatants. The women and children were released. A year
later, William Strickland, a Confederate deserter and organizer
of a band of Union raiders called the Florida Royals, a cattle
thief and sometimes saboteur, was captured and hanged without
a trial.

In 1864, pitched battles in Florida reached their peak. That
January, Union raiders attacked the railroad depot at Baldwin,
and the following month, a federal force of 5,000 men—one
third of whom were blacks—met an equally large Confederate
troop at Olustee on Ocean Pond, fifty miles from Jacksonville,
thirteen from Lake City. The 8th U.S. Colored Infantry absorbed the heaviest casualties in a battle that cost 1,861 dead,
wounded, and missing for the North and 946 for the South. It
was considered a smashing victory for the Floridians who forced
the crippled Union troops to withdraw. The war in Florida then
reverted to its pattern of raid and counterraid. In August, federal soldiers ripped up the tracks between Jacksonville and Baldwin, only to be driven from their position in Gainesville by John
Dickison.

In the waning days of the conflict, Tallahassee was the lone
Confederate state capital not to fall. The only serious attempt
to seize the city, in March 1865, collapsed when a Union force
of 1,000 failed to gain passage along the Natural Bridge across

the St. Marks River and a second troop of 400 running north from Cedar Key ran afoul of John Dickison.

By March 1865 the Confederacy had grown so desperate for soldiers that legislation was introduced to authorize the drafting of 300,000 slaves. Many white Southerners opposed the plan because creation of even segregated regiments would require them to grant blacks a measure of freedom and equality. The whites also recognized that they would be hard pressed to control such a large number of armed and hostile men. Lee surrendered before the conscription became real.

Although the scene of no major battles or invasions, Florida paid a heavy price for its secession. Nearly 13,000 of its men fought for the Confederacy, many of them draftees. Compounding their suffering were the "Merchants" who traveled through the state impressing supplies—often fraudulently—in the name of the Confederacy. In 1864, 25,000 head of cattle, 10,000 hogs, and 100,000 barrels of fish left the state to feed Rebel troops. By that time, 13,248 women and children relied on a public dole for the bare necessities and often people in outlying areas lacked even those. Many Floridians sought rations from Union forces or joined drifting ranks of wounded veterans, draft dodgers, and deserters from both sides whose very existence terrorized the populace.

Material relief for some Floridians came from blockade runners, who carried cotton, tobacco, and turpentine to Havana and the Bahamas, which often wound up in Northern ports, and brought back munitions, food, manufactured goods, and even luxury items. While some of the seamen received at least tacit support from state officials, the majority operated on their own. Smuggling was a risky and profitable business, with ships averaging three trips, at an average profit in excess of a quarter of a million dollars each, before they were caught. Between 1861 and 1865, 160 craft were captured, yet the flow continued, as the smugglers operated out of nearly every bay and inlet in the state.

The same salt shortage that Henry Flagler attempted to exploit for profit in Michigan became the source of a $3-million-a-year cottage industry in Florida that provided exemptions from the draft for all who engaged in it. Saltworks, often little more than shacks with vats for boiling sea water, cropped up along the Gulf coast, with five thousand men and boys engaged in the operations by 1863. Risk accompanied the enterprise, however, for federal troops regularly raided the camps.

Cowmen also were exempted from the draft, as long as they drove their beef north into the South rather than west to the Gulf port of Punta Rassa where ships hauled it south to Key West for shipment to the Union or to Cuban markets. The Confederacy seldom paid, whereas the North and the Cubans delivered gold at the dock, so the cowmen along the Caloosahatchee sold their stock to all buyers throughout the war. They also organized their own "Cow Cavalry" to fight off Union raiders and Confederate deserters who by 1863 were attacking nearly every cattle drive.

Defeat threw Florida and its allied states into severe economic depression, as well as social and political chaos. With Lee's surrender imminent, Governor John Milton committed suicide. His successor, A. K. Allison, attempted to open relations with the conquering government, but he was imprisoned along with David Yulee and Stephen Mallory, the senators at the time of secession.

Even more than during the war years, Florida collected an assortment of refugees. Confederate President Jefferson Davis, who as United States secretary of war launched the last fighting in the Seminole War, and the majority of his cabinet were arrested while attempting to flee to Florida and thence away from North America. Samuel Mudd, the physician who set the leg of John Wilkes Booth, was imprisoned at Fort Jefferson, the Dry Tortugas, from July 1865 to March 1869 when President Andrew Johnson pardoned him. During his incarceration, Mudd first tried to escape, then worked to halt a yellow fever epidemic that struck the military prison. Deserters and veterans from both sides—men and sometimes women—filtered into the peninsula to log and farm and pillage. John Muir, traveling to Cedar Key during the height of Reconstruction, found these transients the roughest lot he had seen, men quick to fight and to flee.

Slaves deserted their plantations en masse whenever Union liberators drew near. Emancipated, they gathered around the garrisons of the victorious troops or gravitated toward towns and cities they had never seen. They were homeless and poor, but among them were the artisans and nurses who had maintained the plantations.

In the immediate aftermath of the war, during the time of Presidential Reconstruction, white Floridians moved to reestablish their power and prerogatives. President Johnson named William Marvin, the former district court judge and Union sympathizer from Key West, acting governor, and in that role he presided over the state's constitutional convention. He failed to curb the more reactionary of the delegates who, after annulling the ordinance of secession and abolishing chattel slavery, moved to impose a system of economic and legal peonage on the freedmen. In 1866, the unregenerate delegates to the convention (and later the legislature) passed a series of "Black Codes," which mandated the death penalty for attempting or abetting the rape of a white woman and for inciting rebellion—both offenses were sufficiently vague in definition to be arbitrary. The codes also prohibited blacks from owning guns, knives, swords, dirks, or any other weapon, and defined vagrancy in such broad fashion that it became possible for local and state authorities to imprison nearly any black for that offense and sentence him or her to forced labor for up to a year.

Existence of the laws in Florida and other southern states provided sufficient cause for the U.S. Congress to impose what became known as Radical Reconstruction, which rode into the Confederacy on April 1, 1867, under the guise of martial law and immediately drove the unrepentent ex-Rebels from power. New officials were named and elected from the ranks of loyalists and freedmen to write a state constitution that would enfranchise freedmen and protect their rights while forming a government that would exact a measure of vengeance on the former leaders of the South. The document they issued in 1868 reflected congressional mandates regarding civil rights and included a "homestead exemption," still a cornerstone of Florida law, protecting debtors from losing all their possessions if they went bankrupt. The cumulative effect of the changes was to accord blacks in the South greater political freedom and opportunity than those in the North during the years of Reconstruction.

Scalawags, carpetbaggers, and freedmen—all played their roles in Florida's political life from roughly 1867 to 1877, when the "Bourbon Restoration" thwarted participation of blacks in the electoral process. In Florida, as elsewhere in the South, the scalawags were whites, often Whigs before the war, who opposed secession and throughout the conflict sided at least tacitly with the Union—at great cost and risk to themselves. Portrayed by unreconstructed whites as traitors, they were usually devoted to their state and its future. Carpetbaggers, the bogeymen of the southern legend who traveled with their satchels for holding stolen money and the family jewels, were immigrants from North to South who came during the postwar years to build new lives. That a number of those achieving high political office were corrupt—including at various times, the governor, lieutenant governor, and assorted delegates and representatives in Florida—makes them ordinary rather than extraordinary politicians for a period defined by corruption. Their criminal activities frequently smelled as much of incompetence as malice. The freedmen—the term is gender specific in this case because neither black nor white women could vote—moved to build a society based as much on their own notions as on manipulations by unscrupulous whites. Their blunders were no greater or lesser on average than those of politicians in any part of the country. One of them, Jonathan C. Gibbs, secretary of state from 1869 to 1872, when he was the only black in the cabinet, and then superintendent of public instruction, is credited with doing more to improve free public education in Florida than any white politicians before and many after him.

The task facing the new legislature was monumental: to rebuild a state with scant resources that was $2 million in debt, to educate and care for some sixty-five thousand newly free people, and to calm the fears and change the attitudes of nearly that number of whites who had just suffered total defeat. The former Rebels struck back at every turn, passively and actively, while at the same time rebuilding their fortunes through implementation in the old plantation country of new forms of tenancy and exploitation of the timber resources on their land.

In the year following the war, planters in conjunction with the federal Freedman's Bureau brought some 90 percent of the former slaves back to the farms to work as contract laborers. By 1870, despite the legal protections of Radical Reconstruction, it was difficult for them to flee their new economic peonage in the turpentine camps and tenant shacks. White vigilantes organized into the Ku Klux Klan and similar racist paramilitary groups enforced that dependence through threats and violence—including lynchings, beatings, and physical mutilations. In 1871, they drove sixty black workers from Henry Sanford's model farm near Fort Mellon. Although historians agree that supremacist attacks in Florida never approached in number or severity those perpetrated in the Carolinas, Mississippi, Louisiana,

Georgia, or Alabama, they were common enough to intimidate many unarmed and defenseless people.

Suppressed shortly after the attack on Sanford's settlement, the Klan raised its bloody, white-hooded head again in the 1920s and late 1930s to spread a message of hate born of fear. Klan members assaulted Earl Browder, the presidential candidate of the Communist party, in Tampa in 1936 and led marches through Jacksonville, Lakeland, Miami, St. Petersburg, and Starke. Legally prosecuted, the KKK and related white supremacist groups never vanished, and in the 1950s and 1960s, they violently opposed efforts to desegregate public schools and facilities. Today, in parts of rural and urban Florida, crosses are still burned in people's yards and threats are leveled by men expressing the ugliest side of the most reactionary of their political leaders.

Some formerly prominent planter families, like that of Napoleon Bonaparte Broward, lost their land to public auction in the early years of Reconstruction, when large farms and plantations were broken up and sold to satisfy the tax claims of state and local government. Others, like Achille Murat's widow, lingered impoverished in their homes. The dispossessions often had more to do with punishing political opponents than with any notion of social justice; yet, conducted under terms of the law, they were unstoppable. Some of the families never recovered their economic standing, but many relied on their social connections to gain access to loans, jobs, schools, and even favorable marriages. Broward became something of an exception politically because of his pseudopopulism, but in all other respects he fits the mold of the resurgent, repackaged planter class.

Florida's scalawag/carpetbag government followed a program of land abuse established before the war and continued well into the present century. That policy involved the exchange of land for construction of railroads, canals, ship's channels, and the assignment of timber and mineral rights for virtually no return to the state treasury. The most active manipulator of this system of largesse throughout the period of Reconstruction, when the ability of Southerners to buy large tracts of property was circumscribed by federal law, was William H. Gleason who moved from Wisconsin to Florida in 1866 to start a tropical fruit plantation. He knew enough to sail for Biscayne Bay, below the frost line, and to approach almost immediately the Internal Improvement Fund trustees with a drainage scheme, something no politician could refuse. The thirty-six-year-old Gleason proposed digging ditches through the east Everglades and Immokalee Rise west of Lake Okeechobee in exchange for the right to buy 1 square mile of land for $40 for each 50,000 cubic feet of earth he removed.[7] The ditch necessary for him to purchase a square mile would have measured 1 mile in length by 3 feet deep and 3 feet wide, no more than a gouge. The Democratic trustees of the fund agreed to the terms and gave Gleason the right to purchase up to 9,300 square miles (5.9 million acres) for $372,000, or roughly $.06 an acre.

The Democrats committed the state to awarding at least 300,000 additional acres to the Florida Canal and Inland Transportation Company for work on what now is the Intracoastal Waterway and to Hubbard L. Hart for dredging the Oklawaha River, which amounted to clearing snags from the twisting channel to permit passage of small steamers, which Hart ran as part of his transportation line.

The state's first Republican governor, Harrison Reed (1868–72), continued the Democrats' policy of liberal land grants and certificates of incorporation. Reed's rise to power in the state was fraught with dissension, with his opponents within the Republican party claiming his election resulted from vote buying and fraud and Democrats seeking to defeat every vestige of Radical Reconstruction. But business proceeded. Reed's lieutenant governor was William Gleason, who used his position to secure more land patents for himself and his partners, including one of Florida's U.S. senators, Thomas Osborn. They proposed to dig a sheltered steamboat channel from Key West to Fernandina through Florida and Biscayne bays, the Halifax and Indian rivers, Mosquito Lagoon, and the St. Johns River—little matter that a charter had already been awarded for making the intracoastal waterway along this same route. Gleason gained his greatest support and largest favors, however, after he dropped his political opposition to Reed—which had led him to claim the governorship for a three-week interregnum and attempt to engineer the impeachment of his fellow carpetbagger—and resigned his post as lieutenant governor. The grateful Reed and his supporters compensated their former adversary well.

After his resignation, Gleason and State Senator William Hunt received state charters to reclaim land along the southeast coast from the Jupiter Inlet south to the Miami River. Through his Southern Navigation Company, Gleason was granted the right to purchase, for four cents an acre, half of the three million acres it was to drain, and he also secured the state's backing in floating bonds to pay for his projects. In the 1870s, he became involved in efforts to dredge a cross-state canal and a protected ship's channel that would run from Texas to New York, the goal being to avoid the dangerous Straits of Florida.

Governor Reed and his fellow Internal Improvement Fund trustees ignored Gleason's bid and awarded to Hart a charter for constructing a cross-peninsula canal identical to the one that was discredited during territorial days. They also agreed to sell 1.1 million acres to the New York and Florida Lumber Company for $.10 an acre and the promise to settle one family on every 320 acres of clear-cut land. At minimum homesteading rates, the land the state was selling for a pittance would have brought $1.25 an acre, and people would have paid.

While promising vast acreage at little or no cost to corporations and entrepreneurs, state officials seldom honored a legislative mandate of 1866 to make land available to homesteaders willing to live beyond the edge of civilization. Blacks were to be given priority in the land purchases, but by 1876, freedmen owned only 2,012 homesteads amounting to 160,960 acres—an insignificant measure.[8] The state offered them swamplands in south Florida and provided neither financial assistance for making them arable nor security against the attacks of white racists.

All the state's plans and charters perished under a court injunction issued on behalf of Francis Vose and other holders of Florida Railroad bonds the state hadn't retired after the line went bankrupt. The court ordered the state to pay the bonds in full or deliver an equivalent amount of land to Vose and later his heirs, neither of which options appealed to state leaders. Although Vose's suit basically froze large-scale development and exploitation until Hamilton Disston was recruited in 1881 to bail the state out of its financial straits, investors continued to join Gleason and others in various development schemes. From England, Sir Edward Reed contributed to Gleason's Southern Navigation Company and bought the bankrupt Florida Railroad. Other investors from Europe and the northern United States followed his lead, Florida's timber being too tempting a bargain to ignore.

New settlers also looked beyond the political turmoil and economic uncertainty as they poured into the state, raising its population from just over 140,000 in 1860 to 187,748 in 1870 and 269,493 a decade later. The richest and most populous city in Florida was the most aberrant—Key West, the southernmost city in the United States, its opening to the Caribbean.

Early in 1822, Lieutenant Matthew Perry took control of Key West (then, Thompson's Island), and by implication all of the Keys, for the United States. At the end of that year, Commodore David Porter assumed command of a squadron of sailing vessels, schooners, rowing barges, and the U.S. Navy's first battle steamboat; established a base on Key West; and began pursuing wreckers relentlessly on open water and in the shoals. After invading Puerto Rico in violation of international law and orders, he was court-martialed, convicted of conduct unbecoming an officer and of exceeding his authority, and suspended from the service for six months. He quit the U.S. Navy to become general of marines for Mexico and in that post harassed Spanish shipping from Key West, becoming something of a pirate himself before returning to the U.S. Foreign Service.

Porter's violence did little more to prevent wrecks than did the lighthouses established during the 1830s on Perry's recommendation at Cape Florida on the southern end of Key Biscayne, at the Dry Tortugas, and later on Carysfort Reef and Sambo Key—which is to say not much. Weather and poor navigation by sailors ruined more ships than pirates; the salvors continued to pick up the pieces as an unofficial coast guard and lifesaving service.

In 1828, the federal courts ruled that the first crew reaching an abandoned ship could claim the cargo for itself and so wreckers kept close and constant watch on the reefs and frequently raced, in a sort of scavengers' regatta, for the prize. Ship captains, manufacturers, and insurers often despised the wreckers and continued calling them brigands, or worse, although the complainers would have liked losing everything they owned far less than dealing with the salvors. By the 1830s, the community of three thousand on Key West had become one of the richest per capita in the United States, a status it retained through the rest of the century. Between 1850 and 1860, $16 million worth of salvage from five hundred wrecks passed through Key West, and in 1873, an astounding seven hundred ships became grounded on the reefs, with many of them abandoned to the wreckers. Buyers came to Key West from around the country for the goods brought in, often luxury objects, and many of the islanders built for themselves fine, eccentric houses of prime lumber pulled from wrecks.

The bazaarlike atmosphere of Key West expressed the state's more exotic side, the allure, be it of wealth or adventure, that drew people to it in ever increasing numbers, and few of those who visited failed to find some bit of reality that exceeded their expectations. John Muir on his 1867–68 walk through the devastated South entered Florida at Fernandina and found the country "so watery and vine-tied that pathless wanderings are not easily possible in any direction."[9] Although he located his personal nirvana in the Yosemite Valley in California, Muir touched a potent mystery in Florida. He wrote in his journal:

> I am now in the hot gardens of the sun, where the palm meets the pines, longed and prayed for and often visited in dreams, and, though lonely to-night amid this multitude of strangers, strange plants, strange winds blowing gently, whispering, cooing, in a language I never learned, and strange birds also, everything solid or spiritual full of influences that I never felt, yet I thank the lord with all my heart for his goodness in granting me admission to this magnificent realm.[10]

FOURTEEN

Rising from the Ruins

*Depression, floods, droughts, and fires ravage the nation's play-
ground. The battle for conservation produces results: a national
park and protected forests. The cross-state canal is reborn, defeated, resurrected. Population rises.*

Many people remember Florida in the 1930s and early 1940s as
a place where one could look across the lake or river or bay at
fish leaping and birds soaring, where the fragrance of orange
blossoms filled the air each spring, where woods or prairies were
open for roaming or hunting in season. Near Miami or Tampa,
Palm Beach or Orlando, one could drive to farms and groves for
vegetables and fruit without passing through miles of suburban
sprawl. Yet there were also days when Tampa Bay or Biscayne
Bay smelled from raw sewage, when the skies over the lower east
coast were darkened not by birds but by smoke from fires in the
Everglades, when the pulp mills popping up around Jacksonville, Fernandina, Pensacola, and Port St. Joe spewed their
stench into the air, their waste into the water, when there was
no money and no work and the whole state appeared doomed
beyond the worst nightmares of anyone.

Ravaged though Florida was in the eyes of those familiar
with its more lush times, it was an exotic, new country to half of
its residents, and compared with the present, the state fifty years
ago was a remarkably scenic and rich blend of rural, urban, and
wild areas, where a person could easily find companionship or
escape. In 1945, Thomas Barbour, a paleontologist and cham-

pion of natural Florida, recalled the excursions he and his wife made in a Model T customized for camping, with a "contraption of little cupboards" for onions, sweet potatoes, and other dry goods strapped on one wooden side; slings for rifles under the top; and a backseat full of tents, cots, mosquito bars, folding chairs, and dogs. "Our procedure was to drive north up the Dixie Highway, then a narrow backroad where at times it was difficult for two cars to pass, but now the great boulevard, route U.S. 1, with its dreary vista of bill boards and hot dog stands." On other excursions, he would travel inland from Melbourne to Kissimmee, where he would "always see from two to a dozen box tortoises warming themselves on the black tarred highway."[1] The Dixie Highway is now four or more lanes, lined not with hot dog stands and billboards but with motels, condominiums, apartments, gas stations, shopping centers, car lots, fast-food drive-ins, and convenience stores for more than one hundred miles, from Homestead to Palm Beach and beyond, and it is merely one manifestation of the growth that has carpeted Florida.

The reason for Florida's environmental decline, simply put, is millions of people and their concentration in cities and resorts along the coasts and around the lakes and rivers of Orlando and central Florida. Often, these burgeoning metropolitan areas are in the places least tolerant of massive numbers of people—the water supply and the amount of arable, developable land being too slight for their weight—while the parts of north Florida and the Panhandle most suitable for urbanization are shunned. The goals of the immigrants are jobs, sunshine, and a body of water. Although the climate remains equable, many lakes have become hazardous to swimmers because of vegetation and microbes that entangle and infect them, while beaches sometimes appear to consist as much of garbage as of sand. Overuse has become such a problem on historic Daytona Beach and its neighbors that officials have begun to talk openly about banning cars on the beach, an act that would effectively end a tradition of driving on hard-packed sand that is as old as the automobile.

The collapse of the real estate market in 1926 and the subsequent economic Depression hardly affected the movement of people into the state; in fact, many came from broken areas to seek a new start where, at least, it was warm. In 1900, the state had 528,000 people. By 1920, the total had reached 968,470, to leap to 1,468,000 in 1930, and 1,800,000 in 1940. Luther Carter

in his study of land use and water policy in Florida has pointed
out that since 1930 Florida has been a predominantly urban
state, with up to three quarters of the population concentrated
on some 6 percent of the land (25 percent of the state is devoted
to agriculture; the remainder to pasture, private lands awaiting
development, and parks).[2]

The Depression in Florida deepened the rifts between rich
and poor, owner and worker, winter visitor and permanent resident. It also fixed in popular imagination, if not reality, the
character of the state's dominant cities and resorts, which air-
lines began to serve on a regular basis, bringing a new influx of
wealthy tourists and investors. The WPA Guide of 1939, an
authoritative look at the condition of the state and its people,
said:

> Florida . . . is a playground for the many rather than for the
> wealthy few; nevertheless, it is around the latter that recrea-

Water Resources Atlas of Florida, Institute of Science and Public Affairs State
University

tion has been publicized into the State's most prominent
industry. To foster this, much costly and elaborate parapher-
nalia has been installed in the resorts. Commercialized recreation, with its attendant spotlighting, nearly obscures the
State's other interests and pursuits, and resort patrons consequently have little acquaintance with these.[3]

Late in the 1920s, Al Capone, the notorious gangster and
bootlegger, bought a Miami Beach mansion, and his colleagues
in vice soon followed. Although his tenancy lasted only until his
imprisonment in 1932, Capone stirred ambivalent feelings in
the community, whose leaders publicly berated him and privately accepted his charitable and even more secret political
contributions.

More significant than Capone's adventures in wonderland
was the rapid expansion of tourism. The population of the lower
east coast regularly doubled during the winter, as part-time
residents migrated from North, South, and Central America. An
additional two million visitors arrived annually to fish and play
in resorts that boarded themselves up in the summer, reverting
to the locals, whose feelings toward their seasonal neighbors
remained ambivalent at best.

An even tan, a quick affair, a trophy-sized catch for mount-
ing, a Bloody Mary dawn—those were the goals of the Panama-
hat, Bermuda-shorts, sun-tan-lotion, libation-ingesting set. The
destination of choice for many was the old crocodile ground and
mangrove island Carl Fisher had converted to Miami Beach.
The place rose from the devastation of the 1926 hurricane more
dramatically than from the sea. During the 1930s, the number
of hotels on the beach increased from 56 to 250, as Fisher's
dream resort became the nation's playground. Capone brought
his gangster friends, but more reputable investors built winter
estates there as well. Florida and Georgia Crackers—which at
the time referred to native-born Anglos of those states—joined
a migration of émigré Jews from Eastern Europe by way of New
York to transform the look and feel of the area below Lincoln
Road called South Beach. Cash more than ethnicity or class
became the criterion for admission to paradise.

Starting in the late thirties, architects—most trained abroad
or heavily influenced by trends there and in New York—eluci-
dated the style that came to be called Tropical Deco. The buildings had the look and feel of the streamlined machine age

tempered to the slow, tropical pace of south Florida. They were four, five, maybe six stories—seldom more—their white stucco walls trimmed with bright pastels. Neon signs and highlights, flamingo-decorated iron doors, glass brick, ornamental but inexpensive windows—common materials turned to decorative appointments helped define the style that shaped the beach until the post-World War II years when the baroque, high-rise, resort hotels of North Beach were built: the Fontainebleau, Eden Roc, Doral, and Sahara. The new hotels locked out all but guests and blotted the rising sun.

Prosperity brought increased corruption, especially to the "Gold Coast," as organized-crime figures entrenched themselves in the resort industry and operated with relative impunity illegal casinos and rings devoted to prostitution, extortion, drugs, and smuggling—to make Al Capone's activities two decades earlier appear minor league. Meyer Lansky, the legendary crime chief of south Florida, supported Fulgencio Batista's presidency in Cuba in the early 1940s, pulled out when Batista was deposed in 1944, and returned with him in 1952 to run profitable casinos until Fidel Castro seized power in 1959. In 1950, U.S. Senator Estes Kefauver brought his Special Committee to Investigate Organized Crime in Interstate Commerce to Miami for hearings to expose corruption. The public drama produced sound, fury, and publicity to match that of the theater surrounding Prohibition. Miami and Miami Beach added to their reputations as wicked cities.

The ocean extracted a heavy toll for the hotelkeepers' extravagance. By 1970, most of the quartz sand of Miami Beach had vanished into the sea. Storms and tides, which had once beat the sand inland only to have it wash back in a constant recycling, began slamming the fine grit into the new hotels and then carrying it into the ocean in the backwash and riptide. Tourism suffered, and the city and state demanded federal action, which came in the form of a ten-year, $68-million "replenishment" of a fifteen-mile stretch of north beach with sand dredged from the sea—not quartz sand but fine-grained bits of marine animals, which, when washed to sea, hangs suspended in the water, like a haze in air. As long as the hotels remain, the beach they guard will go through its cycles of erosion and artificial renewal, and one day even the memory of the clear, warm Atlantic waters will fade away, and visitors to Miami Beach's hotels will think the cloudiness a constant fact of ocean life.

The 1920s through the 1960s were the glory decades when Greater Miami was the destination of choice for many of the visitors to Florida. But other cities appealed to large, if slower and quieter, crowds. On the Gulf coast, St. Petersburg achieved renown not only as the spring-training ground of the New York Yankees (who now train in Fort Lauderdale, while the Boston Red Sox call St. Petersburg their Florida home) but also as a haven for retirees and family health seekers. Advertising itself as "Sunshine City," St. Petersburg boasted five thousand green benches, which turned it into one big rest stop for strollers and an open-air bazaar for deal makers. The city's piers and bridges provided prime stands for fishermen who lined their railings day and night. The parks hosted scores of chess players; the shuffleboard courts became the symbol of the elderly at play.

Just down the coast, following the real estate bust of 1926, John Ringling established a winter home for his circus and an art museum for his collection at Sarasota, which remained for nearly forty years a quiet town. The beach town was a haven for surf fishermen and charter boats until the 1970s, when condominium fever spread from the Atlantic to the Gulf. Sarasota's second most famous citizen—Ringling being first—the late John D. MacDonald created Fort Lauderdale's most notorious beach bum, Travis McGee, whose adventures he chronicled in color-titled books until his death in 1987. MacDonald frequently defended through essays, as well as through the observations of McGee and his alter ego Meyer, the distinctive characteristics of rural and natural Florida, decrying on several occasions the drive to "pave the whole state."

In the Depression days, towns defined themselves according to characteristics they felt would attract tourists. St. Augustine advertised itself, correctly, as the oldest town in North America and, incorrectly, as the landing site of Florida's Spanish discoverer, Juan Ponce de León. Daytona Beach boasted of its hard-packed white sand beaches; Tallahassee of its status as state capital and of its southern gentility among the moss-draped live oak and rolling hills; Winter Park and Orlando extolled their lakes and groves; Fort Myers, its royal-palm lined streets, gardenlike beauty, and the winter home of Thomas Alva Edison; Tampa and Jacksonville advertised their commercial vitality; Key West, its tropical atmosphere, fishing, and piratical past. Festivals, rodeos, harvest fairs, and other special events were organized to attract tourists. Tampa offered its annual Gasparilla festival, begun in 1904 as a publicity ploy by the

society editor of the local newspaper, the *Tribune*. The event
honors José Gaspar, purportedly a henchman of the "bloody
Roderigo Lopez," a pirate in the Straits of Florida who was said
to have taken thirty-six ships in twelve years at the beginning of
the nineteenth century before the U.S.S. *Enterprise*, disguised as
a merchant ship, brought him to bay. The affair became a
Tampa tradition and is celebrated today on a grandiose scale
though Gaspar is no more real now than he was in 1904 or 1812.

Fishing camps drew anglers from around the world. Lake
George on the St. Johns, Lake Apopka in central Florida, the
Kissimmee and Apalachicola rivers, and Lake Okeechobee were
among the most celebrated freshwater fishing spots, while the
Indian River, Mosquito Lagoon, Keys, Ten Thousand Islands,
and every major bay lured the salts. The beauty of the sport in
Florida derived from the simple fact that one could always find
along the shores, causeways, and bridges a place to drop bait
and, although many interior lakes were sealed off from casual
anglers by private homes, others remained accessible by boat or
wading from a public beach. The scenery, the sunrises and sun-
sets, the glint of light on the water, the sight of fish leaping,
made the effort worthwhile. If each year it took longer to bring
home dinner, it could still be done with relative ease.

Canoeists paddled, with only a short portage, 469 winding
miles across the peninsula from White Springs down the Suwannee, up the Withlacoochee to Lake Griffin, then down the Oklawaha to the St. Johns and Jacksonville. Moss-draped trees
overhung the rivers and lakes, dancing shadows and light across
the tannin-stained water. The course bore a deserved reputation
as one of the most splendid canoe routes in the world. For the
less adventuresome, other rivers offered equal beauty. If one
wanted a taste of reptiles or wild animals, there was always an
alligator farm or snake house, a zoo or roadside collection—
usually far less attractive in reality than in the billboards advertising them along the road, with sickly animals crowded into
filthy pens. Along the Tamiami Trail, there were even Indian
villages to visit for a fee.

The Crackers sought to cash in on the tourist traffic, too.
Every junction on the new highways sprouted a gas station; a
cluster of one-room cabins; a citrus stand; a curio shop selling
shells, cypress knees, stuffed and live alligators, shellacked blow-
fish. "Swamps and jungles," according to the WPA Guide, "have
been enclosed and converted into Japanese, cypress, oriental,

and many other kinds of gardens, to which an admission fee is charged. Here have been assembled extensive collections of native and exotic plants."[4]

Silver Springs, the source of the Oklawaha River's major tributary and destination of choice for many nineteenth-century visitors, grew into a major tourist attraction. The beautiful Silver Springs Run became the location for jungle movies and diving adventure movies. Monkeys imported for the Tarzan episodes filmed there through the 1930s and 1940s have naturalized, making themselves pests in the eyes of many environmentalists. In 1929, Ross Allen, a young herpetologist and collector, established at the springs a Reptile Institute devoted to the study primarily of poisonous snakes, but a repository as well for non-poisonous species, alligators, crocodiles, turtles, and tortoises. The institute offered vipers for sale to collectors and also performed daily "milkings" of rattlesnakes and water moccasins for their venom, which was converted to antivenin. Over the years, Allen gained recognition as one of the world's foremost authorities on poisonous snakes.

An Iowan named Richard Pope, Sr., who moved to Florida while a child, created Cypress Gardens in 1936 and built it into a tourist attraction synonymous with bathing beauties and water skiing. For decades movie houses throughout the country featured newsreels and shorts revealing the glories of Cypress Gardens and its water-skiers. The mermaids at Weeki Wachee Spring on the Gulf coast possessed the looks but lacked the high-tech, high-flying charm of slaloms, jumps, and choreographed formations necessary to compete with their eastern neighbors. Near Winter Haven, in the heart of citrus country, Pope's playground, along with Silver Springs to the northeast and Rainbow Springs, preserved and enhanced the tourist tradition inland. Purchased by Harcourt Brace Jovanovich in 1985, Cypress Gardens now competes with a seemingly endless array of central Florida attractions, including Disney World and Harcourt's own Sea World.

The Florida that Depression-era tourists seldom saw was often less amusing and paradisiacal. Malaria occurred at six times the national average while tuberculosis and syphilis were epidemic among blacks, who comprised 30 percent of the population. Only seven of the state's sixty-seven counties had hospitals to serve black people—in an age when segregation either kept them out of white hospitals or confined them to poorly equipped and staffed Negro wings. Fully 20 percent of the state's resident population received relief or work through the Federal Economic Recovery Act or the WPA, which constructed roads, libraries, schools, hospitals, and other public facilities.

By 1938, the federal and state governments had spent $250 million in building nine thousand miles of roads. Buses served nearly every city and town; trucks reached communities that had never seen a railroad. The competition drove the railroads to seek legislative approval to enter the trucking business, which they received. Trains pulling trailer-laden flatcars became common sights until the interstate highway system drove even those services to ground. The centerpieces of Henry Flagler's and Henry Plant's domains—the Florida East Coat Railway and Atlantic Coast Line, respectively—had filed for bankruptcy in 1931; they needed all the breaks and help they could find.

On the prairies, ranchers fought with government agents, with each other, with deer, timber companies, mine owners, and hunters over fever ticks, rights of passage, fencing, screwworms, and quarantines of beef. To protect their interests and allow them to work politically as a group, the cowmen formed the Florida Cattlemen's Association, which became a powerful lobbying force in Tallahassee. The growing availability of trucks and refrigeration plants led to marked increase in cattle rustling for county fairs, dog tracks, and other local black markets. It was clear as well that despite warnings to all motorists to be alert, cattle, hogs, and cars could not share the roads. The 1949 Florida fence law whispered the end of a range that was already largely closed. The cowmen who once had defended the open range as an article of faith, declaring subversive anyone who suggested fencing even a pasture, now employed riders to patrol the miles of barbed wire that bound ranches running into the hundreds of thousands of acres in size. Naturalists and campers who argued for a right to pass across the palmetto prairies were dubbed communists, radicals, moss pickers, and worse.

Throughout the state, political and business leaders moved to suppress workers and reformers. Like other members of the unregenerate Confederacy, Florida was ruled by the Democratic party and within that by a core of rural politicians and the state's economic elite. They would war among themselves for promotion of their special interests, but they tended to show solidarity in their antipathy to unions and people seeking economic and social equality—for all races. In 1935, Joseph Shoemaker, Eugene Poulnot, and Samuel Rogers, leaders of Modern Democrats, a local group devoted to political reform in Tampa, were arrested after a meeting and then turned over to a gang of vigilantes who, without provocation, beat them mercilessly.[5] Shoemaker died as a result of his injuries. Of the eleven assailants arrested and brought to trial, six were Tampa police officers; all were acquitted by the jury. Around that same time vigilantes kidnapped a CIO official trying to organize fruit pickers near Orlando. He was never seen again and was presumed to have been murdered, although the police failed to find any evidence of a crime.

In 1937, the growers' hatchet men drove union organizers out of the groves, where migrant workers were predominantly white. (The migrants on the truck farms and in the sugarcane fields were black and unorganized, subject to the whims of growers and crew bosses.) In 1938, orange pickers actually joined the United Cannery, Agricultural, Packing, and Allied Workers of America, a CIO affiliate, and struck growers near Lake Alfred. Packing plant workers in Winter Haven, the heart of citrus country, walked out in sympathy, but the growers closed their groves and plants until the strike was broken. In the years following World War II, growers increased their economic and political power and effectively shut organizers out of the citrus industry through intimidation and the traditional method of playing blacks, who had come to represent the majority of pickers, Mexicans, and whites against each other, dividing on the basis of race and fear people who shared the same hardships and aspirations.

Volunteer organizations like the Florida Christian Migrant Ministry tried for years to alleviate the poor conditions of the workers, organizing education and nutrition programs, but their efforts could not change the underlying conditions of the camps where the commissary system held sway and exploitation was the order of every day. As more migrant workers have remained in state year round, social service agencies have begun to reach them, although the help they can offer is limited by shortages of funds and professionals and conditions remain disgraceful. The black migrant town of Belle Glade—many of whose residents are Haitian—has the highest AIDS rate per capita in the country and violent crime, drug, and alcohol abuse problems to match. Most migrants do not qualify for social security or Medicare coverage, leaving them more impoverished in old age than when working the fields. Changes in the federal immigration law, which took effect in 1988, are contributing to the hardship of the workers by requiring proof of citizenship that many who are natives of the United States cannot provide. Born at home in rural areas, they never received birth certificates nor do they have social security cards or drivers' licenses.

In 1935, the legislature established the Florida Citrus Board and its supervisory panel, the Florida Citrus Commission, and granted them broad authority to regulate the cultivation and marketing of citrus. Producing some forty million boxes a year of oranges, grapefruit, tangerines, and assorted other citrus, the growers represented the greatest agricultural enterprise in the state. Weather stations, and federal and state experiment and extension services, were geared to their needs, to the protection of groves and the cultivation of new, more durable fruit.

Farming in Florida offered wide discrepancies in holdings and income. Of 73,000 farmers, 80 percent were white and 28 percent were tenant farmers; whereas in the other states of the Confederacy, 48.7 percent were sharecroppers. Among Florida's 12,764 black farmers, however, the tenancy rate was 46.4 percent (compared with 24.1 percent for whites). What the figures failed to reflect was the number of migrant farm workers, white and black, with no stake in the fields and groves they harvested. (In resort communities, their counterparts were a large group of intinerant hotel and restaurant workers who yo-yoed between Florida and the summer resorts in the northeast— the Catskills, Long Island, Maine, New Jersey, and Rhode Island.)

By 1939, unions counted only 20 percent of Florida's 350,000 wage laborers as members, including cigar makers, longshoremen, transportation workers, tradesmen, and phosphate miners who had succeeded in gaining representation after years of often violent struggle. The militant antiunionism of the state's business and political leaders sometimes spilled over to the labor organizations themselves. Late in the 1930s, the cigar workers voiced a desire to switch their union affiliation from the AFL to the CIO, which they believed more activist. They feared for their livelihoods in an industry suffering the full brunt of the Depression and competition from cigarettes. Intent on smashing any semblance of a progressive labor movement, AFL officials called the cigar workers backing the switch communists in order to thwart their campaign. The tactic worked. These mach-

inations further undermined a generally passive labor movement: Between 1916 and 1932 only 159 of 31,625 strikes nation-
wide occurred in Florida.

From the start of the Depression, Alfred I. Du Pont, traveling with his brother-in-law Ed Ball, bought played-out north
Florida farmland, cut-over pine forests, and failing banks. He
wanted to establish across the land- and water-rich, transporta-
tion-poor Panhandle and north peninsula, from Pensacola to
Jacksonville, a quasi-feudal state no less extensive than Flagler's
east coast empire had been. Du Pont's investments propped up
the state's banks at a time when many verged on collapse and
helped establish the pulp industry in north Florida in the 1930s,
which continues to dominate local economies along the lower
St. Johns River and in the Panhandle. After Du Pont's death in
1945, Ball became sole trustee of the Du Pont estate and the
most powerful man in Florida, a racist, union-busting anticom-
munist vilified by his opponents, fawned over by the people he
supported until his death a decade ago. During his thirty-year
reign in the state, Ball became so powerful that it was, in the
words of his biographer, "difficult to go 50 miles in any part of
Florida without coming in contact with a portion of the empire
[he] built."[6]

Du Pont started the St. Joe Paper Company in Port St. Joe,
and his estate eventually came to own one million acres of pineland in the Florida Panhandle and south Georgia, along with
twenty-three box plants in the United States and Europe, thirty-
one banks in Florida, the Florida East Coast Railway, and its
assorted properties. Ball bought the railroad's bonds at sixteen
cents on the dollar when it was in receivership in the 1930s and
gained control of it, after long court and congressional battles,
which included financing the electoral defeat by George Smath-
ers of his nemesis U.S. Senator Claude Pepper, whom he tarred
through henchmen as a communist sympathizer—"Red Pepper"—and a consort of "thespians." (Pepper, after his defeat in
1946, became a United States congressman and served in the
House of Representatives until his death in 1989.) Ball broke the
railroad unions in Florida during the 1960s by provoking a
strike noteworthy for its duration, violence, and lack of substan-
tive negotiations.

For three decades the Du Pont estate, as a "testamentary
trust," was exempt from provisions of the federal Bank Holding
Act prohibiting banks from owning other major businesses, a bit

of largesse that allowed Ball to purchase the railroad. In 1965, after a lengthy congressional battle initiated by the railroad unions with whom the estate was fighting, the exemption was revoked and Ball was given five years to sell either the trust's Florida banks or the Florida East Coast Railway. The unions believed he would choose the latter course because the line was a perpetual money-loser, but he opted to sell the banks and bust the union.

The Du Pont trust was accused in the 1960s of thwarting development in the Panhandle and Big Bend because Ball preferred pine trees—for their pulp—to humans.[7] In truth he preferred profit and power to either forests or people, and since money lay in the pines he kept the acreage out of the hands of developers. Although its leaders continue to follow Ball's precedent and maintain their tree farms, St. Joe Paper Company has begun making selective land sales and joining development ventures.

Du Pont's pulp mill followed the opening in 1931 of the International Paper Company facility in Panama City, the first in the state. With less than a quarter of Florida's first-growth timber still standing and millions of acres clear-cut and abandoned, the new pulp industry offered to state officials hope for revitalization of the forest. In uniform rows, fast-growing slash and pond pine were set out by the companies, the Civilian Conservation Corps (CCC), and the State Forestry Department, established in 1935 to manage the trees as a cash crop. In 1937, the legislature passed the Murphy Act, which allowed the pulp companies to purchase land that loggers had clear-cut and abandoned for taxes due—a fraction of its value. The pinelands themselves became little more than cultivated fields of trees, all the same age, the same height and girth, planted close and cut clear according to schedule.

The CCC joined with the WPA, the National Forest and Park Service, the various agencies of the State Conservation Board and Forestry Department in an effort to improve the look of the abused peninsula. Early steps in that direction had been taken during the first decades of the century, when the federal government expanded its forest reserves into a national system set aside for logging, hunting, and recreation. During the Depression, the Civilian Conservation Corps established the 157,000-acre Osceola National Forest in north Florida and the 557,000-acre Apalachicola National Forest in the Panhandle, and worked to improve the 366,000-acre Ocala National Forest. (Today, with so much of Florida's pinelands and scrub vanishing and so much woodland still in private hands, these forests should be exempted from logging and restored to vital natural systems benefiting people and animals, but the federal government remains intent on leaving them open to exploitation by lumber and mineral companies, for the profit of a few in the name of the public good.)

The federal conservation workers also landscaped Fairchild Tropical Garden in Dade County, conceived by winter residents Robert Montgomery, a New York accountant, and George Brett, president of Macmillan Publishing Company, as a tribute to the plant explorer David Fairchild and as a showcase for plants that would flourish in tropical south Florida, including fine collections of cycads and palms from around the world.

In other areas of the peninsula, newcomers worked to establish preserves and gardens, continuing efforts that had, in some cases, begun years before. On Iron Mountain, the highest point on the peninsula, in the Lake Wales Ridge not far from Sebring and Avon Park—a site where Indians were said to have held a rising-sun ceremony every spring—Edward W. Bok, freshly retired as editor of *Ladies' Home Journal*, built during the 1920s a Singing Tower and formal garden. He called the whole the Mountain Lake Sanctuary and dedicated it to spiritual repose, adorning his tower with a frieze portraying birds and animal fables, carving on the doors biblical and mythological legends. He installed a seventy-one-bell carillon and a crypt for himself at the base of the tower, which President Calvin Coolidge dedicated in 1929. This sedate sanctuary was the site in 1931 of a sing off between imported European nightingales and native mockingbirds, which in 1927 had been voted the official state bird by Florida's schoolchildren. The mockers copied every tune the nightingales could sing and then proceeded to run through their own creations.[8] (The mockingbird's singing prowess is matched only by its aggressiveness toward other birds when nesting—including hawks—cats, dogs, and people, all of whom it attacks without regard for its safety.)

In the aftermath of the real estate market's collapse in 1926, Mrs. John A. Roebling, the granddaughter-in-law of the builder of the Brooklyn Bridge, and a few other concerned winter residents in the area around Sebring, acted to save from axes and plows a thirty-eight-hundred-acre tract that included nearly every major plant community in Florida—cypress swamp, pine flatwoods, scrub, bayhead, marsh, and above all, hardwood hammocks. In 1931, they opened their Highlands Hammock to the public and in 1935 deeded it to the state as one of its original parks. The preserve contains one of the few virgin hardwood hammocks left in Florida, an awe-inspiring collection of live oak, sabal palm, naturalized oranges, and some 350 other species of trees, ferns, moss, and vines, a place of deep shadows and calm, of insects one forgets while contemplating the foliage, listening to wind on the leaves, skinks skittering across the debris rotting on the forest floor. Highlands Hammock is a sanctuary in a rapidly urbanizing area: Rare is the quiet visitor who, hiking through the woods, will miss seeing deer or, strolling the board-walk through the cypress swamp will fail to observe an alligator basking on the sun-bathed shore. Scores of bird species call the hammock home.

The 1928 hurricane that killed two thousand people south of Lake Okeechobee headlined the shortcomings of a drainage campaign that had always been long on promise and short on anything other than destruction. Yet the most sensible solution from the standpoint of the environment and even future economic savings—to fill the canals, break down the inefficient mud levee bordering the lake, and let the water resume its gentle flow down the peninsula—was precisely the one never considered. Officials and most residents firmly believed the Everglades of use and benefit only if drained and converted to farmland; otherwise, they were the domain of all sorts of vermin, including outlaws and naturalists—all disreputable and antisocial. Land-owners in the region of Lake Okeechobee, near Miami and Fort Lauderdale, who swore at the shortcomings of the program, nonetheless believed that long-term gain from their investments depended on more, not less, drainage. Although they frequently balked at the taxes levied by the Everglades Drainage District to pay for the dredging and diking, they objected to the execution, not the conception of the campaign.

From the disaster of the hurricane rose President Herbert Hoover's offer of federal and technical aid, which rescued the bankrupt and discredited state reclamation program. Through its various agencies, Florida had spent $18 million by issuing bonds it couldn't properly service or redeem only to learn that at least $20 million more in canals and levees were needed to prevent flooding. The state sugarcoated its appeal to the federal government for the funds by organizing the Okeechobee Flood Control District, which basically encompassed all of south Florida from just north of the lake to the Keys. No longer were the waterworks justified in the name of land reclamation, though that remained their goal; now, they were called necessary to protect people and property, who were beneficiaries and victims of the earlier efforts. The ploy worked; and from its initial entry into the fray in 1930 until the outbreak of World War II, the federal government, through the U.S. Army Corps of Engineers, invested $23.4 million in an increasingly elaborate plumbing system in south Florida.

The first, most highly visible, and most destructive project was the Hoover Dike. The earthwork towered from 34 to 38 feet around the south and southwest shores of Lake Okeechobee to slightly lower elevations in the north and northwest. Totaling 85 miles in length, ranging from 125 to 150 feet in width at its base, 10 to 30 feet at its peak, the levee effectively imprisoned the Big Water, sealing it from vision except from a few select points and the areas, later closed, where the dike did not extend. As part of its initial work, the corps also created a 155-mile-long, 80-foot wide, and 6-foot-deep channel through the St. Lucie Canal, Lake Okeechobee, and the Caloosahatchee River (later expanded to 100 feet wide and 8 feet deep) for ships and barges. Where the canals met the lake, huge locks and hurricane gates rose. The other existing canals were cleaned of silt, and spur ditches were dug to improve the system.

Even in the early stages of construction, the new program proved so efficient in drying out the area that the level of Okeechobee dropped to a record low of 10.2 feet above sea level from a predrainage maximum of two times that. The 10-foot drop in the water table left the Everglades dry for half the year where historically it had been covered even in the driest times by at least a thin sheet of water. The 1930s were years of low rainfall, to be sure, but the works of engineers and the growing demand for water among farmers and city dwellers amplified the poor natural conditions in a most dangerous way. By 1940, the farmlands around Lake Okeechobee had lost at least half of their initial 14 feet of soil.

With its natural water flow blocked and its animal water conservers—its alligators—shot, the parched Everglades began to burn, down to bare rock. The Everglades keys, those islands of oolitic limestone hosting hardwood hammocks and pinelands in the sawgrass, burned too, aided by man, who torched them to create farms, improve hunting, and guarantee the rarity of his tree snails. The smoke clouded the sky over the east coast resorts. Miccosukee Indians reported that the muck was on fire deep in the lower Everglades, where few people ever journeyed, proving no place was safe.

The fires flared with distressing regularity—1926, 1928, 1931–32, 1935, 1937, 1943, 1945–47, 1950–52, 1962, 1965, 1971, 1973—often igniting in the dry season only to be followed in the late summer by a hurricane and flooding.[9] The extreme swings proved a double whammy to wildlife and farmers, while underscoring the problems with the reclamation program in south Florida. When dry, the sawgrass and peat burned until sufficient rain fell to quench the fire, and sometimes immense quantities were required. Countless plants and animals died in the conflagrations. With the coming of the rains, especially hurricanes, the canals quickly became overburdened and the dry, burned-over land flooded, catching animals unaware, destroying homes and crops.

Fire defined the pinelands and sawgrass seas long before white men began attempting to remake the landscape, but it came most frequently from lightning and would burn briefly and fast, clearing detritus from the understory of forests, dead grasses and unwanted saplings from the prairies, killing insects and fungi that infected the plants. Indian hunters also used fire to flush game, although until the canals were cut and the water table lowered, the land remained damp enough to limit the extent and damage of those flames. Similarly, even heavy rains in the predrainage period would not have created the great shock that flooding brought after the muck had dried and blown away, because the sawgrass marshes and prairies served as sponges whereas the water simply ran off the bare rock.

No one knew the exact depths of water in the dry seasons of the Everglades before the dredges started crunching through rock, but they were substantial enough to allow the passage of dugouts and canoes through the sloughs. After the canals and dike were in place one crossed the same region on foot or in a car modified with airplane tires.

While state and federal engineers replumbed south Florida, conservationists fought two major, quite different battles to save portions of natural Florida from dynamite and the maws of dredges. These botanists and biologists, fishermen and hunters,

landscape architects and artists battled in south Florida to preserve portions of the Everglades as a living system. In north
Florida, they worked to block construction of a cross-peninsula
ship canal and thereby save the Floridan Aquifer—the main
source of fresh water for many of the state's people—and the
scenic Oklawaha River and Silver Springs from despoliation.

With Ernest Coe as chairman and David Fairchild as president, the Tropical Everglades National Park Association issued
a report in 1932 urging creation of a vast preserve in south
Florida, the nation's first biological and botanical park. Authorized by Congress and President Franklin Delano Roosevelt, the
Everglades National Park was to be held inviolate from any
development or act that would "interfere with the preservation
of the unique flora and fauna of [its] essential primitive natural
conditions."[10]

Initially, the park was to include within its boundaries
2,104,500 of the 8,000,000-plus-acre Everglades region of
south Florida. As approved in 1934, the park would have encompassed the sawgrass marshes that many people consider the
true Everglades, most of the Big Cypress Swamp, south Biscayne Bay and its sand keys, Key Largo and a large section of
the coral reef lying off its shore, Florida Bay, and Marco Island.
Daniel Beard, an assistant wildlife technician for the National
Park Service, surveyed the proposed area in 1938 and urged
prompt action. "The southern Florida wilderness," he said, "is
a study in halftones, not bright, bold strokes of a full brush as
is the case of most of our other national parks. . . . there are
lonely distances, intricate and monotonous waterways, birds,
sky, and water."[11]

A careful, thorough investigator, Beard recognized immediately the unique characteristics of the region and the need to
act decisively to protect them. "The reasons for considering the
lower tip of Florida as a national park are 90 percent biological
ones," he said, "and hence highly perishable. Primitive conditions have been changed by the hand of man, abundant wildlife
exploited, woodland and prairie burned and reburned, water
levels altered, and all the attendant, less obvious ecological conditions disturbed."[12] Like other prescient observers, Beard recognized that the health of the Everglades served as a barometer
for the well-being of humans in south Florida.

The federal legislation required the state to purchase the
land designated for the Everglades National Park and to deed

it to the federal government, but for want of funds and desire, officials in Florida and Washington, D.C., dragged the process out for a decade. Speculators and con artists had a fine time buying lands, especially after drillers struck oil in the pinelands around Sunniland on the north edge of Big Cypress in 1943. Suddenly everyone wanted to own and not renounce mineral rights to the lands marked for the national park. (The park's observation tower overlooking the Shark Valley Slough is built on the site of an exploratory oil well, which, fortunately for the Everglades, failed to produce.)

Cypress, mahogany, and other trees also became objects of lust in the early 1940s. During World War II, cypress was used to make PT boats, and loggers began to move into the Big Cypress Swamp to destroy its centuries-old trees. A few years later, after World War II, manufacturers demanded cypress for coffins, barrels, decks for houses, stadium bleachers, boats, and paneling; and the timber companies—the Lee Tidewater, and J. C. Turner companies chief among them—pushed deeper into the wilderness. They built roads and tramlines and attacked the most remote strands. In 1952, when it was clear that logging threatened virtually all of the first-growth cypress in south Florida, the Collier family and Lee Tidewater Cypress Company donated Corkscrew Swamp to the National Audubon Society as a sanctuary for wood storks and other wading birds, whose rookeries society wardens had begun protecting in 1912. Consciences satisfied, the timber companies redoubled their logging efforts. They hauled out nearly forty thousand railroad car loads of cypress in less than two decades.

Fire swept the cut strands, making it difficult to impossible for the bald cypress to come back, because the thin soil was consumed. An altered landscape was left to hunters, land agents, and a few settlers content to dwell in the backcountry. In the Big Cypress country at Ochopee, which now boasts the country's smallest post office (approximately the size of a large privy), farmers drilled wells and plowed fields for growing vegetables. A packing plant opened at nearby Monroe, off the Tamiami Trail. The intensive cultivation so depleted water supplies that wells along the Gulf coast turned brackish.

The delays in establishing a park caused by timbermen, farmers, and oilmen, when combined with the natural vagaries of the weather and human depredations, made the situation in the Everglades more critical yearly. In the fading days of World

War II, state officials, bowing to the pressure of mineral-hungry landowners, negotiated a reduction by one third of the park's authorized size and then in Solomonic fashion promised to donate to the park 850,000 acres—the last of the swamplands deeded by the federal government in the nineteenth century— and to appropriate $2 million for the purchase of the rest of the area. The park, as reconfigured, would contain 1,337,000 acres, with the east Everglades and assorted sawgrass marshes north of the Tamiami Trail, Key Largo, and the coral reef lying off its shore, Marco Island, Big Cypress Swamp, and Biscayne Bay being left out. The Izaak Walton League and lobbyists for recreational fishermen argued that Florida Bay should be excluded from the park because they feared regulations would eventually curtail anglers' access to the rich fisheries along the coast. That was one of the few fights for exclusion of property that any special interest group lost! According to William Robertson, Jr., a biologist with the park for more than thirty years, virtually every major conservation battle in south Florida since creation of the Everglades National Park has centered on one or more of the tracts that were kept outside its boundaries for political reasons.[13]

The negotiations over specific parcels of land gave state officials additional opportunities to renege on meeting their pledge to create a park. Powerful north Florida legislators balked at appropriating the agreed-to funds. To break the impasse, the president and chairman of the state's largest utility, McGregor Smith of Florida Power and Light, arranged a meeting between the reluctant legislators and John Pennekamp, editorial director of the *Miami Herald* and a leader in the park movement. Only after Pennekamp broke the park's opponents in a late-night poker game did they decide to honor their commitment.[14]

President Harry S. Truman dedicated the Everglades National Park in 1947; it had as its first director Daniel Beard, who brought on staff a biologist to help survey and manage the area's unique, often nearly inaccessible resources. Now, scientists and rangers can travel over the park in a helicopter equipped with pontoons that allow it to land in water or on the dense sawgrass. They rely as well on airboats and " 'Glades buggies," vehicles with airplane-size tires that enable them to traverse the muck. Private travel in the park by those means is prohibited because the airboats smash down the sawgrass with their broad bows, leaving trails that become scars of broken sedge, and the off-track vehicles, as they are called today, rip away vegetation and carve deep furrows in the soil. These restrictions mean that most of the million or so park visitors a year never see the heart of the Everglades except from one of the overlooks or observation towers. To skim through the sawgrass, one must go to the conservation areas or parts of the Everglades lying outside the park where privately operated airboat tours are available.

The new park's boundaries continued to shift until 1958 when its perimeter, at last, was fixed. An area of pineland, known as the "hole in the doughnut," was logged, rock-plowed, and farmed into the 1970s when it finally became part of the park. Now, the Everglades Research Center occupies what was formerly a dormitory for migrant workers and, among its many projects, attempts to restore the surrounding pinelands, an effort that involves fighting back invading *Schinus*—Brazilian pepper—and fans of the Florida panther who believe knocking down the pine and sowing grain will bring a population explosion among deer that will then fuel a comeback by the big cats—an odd notion that would destroy one of south Florida's most endangered ecosystems.

The opening of the park coincided with a renewed push for federal intervention in the canal and levee business of south Florida, a campaign that became a final, mad assault. As in the past, the cause for alarm was flooding—massive, development-eating inundations in Palm Beach, Hialeah, Miami Springs, Opa-Locka, Fort Lauderdale, along the Kissimmee River, at the headwaters of the St. Johns, on the farms, and in the Everglades. The flooding came from rain and hurricanes—facts of south Florida life, nemeses of the drainage engineers.

The year 1947 had begun with fires in the Everglades, started in the dried-out beds of sawgrass by careless humans. In the summer, heavy rains had doused the flames and filled the canals to capacity when a hurricane began drifting up the coast on September 10 and crossed the peninsula from Fort Lauderdale to Naples the following week. The storm dumped a foot or more of rain on some areas, causing tremendous flooding, and a second storm, crossing from Cape Sable to the east coast on October 11, amplified the disaster. Nearly twelve thousand people were evacuated, and eleven died. Property damage amounted to $59 million. Septic tank failures fouled flood wa-

ters and added to a generally unhealthy environment in the
waterlogged communities. People screamed for control of the
Everglades, and the state moved to wrest more financial and
technical assistance from the federal government.

A Central and Southern Florida Flood Control District was
created in 1949, the forerunner of the state's water management
districts and the agency that would oversee one of the most
comprehensive and environmentally ruinous water control projects in the nation's history. Conceived to correct through more
engineering the damage wrought by haphazard, piecemeal canal
and levee building around Lake Okeechobee and the Everglades, the project engulfed the Kissimmee River and the marshes at the headwaters of the St. Johns River. When completed,
the project had nearly destroyed the ecological viability of a
third of the peninsula.

Canals, like roads and railroads, airports, harbors, and subdivisions were good for business. The profit motive was often
coated in homilies about progress and the greater good of society, and they worked.

In the sixteenth century, the lords of Spain conceived a
canal across the peninsula as a means to protect the fleet bearing
gold from the evils of hurricanes, pirates, and incompetent
navigators. But Spain could barely hold Florida, much less
mount a major public works project across its midsection. The
fantasy lived on through English possession, Spanish reposses-
sion, and American annexation, when it became, according to
Nelson Blake, "a hardy perennial of Florida politics."[15] In the
1920s, business leaders in Jacksonville and Yankeetown, the
likely Gulf coast terminus, began one of the periodic agitations
and succeeded in gaining money for additional studies. No action was taken because the resulting report did not support the
scheme. Undeterred by failure, in 1932, promoters of the ditch
organized the National Gulf-Atlantic Ship Canal Association,
with representatives from Alabama, Louisiana, Mississippi,
Texas, and Florida, all of whom saw an opportunity to coun-
teract the effects of the Depression and bring some business to
themselves. Building on its experiences in the Everglades, the
Florida legislature organized a Ship Canal Authority, a special
taxation district headquartered in Jacksonville and encompassing the six counties that stood to benefit and suffer most from
the canal. The deeper county residents became financially in-

volved through taxes and bond obligations, the thought was, the
less likely they would be to drop their support for the project.
Ed Ball, trustee of the Du Pont estate, bought bonds for the
canal and proclaimed it a significant boon to the state's development.

The proposed route followed a dredged channel from Jacksonville up the St. Johns River to Palatka, then ran through a
newly dug canal to the Oklawaha River and proceeded along a
straightened version of that waterway to just south of Silver
Springs whence it crossed the Central Highlands for thirty-five
miles to the Withlacoochee River and a channelized straight
shot to enter the Gulf of Mexico at Yankeetown. At best, the
route was circuitous and therefore potentially difficult for large
ships to traverse. Also unclear to all but the most rabid backers
of the scheme was how it could succeed while the south Florida,
cross-peninsular waterway through Lake Okeechobee along the
Caloosahatchee River and St. Lucie Canal remained underuti-
lized at its busiest times.

With Senators Huey Long of Louisiana, Duncan Fletcher of
Florida, and their Gulf state colleagues in the House and Senate
lobbying for work to begin, President Franklin D. Roosevelt
agreed to support the project under the newly passed Emer-
gency Relief Appropriation Act. Within two months, the Army
Corps of Engineers had hired forty-six hundred men and established five base camps for its assault. But Roosevelt had received
bad advice from politicians supporting the canal, who led him
to believe he was funding a great and beneficial public project
that would fight unemployment in the present and future.

The Seaboard Air Line, the Florida East Coast Railway, and
the Atlantic Coast Line, as well as the state's smaller carriers,
vigorously opposed the canal on the grounds that it would undermine their business, an accurate assumption but not one to
elicit much sympathy among people who recalled their discriminatory ways. More significant from an environmental
standpoint, the U.S. Geological Survey reported that the canal,
as designed, would slice eighty-five feet into the Floridan
Aquifer in the Central Highlands, thereby allowing salt water to
intrude into the major source of fresh water underlying the
peninsula and cutting off the flow of water at Silver Springs and
Rainbow Springs. In effect, the canal would cut in half the state's
underground water supply and create an ecological disaster to
make those already manifest in the Everglades appear insignificant.

In Henry Sanford's former colony, which had become the major celery-producing area in the country, outraged citizens formed the Central and South Florida Water Conservation Committee. Another coalition came together in Bradenton on the Gulf coast, and soon the two groups presented a united front of citizens who lent their voices to those of the railroads and businessmen in the port of Tampa who felt threatened by competition from the canal. The Army Corps of Engineers issued a report claiming the damage would be minor, especially when compared with the economic benefits to Jacksonville and Pensacola, two port cities out to reassert their economic dominance in the state. But the corps's report was not widely believed.

Congress refused in 1936 to vote funds necessary for the canal, not out of environmental sensitivity, but out of a desire to teach Roosevelt that he could not start major public works projects without first gaining its approval. The result was a plus for the defenders of Florida. But the defeat of the canal proved temporary, for during World War II when German U-boats prowled off the Florida coast, patriots began to agitate again for the direct line across the peninsula.

The new incarnation was a barge canal, with a twelve-foot channel, locks to prevent saltwater intrusion, and a promise to slice into the Floridan Aquifer to a depth of only twenty-seven feet. Congress approved the revised project, which was to cost nearly $45 million, but refused to appropriate the necessary funds because of a wartime shortage of men and equipment and a backlog of Army Corps of Engineers projects. Even after the war nothing was done, as the corps dug its way through other areas, including south Florida, but the Cross-Florida Barge Canal remained on the books, waiting for someone with power enough to start the money flowing.

FIFTEEN

Florida Takes Off

The population explodes out of World War II. Florida enters the space age but can't keep itself together. Mass migrations bring unequal prosperity. Quality of life falters.

During the Second World War, playground Florida became campground U.S.A. as airmen and sailors came to train quickly in the warmth and ship out. Resort hotels on both coasts were converted to barracks; calisthenics were conducted on the beaches where the beauties bathed; jungle survival and landing courses met in the Everglades and along the Keys, where poisonous plants and snakes were among the hazards. At Miami Beach, seventy thousand hotel rooms were requisitioned by the Army Air Force; Flagler's Ponce de Leon Hotel in St. Augustine served the Coast Guard. There were new military bases at Tampa and Orlando, revived ports at Key West and Pensacola, an airfield at Homestead. Dirigibles patrolled the coast, looking for U-boats, while destroyers stood offshore to intercept them. Airmen on training flights over the Everglades dumped their cigarette butts out the bomb bays and ignited the dried-out sawgrass and muck. Farm workers deserted the fields for factory jobs or military service in such great numbers that migrants were brought from the Bahamas and other islands to cut sugarcane and pick fruit and vegetables. Students too young to fight were sent along with prisoners to help in the harvest. Women worked the factories and mills. Shipbuilding contracts brought new wealth to the dry docks at Tampa and Jacksonville.

The most exciting military operation in the state since the Civil War occurred when four German saboteurs were landed from a submarine onto the beach at Ponte Verda. No one knew about their existence until the leader of another German commando team, which landed at Long Island, exposed the operation to the FBI. The foursome from Florida, having split into pairs, was arrested in New York and Chicago. Only then did the state learn of its invasion. The episode combined with German U-boat raids on ships off the Florida coast to leave people with a sense of apprehension and vulnerability that would rise again during the Cuban missile crisis of 1962 when panicked patriots dug bomb shelters in anticipation of a nuclear attack. The most famous of these bunkers was blasted into limestone at Palm Beach near the winter home of the parents of President John F. Kennedy.

The state welcomed the military recruits and their visiting families, many of whom complained about the food, the prices (vendors gouged tourists, even if soldiers and sailors, whenever possible), the heat, and the bugs. Despite their complaints, many decided to migrate. The state's population grew from 1,897,414 in 1940 to 2,771,305 in 1950. It was an odd migration into Florida—the Panhandle and northern counties being largely forgotten until the last half of the 1980s when they were rediscovered as "unspoiled"—of retirees living on pensions, social security, life savings, and home profits; of young couples taking advantage of the VHA and FHA to buy tract houses in new developments and start families and careers; of professionals and entrepreneurs establishing businesses; and of military families.

Cape Canaveral was selected in the postwar years to serve as the launchpad for the nation's space program, a move that led to demand for engineers and technicians not available locally. Sleepy beach communities like Titusville, Cocoa Beach, and Merritt Island became space age boomtowns through the heyday of rocket testing and NASA's manned space flights. During the 1960s, the population of Brevard County more than doubled, and although the prosperity of the area since then has tracked the fits and starts of the nation's space program, it has continued to spread into the marshes inland from the coastal ridge.

Nothing dimmed the allure of Florida. By 1960, the population had reached nearly 5,000,000; ten years later, 7,000,000;

and by 1980, 11,000,000-plus. Reversing historic patterns, new-comers in the postwar years settled south to north, with the southeast coast and Tampa Bay regions receiving the majority of immigrants. Population growth in these areas defies comprehension: Dade County, 495,000 in 1950 to 1,250,000 in 1970 to 1,700,000 in 1986; Broward County (Fort Lauderdale), 84,000 in 1950 to 612,000 in 1970 to 1,200,000 in 1986; Palm Beach, 115,000 to 346,000 to 720,000; Pinellas (St. Petersburg), 159,000 to 515,000 to 816,000; Hillsborough (Tampa), 250,000 to 484,000 to 775,000; Orange, 115,000 to 345,000 to 578,000.

The number of tourists quadrupled between 1960 and 1988: 10.7 million in 1960; 20 million in 1968; 34 million in 1978; and 44 million in 1988. Mobile homes increased during the same period from 89,000 to 515,000—not including recreational vehicles that vacationers drive through the state for visits. The expanding tourist and resident populations spurred construction of 130 new airports during the 1960s alone. (More foreign visitors to the United States land at Miami International Airport than any other outside of New York City's Kennedy Airport.)

In the 1960s and 1970s, condominiums and apartments sprouted along the coast, from Miami north and Jacksonville south, looming, steel-and-glass cliff dwellings with views of the water for their inhabitants alone. Their march swallowed old beach towns and created new ones indistinguishable except for road signs along U.S. 1 or A1A—Surfside, Sunny Isles, Hallandale, Fort Lauderdale, Pompano, Boca Raton, Delray Beach, Boynton Beach, the Palm Beaches. The southeast Gold Coast became so overbuilt and expensive that developers switched their attention to small Gulf communities like Sarasota, Bradenton, Naples, and to small towns farther up the east coast—Vero Beach, New Smyrna Beach, Daytona Beach, and Ormond Beach.

Gas stations and fast-food outlets at every corner, strip shopping centers—usually with a food store, five-and-ten, drugstore, beauty parlor, and one or two other specialty shops—and later climate-controlled malls lined the major thoroughfares leading out of towns and cities, serving the new subdivisions—the Estates, Gates, Woods, Lakes, Whispering Pines, Seasides, Glades, Sweetwaters, and Springs, and names using every other natural and bucolic noun that had nothing to do with the actual setting. At their most luxurious the shops, like the subdivisions, were expensive, architect-designed, professionally decorated.

At their tackiest they were cinder blocks thrown on slabs or factory-prefabricated structures or trailer parks a severe storm would smash and scatter. The common construction practice was to bulldoze the lot clear of trees and scrub or, as a concession to nature, leave a few scrawny pine and oak trees, then lay rectangles of wiry St. Augustine grass, a few shrubs, and trees and let the newcomers do the rest on a field that had sprouted identical houses under a wide dome of sky with air conditioners humming to break the calm.

There was no way to gain control of a state growing by 3 million and, since 1970, 6 million people every two decades— 300,000 a year, 6,000 a week. The state built tens of thousands of miles of roads, counties built roads and schools, cities built roads and sewers; the federal government built roads and dug ditches and dredged channels, until from Jacksonville to Homestead, the Atlantic coast was a stretch of people broken occasionally by a public beach or vacant lot. From Tampa and St. Petersburg to Naples and from Orlando west to the Gulf and east to the Atlantic similar strips of urbanization arose.

For people accustomed to two-lane roads running through stretches of open country and to ocean views uncluttered by houses or hotels, the intersections and exchanges of the interstate highways and expressways represented surreal fantasies, swirling and twisting in an impossible-to-navigate display. They filled with traffic, they expanded. Interstate 95, ranging from four to eight lanes, followed the western rim of the coastal ridge, running back of "civilization" until the suburbs spread to bridge its banks, making it a blacktop river. It is being expanded again through densely populated south Florida with wags joking seriously that one day the road will have forty lanes from Palm Beach to Miami. Interstate 4 was a speedway from Daytona to Tampa for a decade before it became choked with traffic from the explosive growth of central Florida. By 1986, nearly 100,000 miles of roads laced the state, clogged with eight million cars of Floridians, as well as those of twenty million-plus tourists, who arrive in the state in automobiles.

As important as gross numbers in shaping the state in the postwar decades was the demographic breakdown. By 1980, 18 percent of the population was over sixty-five, up from 14.5 percent ten years earlier and nearly 5 percent above the national average. In twelve counties along the east and west coasts and in central Florida, the population of retirees ranged from 33 to

50 percent; and their concerns were more often with proper facilities for care and entertainment of the elderly than for the young.

The state was no better prepared for young families than for the elderly. Now, with the fourth largest population in the nation, Florida has no college or university to match in quality those of California, Texas, New York, Illinois, Pennsylvania—to name states close to it in size. Its primary and secondary schools rank no better, yet state leaders for forty years have failed to address the issue in coherent fashion, ducking responsibility by proclaiming that the people of Florida will not accept the taxes necessary to pay for quality universities and leaving the issues at the primary and secondary levels up to the individual counties, which often lacked the resources and the will to address them. Governor Claude Kirk in 1968 announced grandiose plans to create in central Florida a university devoted to engineering and technology that would rival any in the country. The University of Central Florida—originally Florida Technological University—was never provided funding or leadership to meet its charter, but Kirk's instincts were correct.

Conventional wisdom holds that the proliferation of air-conditioning and mosquito control, especially that involving "fogging" with DDT, made this sudden influx of people possible. Although convenient, that explanation fails to take into account the state's habit·of doubling its population roughly every two decades since the Civil War. Each new technological advance helped bring new settlers and, increasingly, tourists—steamboats, trains, cars and buses, airplanes.

Beginning in the 1950s, expansion of air-conditioning technology permitted construction of larger hotels, stores, office and industrial facilities, apartment buildings, and condominiums that could offer tenants a controlled climate throughout the year. Through the mid-1960s, central home air-conditioning, while growing in use, remained a major economic investment, a monthly expense that only the solidly middle and upper-middle class could afford. Over time, builders, as a marketing device, placed central units in their homes, which they designed as if they would be open to real air only on cool, dry, and breezy days. Windows became smaller, houses were placed on lots with no regard for the prevailing winds, no shade—given the universal habit of stripping every homesite bare, there could be none—no sensitivity of any sort to the climate. If people wanted comfort in summer, they had to use air-conditioning and bear the costs.

Screens for keeping mosquitoes and other insects at bay were as important to human habitation of Florida early in this century as pesticides became in the 1940s, and far less damaging to human and animal health. Screens allowed people to stay outside even during summer mornings and evenings and on breezeless days when mosquitoes swarmed. Drainage of wetlands for development also drastically reduced the mosquito population, as have recent efforts to keep water running through canals and ditches, because mosquitoes lay their eggs in stagnant water. But it is nonetheless true that pesticides for home and outdoor use made Florida more tolerable to many people than in years past.

Early in the 1940s, researchers at the federal Agriculture Department's entomology office in Orlando proved the efficiency of DDT—a German chemical discovered a decade earlier against mosquitoes, lice, and other insects, and manufacture and use of the insecticide on a massive scale followed almost immediately. Trucks and planes began spraying clouds of the toxin through neighborhoods and across the countryside. Houses and lawns, farms and gardens, were treated monthly, with the residue building up not only in the homes and their residents but also in the environment.

The destructive side effects of DDT on fish-eating birds and potentially on humans were apparent by the 1960s and finally led to a ban on nearly all uses of it despite protests that insects would assume control of the world. That other chemicals may be equally hazardous in aggregate, if not alone, has become clear during the past decade. Residents of the Florida Keys are subjected after every rain—almost daily for more than half the year—to heavy doses of poison spread by insect control squads. The pesticides have entered the aquatic food chain near the Keys and may one day force closure of the lucrative shrimp industry, as residues in the animals become too large to tolerate. On the peninsula, the chemicals—most of them known or suspected carcinogens—enter ground and surface water supplies, as well as fish and wildlife. The irony is that one can live in Florida with a minimum of chemical allies, providing one is willing sometimes to tolerate biting insects while encouraging insect-eating reptiles, birds, and spiders to live nearby.

*   *   *

Through the late 1960s, state and local officials actively promoted growth. Developers platted millions of lots and subdivisions across the state. Elaborating upon techniques pioneered by Richard Bolles, George Merrick, and Carl Fisher, they sold subdivision lots by mail, by phone, and by agents operating in major northern cities. They offered enticing and misleading financing and brought people by plane, bus, car, and train to view the marvelous unbuilt communities.

Leonard and Jack Rosen, appliance salesmen from Baltimore who saw quicker profit in the south Florida swamps, established the Gulf American Corporation in the late 1950s and on a point southwest of Fort Myers platted a community they called Cape Coral. Sales of lots fueled creation of more lots, and the Rosens soon moved from the coast into the logged-out wilds of Big Cypress Swamp to create a 173-square-mile subdivision called Golden Gate Estates. The Gulf American Corporation in the 1960s dug 183 miles of canals, constructed twenty-four water spillways, and laid 807 miles of road. Although the lots in Golden Gate Estates remained subject to flooding during periods of high rain, the massive development thoroughly disrupted the flow of fresh water through much of Big Cypress into the Everglades and estuaries, dropping the water table in the region an average of two to four feet—up to fifteen feet near Corkscrew Swamp and Immokalee. Golden Gate Estates was finally arrested after several thousand unwary investors bought its submerged lots, only to arise again in 1987 when attorneys for Avatar Properties in Miami began buying at a low cost the parcels those early investors had been unable to unload. Avatar, in turn, resold the lots for high profits to unsuspecting people, primarily Hispanics, seeking refuge from urban southeast Florida.[1]

From Golden Gate Estates, the Rosens, through their Gulf American Corporation, moved on to the Fakahatchee Strand, where some of the state's most glorious cypress and royal palms had once grown. The Rosens bought the strand and set out to market a subdivision called Remuda Ranch. They sold submerged lots, unimproved and isolated, and made millions of dollars before selling their Gulf American Corporation to the General Acceptance Corporation, which went bankrupt as a result of scandal associated with the Rosens' activities.[2] The undeveloped subdivision became a state preserve adjacent to Big

Cypress National Preserve; the cypress and wild animals again flourish there.

Another large construction firm, the Mackle brothers' Deltona Corporation of Miami, converted Key Biscayne from a sleepy barrier island with a mangrove coast and coconut groves inland into a flourishing residential colony, which subsequent developers expanded into an upscale resort for condominium dwellers in the 1970s. At the tip of the key is Cape Florida, now a state park, where one of the first lighthouses on the east coast of the peninsula was constructed early in the nineteenth century. Seminoles attacked the lighthouse in 1836 and brought it lasting fame. The park is filled with towering casuarina that have driven out native vegetation and altered the look and feel of the cape. Along the Atlantic shore is a white sand beach created and periodically replenished by the U.S. Army Corps of Engineers. Condominiums face the ocean while the bay side is dotted with natural anchorages and laced with unnatural canals to provide private moorings for people in their waterfront homes.

The Mackle brothers also platted around a small cluster of lakes named the Butler Chain, which they enlarged, between Sanford and Daytona Beach a new town they called Deltona. The community languished for several decades until the building boom that followed the opening of Walt Disney World finally gobbled it up during the past five years, but by then the Mackles had sold their interest. Recently, a series of years with below-normal rainfall and an increasing number of homes served by wells have depleted the aquifer and caused water levels in the lakes to drop so much that some are becoming large mud holes not an uncommon problem in other parts of the state as well.

The Mackle brothers are most notorious for their ambitious resort that ruined Marco Island, the largest of the Ten Thousand Islands, site of the tallest and most beautiful sand dunes in south Florida. Like the Rosens, the Mackle brothers sold lots on Marco Island before they received the necessary permits to dig canals and fill wetlands. Beginning in 1964, they spent $500 million on homes, shops, high-rise condominiums, waterways, and artificial roosting towers for bald eagles designed to appease people more than to attract birds.

By the late 1960s, public opposition to the rape of Marco, led by the Audubon Society and Environmental Defense Fund, grew loud enough that political leaders had to listen. The Del-

Current Population Distribution

One dot represents 1,000 persons

Water Resources Atlas of Florida, Institute of Science and Public Affairs State
University

tona Corporation wanted to start work on three new phases of
the resort community that required destruction of fifty miles of
mangrove swamps and extensive dredging of the island's embayments. After prolonged court hearings and proposed land
swaps that would have permitted the Mackle brothers to continue their work on Marco, although on a smaller scale than
initially planned, the U.S. Army Corps of Engineers in April
1976 refused to grant them permits to alter any of the island's
remaining wetlands, thereby halting conversion of mangrove
swamps into about thirty-seven hundred already sold lots
(repurchase of which remained the subject of several court cases

in 1988). Conservationists considered the corps ruling a victory, but the bulk of the damage to Marco Island was done, and now the fancy resort experiences periodic water problems because it has pumped out its groundwater supply.

In Flagler County, on a stretch of scrub between St. Augustine and Daytona Beach, International Telephone and Telegraph set out to create Palm Coast, a city that would hold 750,000 people by 2010 and stretch from the Atlantic Ocean inland toward the St. Johns. The plans called for connecting twenty-eight miles of canals to the Intracoastal Waterway, but, reflecting new awareness of the environmental impacts of such projects, the Army Corps of Engineers approved only thirteen miles of the total. Begun in the 1970s, work has progressed slowly on the golf courses and homes, which a driver speeding down Interstate 95 can see, forlorn, stranded in the scrub. Fire sweeping across that country, as is its habit, nearly consumed Palm Coast early in this decade, lending a certain ruggedness and hint of danger to the place. But if Florida patterns hold to form, the flood of people heading for Jacksonville or Miami or Tampa or Orlando will soon reach Palm Coast.

Just south of Fort Lauderdale, the Arvida Corporation, once a Disney subsidiary, is building an elaborate new town called Weston, which stretches from the ocean to the edge of the Everglades and offers nearly every style of "contemporary living" for the appropriate price: condominiums overlooking the Atlantic, houses on the golf course, lakefront homes, shops, marinas. General Development Corporation, which in 1987 became the largest subdivision builder in the state, has projects in various stages of completion, including one at North Port on the west coast in southern Sarasota County, site of Little Salt Spring, the most important Paleo-Indian site in the country.

Other large-scale plans are floated around the state but they are increasingly difficult to launch and sustain because of ethical and environmental regulations. Little, however, stands in the way of smaller subdivisions and model communities leapfrogging across formerly undeveloped land. So-called impact fees, which require builders to pay for essential services so that county residents no longer have to underwrite their own ruination, are assessed as a way to gain control of growth, but they are generally too low and inconsistently applied to be effective.

* * *

Savvy developers learned to use master plans and environmental concerns to their advantage. In the 1980s, Seaside, designed by Miami architects Andres Duany and Elizabeth
Plater-Zyberk, began to grow near Fort Walton Beach in the
Panhandle. It is a community of natural landscaping—no grassy
yards—of architect-designed houses that conform to rigorous
standards, of planned roadways, passageways, shopping areas,
parks, and neighborhoods, residential areas, of front porches,
and gazebos. Praised as a model for other communities, the
beachfront town is an enclave for the comfortably upper-middle
class; but for all its publicized uniqueness, it is not much different in concept from Coral Gables or other, older planned communities around the state.

The use of native plants and the refusal to put down water-
consuming lawns at Seaside represents a significant advance in
landscaping aesthetics. The houses fit more easily into their
surroundings, and the development both consumes less water—
an increasingly precious commodity in that area—and contrib-
utes fewer fertilizers and pesticides to the surface and ground
water. A Native Plant Society and a few nurserymen have kept
Florida's flora alive and have begun recently to win converts to
their cause. The South Florida Water Management District and
others around the state also have introduced programs to encourage landscaping with native plants adapted to wet and dry
seasons as a way to conserve water, but they receive too little
financial support to change the attitudes of most people toward
what makes a yard "pretty."

On a smaller scale—so isolated it doesn't rate as a trend—
bold architects and engineers have turned back to the old
Florida Cracker houses with their middle, bisecting breezeways
and wraparound porches, their stilt bases, and high ceilings,
creating houses that require little or no air-conditioning.
Breezes and well-placed fans, perhaps a dehumidifier, provide
cooling through the hottest summer days. Shade and decoration
come from native plants. Energy- and water-conserving appli-
ances are used exclusively. The homes are expensive and defy
conventional wisdom about the absolute necessity of air-conditioning, but they point to recognition among some Floridians
that alternatives exist. In south Florida, they often employ, as
well, solar panels for generating hot water, the way residents did
in the 1930s and 1940s when electric service was limited and
costly.

*   *   *

Unprepared as it was for the numbers of immigrants in terms of its infrastructure and planning, the state welcomed them with open wallets, in keeping with its tradition of encouraging population expansion, as long as the newcomers were white. In 1951, as voting rights and integration became issues throughout the United States, bombers struck synagogues and black homes in Jacksonville, a black community named Carver Village, and a Catholic church and synagogue in Miami. The state coordinator of the National Association for the Advancement of Colored People was murdered in Mims, a small town just north of Titusville, shortly thereafter. The Ku Klux Klan took credit for the terrorism and a number of its members were indicted for various petty offenses because the major charges wouldn't stick. In the early 1960s, civil rights advocates protested in Tallahassee, Jacksonville, and St. Augustine, where in March 1964, Martin Luther King, Jr., spent the night in jail after leading a demonstration against the old Spanish town's restaurants and hotels. Although overt violence dwindled, white supremacists' opposition to every manner of desegregation remained a matter of faith after *Brown* v. *Board of Education* in 1954 ended separate and unequal education and the landmark Supreme Court rulings and civil rights legislation of the 1960s laid legal discrimination to rest.

Schools are integrated now, after a fashion, which often means not much because they tend to follow neighborhood boundaries. In Winter Park, the high school in the middle of town, integrated enough in the late 1960s to improve its athletic program, was moved in the early 1970s to a much needed new facility located in an exclusively white part of town. In the larger cities—Miami, Tampa, Orlando, Jacksonville—poor blacks are isolated and often ignored in ghettos. Henry Sanford's farming capital on Lake Monroe has a large, poor black population, often celery and lettuce pickers who have settled in year round. From nearly half the population one hundred years ago, blacks now comprise only about 15 percent of the state's people; they live primarily in the cities or rural areas beyond the pale of suburban society.

Black people in Florida, many of whom have roots running several centuries deep, have not benefited from the state's economic development. Their neighborhoods have received the least and worst of schools and services. Police and fire protection lag. Poverty, drugs, and crime run high, as does resentment against a white society that pays scant heed to the needs and

aspirations of the people and their neighborhoods. Unemployment among blacks is twice the state average, with the level for
teenagers exceeding 33 percent. An equal percentage live in
poverty and nearly half of them suffer from hunger. Inadequate
medical care and housing are epidemic. The legal system reveals
racial bias as well, with blacks representing 49 percent of the
state's prison population.

In the cities, public housing projects and industrial parks to
revitalize the ghettos are discussed and planned, then forgotten;
codes are not enforced to bring existing structures in black
neighborhoods up to standard. In Coral Gables—notorious for
its enforcement of strict regulations regarding paint color for
homes indoors and out, tree cutting, placement of boats, height
of walls around yards, and all other such matters great and
minute—city investigators do not enforce zoning and sanitation
codes in the old black section, allowing it to deteriorate. Nor
does the city maintain adequate water pressure in that area's
hydrants to power firemen's hoses. In consultation with area
residents, Arquitectonica, the premier architectural firm in
Miami, designed traditional Cracker-style Florida homes to be
built in the neighborhood as low-income housing, but the city
and county have thwarted the construction of the homes at every
turn. (Coral Gables officials acted quickly in 1988 to arrange
financing for work on the exclusive Coral Gables Country Club,
which grants free membership to each of them.) In Ybor City,
the capital of the old cigar industry in Tampa, blacks, many of
them descendants of the factory workers, find their homes
threatened by encroaching gentrification, which has run up real
estate prices and rents. Many can ill afford to move elsewhere.

The inequities have periodically led to violence. Race riots
rocked Miami and Tampa in 1968 in the wake of the assassination of Martin Luther King, Jr., as they did cities throughout the
United States. Few steps were taken to improve race relations or
living conditions, and riots and upheaval have also periodically
swept the cities since then, often over issues of police brutality
and poverty. In May 1980, perhaps the worst race riot in the
nation's history turned large sections of Miami into a combat
zone and left 18 people dead, several hundred injured, 1,100
arrested, and $200 million in property damaged as blacks as-
saulted whites, their cars, and businesses. The apparent cause
of the riot was acquittal by a Tampa jury of four white Miami
policemen who had, without provocation, cause, or warning,
beaten and stomped to death a black insurance agent, Arthur

McDuffie. The case was the most egregious of a series of incidents involving police brutality against blacks.

On January 16, 1989, after ceremonies commemorating the birth of the late Martin Luther King, Jr., violence again engulfed Miami. That evening a police officer shot and killed a young black motorcyclist being pursued for speeding; and a passenger on the motorcycle was fatally injured when the machine collided with an automobile. The bloodshed, arson, and looting that followed almost immediately continued for several consecutive nights in Overtown and adjacent Liberty City.

The circumstances of south Florida's recent history contributed greatly to these periodic outbreaks. For twenty years, black Floridians had watched in dismay as waves of Cuban immigrants received abundant government assistance and were hired into low-paying jobs as clerks, security guards, janitors, and maids to which they felt entitled, even if they thought them undignified. Blacks came to believe that United States immigration policy, which classified the Cubans as political refugees, did not accord the same respect to Haitians or Jamaicans or blacks from anywhere who fled oppression and poverty. As the years passed, many of south Florida's native blacks began to feel that their needs were again being neglected by state and federal programs designed to aid immigrants from Haiti, Jamaica, and other islands, and their sense of injustice resulted in schisms within the black community itself.

In the spring of 1980, as south Florida was making room for the influx of Cubans coming from the port of Mariel, the United States government was turning away from the Florida coast at gunpoint tramp steamers and makeshift craft overloaded with Haitians who had paid, often dearly, for passage to freedom from the terrorism of the Duvalier dictatorship and the grinding poverty of their homeland. Some of the ships grounded, and their captains threw the unwanted refugees into the ocean and their death. Others of the freedom seekers died when their fragile craft sank. Occasionally the bodies of victims washed onto the sands of Palm Beach, Miami Beach, and other Gold Coast cities. In the winter of 1988–1989, Miami's black leaders reacted angrily when busloads of Nicaraguan refugees were welcomed to Miami with jobs, food, and money, while promises from civic leaders to improve coniditions in black communities remained unfulfilled.

The problems reach throughout the state. Florida ranks fiftieth among fifty states in the amount it spends each year on health and human services, and thirty-second in average teacher salaries. The state's dropout rate is the sixteenth highest in the nation, and most of those who quit school are black teenagers.[3]

The situation among many black Floridians stands in stark contrast to that of another large ethnic group with a long historical relationship to the peninsula—Cubans. Given that long history, it was not surprising when many middle-class Cubans following Fidel Castro's successful revolution in 1959 chose exile in Florida. Their destination, however, proved to be not Key West or Tampa, but the state's major city—Miami, and not all of those coming in the wake of the political fugitives were refugees from communism. Many came to rejoin their families or to seek better economic opportunities. Since the 1930s, Miami had been attracting Latin Americans—including Cubans—and, in the opinion of many observers, it has become the economic capital of Latin America, a place that attracts exiles and business leaders from throughout the region.

The Cuban migration to the United States has drawn the attention of scholars and journalists for nearly thirty years, with the most noteworthy 1987 additions to the literature being Joan Didion's *Miami* and T. D. Allman's *Miami,* which have little in common beyond their titles. Didion's monograph is a serious examination of the relationships—often strained and always conflicted—between Cuban exiles eager to return victoriously to their homeland and various administrations in Washington, D.C., more concerned with geopolitics than political principle— no matter which part of the spectrum they occupy. Sociologists Alejandro Portes and Juan Clark, among others, have conducted extensive studies of the adaptation and acculturation of Cubans to the United States that speak to successes remarkable among immigrant groups and failures that no one wants to recognize. The history of recent Cuban migration is filled with mercenaries, patriots, ambitious and talented businessmen and women, who have transformed south Florida, making it at once more cosmopolitan and more narrowly parochial.

Between 1959 and 1966, some 400,000 of the Cubans leaving their homeland, for whatever personal or political reasons, settled in Miami, causing a dramatic increase in population in a city accustomed to rapid growth. The federal government officially contributed $2.1 billion to their resettlement during the period 1962–76, and state and local agencies added more. As the numbers of Cubans rose in the Miami area, many Anglo-

Americans began moving to unincorporated areas south of the city or north into Broward and Palm Beach counties, dithering about a loss of their "quality of life" and crime.

In the spring of 1980, the exodus of 120,000 Cubans from the port of Mariel aboard a makeshift flotilla of sinking pleasure and fishing boats contributed to the Cuban explosion. The Mariel exodus arose from a game of international brinkmanship between President Jimmy Carter and President Fidel Castro, which the latter won, as he threw unwanted convicts into the crowd of people waiting to emigrate. There was great confusion over the event, to be sure, as the Carter administration first urged boat owners in the Keys to sail for Cuba and then seized boats and persecuted their owners for carrying the refugees. (The fiasco contributed to Carter's defeat in the 1980 presidential election.) Carter's equivocation reflected that of the already existing exile community, which until 1987 considered many of these newcomers anathema. Only after a new federal immigration law mandating the deportation of criminals among the Marielitos caused those incarcerated in federal prisons in Atlanta and Louisiana to riot did Miami's Cuban establishment suddenly discover them as a cause célèbre.

Most of the refugees arriving in April 1980 were sent to a tent city in the Orange Bowl, because there was literally no room in Miami for them. From that camp, Marielito sociopaths created in Miami a crime wave of unprecedented proportion that tarred the image of Cubans and panicked an already frightened Anglo community. By the early 1980s, the former paradise on Biscayne Bay had the highest rate of murders and other violent crimes in the country and a reputation as the drug capital of the hemisphere.

With several hundred thousand Nicaraguan refugees expected to arrive by 1991, the ethnic mix and economic situation will become even more complex. Despite federal aid, the county's residents will bear the burden of caring for the basic social needs of the newcomers, and the environment, which many experts believe has already reached its carrying capacity, will deteriorate even more rapidly.

Because outside of Dade County, immigrants to Florida are predominately white, middle-class Americans, less attention accompanies their arrival, which resembles more a constant flow than a flood tide. But for nearly all areas of Florida, the problems of growth and pollution, of where to put people, their aspirations, and their trash are the same.

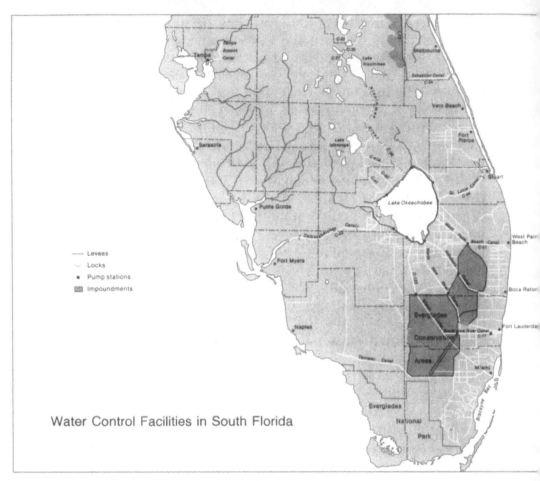

Water Control Facilities in South Florida

Water Resources Atlas of Florida, Institute of Science and Public Affairs State University

SIXTEEN

In Defense of
the Environment

Fearing for their state, Floridians fight against more canals and a huge jetport to preserve swamps and springs. The natural vanishes unless locked in parks and preserves. The legislature attempts solutions.

On June 17, 1962, Ross Allen and nine young men left Daytona Beach for Yankeetown, 153 miles to the west, a peninsula away. Allen, fifty-four, and his assistant, John Street, twenty-one, were the only certified adults on the trip; the remaining eight were teenagers, aged fourteen to seventeen. They carried no food and no weapons, except their hunting knives. Each bore a shoulder bag containing all his gear: mosquito netting, canteen and cup, pocket knife, compass, whistle, snakebite kit, two muslin sacks "for toting animals," headlamp and battery, a waterproof match case, a large plastic bag to keep his pack dry, six small plastic bags for storage, salt, water purification tablets, one spoon, aluminum foil (for cooking), notebook, pencil, handkerchiefs, and a change of socks and underwear. Camp equipment consisted of one shovel, one machete, maps, and a first-aid kit. The packs weighed ten pounds each. The Boy Scouts, according to their leader, were out to prove:

1. Survival by living off the land is possible, should such an occasion become necessary in our modern world.
2. The physical fitness of our youth (Boy Scouts in particular) can measure up to any in the world.

353

3. Many personal adjustments and requirements are necessary in order to survive any eventuality.[1]

The band crossed the peninsula in thirteen days on a diet that included berries, heart of palm, yucca seed pods, cattail, cactus, wild plums, wild oranges, bamboo shoots, and wild cherries; melons, corn, tomatoes, carrots, onions, and squash from abandoned fields; armadillos, frogs, snails, mussels, squirrels, grasshoppers, gopher tortoise, freshwater eels, skunk, rabbits, freshwater clams, fish, crabs, soft-shell turtles, wild hogs, rattlesnakes, coral snakes, and various other serpents. All but one lost weight, ranging from three pounds for one of the boys to 15 pounds for Ross Allen. But they made the crossing in good shape, proving, Allen said, that American youth were physically fit and that people could survive off Florida's natural bounty.

Allen, the internationally known snake hunter, was founder in 1929 of the herpetology institute at Silver Springs. At his institute he demonstrated techniques for handling and milking rattlesnakes—taking the venom for the manufacture of antivenin—and legend holds that he was struck more times than any man alive, with each next bite to have been his last. (He died of natural causes.) Communities in Florida in the 1960s would call Ross Allen and his crew to rid them of snakes real or imagined, for no new subdivision rose during that time that did not host a fair population of the reptiles, most of them nonpoisonous, but not many newcomers bothered to understand the difference. Of the six venomous inhabitants of the state—eastern diamondbacks, canebrakes, and pygmy rattlesnakes, water moccasins (cottonmouths), copperheads, and coral snakes—the diamondback is the most aggressive and largest, commonly exceeding six feet, although by now collectors, builders, and new settlers have managed to kill most of the large snakes. A hunter would be hard pressed to find rattlesnakes, or even nonpoisonous snakes, in most places today. Ten people would have an even greater difficulty crossing the peninsula on open ground, much less surviving off the country, from Daytona Beach to Yankeetown.

In 1962, there were still places in Florida people could go to escape other people and live from the land's bounty. Sandy Dayhoff moved with her husband Fred to the Big Cypress Swamp, off the Loop Road that runs out of the Tamiami Trail at Forty Mile Bend, near the Miccosukee reservation. No electric lines reached that far west from Miami; the Dayhoffs had no car. Land in the area belonged to the heirs of Jean Le Chevelier, the infamous plume hunter and bird collector of the turn of the century, who had bought it to create a canal-laced community. None of that came to pass, although in the 1940s and 1950s, loggers ripped out the old cypress, oil companies punched exploratory wells in the limestone, and vegetable farmers began tilling several thousand acres around nearby Pinecrest and Ochopee, places hardly large enough to warrant names. For many people with a love of the outdoors and hunting, Big Cypress Swamp was the last wild place in south Florida. (People can neither live nor hunt in the Everglades National Park.)

Sandy Dayhoff remembers flocks of fifteen to twenty wild turkeys foraging around their house, with some occasionally flying through the open windows, and herds of up to fifty deer browsing in their clearing. She could see hundreds of wood storks at a time and similar numbers of alligators. Snakes, turtles, frogs, and raccoons were ubiquitous. The Dayhoffs and their neighbors—there was a chicken farm across the street and other houses were scattered along the sand road—lived by barter, hunting, raising garden crops. They sold chicken eggs and raccoon meat and pelts for cash. They collected frogs by the wheelbarrowful for their legs.*

"This is a subtle place," Dayhoff says of the Big Cypress and Everglades region. "I learn something new about it every day." Life is easier now than twenty-five years ago, too, and a bit too crowded for people like the Dayhoffs. "We had hard times then. But I'm glad we could live that way." She possesses a deep love for the land that supported her and now, as a ranger for Everglades National Park and head of its Loop Road Interpretative Center, she works to instill that emotion in schoolchildren who come to learn about nature they never see in the suburban sprawl of Dade and Broward counties. "A feeling for the land," she says, "has to come from deep inside you."

There's little wild about Florida today; there are few un-

---

*Frogs appear as prevalent as ever; the *Miami Herald* in 1987 ran an article explaining to people in the new subdivisions in west Dade and Broward counties—literally in what once was classed as Everglades—that the frogs begin to swarm with the start of the rainy season. After each rain, they will croak through the night and invade swimming pools and Jacuzzis, where they deposit their eggs, which, unless cleaned out, produce filter- and pump-clogging tadpoles.

spoiled places, especially in the tropical southern half of the peninsula. In many areas a child can't find a forest or clean water to play in: There are too many houses. Even the once isolated Loop Road felt the press of people and development before coming under the protection of the National Park Service after one of the major environmental battles in Florida's history and one of the few notable victories for conservationists.

In the 1960s the Loop Road became the site of a mini-population boom as whites fled Miami, because of fear of Cuban refugees, civil rights legislation demanding integrated schools and housing, and a perception that government was reaching too deeply into their lives. They settled in the Big Cypress country because of its relative isolation and because it was to be the site of a massive jetport that the Dade County Port Authority planned to build to serve all of south Florida through a network of roads and rapid transit lines. The rogues and bigots among the newcomers turned Pinecrest into what many Miamians considered a lawless "redneck" town. To defenders of the place, the real villains were the developers and government officials moving to destroy every last vestige of Big Cypress.

The Port Authority had already started work on the thirty-nine-square-mile regional jetport when, in late 1968, a coalition of environmentalists, Indians, water managers, and politicians began arguing to stop the project on the grounds that it threatened the integrity of south Florida's water supply and the ecology of the entire region. The county's initial response was to slander and ignore the jetport's opponents, with Allen C. Stewart, head of the Port Authority, referring to them in 1969 as "butterfly chasers" and "yellow-bellied sapsuckers." At the same time the mayor of Metro-Dade (the hybrid government organized to manage a fast-growing, heavily urbanized Dade County), Chuck Hall, called Governor Claude Kirk's aide Nathaniel Reed and environmentalist-activist Joe Browder "white militants" for publicly objecting to the massive project. Hall voiced no concern when the Port Authority admitted at the same meeting that it had not conducted requisite studies of the impact of the airport on Big Cypress Swamp, the Everglades, and Water Conservation Area 3, which recharged the Biscayne Aquifer and provided surface water to the national park.[2]

Protests, a series of scientific studies, and domestic politics finally convinced President Richard Nixon's secretary of transportation John Volpe to order the construction halted in 1970, leaving in place a completed runway for use as a training facility. The battle led to creation of the 540,000-acre Big Cypress National Preserve, which in 1988 was increased in size by nearly 300,000 acres. (Ironically, the 1988 vote by Congress to approve expansion of the preserve drove Gulf Oil Company surveyors to move quickly into the designated area to examine it for oil, in order to avoid environmental restrictions that would be placed on their seismic blasting once the Park Service took control.)

By 1973, after the jetport project was canceled and the Big Cypress National Preserve established, the population boom along the Loop Road had busted, but so much damage had been done that the area, which has become a sort of natural laboratory for measuring the resilience of the south Florida environment, has not yet recovered. Wildlife populations remain suppressed. Although off-track vehicles have been banned from the Loop Road area for nearly a decade, the earth remains scarred from their tires, defying the assumptions of many experts that the land, left alone, would recover.

In 1962, the year of Ross Allen's hike and the Dayhoffs' move into Big Cypress, the U.S. Army Corps of Engineers commenced work on the last phase of its massive south Florida water control project—conversion of the meandering ninety-mile Kissimmee River into a fifty-two-mile ditch, C-38 (Canal-38), a superhighway of a waterway rammed through the oxbows and floodplains of the old wanderer, past dairy farms into Lake Okeechobee: There was no way the big concrete ditch could overflow. Since water began flowing through C-38 in 1971, the wetlands along the riverbanks have dried into pasture; the oxbows have stagnated and become clogged with plants that belong to alien ecosystems. Water bird populations have fallen to levels that disturb nearly everyone except bird haters. The C-38 aroused immediate opposition that reached a crescendo in the late 1970s when the full extent of its destructiveness became clear.

At the same time, water managers and conservationists became alarmed at the failing health of Lake Okeechobee, and the C-38 fell under suspicion as the agent of its near suffocation from too many nutrients. Careful investigation revealed that although fertilizers do course through the fifty-two-mile ditch, wastes from dairy farms just above the lake contribute most greatly to its overenrichment and would do so regardless of whether they flowed through C-38 or the Kissimmee River. Along with effluents from the dairies, the chief culprit in Okee-chobee's eutrophication is phosphorus- and nitrogen-enriched water pumped into it from the Everglades Agricultural Area. The diked lake can't handle the fertilizer and in recent summers has experienced algae blooms that have killed hundreds of thousands of fish and reminded biologists of 1966 when one million fish perished in Lake Apopka in central Florida from the same causes. Nearly 200,000 of the 775,000-acre agricultural district surrounding Lake Okeechobee are devoted to sugarcane, which survives as a cash crop in the United States because of federal price supports. In effect, the U.S. Department of Agriculture is subsidizing the destruction of south Florida's environment.

The drive to restore the Kissimmee River, organized and husbanded for years by a West Palm Beach plumbing contractor and leader of Florida Wildlife Federation named Johnny Jones, had become by the late 1970s a major cause for a coalition of environmentalists, hunters, fishermen, and water managers. The campaign achieved success in 1983 when Governor Bob Graham announced a Save Our Everglades program, which featured as its centerpiece restoration of the Kissimmee River and included plans to protect the vanishing Florida panther by, among other steps, placing culverts under a widened Alligator Alley, as it passes through Big Cypress on its run from Fort Myers to Fort Lauderdale; the cats are supposed to know to walk under rather than across the highway. (A program was also launched to restore marshlands at the headwaters of the St. Johns River.)

Bold though Graham's plan appeared at the time, it represented a fragile political compromise between those demanding a radical restoration of the Kissimmee River to its natural flow and those, like the cattlemen and Army Corps of Engineers, who favored the ditch. The partial restoration that began in 1983 involves the placing of weirs in the canal to divert water into the oxbows, thereby washing them clean of detritus and rejuvenating the wetlands on their banks. If completed, the rechannelization of the Kissimmee River would represent the first reversal in history of a major waterworks project. That a $150-million program dedicated to plants and animals was initiated on even a small scale represents a significant turn of mind and policy— nature becomes the justification, not man.

The saga of the Kissimmee River expresses many of the

contradictory notions and forces at work in Florida today. The Kissimmee River canal itself was the final, crowning glory of the Army Corps of Engineers' replumbing of the Everglades region. Between 1948 and 1971, the corps, with the state-created Central and South Florida Flood Control District staff, which ran the waterworks, built and improved fourteen hundred miles of canals, levees, and spillways (designated on maps "C," "L," and "S," respectively and numbered). The gridwork of canals emanates from Lake Okeechobee, whose depth is regulated in anticipation of south Florida's wet and dry seasons.

A levee built in the late 1940s runs along the border of the east Everglades from Palm Beach to South Dade, forming a wall the grassy water cannot overflow. The levee helps seal in manmade Water Conservation Areas 1, 2, and 3, lying south and east of Lake Okeechobee and completed from the late 1940s to the early 1960s. Collectively, they cover nearly 900,000 acres, with number 3—subdivided into A and B—alone larger than Lake Okeechobee. Conservation Area 3A feeds water directly into the Shark Valley Slough near its juncture with the Tamiami Trail, while a lock sits above Taylor Slough in the east Everglades, regulating its levels. All three impoundments are designed as storage basins to serve farmers, ranchers, the Everglades National Park, and urbanites in south Florida. The U.S. Fish and Wildlife Service manages number 1 as a part of the Loxahatchee National Wildlife Refuge, while the State Game and Fresh Water Fish Commission supervises hunting, fishing, and recreation in 2 and 3. Water Conservation Area 2, which receives runoff from the agricultural district, has become the habitat of cattail and other nutrient-loving species that have supplanted the native sawgrass. The other two have also suffered such severe changes in vegetation that the South Florida Water Management District, the successor to the Central and South Florida Flood Control District, plans to draw water out of them in an attempt to restore them to their natural conditions.

In years of heavy rainfall—from 1966 through 1970, for example—the District pumped excess water off the farmlands into the conservation areas and thence to the Everglades National Park, creating a flow of water faster and higher than existed under similar climatic circumstances in the years before drainage. Animals trapped in the man-made flood drowned by the thousands. The deer population declined sevenfold, from an estimated 7,000 to 1,000. Eyewitnesses reported that some hunters, encouraged by the state, went to the hammocks where deer congregated, turned their dogs loose, then shot from their airboats those animals running into the water to escape the hounds. The articles aroused the ire of antihunting groups, which nonetheless were hard pressed to solve the problem of deer starving on small islands in high water. Bitterness and accusations ruled debate over the situation, which clearly arose from the nature of the water control system.

Drought followed the flood, just as dry years had preceded it. By 1971, south Florida was locked in one of the most severe droughts on record; and the shock of several years of abnormally high water followed by no water stressed plant and animal life to near the breaking point. In 1970, the U.S. Congress had mandated that the Everglades National Park receive 315,000 acre-feet of water or 16.5 percent of the total discharge from the system in any given year, whichever was less. Reluctant state officials complained that the park should build levees and storage facilities just north of Florida Bay to impound fresh water, without caring or thinking that those structures would obliterate the last remnants of the natural system, which the park was designed to preserve. Water was released during the drought, but not enough to prevent 400,000 acres of the Everglades from burning.

No region of Florida escaped the push in the post-World War II years for massive, pork barrel waterworks. Natural disasters provided the opening for introduction and rapid movement of these projects through Congress. For Tampa—indeed for much of peninsular Florida—the signal event was Hurricane Donna's assault in 1960. In 1961, the Florida legislature created the Southwest Florida Water Management District to work with the Army Corps of Engineers to establish flood control structures around Tampa Bay. The District covers sixteen counties in the Gulf coastal lowlands and the De Soto Plain inland, along with the Lake Wales Ridge, Brooksville Ridge, Polk Upland, and Green Swamp and contains 25 percent of the state's people.

The corps planned an elaborate Four River Basins Project to complete a chaotic network of canals that had been growing in the Tampa Bay area since the late nineteenth century when settlers dug irrigation ditches for their farms. The Withlacoochee River was dammed in 1910 for a hydroelectric plant with the resulting reservoir being named—not ironically—Lake

Rousseau, for the celebrant of nature. In the 1920s, as in Miami and other booming communities, developers began more intensive dredging and filling that created water shortages and disastrous floods. The Army Corps of Engineers based its plan to protect six thousand square miles around Tampa on the highest water level recorded during one hundred years of record keeping, meaning the corps planned to replumb the Tampa Bay region as thoroughly and as unnecessarily as it had south Florida.

The design called for canals, spillways, and levees radiating from the Green Swamp, northwest of Tampa, where the corps intended to establish water conservation areas. The swamp was the marshy headwaters of four major rivers: the Oklawaha, flowing north-northeast; Withlacoochee, north-northwest; Hillsborough, southwest to Tampa; and, Peace, south-southwest through phosphate country. A major canal and several shorter waterways were constructed to divert floodwaters around Tampa and to drain other low-lying land. Other canals would straighten the rivers at their headwaters to allow for the rapid pumping of fresh water into Tampa Bay, where it served no one and killed creatures dependent on certain levels of salinity.

Profligacy brought the Four River Basins Project to a halt in 1970. The urban dwellers of Tampa, St. Petersburg, their northern neighbors at Clearwater, and their southern coastal neighbors of Sarasota and Bradenton, along with phosphate miners, grove owners, and farmers, used water in quantities the annual rains could not replenish. Dry years in the early 1960s and the beginning of the 1970s convinced local officials that the problem was less flood control than retention and conservation of water. Declines in the Floridan Aquifer during those droughts ranged from forty to sixty feet, and saltwater intrusion into well fields became a recurring problem. The flow of water in local springs diminished or died altogether. Tampa, which drew its drinking water from the Hillsborough River, could barely pump enough to supply its people and feared that its burgeoning population would outstrip supplies. As that dire prophecy now threatens to become real, the city has begun desperately to seek new sources of fresh water: One plan that has met strong opposition calls for diverting flow from the Suwannee.

Ignoring all evidence that more water was needed in the aquifer, rivers, and lakes, the U.S. Army Corps of Engineers proceeded with its plan to alter the Green Swamp, one of the prime recharge areas for the depleted supplies, until the Southwest Florida Water Management District board, under pressure from environmentalists, requested a new analysis of the scheme. Rather than respond to the request, the corps quit, leaving the project less than 20 percent complete. Nearly two decades later the water district board—political appointees, as are those in every one of the state's five districts—continue to debate various alternatives for flood control, including one that would leave about 90 percent, approximately 453 square miles, of the Green Swamp much intact as a naturally operating system. The board also kept alive the option of completing most of the discredited Four River Basins Project, proving again that in Florida major water control programs are nearly impossible to kill. While options are drawn and redrawn, the swamp is somewhat protected by the state cabinet's designation of it in 1974 as an Area of Critical State Concern, although builders pushing west from Walt Disney World have encroached on its edges.

In the boom times following World War II, expansion remained an article of faith. New schemes were launched and old scams rerun without regard to the needs of the state or its people. Early in 1960, dedicated north Florida Democrats, businessmen like Du Pont estate trustee Ed Ball, and labor leaders eager for public-dole jobs gained the support of presidential candidate John F. Kennedy for resurrecting the discredited cross-peninsula canal, not as a ship channel but as a waterway for barges, with locks to prevent saltwater intrusion and other environmental safeguards. The U.S. Army Corps of Engineers produced an analysis proving that the canal would return 5 percent a year on an estimated investment of $164.6 million, and a boondoggle that had languished for twenty years because of environmental concerns and lack of money was rededicated. In 1962, Marjorie Carr, wife of wildlife biologist Archie Carr and an outstanding ecologist in her own right, with two colleagues from the University of Florida faculty—David Anthony and Jack Ohanian—started a battle against the canal that they would wage for ten years before achieving a tenuous victory.

In February 1964, President Lyndon Baines Johnson triggered a blast starting work on the barge canal that would destroy forty-five of the wildest miles of the Oklawaha River and twenty-seven thousand acres of river swamp and hydric hammock.[3] From Yankeetown on the Gulf coast and the confluence of the

Oklawaha and St. Johns rivers to the east, the Corps of Engineers commenced work on the canal and lock system that would bisect the Ocala National Forest, curtail the flow in Silver Springs, befoul the Floridan Aquifer, and slice the Central Highlands like a loaf of bread, not to mention turning the Oklawaha and parts of the Withlacoochee rivers into silt-gathering ditches. The project was so massive that initially even the environmentalists weren't sure whether to petition for a route change to protect the Oklawaha or press against the odds for termination of the whole.[4]

While they debated, a 306-ton crusher-crawler, a huge diesel-powered tree-mashing machine, flattened 6,445 acres of riverine forest between two dams—Rodman and Eureka. Work progressed rapidly enough that Rodman Dam successfully blocked the flow of the Oklawaha's waters into the St. Johns near Palatka, backing them up for sixteen miles into a 13,000-acre reservoir, sometimes called Lake Oklawaha. A lock and canal connected the reservoir to the St. Johns to permit the passage of boats and barges. Although finished farther upstream, Eureka never dammed a drop.

Carr, Anthony, Ohanian, and their colleagues by 1969 had organized the Florida Defenders of the Environment and, along with the national Environmental Defense Fund (FDE was chosen because it is EDF backward) set out to educate the public and the politicians. The Florida Defenders of the Environment's 1969 report, *Environmental Impact of the Cross Florida Barge Canal with Special Emphasis on the Oklawaha Regional Ecosystem*, recommended that the canal be halted and Rodman Reservoir and Dam be dismantled and filled, a difficult task, given that much of the sand excavated to make room for the impoundment was used to build Interstate 95 down the east coast. The study galvanized opponents to the project, who had always been relatively numerous in south and central Florida, and the activists appeared to have achieved a remarkable victory in 1971 when President Richard Nixon directed the Army Corps of Engineers to abandon the canal.

In 1974, a federal judge ruled that Nixon had acted illegally in terminating a project approved and funded by Congress, but work did not resume on the barge canal. The federal government had spent in excess of $70 million for an incomplete ditch; it began paying more than $1 million a year to keep the locks working, the dams and channels in repair.

The battles dragged on. The 1969 Federal Environmental

Policy Act had required an environmental impact study for all
public works, and so the Corps of Engineers issued one for the
barge canal in 1974. But the project proved difficult to restart.
At the urging of Governor Reubin Askew, the state cabinet—its
officers are elected, not appointed by the governor, and thus
exercise considerable autonomy—voted in 1976 to oppose any
more work on the canal and to plan for restoring the Oklawaha.
In 1977, President Jimmy Carter sent to Congress a new Corps
of Engineers study urging the same approach—demolition of
Rodman Dam, back-filling of the reservoir, and designation of
the Oklawaha as a "wild and scenic river." To no avail: The
Cross-Florida Barge Canal remained on the active public works
list until 1985, meaning Congress could at any time have appropriated money for its continued construction. That year it was
dropped from the list, but through a compromise, Congress
agreed, because of the influence of representatives from the
region, to leave existing structures in place and maintain them
indefinitely in working order. Although a popular fishing and
duck-hunting site, which proponents of the canal trumpet with
glee, as if those attributes made it environmentally sound, the
reservoir is choked with hydrilla, hyacinths, and downed wood.
It is regarded as a hazard and eyesore.

South Florida was the sight of another major environmental
battle in the 1960s, when conservationists and sailors organized
against a baroque plan to create a community called Islandia,
which was to consist of Elliott and neighboring sand keys in
south Biscayne Bay linked to each other and the mainland by a
bridge and causeway. The plan, which included construction of
huge oil refineries in addition to homes and stores, was abandoned after prolonged and bitter political battles between residents and the Metro-Dade County Commission, which favored
the construction projects, and after passage of the state and
federal conservation measures that required environmental impact studies. In 1964, the only proenvironmental county commission in the region's history passed a proposal to establish a
Biscayne National Monument, and ten years later the lower bay
became a marine preserve under the supervision of the National
Park Service. (By that time developers were back in control of
the county government and they have remained there since.)
In 1968—before the marine park was formally established—landowners on Elliott Key plowed a road through the

middle of the hardwood hammock that filled the island, nearly destroying the last wild stand of Sargent's palms (sometimes called cherry palm) in Florida. They believed erroneously that if they tore up the hammock, they would block creation of the preserve: It mattered little that the government paid fair value for their property. The landowners lost on Elliott Key and were ordered to pay for replanting the palms and hammock, but elsewhere they have won.

Although the commercial oil refineries and causeway- and bridge-linked projects were defeated for Biscayne Bay, major electrical power plants were erected on the shores of the south bay at Turkey Point, including two relying on nuclear fuel. Constructed without proper environmental assessments, these plants contribute significant amounts of pollution to the water and air of southeast Florida. Should an accident occur, the fallout would travel on the prevailing winds—usually from the south-southeast—up the densely populated east coast. (A nuclear power plant was also built on the Crystal River above Clearwater, and it too has been plagued by problems ranging from improperly trained staff to thermal pollution of the river and leaks of "small amounts" of radioactive waste.)

State-mandated sewage treatment plants began in the late 1970s to improve water quality in bay waters around Miami and adjacent cities, many of which had sprung up without planning or control in the 1940s through the 1960s. Marine biologists say now that the programs have produced some limited positive results, but they have been achieved by moving the largest problem—sewage—a mile offshore so that currents sweep it to sea rather than to the bay. No one knows what will happen when the oceans rebel at serving as cesspools for humans. Improvement often proves transitory, as leaks of untreated sewage and other wastes can wipe out in a day the gains of a decade.

The issues that gave rise to the degradation of water quality—sewage, storm runoff from cities and farms, industrial pollution, garbage, spoil from dredging operations—have been treated to date with Band-Aids and prayers or ignored. Florida contains 286 toxic-waste dump sites, 29 of which qualify for the federal Environmental Protection Agency's list of those most threatening to human health—the "superfund" sites eligible for federal aid to clean them up: 8 in southeast Florida between Miami and Fort Lauderdale; 1 west of Palm Beach; 10 spread in a line from Tampa to Daytona Beach, roughly following Interstate 4; 4 around Jacksonville; 2 at Pensacola; and 4 in the pulp mill and mining country of middle Florida. Most of these dumps present clear threats to the aquifers underlying them and neighboring surface waters, including those of the Everglades. The canals of the water control systems present additional threats, which many officials have underestimated. In the fall of 1988, south Florida water managers flushed the canal (C-111) that flows through the rich agricultural land north of Homestead and were shocked when muck and stagnant water laced with herbicides and pesticides, including DDT, killed marine life in a mile-wide swath in lower Biscayne Bay.

No body of water in Florida is free of pollution and death. The Peace River in west-central Florida ran yellow twice during the 1960s from the discharge of the phosphate mines, and the water table in the aquifer dropped precipitously while the companies, many of them under the ownership of multinational corporations—Mobile and Monsanto being two of the largest—fought any attempt to require them to restore the land or pay a fee for the mineral they removed from the state. For the time these issues are resolved, with the state finally imposing a severance tax in 1971, modest by standards of the profits, and the companies moving to make the pits at least recreationally useful because of federal legislation requiring restoration of mined-out land. But successful reclamation remains the challenge rather than the rule: Waste clay from phosphate mining covers sixty thousand acres, while heaps of radioactive gypsum that threaten groundwater fill another four thousand. While ways are sought to seal them, radioactive particles seep into the earth with every rain.

The Panhandle and north Florida have also fared poorly. In the early 1970s, Escambia Bay in the Panhandle suffered repeated, massive fish kills because of discharge from factories of the Monsanto Chemical Company, Escambia Chemical Company, and American Cyanamid Company.[5] Pulp mills have turned the Fenholloway and Amelia rivers into open sewers. Pollution in the Apalachicola Bay regularly forces the closing of oyster beds, while on the opposite side of the peninsula, the toxin-laced waters around Jacksonville and at the mouth of the St. Johns River produce mutant fish.

Throughout the Orange Belt, processing plants for frozen orange concentrate have contributed substantially in central Florida to the eutrophication of Lake Apopka and the near death of Lake Griffin. Muck farms add their fertilizer-laced waste water to the overenrichment of these lakes, just as they feed unwelcome nutrients into Lake Okeechobee and the upper St. Johns River. By most counts fifty lakes need cleansing and restoration, and fifty more require protection from pollutants, with the majority of both groups lying in the Lake District of central Florida. Urban waste water from Orlando, Winter Park, and environs has contributed to the problems of lakes in that vicinity and poisoned the Econlockhatchee River and through it the St. Johns River in and around Lake Harney. Runoff from central Florida's growing cities also threatens the oyster beds of the Indian River.

Though the results are mixed, the environmental battles fought in Florida since the mid-1960s represent a significant change in the terms of public discussion, with citizens far outstripping their leaders in their desire to preserve and enhance natural Florida. The reform movement received a boost from Claude Kirk, the first Republican governor of the state since Reconstruction and a man who had portrayed himself as a conservative answer to the "liberalism" of Mayor Robert King High of Miami—his Democratic opponent. Kirk surprised everyone, including his supporters, by siding against developers on several major issues, including construction of the south Florida jetport, and signing environmental legislation to protect water quality and wetlands around the state. During Kirk's four-year term (1967–71) and sometimes over his opposition, the legislature adopted a "sunshine law" requiring that politicians discuss official business only in public, under the eye of people and press, and, reluctantly obeying a federal court order, reapportioned itself to give more equal representation to the fast-growing suburban areas of south and central Florida. The state's voters also adopted a new constitution, which strengthened the governorship, allowing the incumbent to succeed himself, reorganized the cabinet, established a state planning office (now Department of Community Affairs), and granted political autonomy to the counties.

Kirk's successor, Reubin Askew, served two terms (1971–79) and earned a strong reputation as a champion of the environment and planned growth. (He also established a record of support for civil rights in politics and education that was liberal by Florida standards.) During his administration, Big Cypress National Preserve and Biscayne National Monument were established, the barge canal was laid to rest, state parks grew in size and number (from 87,751 to 155,585 acres and 63 to 87, respectively), and the five water management districts were organized to safeguard the state's freshwater supply.

The legislation passed during Askew's administration to preserve land and water was as significant as the conservation laws passed earlier in the century to protect fish, birds, and animals, and its results have been as spotty because of erratic enforcement and inadequate funding. In 1972, the Environmental Land and Water Management Act gave state officials the authority to designate and then closely monitor land use in "areas of critical state concern" and approve plans for "developments of regional impact." A Land Conservation Act of 1972 authorized the state to issue bonds to raise as much as $240 million for the purchase of environmentally endangered lands and recreational areas, and in 1979 a Conservation and Recreation Lands (CARL) Trust Fund was established to finance protection of environmentally sensitive lands and to restore man-damaged systems. In 1975, an Aquatic Preserves Act approved the setting aside "forever" of lakes, bays, or rivers for the public use but not for mineral exploitation and, theoretically, not for extensive development. In 1981, the Water Management Lands Trust Fund was established to handle purchases under the state-sponsored Save Our Rivers Program.

The funds put the state in the business of buying at a premium lands it previously had given away in exchange for railroads and canals. During the Askew administration, twenty-two tracts totaling 363,200 acres were purchased and marked for protection, a worthy number compared to zero, but only about 1 percent of the state's acreage. Those modest achievements mark the high point of the programs, which operate according to an elaborate system of politically determined priorities. Nearly every county has a site worthy of protection, but even where officials are willing to acquire land threatened with development, they are unable, despite the state programs, to raise sufficient funds to do so and therefore must postpone the purchase. The delays result in higher prices or in sale of the publicly sought acreage to private investors. Another impediment to land acquisition is a provision in the conservation laws prohibiting officials from taking endangered areas under the right of eminent domain.

In rapidly growing central Florida, the Wekiwa River, a beautiful spring-fed tributary to the St. Johns, is threatened on all sides by development, despite its designation as an aquatic preserve and a "wild and scenic river." For years, the state has refused to buy land along the Wekiwa's banks, in defiance of its own public recognition of the river's importance, using as an excuse the river's relatively low position on a list of priority sites for state purchase. The list, which includes the east Everglades, is purely a political creation.

The springs at the headwaters of the Wekiwa are part of a typically overcrowded state park, although twenty years ago they were still undeveloped, having returned to their natural condition after hosting a spa in the late nineteenth century. The river forest, logged out at the same time, had regenerated itself and one could canoe and fish there for days seeing few people. Limpkins occupy the marsh, along with alligators, snakes, turtles, bears, raccoons, possums, bobcats, hawks, osprey, perhaps a few eagles, and, according to unconfirmed reports, several panthers.

Human squatters have settled along the river in increasing numbers, seeking a place to live in the wild, befouling the water. The squatters add a social and economic class element to the battle for the river. Undereducated and poor, they claim a right to settle along the river, to hunt, trap, and fish because they can find no life in the booming suburbs of central Florida—an argument similar to that made by squatters in the Big Cypress National Preserve in south Florida. Opposed by all other groups with an interest in the river, the squatters ironically serve the cause of developers because they disturb the forests and water, making it difficult for state officials and environmentalists to argue that the area is unspoiled. Pressure of another sort comes from the canoeists who flock to the Wekiwa to enjoy its beauty and charm in such great numbers that they seldom are out of sight of each other and on busy weekends scare much of the wildlife into hiding. They are bound in any event always to hear the hum of traffic on nearby roads and to see through the pellucid water the beer cans of their cohorts. The river cannot survive the developers, no matter how ecologically enlightened they purport to be; sometimes, one wonders whether it will survive its admirers. But there are no other places like it left in central Florida.

The environmental and land-use legislation enacted during the past two decades has shown that many Floridians believe such issues transcend parochial interests, and they have succeeded in stopping egregious projects that obviously would harm a major natural system, like the Big Cypress Swamp. The laws reflect a desire for what Luther Carter described in his 1976 study of the state as "an environment in which the natural and the man-made are treated as complementary, with the choice wild places preserved and the cities becoming more garden like."[6] Strong though that longing may be, according to public opinion polls, it is coupled with its opposite—a desire for the economic prosperity that growth brings. The cry of the conflicted is for an undefined "controlled" growth.

This attitude was forcefully expressed in December 1987 when the final 33.8 miles of Interstate 95 in Florida were opened through Martin, St. Lucie, and Palm Beach counties, providing multilane, high-speed highway travel from Houlton, Maine, to Miami. The last gap cost $221.9 million to close; the entire 382.4-mile stretch down Florida's east coast took fifteen years and $1 billion to build—roughly twenty times what Henry Flagler spent on his railroad along the same coast less than a century before. Even the normally proconservation *Miami Herald* hailed the completion as a great moment in south Florida's history, one that would improve life for commuters and tourists, while fostering growth. The roadway also brought up for development several hundred thousand acres of land. The John D. and Catherine T. MacArthur Foundation, noted for its support of conservation projects as well as for the genius fellowships it awards, unsolicited, to intellectuals and artists, announced plans at the time to sell a 46,000-acre parcel of the most prime of that real estate.

The equivocation has made it difficult for conservationists to consolidate fully their gains during the past two decades, despite passage in 1985 of a tough state law, the Growth Management Act, which mandated the most detailed plans ever drawn for Florida counties and municipalities. The act's intent was to assure that services would be provided for each new development, that adequate transportation, schools, hospitals, roads, parks, libraries, sewers, and water supplies would exist before homes and condominiums were built and occupied. The plans themselves would show the size and extent of permissible suburbs, as well as the location of the facilities that would serve them. Among the most advanced land-use legislation in the nation, the Growth Management Act has not lived up to the expectations of its promoters.

The difficulties are familiar. Because county and city commissioners often support developers and real-estate agents—are members of those professions themselves—they proceed reluctantly in preparing land-use plans, and when they finally act, they pay close attention to the desires of builders. Should the commissioners bow to public pressure and impose strict codes, they frequently amend them at a later date. Even destruction of wetlands is permitted, providing developers agree to set aside certain portions as undeveloped or to restore plowed areas as "natural landscapes." Industries devoted to this ecological landscaping have sprung up around the state, though their success rates, credentials, and methods are seldom examined critically. The justification for granting these exceptions is usually that the projects bring jobs and therefore wealth to the communities. In areas where both are not particularly abundant, the explanation usually goes unchallenged, although the people most in need seldom benefit.

Abundant evidence exists that planning enhances every aspect of life and furthers economic growth. The argument that such regulations run counter to individual freedom simply doesn't hold; the codes serve rather to create a viable community in place of tract houses thrown cheek by jowl with no sense of design, no parks, no focus, no plan other than a grid permitting the maximum number of units in the available space or a golf course open to members only. That ruins hundreds of thousands of acres a year, and nothing can be done to restore them until the land is somehow swept clean.

No place in Florida more clearly reveals the absolute necessity for a comprehensive development plan, along with the many obstacles to preparing and implementing such a plan, than the Keys. The Keys and the neighboring reef are unique, yet fragile ecological communities, as well as symbols of the American tropics, a way of life different from that found anywhere else in the United States. The Keys suffer from their popularity and the desire of people to cash in on the qualities that make them special by building condominiums, strip shopping malls, motels, and luxury vacation homes.

Nearly ruined during the Depression, Key West recovered economically in World War II, as the U.S. Navy expanded its base there. Military spending remained the chief constant of the local economy until the 1970s, when reductions again drove the

city close to bankruptcy. The tenuous finances of Key West
magnified problems arising from its increasing popularity
among counterculturists, artists, and wealthy northerners looking for a retreat. The island's population had risen from 30,000
to 52,000 between 1950 and 1970, and the pipeline from the
mainland no longer carried sufficient water to meet its needs.
Land companies dredged mud flats and shallow embayments to
make navigable canals for pleasure boats and filled wetlands for
homesites and trailer camps. Septic tanks malfunctioned and
combined with silt from the dredge and fill operations, raw
sewage from the city of Key West, and toxic wastes to befoul and
cloud the waters, killing coral and destroying fish breeding
grounds.

A desalinization plant and improved flow through the pipeline alleviated the immediate water problem, but the Monroe
County commission evinced no interest in any form of zoning.
In 1975, the state cabinet under Governor Askew declared the
Keys an area of critical state concern and took control of planning and zoning. The state also began to acquire land on Key
Largo for addition to the park and preserve system. Despite
those actions, the situation continued to deteriorate. By the
mid-1980s, after another military buildup and the increasing
gentrification of Old Town Key West, as hotels, homes, guesthouses, and restaurants were bought and renovated, the island
had become too expensive for many of its working-class residents.

In 1987, after a dozen years of political battles, master
development plans were adopted for Monroe County and the
city of Key West. Although more stringent than what had existed, the state's plans favored individuals and contractors with
the financial resources to meet environmental strictures. Local
officials promptly set out, not to correct the class imbalance, but
to loosen restrictions on condominium and luxury-home builders. Governor Bob Martinez, the former mayor of Tampa, refused to allow his Department of Community Affairs to exercise
its power of review and approval of the changes.

The land-use plans offered little relief to the stressed environment of the islands and neighboring coral reef. Although
Key West opened a sewage treatment plant in 1987, toxic wastes
continued to pour into the surrounding waters from private and
governmental sources, leaving the beaches around the city un-
safe for swimming, the sponges, corals, and fish poisoned. That

same year, the federal government introduced another grave threat to the Keys when it announced plans to lease tracts off the Atlantic coast of the Keys to companies with plans to drill for oil. The pressure of conservation-minded citizens and state officials forced a delay until environmental impact studies—notorious for their understatement of potential problems—are completed, and then the battle will be rejoined.

Nearly everyone agrees that neither the islands nor the surrounding water can bear much more human abuse. The most practical and difficult solution is purchase of all remaining undeveloped land on the islands for an estimated $600 million. Although large, the price is a bargain compared with the cost of the damage to all forms of life from continued development.

For any plan for the Keys or any other area in Florida to be viable, it must assure that a wide range of life-styles are open to state residents, that it is possible for men and women to become growers of citrus or rare fruit, to become farmers or ranchers, fishermen or spongers, as well as managers and laborers, police and firemen while safeguarding the environment. To fulfill that goal requires an expansion of opportunity beyond any that now exists, but to ignore it is to divorce everyone eventually from the land and water.

SEVENTEEN

Tomorrowland, Today

Walt Disney World redefines tourism and development patterns in Florida. For many people the future is now in a paradise lost. Does redemption follow the fall?

A nine-hundred-room Victorian-style hotel, called the Grand Floridian Beach Resort, occupies forty acres fronting the Seven Seas Lagoon between the Magic Kingdom and Polynesian Village. Coconut and canary palms wave at the breeze from the pristine white sand lining the canal. The place is not the South Pacific or even south Florida, and there's no ocean within several score miles of the beach. This Grand Floridian Beach Resort is in central Florida, specifically the Reedy Creek Improvement District, a special construct bridging parts of Osceola and Orange counties, the legislative umbrella for Walt Disney World, the vacation destination of choice for twenty-five million travelers a year from around the globe. Like the Standard Oil can and Coca-Cola, Mickey Mouse has achieved total market penetration. When Mickey wiggles his ears, the world squeaks.

According to the official guide to Walt Disney World, the Grand Floridian Beach Resort harks back to the turn of the century when

Standard Oil magnate Henry M. Flagler saw the realization of his dream: The railroad he had built to "civilize" Florida had spawned along its right-of-way an empire of grand ho-

374

tels, lavish estates, prominent families, and opulent life-
styles. High society blossomed in winter, as the likes of John
D. Rockefeller and Teddy Roosevelt put up at the Royal
Poinciana in Palm Beach, enjoying the sea breezes from
oceanside suites.[1]

The Royal Poinciana stood on the shores of Lake Worth,
not the Atlantic, but no matter. The Disney guide presents history in the grand tradition of Florida promotional literature,
which at its best has spawned such classics as Sidney Lanier's
Florida: Its Scenery, Climate, and History and the WPA Guide.

The Disney "official guide" tells its readers that the Grand
Floridian possesses all the opulence of "yesteryear" and adds to
it the conveniences of the twenty-first century—air-conditioning
and monorail service. They're available now, which means that
visitors to Disney World are running twelve years ahead of
schedule. . . . The architecture expresses a "strong" Key West
influence "but with a delicate touch," presumably meaning that
the only wreckers present are Audio-Animatronics or, at least,
Disney's costumed, clean-cut staff members (uniformally young
and trim).

Disney World is that way—a scrubbed, sterilized, dena-
tured, sexless fantasyland built on idealized notions of a roman-
ticized past. History serves the illusion or doesn't exist. On the
Caribbean cruise, the pirates—Audio-Animatronics that do the
same thing for everyone in the same way—sing about bottles of
rum, rape, and pillage, while tippling from dry bottles and chas-
ing buxom lasses round and round the sleeping quarters of
houses in a burning town. There are flames but no fire; mayhem
but no blood and guts; rapine but no touching, and certainly not
a hint of penetration. One travels through this "adventure" in
a plastic, boatlike car linked to five or more others, all riding
submerged rails. The speed is regulated so that the water train
slows and even stops at appropriate intervals to allow passengers to savor the delights and terrors of the voyage—and the
terrors are about as horrible as a bowl of Wheaties with milk but
no sugar. People regularly wait in line for a longer period of
time than their adventure takes—and 90 percent of them do so
without complaint: most unusual behavior for Americans accustomed to pushing and shoving for every square inch of space at
the entrance to a place, then attempting to enter simultaneously.
(At Disney World, the large number of foreign tourists may be

sufficiently interspersed through the crowd to help impose manners, but the primary enforcer appears to be well-designed rope mazes, signs that tell customers how long a wait to expect, and the expectation among most visitors that no matter what happens they will have a good time.)

A riverboat, stern wheel churning, rides a rail—like every other Disney World conveyance—in a man-made river that is the Mississippi or Missouri of the mind running around an artificial island inhabited by Audio-Animatronic Indians, station masters, and cavalry charging to rescue helpless white settlers from those noble savages. The Swiss Family Robinson lives in a superrealistic fake tree. Gold rush trains run amok through Thunder Mountain at controlled breakneck speed while their aerodynamic cousins hurtle through the spirals of Space Mountain. The attractions of Disney World, in short, offer little of Florida, and no one seems to care. But by establishing this 27,400-acre fantasyland in Orange and Osceola counties, in the old Disston purchase, Walt Disney did more to redirect the development of Florida than any individual since Henry Flagler. And he did more for the state's tourist industry than Carl Fisher, Flagler, Plant, and all the other promoters combined. It is fitting therefore that Disney's dreamland should build a hotel commemorating the efforts of Flagler and his friend and rival Henry Plant and convert their history into promotional fantasy. That's what Disney did with his proletarian rat, turning him into the sexless Mickey Mouse, and what Disney's heirs and successors in the Disney empire did to Disney himself, elevating him to kindly sainthood while ignoring his most grandiose and redeeming visions.

Through dummy corporations and trusted lawyers and bankers, Walt Disney assembled his kingdom of swamp, flatwoods, lakes, and creeks in 1965, buying it for $5 million, an average of $180 an acre. Only a handful of people—including the publisher of the *Orlando Sentinel,* who agreed to embargo the news—knew what Disney was doing, and Disney kept it that way by threatening to scrub the entire deal if word leaked out. He had already rejected St. Louis after a well-publicized flirtation and falling out triggered by Augustus Busch, who said a man wanting to build a theme park that didn't sell beer and booze was loco.[2] Disney didn't want a replay in central Florida of that aborted courtship or of the run-up in land prices that would surely follow news of his intent. His secrecy, threats of early Mouse withdrawal, and fronts buying small parcels worked well—too well for those who lust for a larger slice of the riches his domain has wrought.

Orange County hadn't scored a major economic coup since 1957 when defense contractor Martin Marietta moved to town with a work force of ten thousand, many of them from its original plant in Baltimore. Landowners were eager to ride a new boom because often their chief and only assets were their acres. (After the news of Disney World broke, land adjacent to it sold for $80,000 an acre.) But Disney planned more than just an amusement park, and to guarantee absolute control over his domain, he ordered his attorneys to draft legislation establishing the Reedy Creek Improvement District (named for the creek running through the property), which the legislature passed with barely a whimper of dissent in 1967.

The district effectively creates a company fiefdom, giving the board of supervisors—comprised only of representatives elected from among landholders in the district, by the formula one vote to each acre—power to drain, ditch, run power lines, create a fire department, provide a security force, assess taxes, develop and impose a master plan and building codes, construct roads and towns and theme parks. Reedy Creek officials say the legislation was necessary because Orange and Osceola county officials had no way to judge the structural integrity and safety of oddities like fiberglass mountains and therefore Disney required authority to regulate itself according to standards it set. Equally important was Walt Disney's desire to create a buffer zone shielding his theme parks from the ticky-tack that surrounded Disneyland in Orange County, California. Through Reedy Creek, the Disney engineers and imagineers, as they are known, could create the world they dreamed, and the resort's safety record points to the skill with which they built. On the other hand, opponents like to argue, Disney has virtual police-state powers in Reedy Creek, which complaint, although not fully accurate, carries a ring of truth because Disney World is classed as private property and, in most instances, it gets what it desires from the state and county governments.

Walt Disney died in 1966, two years after taking the New York World's Fair by storm with his robotic Animatronics, five years before his Florida dream opened. Fortunately for the Mouseketeers, he completed the master plan for his central

Florida kingdom, although on his deathbed. Admiral Joseph W. Fowler, who directed construction of Disneyland and later Disney World, told the *Orlando Sentinel* of a meeting with the dying showman:

> Early in the visit, Walt pointed up to the ceiling and verbally started sketching how the park should be laid out, pointing this way and that way, improvising all the time. As ill as he was, he acted like a boy just let out of school. Finally, the last draft of what is now Disney World was sketched out, figuratively, on that ceiling. And the next day he died. There were many times later, when I was walking the property, that I felt him looking over my shoulder.[3]

The company spent $400 million—$275 million more than originally estimated—in creating the Magic Kingdom and the rest of Disney World. It formed its own construction company to complete the work after the initial contractor swore he would never meet his 1971 deadline. Disney did, by working crews seven days a week and paying top dollar.

Under the direction of a retired major general of the U.S. Army Corps of Engineers, the chief engineer for Robert Moses on the 1964 New York World's Fair, and former governor of the Panama Canal Zone, William Everett "Joe" Potter, Disney's crews constructed 26.1 miles of canals, 19.3 miles of levees, and twenty-seven flood control structures to prepare the land for the Magic Kingdom with its assorted hotels, campgrounds, monorail, trains, rides, towns, restaurants, and parking lots. Unlike other artificial waterways in Florida, the ones in Reedy Creek looped and curved enough to appear natural. Bay Lake, the central body of water in the World, looks real too, and it is, in a way: Tannin from cypress trees gave the water the brown tea color common to Florida fresh water and evocative to many urbanites of pollution, so the engineers drained the lake, cleaned out the muck, created a sand bottom, and refilled the basin, following a procedure that may be the only way to restore eutrophied lakes like Apopka. The cypress vanished as the Magic Kingdom, Discovery Island, and the Polynesian Village rose. While doing the resculpting, the crews managed to create a model water network—installing extensive recirculation sys-tems for the well water used to fill the ponds and streams from which customers view the mysteries of the kingdom; establishing state-of-the-art water treatment facilities, which include use of 100 acres of wetlands to filter wastewater; and setting aside 7,500 acres for conservation, which serve as a buffer zone between Walt Disney World and the rest of central Florida.

The conservation areas and treatment facilities, the curving lagoons and environmental safeguards, are no accident. Unlike other developers in Florida, Walt Disney hired a group of environmentalists to serve as an advisory board while he planned Disney World. He and his successors also embedded in the master plan for Reedy Creek an aesthetic component, which dictates not only the look but also the placement of development in the district and requires attention to the land's contours, to wildlife, vegetation, and water quality. Sanitation, waste disposal, road and sidewalk location—all are detailed because Walt Disney long ago decided that appearances were nearly everything.

Plans alone do not dispose of waste, and Disney in recent years has run afoul of its own astonishing growth and corporate negligence. Early in 1988, Walt Disney World was cited for improper storage of hazardous material in the nether reaches of the Magic Kingdom. Over the past few years, the expansion of attractions and guest facilities has resulted in the dumping of more sewage into the artificial wetlands than they could handle, and Disney World has become another large industrial polluter of the water supply of Osceola and Orange counties. Disney and conservationists have a stake in making these artificial swamps and bogs, which many experts have promoted as a safe and ecological solution to disposal of human waste, function properly. Orange County has already created an elaborate wetland, stocked with native plants and named, with no apparent irony, Wilderness Park, to complete the treatment of wastewater before releasing it to the St. Johns River; and other areas watch its performance.

In laying down an infrastructure that was functional and nonobtrusive, Joe Potter accomplished something of an engineering miracle by placing all the utility lines underground, a feat believed impossible because of Florida's high water table. "I went out and got three crackerjack college professors to show me how to do it," he said. "And then I got me another professor to help put the utilities underground."[4] Many local governments in Florida refuse to listen to academics, preferring to view them as abstracted intellectuals, impediments to progress.

Landscapers and builders moved live oaks, rather than cut them down, and they saved a significant number of the one-hundred-year-old longleaf pines that occupied the property. Few people go to Disney's domain for the growing trees and shrubs, the vines and flowers, but they are well planted and labeled. Disney's gardeners propagate plants in their greenhouses and often choose tropical vegetation to adorn the grounds. (Visitors do, however, look for trash as if to prove the place can't be as clean as reported, and they comment loudly on the rare occasions when they find it, tolerating much less refuse in the well-traveled theme park than they do in their homes and neighborhoods.)

Disney World is a study in contradiction. The facades, costumes, scene design, the Audio-Animatronics, the rides and attractions themselves, are remarkable for their exquisite detail: The fake trees look real, the castle appears made of stone not fiberglass and steel, and although no one will confuse the androids with humans, their appearance from afar is at least disconcertingly real. Some of the monorail cars looked, at the end of February 1988, a little worse for wear (by Disney standards; by those of public transit, the cars were immaculate) but new ones were on order and the system works. Service was prompt and courteous; attendants and stanchions managed a crowd with ease. Disney World is the shining example of a service industry—the leader in the new world economy, according to some experts. Ordinary workers find it a future to dread—low pay for work that is mind-numbing at its most stimulating moments. Nothing is left to chance: The ushers, usherettes, and guides on the river craft that travel at a set speed with preprogrammed pauses, bumps, and stops, utter the same phrases in the same tones on every cruise.

Even the mistakes turned to magic in the world according to Disney. On an island in Bay Lake, Disney's planners created a semitropical jungle and bird sanctuary, a place of bamboo and palms, of plants from Central and South America, India, China, and the Canary Islands. Parrots, macaws, cockatoos, trumpeter swans, brown pelicans, flamingos, and a pair of southern bald eagles were imported or settled on their own, finding a haven in the midst of the tourists. As a sort of ironic commentary on the value of Audio-Animatronics, the living birds and plants took over what was initially built as an attraction called Treasure Island, to be filled with mechanical creatures.

Walt Disney World opened with a bit of a whimper in October 1971, when central Florida was still calm and quiet, its landowners, businessmen, and bankers eager for growth but uncertain of its extent. Many of them believed Disney officials overly optimistic in their projections: They should have listened more closely. From its slow start, attendance gathered momentum and accelerated, drawing first 8, then 10, 12, 20, 25 million visitors a year, 250 million since it opened—and central Florida scrambled to cash in, building motels and hotels, fast-food outlets, gas stations, subdivisions, strip shopping centers and huge malls, roads and more roads. (California's Disneyland, by comparison, draws less than one half the total of its Florida counterpart.) Even the oil embargo and recession occurring shortly after opening day proved minor setbacks to the booming corridor along Interstate 4 (I-4) between Daytona Beach and Tampa. Before the place opened, company officials sent monitors to count traffic on I-4, only to find them asleep after a few hours of watching empty highway. Now the road is never still, and on December 23, 1986, it was impossible for travelers between New York and Winter Park to find a motel room out of tens of thousands along Interstate 95 between Richmond, Virginia, and Savannah, Georgia, unless they had reservations. The bulk of the cars were heading for Disney World and other nearby theme parks, like Sea World; on December 29, Disney set its single-day attendance record, 148,500, waiting in line.

The allure by then was not only the fantasies of the Magic Kingdom—Frontierland; Adventureland; Main Street, USA; Fantasyland; and Tomorrowland—but also Epcot, described in Disney promotional releases as "a permanent international showplace covering 260 acres." From the beginning, Walt Disney planned to create on his central Florida spread an Experimental Prototype Community of Tomorrow (Epcot), a place people would live and work in a weird amalgam of past, present, and future, testing each marvelous new machine and appliance. The man who brought Davy Crockett, Zorro, Bambi, Thumper, Goofy, Donald Duck, Mickey, Minnie, Dumbo, and 101 dalmatians to millions, who defined American animated films, believed technology would create a new world, clean and healthy, free of care and trouble, like the old one only better.

A bit of Disney lore holds that Walt walked his 27,400 undeveloped acres and picked the site of Epcot. After his death and the successful opening of the Magic Kingdom, company officials set out to build the experimental city. Looking for an appropriate location, they took and examined rolls of aerial photographs, hauled out consultants, and conducted surveys only to conclude that Walt had chosen correctly after his stroll.

Epcot opened on October 1, 1982, eleven years to the day after the World. (Separate admission fees are charged for the Magic Kingdom and Epcot.) But Epcot is not Walt Disney's experimental city; no one lives within its boundaries. His heirs abandoned that vision as too costly—a reason the creator of Mickey Mouse would have rejected—and settled instead for a polygamous marriage to other major United States corporations, each of which sponsors a theme area or attraction: AT&T's "Spaceship Earth"; Exxon's "Universe of Energy"; General Motors's "World of Motion"; Eastman Kodak's "Journey into Imagination"; Kraft's "Land"; Unisys's "Computer Central"; General Electric's "Horizons"; United Technology's "Living Seas"; and Metropolitan Life's "Life and Health."

Across a lake from the self-promotional corporate displays lies a "World Showcase" where ten nations have built pavilions said to be representative of their history, culture, and commerce, but not their political and economic systems; even the People's Republic of China offers a temple free of the sayings of Mao or Deng. On close inspection, the pavilions of the "World Showcase" become little more than souvenir shops wrapped in architectural models of what Americans are supposed to fantasize about the sponsoring nations—Chinese temple, Japanese temple and garden, southern Italian piazza, French sidewalk café, British pub, Canadian trading post. The great dome of central Florida sky and distant pines make the scene thoroughly surreal and unsettling.

Epcot is billed as a permanent World's Fair, patterned after the 1964 bash in New York. The corporate attractions are more shoddy in their execution and detail than the fantasies of the Magic Kingdom, more ponderous and propagandistic in their claims. Thus, Kraft, as it takes riders on a waterborne tour through a tunnel lined with discrete and well-made model eco-systems—the desert and rain forest are most notable—intones through its recorded narration that man cannot inhabit those areas without modern technology. The journey ends with a trip through hydroponic heaven, an experimental greenhouse where bland vegetables and fruit grow out of anything but soil. Everywhere the message is the same: Technology will solve all human problems, including those it has created (but that caveat is unstated, if even recognized by the people putting together the show).

Humorist P. J. O'Rourke summarized the Epcot experience in the August 1983 issue of *Harper's:*

> At Epcot Center the Disney corporation has accomplished something I didn't think possible in today's world. They have created a land of make-believe that's worse than regular life. Unvarnished reality would be preferable. In fact, it might be fun.
>
> "America," for instance, could be the very stretch of highway through Kissimmee, Florida, that leads to Epcot's gates—a thousand Dairy Queens, RV parks, peewee golf establishments, and souvenir stands selling cypress knee clocks and shellacked blowfish. We could buy cars from General Motors, gas up at Exxon, and drive over to the Bell System, where, if they have any sense, they'll give us free whiskey so we'll make nine-hour phone calls to old girl friends in Taos. When we've spent all our money doing this, we could go to Kraft and get free government surplus cheese-food substances. And if Disney still wants to make Epcot Center futuristic, they could do so by blowing the place up with an atom bomb.[5]

Walt Disney World draws nearly 60 percent of the 44 million tourists who dump more than $20 billion into the Florida economy each year, compared with the $300 million that one tenth that number of tourists spent fifty years ago. The 22 million-plus people who walked through the gates of Disney World in 1986 equaled the number who visited the entire state of Florida in 1972. Almost alone, Disney created a summer tourist season in Florida, drawing most of its visitors during those warm and rainy months. Although winter remains the tourist season in many coastal communities—especially wealthy towns like Palm Beach, where many hotels and homes close for the summer—the steady flow of travelers throughout the year means that in gross annual numbers the state's population is not 12 million but 56 million. Tourists, like residents, consume food, water and energy, generate garbage, and use the public parks and beaches, the roads and medical facilities, the jails, exempting the schools and most social services. The visitors' environmental impact is profound and surprisingly unexamined.

Walt Disney World dominates a belt of playgrounds and wonderworlds that runs from Busch Gardens in Tampa to the Kennedy Space Center at Cape Canaveral, which in addition to its rocket launches sponsors various tours and museums. Of course, most people in Florida travel by car, even if they arrive by plane, and they doubtless visit at one time or another an Atlantic or Gulf beach between bouts with Disney World, Epcot, Sea World (which borders no ocean), Baseball and Boardwalk, Busch Garden. If the attractions are alluring enough, they will draw visitors again and again because Florida remains a relatively inexpensive vacation destination for many people driving from the Northeast, Midwest, and Canada, who want to know they are attending a clean and well-regulated amusement park that also purports to educate and enlighten them. Others want to golf while their hometown is locked in cold, comb the beach for shells, go to the Everglades and see an alligator (the creature of choice for 90 percent of the visitors), dive along the coral reef or in the crystalline water of the springs, fish on lakes, rivers, in the ocean. Not many states offer such a variety of experience inside and out.

Among the counties of destination, Orange and Osceola, the homes of Disney World, rank first, followed by the coastal counties of Dade, Broward, Palm Beach, Pinellas, Hillsborough, Duval, Sarasota, Lee, Monroe, and Volusia. The national seashores at Cape Canaveral and the Gulf islands off the Panhandle draw eight million visitors a year, with all national parks and monuments attracting twelve million, and state parks hosting another fourteen million. During the winter tourist season, the most popular parks and beaches must close their gates because of overcrowding, shutting out local people who rely on them year round for recreation and relaxation. In recognition of that inequity, the state has imposed higher fees for tourists than residents, a small positive step in the direction of making visitors pay a just amount for the services they use.

In 1987, Orange County asserted that the Disney Corporation should help pay for roads, schools, and other infrastructure improvements because it was responsible for bringing so many people into central Florida, and Osceola County soon made a similar argument. Disney officials countered that they would discuss the matter if the county commissions produced data showing who was using how much of what, but those figures didn't exist. As the situation stood in the first half of 1988, county officials and business leaders were concerned that expansion at Walt Disney World, which included the Grand Floridian and additional hotels, a convention center, and new attractions like Typhoon Lagoon, which offers the wonders of the sea inland, and the extravagant Disney-MGM film studios, a fantasy world for film fanatics rising under a mouse-ear adorned water tower, would draw more business directly into the park from the airport and highways, thereby cutting revenues for their non-Disney enterprises. A Japanese company's proposal to build a high-speed railway from the Orlando International Airport to Disney World heightened their fear that tourists would make no interim stops.

Central Florida's counties—Orange, Osceola, and Seminole—failed to control and regulate development. They succumbed to the greed of landowners and developers, suspending when beneficial those regulations on the books, making a mockery of their master plans as soon as they adopted them. As a result, central Florida has repeated in the last two decades the patterns of unrestrained construction that tore up Dade County through the years following World War II and ravage Broward and Palm Beach counties now. Many of the new businesses and attractions, as well as the people they employ directly and indirectly, came to central Florida because of Disney World's success, but Disney did not encourage or allow them to build wherever and however they wanted—those were county decisions.

The waves of development ripping across central Florida have consumed hundreds of thousands of acres of forests, fields, and orange groves—thousands of acres that once served to filter water recharging the Floridan Aquifer. The rise and fall of citrus production over the past fifty years clearly shows the interrelationship between land use, natural disaster, and tourist-related growth. The orange groves of the Central Highlands, which supplanted the sandhill pine and hammocks, suffered from two severe freezes in the early 1980s, and growers refused to replant the decimated trees, finding the land too valuable for its development potential and being thwarted in their search for young trees by an outbreak of citrus canker that forced the state Agriculture Department to destroy infected nursery stock. Thousands of acres of groves now sit barren, waiting for bulldozers to begin the process of converting them into apartments, stores, or housing developments, while former Orange County agricultural agent Henry F. Swanson and other experts preach that paving of the groves will harm groundwater quality and supplies. The sand and vegetation filter out impurities; when the land is paved, it not only no longer acts as a filter but also produces more pollution that flows into the ground and surface water.

In 1940, 226,000 acres were planted in oranges; 82,500 in grapefruit. By 1970, the figures had reached 601,600 and 91,200, respectively. Ten years later, the totals stood at 576,600 for oranges and 126,400 for grapefruit. In 1985, after the freezes, they were 367,600 and 105,100 respectively. Those growers who did not quit moved south for warmer weather, just as they did after the disastrous freeze in 1895–96, only this time they have relocated in the southwestern part of the peninsula in Collier, Glades, Hendry, Lee, and Charlotte counties, converting vegetable farms, rangeland, and pine flatwoods to groves (or left the state for the rain forests of Central and South America). The shift resulted in a near doubling of acreage devoted to citrus in southwestern Florida between 1986 and 1988, when it stood at 130,000 acres.

Despite the overall decline in total acreage since the peak decade of the 1970s, the $2.7-billion citrus industry remains among the most lucrative in Florida, followed closely by cattle. Both are exceeded slightly by the nursery business—especially the cultivation of houseplants in south Florida. Winter vegetables and corn trail behind but contribute significantly to the economies of nearly every region of the state, including urbanized counties like Dade and Palm Beach.

Throughout the state, agricultural and range lands that replaced natural ecosystems during early waves of human expansion are feeling the pressure of more recent growth. Between 1940 and 1964, the number of farms in the state declined by one third, with most of the drop coming among those that were small and privately held. Total acreage, on the other hand, has remained constant as corporate farmers have opened new lands to production. But affordable land is becoming scarce, and experts expect the numbers of farms and groves to decline in the next two decades unless steps are taken to relieve real estate pressure near expanding cities and encourage people to remain in the business. Around lakes Okeechobee, Apopka, Griffin, in the marshes of the St. Johns and the east Everglades, the loss of farms could produce ecological benefits of greater value than that of the lost crops—providing the acreage was restored to natural conditions and not converted into golf-course-centered subdivisions. Restoration of native vegetation would improve the quality and quantity of surface and ground water by removing major polluters and users and re-creating conditions ideal for water purification and aquifer recharge.

For nearly five hundred years, whites have abused Florida's land, water, vegetation, and animals, treating them as if they were limitless; moving to another species of fish, bird, or mammal if the one they had been hunting vanished; draining and filling more distant marshes for new farms and communities. In some areas of the state, there still don't seem enough people to make a dent in the lushness of the place. But even there Florida has changed, moved from a natural to a man-made state.

The three Henrys—Sanford, Plant, and Flagler—and Hamilton Disston controlled vast stretches of the peninsula at various times and sought to build not just cities but experimental farms and citrus groves. They wanted to attract settlers and visitors to make their investments pay, but they also operated under the nineteenth-century view that economic development was a necessary and noble end. God and man's innate superiority had charged the latter with exercising dominion over the world, and therefore he built. That the building created millionaires who then bought yachts, trotters, private railroad cars, and automobiles and needed places to play with them, so much the better. Florida existed for pleasure: Its hard-packed sand at Ormond Beach and Daytona Beach provided a natural track for bike and auto races; its coasts, lagoons, rivers, and lakes, later its intracoastal waterway, offered sailing and, when powerboats arrived, cruising in all types of water; its fishing was unsurpassed; its hunting exotic.

The lore of the water remains, despite the growth and deterioration of quality in lakes, rivers, bays, and the decline of the reefs. Though besmirched, they remain consistently cleaner than most of their northeastern and midwestern counterparts, and the shifting tones of light playing on the water and refracting through it continue to amaze all who see them. Sailing on Biscayne Bay on a stiff breeze can still drive all sense of Florida's demise and ruin away and allow one to see why the sailors have always come here. In the early part of this century Ralph Munroe and his friends steered for their moorings by the light of the Coral Gables water tower and then the Biltmore Hotel in that city, wonderful, Mediterranean-style structures that dominated the horizon. A score of condominiums and office towers now perform that function in Miami, but the dominant features on the landward horizon of south Biscayne Bay are the giant Dade County landfill and Turkey Point, with its four power plants— the underbelly of modern civilization.

Snorkel above the flats around Elliott Key to see the sponges and bits of coral, the fish, and lobster (protected in the waters of the national park), maybe a stray conch, and even the dump and power plants that mar the shore lose their meaning. It's a life of wind, sea, and air. The bay and, farther south, the coral reefs sometimes draw more divers and sailors than they can bear, but the fault is neither theirs nor the people's. The solution, if possible, is more public marine preserves, more protected areas for people who require for their mental and physical well-being a refuge, however temporary. Many of those seeking lasting escape from Florida's development, having fled first north, into the center of the peninsula and the Panhandle or deep into southern Dade County and the isolated Keys, now go to the Ozarks in Arkansas and Missouri or to the rain forests of Central and South America where the same tired tale of resource exploitation followed by agricultural and population settlement is being told.

Inland and north from tropical Florida are the springs that continue to defy the imagination with their pellucid, cooling waters, their boils from the depths. To go to a place like Silver Springs and look forty feet through water so clear one has to touch it to make certain it is there is an experience to remember for a lifetime. To dive into liquid crystal on a hot summer day, to stare into the face of a fish, is to look into life itself. And a slow canoe ride down one of the clear spring runs or larger rivers overhung with oak and cypress full of moss, with a pair of pileated woodpeckers marking your passage, ospreys crossing the river above, and a swallow-tailed kite cruising back of the river swamp brings peace that is seldom found in the crash of car culture. When people who knew these places speak of their loss to development and overuse, they do so with sadness.

For the more pedestrian among us, a walk on the sand— even along Disney's freshwater Typhoon Lagoon and Victorian beach resort—maybe a ride on a glass-bottom boat over Silver

Springs or the coral reef at John Pennekamp State Park, must suffice. Visitors to the Kennedy Space Center may tour the wildlife preserve on Merritt Island, the nearly unspoiled beaches of Cape Canaveral—secured from condominiums by the NASA facility—and imagine another planet with a frontier to explore and settle.

Paradox defines Florida. During the past twenty years, while state politicians have enacted legislation they claimed would protect the environment and control growth, the state has experienced the most dramatic population increase in its history and acceleration of a precipitous decline in the quality of its water and the viability of its land. People of sufficient financial resources can buy a house or condominium on the Atlantic, the Gulf, an interior lake or river, but the vast majority of people settle for a tract home and weekend trips to overcrowded parks—hoping they can get in before the gates close. Most of the lakes in central Florida, which hosts a majority of the nearly eight thousand in the state, lack public access in the form of beaches or boat ramps—they are private preserves. The St. Johns River on the weekends is a clogged speedway for powerboats, while reverting on weekdays to a slow if muddy river. Golf courses outnumber parks; bike paths exist, if at all, as afterthoughts.

Depending on one's perspective, Florida is a retirement haven with golf course, clubhouse, swimming pools, and assorted strange fruit trees in the yard or a strip of tract homes waiting for the next big hurricane that ten million of the people in the state have never seen and think is as threatening as the California earthquake that never consumes Los Angeles. Immigrants from strife-torn, impoverished Caribbean and Latin American nations come for refuge and economic opportunity, as do young Anglos from northern states and a few blacks, although their migration is primarily northward. There are as many reasons for moving to Florida as there are people, and the problem becomes less one of controlling the influx than of assuring that the state's prime resources are cared for and respected—for a host of different goals. That can come about only if those officials and voters shaping the state's destiny approach their responsibilities with a feel for the land and water that transcends desire for quick profit. Once used up and despoiled, it is paradise no more.

NOTES

CHAPTER ONE: THE END OF THE LINE

1. David Leon Chandler, *Henry Flagler* (New York: Macmillan, 1986), p. 213.

2. *Bellevue Gazette*, December 28, 1906, cited in Chandler, p. 60.

3. *Jacksonville News-Herald*, June 20, 1887, in Chandler, p. 94.

4. Edward Nelson Akin, *Henry Flagler: Rockefeller Partner and Florida Resort King* (Kent, Ohio: Kent State University Press, 1988). Originally a Ph.D. dissertation, "Southern Reflection on the Gilded Age: Henry M. Flagler's System, 1885–1913," University of Florida, 1975, p. 37

5. Larzer Ziff, *The American 1890s* (Lincoln: University of Nebraska Press, 1979).

6. David Fairchild, *The World Was My Garden* (Miami: Banyan Books, 1982): reprint of 1938 edition, p. 389.

7. Charles Torrey Simpson, *Florida Wild Life: Observations on the Flora and Fauna of the State and the Influence of the Climate and Environment on Their Development* (New York: Macmillan, 1932), p.191.

8. Charles Torrey Simpson, *In Lower Florida Wilds* (New York: G. P. Putnam's Sons, 1920), p. 47.

CHAPTER TWO: THE AMERICAN RIVIERA

1. George M. Barbour, *Florida for Tourists, Invalids, and Settlers*, rev. ed. (New York: D. Appleton and Company, 1884), p.16.

2. Charles W. Pierce, *Pioneer Life in Southeast Florida*, ed. Donald Walter Curl (Coral Gables, Fla.: University of Miami Press, 1970), p. 251.

3. Ibid., p. 210.

4. Cleveland Amory, *The Last Resorts: A Portrait of American Society at Play* (New York: Harper & Brothers, 1952), p. 329.

5. Ibid., p. 337.

6. Ibid., p. 347.

7. James E. Ingraham, speech to the Women's Club of Miami, November 12, 1920, in John Sewell, *Memoirs and History of Miami, Florida* (Miami: privately printed, ca. 1933), p. 51.

8. Ibid.

9. Akin, p.133.

10. Chandler, pp.115–116.

11. Akin, p.129.

12. John Sewell, *Memoirs*, p. 28.

13. Ibid., p. 46.

14. Ralph Middleton Munroe and Vincent Gilpin, *The Commodore's Story: The Early Days on Biscayne Bay* (Miami: Historical Association of Southern Florida, 1985), p. 79.

15. Ibid., p. 65.

16. Interview with the author, February 1987.

17. Lloyd L. Loope and Vicki L. Dunevitz, *Investigations of Early Plant Succession on Abandoned Farmland* (Homestead, Fla.: Everglades National Park, n.d.)

18. Munroe, p. 79.

CHAPTER THREE: ALLIGATORS AND ORANGES

1. Robert Barnwell Roosevelt, *Florida and the Game Water-Birds of the Atlantic Coast and the Lakes of the United States* (New York: Orange Judd Company, 1884), pp. 9–10.

2. Harriet Beecher Stowe, *Palmetto Leaves,* Floridiana Facsimile and Reprint Series (Gainesville: University of Florida Press, 1968), p. 257.

3. Ibid., p. 277.

4. W. J. Cash, *The Mind of the South* (New York: Alfred A. Knopf, 1941), p. 31.

5. George Barbour, p. 54.

6. John C. Gifford, *On Preserving Tropical Florida,* compiled and with a biographical sketch by Elizabeth Orgen Rothra (Coral Gables, Fla.: University of Miami Press, 1972), p.194.

7. *Campfire Life in Florida: A Handbook for Sportsmen and Settlers,* compiled by Charles Hallock (New York: Forest and Stream Publishing Company, 1876).

8. George Barbour, p. 35.

9. Ibid.

10. Sidney Lanier, *Florida: Its Scenery, Climate, and History,* facsimile reproduction of the 1875 edition, introduction and index by Jerrell H. Shofner (Gainesville: University of Florida Press, 1973), p.18.

11. Ibid., p. 20.

12. Ibid., pp. 28–29.

13. Ibid., p. 29.

14. Ibid., p. 35.

15. Edward A. Mueller, *Steamboating on the St. Johns: Some Travel Accounts and Various Steamboat Materials,* vol. 7 in local history series (Melbourne, Fla.: South Brevard Historical Society, 1980). Materials on De Bary and Baya are from Mueller's study.

16. Louis W. Ziegler and Herbert S. Wolfe, *Citrus Growing in Florida* (Gainesville: University of Florida Press, 1961).

17. John McPhee, *Oranges* (New York: Farrar, Straus and Giroux, 1966), pp. 89–91, 94.

18. Zora Neale Hurston, *Dust Tracks on a Road* (Philadelphia: J. B. Lippincott Company, 1942), p.18.

19. Ibid., p. 44.

20. Ibid.

21. *Florida: A Guide to the Southernmost State,* compiled and written by the Federal Writers' Project of the Work Projects Administration for the State of Florida (New York: Oxford University Press, 1939), hereafter the *WPA Guide,* p.151.

CHAPTER FOUR: THE MIDDLE KINGDOM

1. Nelson Manfred Blake, *Land into Water—Water into Land: A History of Water Management in Florida* (Tallahassee: Florida State University Press, 1980), p. 75.

2. Alfred Jackson Hanna and Kathryn Abbey Hanna, *Lake Okeechobee: Wellspring of the Everglades* (Indianapolis: Bobbs-Merrill Company, 1948), p. 94.

3. *Campfire Life in Florida*, p. 294.

4. Charles Torrey Simpson, *Out of Doors in Florida: The Adventures of a Naturalist, Together with Essays on the Wild Life and the Geology of the State* (Miami: E. B. Douglas Company, 1923), p.110.

5. Joe A. Akerman, Jr., *Florida Cowman, A History of Florida Cattle Raising* (Kissimmee, Fla.: Florida Cattlemen's Association, 1976), p.172.

6. George Hutchinson Smyth, *The Life of Henry Bradley Plant* (New York: G. P. Putnam's 1898).

7. Ibid.

8. Ibid.

9. Stetson Kennedy, *Palmetto Country*, ed. Erskine Caldwell (New York: Duell, Sloan & Pearce, 1942), p. 273.

10. William J. Schellings, "The Role of Florida in the Spanish American War, 1898," Ph.D. dissertation, University of Florida, 1958, pp.13–15.

11. Fairchild, p.115.

CHAPTER FIVE: A SCARRED AND BARREN LAND

1. Simpson, *Out of Doors in Florida*, p.137.

2. Thomas Barbour, *That Vanishing Eden: A Naturalist's Florida* (Boston: Atlantic Monthly Press, 1945), p. 232.

3. Lanier, p. 71.

4. Ibid.

5. Simpson, *Out of Doors in Florida*, p.111.

6. Virginia Steele Wood, *Live Oaking: Southern Timber for Tall Ships* (Boston: Northeastern University Press, 1981), p. 59.

7. From *Pioneer Florida*, ed. D. B. McKay (Tampa, Fla.: The Southern Publishing Company, 1959).

8. Simpson, *Out of Doors in Florida*, p.130.

9. Lanier, p.76.

10. *WPA Guide*, p. 240.

11. Akin, pp. 113–114.

12. John H. Davis, Jr., *The Natural Features of Southern Florida, Especially the Vegetation, and the Everglades*, Florida Geological Survey Bulletin No. 25 (Tallahassee: Florida Geological Survey, 1943).

13. John C. Powell, *The American Siberia or Fourteen Years Experience in a Southern Convict Camp*, facsimile reproduction of the 1891 edition, introduction and index by William Warren Rogers (Gainesville: University of Florida Press, 1976), p. 332.

14. Ibid., p xii.

15. Kennedy, p. 205.

16. Ibid., p. 239.

17. Arch F. Blakey, "A History of the Phosphate Industry," Ph.D. dissertation, Florida State University, 1967, p. 44.

18. Ibid., p. 67.

19. Ibid., p. 71.

20. Kennedy, p.186.

21. Hurston, p. 94.

22. *WPA Guide*, p. 445.

23. Kennedy, p. 318.

24. Ibid., p. 305.

CHAPTER SIX: LIFE ON THE WET FRONTIER

1. Harry A. Kersey, Jr., *Plumes, Pelts, and Hides: White Traders among the Seminole Indians, 1870–1930* (Gainesville: University Presses of Florida, 1975). Kersey's is the best and only detailed study of the Seminole trade and serves as the basis for this summary.

2. Charles William Pierce, "The Cruise of the Bonton," reprint from *Tequesta*, ed. William Robertson, Jr. (Miami: Historical Association of Southern Florida, n.d.).

3. William T. Hornaday, *Our Vanishing Wild Life: Its Extermination and Preservation* (New York: New York Zoological Society, 1913).

4. W.E.D. Scott, *The Auk: A Quarterly Journal of Ornithology*, two papers, April and July, 1887.

5. Hornaday, p. 3.

6. Patrick J. Gleason, ed., *Environments of South Florida*, Memoir 2, Miami Geological Society, November 1974.

7. Archie Carr, *The Windward Road: Adventures of a Naturalist on Remote Caribbean Shores* (Gainesville: University Presses of Florida, 1979), p. 239.

8. Robert M. Ingle and G. G. Walton Smith, *Sea Turtles and the Turtle Industry of the West Indies, Florida and the Gulf of Mexico, with Annotated Bibliography* (Coral Gables, Fla.: University of Miami Press, 1949), p. 46.

9. Carr, p. 8.

CHAPTER SEVEN: "WATER WILL RUN DOWNHILL"

1. Hugh L. Willoughby, *Across the Everglades* (Philadelphia: J. B. Lippincott, 1900), p. 13.

2. Ibid., p. 64.

3. Ibid., p. 62.

4. Buckingham Smith, Esq., *The Everglades of Florida* in *Acts, Reports and Other Papers, State and National, Relating to the Everglades of the State of Florida and their Reclamation*, U.S. Congress, 1st Session, 62nd Congress, Senate Document No. 89, p. 51.

5. Willoughby, p. 13.

6. Smith, p. 54.

7. Blake, pp. 92–94.

8. Ibid., p. 97.

9. Ibid.

10. Ibid., p. 117.

11. John Rothchild, *Up for Grabs: A Trip Through Time and Space in the Sunshine State* (New York: Viking, 1985), p. 74.

12. Hanna and Hanna, p. 146.

13. *WPA Guide*, p. 406.

14. Simpson, *In Lower Florida Wilds*, p. 126.

15. Ibid., p. 140.

16. Simpson, *Out of Doors in Florida*, p. 16.

17. Hanna and Hanna, p. 217.

18. Ibid., p. 187.

19. Lawrence Will, *Cracker History of Okeechobee: Custard Apple, Moonvine, Catfish and Moonshine* (St. Petersburg, Fla.: Great Outdoors Publishing Company, 1964), p. 120.

20. Ibid., p. 118.

21. Hanna and Hanna, pp. 24–28.

22. J. Carlyle Sitterson, *Sugar Country: The Cane Sugar Industry in the South, 1753–1950*, reprint of 1953 edition (Westport, Conn.: Greenwood Press, 1973). Sitterson provides the best summary of sugarcane cultivation.

CHAPTER EIGHT: FOOL'S GOLD

1. Simpson, *In Lower Florida Wilds*, p.141.
2. Amory, p. 352.
3. *WPA Guide*, p. 270.
4. Fairchild, p. 419.
5. Rex Beach, *The Miracle of Coral Gables* (Coral Gables, Fla.: printed privately by George Edgar Merrick, 1926), pp. 11–19.
6. *WPA Guide*, p. 320.
7. *The New York Times*, September 17, 1926, quoted in Blake, p.134.
8. Frank Conroy, *Stop-time* (New York & London: Penguin Books, 1977), p. 25.

CHAPTER NINE: TROPICAL SANDBAR

1. *Water Resources Atlas of Florida* (Tallahassee: Florida State University, Institute of Science and Public Affairs, 1984), p. 39.
2. Ibid., pp.15–16.
3. Simpson, *Out of Doors in Florida*, p. 256.
4. *Water Resources Atlas of Florida*, p. 122.
5. "Climate of Florida," *Climatology of the United States No. 60*, n.d.
6. Charlton W. Tebeau, *A History of Florida*, 7th ed., (Coral Gables, Fla.: University of Miami Press, 1980), p.16.
7. Stefan Lorant, *The New World: The First Pictures of America Made by John White and Jacques Lemoyne and Engraved by Theodore de Bry with Contemporary Narratives of the French Settlement in Florida, 1562–1565, and English Colonies in Virginia, 1585–1590* (New York: Duell, Sloan & Pierce, 1965).
8. Joseph Campbell, *The Way of the Animal Powers: Historical Atlas of World Mythology*, vol. 1 (San Francisco: Alfred Van der Marck Editions, 1983), p. 217 ff.

CHAPTER TEN: FATAL FANTASIES

1. "The Narrative of Alvar Núñeza Cabeza de Vaca," ed. Frederick W. Hodge, in *Spanish Explorers in the Southern United States: 1528–1543* (New York: Barnes and Noble, 1965). All quotes and descriptions of Cabeza de Vaca come from this translation.
2. "The Narrative of the Expedition of Hernando de Soto by the Gentleman of Elvas," ed. Theodore H. Lewis, in *Spanish Explorers*, op. cit. Quotes and descriptions of De Soto's expedition are from this translation.
3. Jean Ribault, *The Whole and True Discoverye of Terra Florida*, ed. David L. Dowd (Gainesville: University of Florida Press, 1963).
4. Francis Parkman, *Pioneers of France in the New World* (Boston: Little, Brown, and Company, 1886), pp. 43–47.
5. Ibid., p. 50.
6. Bartolome Barrientos, *Pedro Menéndez de Avilés: Founder of Florida*, facsimile, ed. and trans. Anthony Kerrigan (Gainesville: University of Florida Press, 1965); and Gonzalo Solis de Merás, *Pedro Menéndez de Avilés Memorial*,

1567, trans. Jeannette Thurber Connor (Gainesville: University of Florida Press, 1964).

7. Charles H. Fairbanks, *Florida Indians III: Ethnohistorical Report on the Florida Indians,* (New York & London: Garland Publishing, 1974). Fairbanks provides an excellent summary, from which these statistics are culled.

8. Lana Jill Loucks, "Political and Economic Interactions Between Spaniards and Indians: Archaeological and Ethnohistorical Perspectives of the Mission System in Florida," Ph.D. dissertation, University of Florida, 1979.

9. Marjory Stoneman Douglas, *The Everglades: River of Grass* (Simons Island, Ga.: Mockingbird Books, 1974), p.134.

10. Kathleen Deagan, "Sex, Status and Role in the Mestizaje of Spanish Colonial Florida," Ph.D. dissertation, University of Florida, 1974.

11. Fairbanks, pp.100–101.

12. *Orlando Sentinel,* August 8, 1987.

13. Fairbanks, pp. 4–6.

CHAPTER ELEVEN: A NATURAL EYE

1. Conversation with the author, August 1986, St. Johns River.

2. Conversation with the author, August 1986, University of Florida.

3. All Bartram quotes are from Francis Harper, *Naturalists Edition* (New Haven: Yale University Press, 1958), pp. 57, 75–79, 101–107, 119, 158. Sadly, this invaluable work is no longer in print.

4. Ibid.

CHAPTER TWELVE: THE SEMINOLE WAR

1. John T. Sprague, *The Origin, Progress, and Conclusion of the Florida War,* quoted in John K. Mahon, *History of the Second Seminole War, 1835–1842* (Gainesville: University of Florida Press, 1985), p. 286. Mahon's comprehensive study serves as the basis for this summary.

2. Ibid., p. 299.

3. Fairbanks, p. 231.

4. Ellen Call Long, *Florida Breezes, or, Florida, New and Old* (Gainesville: University of Florida Press, n.d.; facsimile reproduction of 1883 edition), p. 46.

5. George A. McCall, *Letters from the Frontier* (Gainesville: University of Florida Press, 1974; facsimile reproduction of 1868 edition), p. 301.

6. Mahon, p.196.

7. Ibid., p. 218.

8. Charles H. Coe, *Red Patriots: The Story of the Seminole* (Gainesville: University of Florida Press, 1974; facsimile reproduction of 1898 edition), p.113; and, Mahon, p. 218.

CHAPTER THIRTEEN: A SLAVE STATE

1. W. W. Davis, *The Civil War and Reconstruction in Florida* (New York: Columbia University Press, 1913), p. 52. Still the most comprehensive work on this period.

2. Julia Floyd Smith, *Slavery and Plantation Growth in Antebellum Florida: 1821–1860* (Gainesville: University of Florida Press, 1973), p. 27.

3. Philip D. Curtin, *The Atlantic Slave Trade, A Census* (Madison: University of Wisconsin Press, 1969), p.72–75.

4. Davis, p. 43.
5. Ibid., p. 141.
6. Ibid., p. 235.
7. Blake, pp. 43–48.
8. Tebeau, p. 266.
9. John Muir, *A Thousand Mile Walk to the Gulf* (Dunwoody, Ga.: Sellanraa, n.d.; reprinted from Houghton Mifflin Company), p. 89.
10. Ibid., p. 93.

CHAPTER FOURTEEN: RISING FROM THE RUINS

1. Thomas Barbour, *That Vanishing Eden*, p. 87.
2. Luther Carter, *The Florida Experience: Land and Water Policy in a Growth State* (Baltimore: The Johns Hopkins University Press, 1976), p. 23.
3. *WPA Guide*, p.114.
4. Ibid., p. 4.
5. Ibid., p. 97.
6. Leon Odell Griffith, *Ed Ball: Confusion to the Enemy* (Tampa, Fla.: Trend House, 1975), p.17.
7. Ibid., p. 53.
8. *WPA Guide*, p. 26.
9. Ronald Hofstetter, "The Effect of Fire on the Pineland and Sawgrass Communities of Southern Florida," in Gleason, *Environments of South Florida.*
10. *Final Environmental Statement, FES-78-7: Proposed Wilderness Recommendation, Everglades National Park*, prepared by the Denver Service Center, National Park Service, 1978.
11. Daniel B. Beard, *Everglades National Park Project*, special report for the National Park Service, 1938, p.100.
12. Ibid., p.1.
13. Conversation with the author, February 17, 1987.
14. Carter, p. 113.
15. Blake, p 151.

CHAPTER FIFTEEN: FLORIDA TAKES OFF

1. *Miami Herald*, December 3, 1987.
2. Rothchild, pp. 98–101.
3. *Keys to Florida's Future: Winning in a Competitive World*, The Final Report of the State Comprehensive Plan Committee to the State of Florida, February 1987.

CHAPTER SIXTEEN: IN DEFENSE OF THE ENVIRONMENT

1. Ross Allen, *Survival Safari: Cross-country from the Atlantic to Gulf of Mexico* (Silver Springs, Fla.: Ross Allen's Reptile Institute, n.d.).
2. Carter, pp. 194–202.
3. Ibid., p. 278.
4. Ibid., pp. 279–280.
5. Ibid., p. 38.
6. Ibid., p. 14.

CHAPTER SEVENTEEN: TOMORROWLAND, TODAY

1. Steve Birnbaum, *Walt Disney World* (Houghton Mifflin Company & Hearst Professional Magazines, 1987), p. 50.

2. John McAleenan, "Building the New World," *Florida Magazine, Orlando Sentinel,* April 10, 1988.

3. Ibid.

4. Ibid.

5. P. J. O'Rourke, "Inside Epcot Center," *Harper's,* August 1983, pp. 42–43.

BIBLIOGRAPHICAL NOTE

Florida has inspired a literature as varied as its flora and fauna, from advertising supplements to technical reports, thoroughly researched histories to anecdotal retellings of old gossip. Specific references are listed in the notes to each chapter. Following is a listing of texts most consulted for this study. It clearly is not exhaustive.

The best-known general history is Charlton W. Tebeau, *A History of Florida* (Coral Gables, Fla.: University of Miami Press, 1971), which focuses primarily on the state's economic and political development, and Tebeau's three-volume treatise, in conjunction with Ruby Leach Carson, *Florida: From Indian Trail to Space Age* (Delray Beach, Fla.: Southern Press Publishing Company, 1966). Other general works and their authors are: William T. Cash, *The Story of Florida*, in four volumes (New York: The American Historical Society, 1938); Marjory Stoneman Douglas, *Florida: The Long Frontier* (New York: Harper and Row, 1967); Gloria Jahoda, *Florida: A Bicentennial History* (New York: W. W. Norton, 1976); W. B. McKay, editor, *Pioneer Florida*, in three volumes (Tampa: Southern Press Publishing Company, 1959); Rowland H. Rerick, *Memoirs of Florida*, two volumes (Atlanta: Southern Historical Association, 1902). *Florida: A Guide to the Southernmost State* (New York: Oxford University Press, 1939), along with other productions on Key West and the Seminole by the Federal Writers' Project, is an invaluable source of folklore and history. Valuable journals and periodicals include: *Tequesta, Florida Historical Quarterly, Florida Anthropologist, Harper's, Scribners'*, and *Niles' Weekly Register*.

Folklore and history shape Stetson Kennedy's *Palmetto Country*, edited by Erskine Caldwell (New York: Duell, Sloan & Pearce, 1942), and combine with autobiography to bring a special flavor to Zora Neale Hurston's *Dust Tracks on a Road* (Philadelphia: J. B. Lippincott, 1942). While strictly speaking a travel guide, Sidney Lanier's wonderfully eccentric treatise, *Florida: Its Scenery, Climate, and History* (Philadelphia: J. B. Lippincott and Company, 1876), falls into this category. In the 1960s, Lawrence E. Will wrote for the Great Outdoors Publishing Company, St. Petersburg, a series of amusing and informative tales: *Okeechobee Hurricane and the Hoover Dike* (1961), *A Cracker History of Lake Okeechobee* (1964), *Okeechobee Boats and Skippers* and *Okeechobee Catfishing* (1965), *A Dredgeman of Cape Sable* (1964), and *Swamp to Sugar Bowl: Pioneer Days in Belle Glade* (1968). In a similar vein is *Cracker Florida: Some Lives and Times* by Ray Washington (Miami: Banyan Books, 1983). Gene M. Burnett profiles people and events in *Florida's Past* (Englewood, Fla.: Pineapple Press, 1986). While not in the same genre, *Okeechobee: Wellspring of the Everglades* by Alfred J. and Kathryn Abbey Hanna (Indianapolis: Bobbs-Merrill Company, 1948) provides glimpses of the people of the "Big Water." Betty Miller Brothers provides some interesting bits in the privately printed *Wreckers and Workers of Old Key West* (1972), and Charles M. Brookfield and Oliver Griswold look at south Florida legends in *They All Called It Tropical* (Miami: Historical Association of Southern Florida, 1985). Charlton Tebeau examined the southwest coast in *Man in the Everglades: 2000 Years of Human History in the Everglades National Park* (Coral Gables, Fla.: University of Miami Press, 1976).

For a look at Henry Flagler and his contemporary capitalists who bought and developed the state, there are: *Florida's Flagler* (Athens: University of Georgia Press, 1949) by Walter Sidney Martin, a limited but still the best biography of the master builder; *Henry Flagler* (New York: Macmillan, 1986), by David Leon Chandler, a disappointing reappraisal; *Southern Reflection on the Gilded Age: Henry M. Flagler's System* by Edward Nelson Akin (a doctoral dissertation in the Department of History at the University of Florida, 1975) that was published in book form in 1988 as *Henry Flagler: Rockefeller Partner and Florida Resort King* (Kent, Ohio: Kent State University Press), an interesting examination of the business of railroad and hotel building. Samuel Proctor wrote *Napoleon Bonaparte Broward: Florida's Fighting Democrat* (Gainesville: University of Florida Press, 1950), an uncritical biography but the only one to date. *The Life of Henry Bradley Plant* by G. Hutchinson Smyth (New York, 1898) is even more uncritical but also the only biography of Flagler's chief railroad and hotel-building rival. William Dudley Chipley and the Pensacola and Atlantic Railroad are the subjects of *Iron Horse in the Pinelands* by Jesse Earle Browden, et al., edited by Virginia Parks (Pensacola, Fla.: Pensacola Historical Society, 1982). The machinations of the railroad men during the Spanish-American War are the subject of William J. Schellings's Ph.D. dissertation at the University of Florida in 1958, "The Role of Florida in the Spanish American War, 1898." Nelson Manfred Blake in *Land into Water—Water into Land: A History of Water Management in Florida* (Tallahassee: Florida State University Press, 1980) discusses Florida's developers' plans for draining the Everglades and building canals.

Edward A. Mueller and Barbara A. Purdy edited *Proceedings of a Conference on the Steamboat Era in Florida* (Gainesville: University of Florida Press, 1985), and Ella Teague De Berard described the scene on the St. Johns in *Steamboats in the Hyacinths* (Daytona Beach, Fla.: College Publishing Company, 1956). Floyd and Marion Rinhart compiled interesting photographs for *Victorian Florida* (Atlanta: Peachtree Publishers, 1986). Few contemporary accounts from the period fail to mention the value of the paddle wheelers and the expanding railways. Sidney Lanier, of course, made the Oklawaha River steamers famous, but others are: Harriet Beecher Stowe, whose *Palmetto Leaves*, edited and reprinted from the 1873 edition for the Floridiana Facsimile and Reprint Series (Gainesville: University of Florida Press, 1968), provides an overview of the St. Johns region during the years of Reconstruction, and Charles W. Pierce, *Pioneer Life in Southeast Florida*, edited by Donald W. Curl (Coral Gables, Fla.: University of Miami Press, 1970), which is one of the primary sources for understanding the life of settlers on that underpopulated coast during the 1870s and 1880s, as well as the immediate impact of Flagler's railroad on the Lake Worth area. Promoters and travelers of the period, which produced a rich if varied literature, are: George M. Barbour, *Florida for Tourists, Invalids, and Settlers*, revised edition (New York: D. Appleton and Company, 1884); Daniel G. Brinton, *A Guide-Book of Florida and the South for Tourists, Invalids and Emigrants* (Philadelphia: G. Maclean, 1869); F. Trench Townshend, *Wild Life in Florida* (London: Hurst and Blackett, 1875); Charles Hallock, *Camp-fire Life in Florida: A Handbook for Sportsmen and Settlers* (New York: Forest and Stream Publishing Company, 1876); John Whipple Potter Jenks, *Hunting in Florida in 1874* (privately printed); Frederick A. Ober, *"Rambler," Guide to Florida, 1875*, edited by Rembert W. Patrick, Floridiana Facsimile and Reprint Series (Gainesville: University of Florida Press, 1964); and Robert Barnwell Roosevelt, *Florida and the Game Water-Birds of the Atlantic Coast and the Lakes of the United States* (New York: Orange Judd Company, 1884). *The Commodore's Story* by Ralph Middleton Munroe and Vincent Gilpin (Miami: Historical Association of Southern Florida, 1985) provides a look at Biscayne Bay from the late nineteenth century through the Depression. Winthrop Packard, *Florida*

Trails (Englewood, Fla.: Pineapple Press, 1983; reprint of 1910 edition, Small, Maynard and Company), provides an early-twentieth-century view.

The most outstanding works on Florida have come from the naturalists who have visited and sometimes settled down. Whichever the case, the best works reveal a spontaneous and enduring love for the place. William Bartram tops the list with his *Travels,* which is best known today in the edition prepared by Mark Van Doren in 1951 for Dover Publications. The outstanding *Naturalists Edition* of Francis Harper (New Haven, Conn.: Yale University Press, 1958) is not available, even through rare booksellers, a sad situation because Bartram remains the point of departure. Also of interest is the work of William's father, John Bartram, *Diary of a Journey Through the Carolinas, Georgia and Florida* (Philadelphia: American Philosophical Society, 1952). Joseph Ewan edited *William Bartram: Botanical and Zoological Drawings, 1756–1788* (Philadelphia: American Philosophical Society, 1968). Books about William Bartram include: Nathan Bryllion Fagin, *William Bartram: Interpreter of the American Landscape* (Baltimore: The Johns Hopkins University Press, 1933); Josephine Herbst, *New Green World* (London: Weidenfeld and Nicolson, 1954). More than a century after Bartram, Charles Torrey Simpson distinguished himself with *In Lower Florida Wilds* (New York: G. P. Putnam's Sons, 1920); *Out of Doors in Florida: The Adventures of a Naturalist Together with Essays on the Wild Life and the Geology of the State* (Miami: E. B. Douglas Company, 1923); and *Florida Wild Life: Observations on the Flora and Fauna of the State and the Influence of Climate and Environment on their Development* (New York: Macmillan, 1932). His contemporary, John Kunkel Small published in New York *Ferns of Tropical Florida* (1918) and *Florida Trees* (1913); and *From Eden to Sahara: Florida's Tragedy* (Lancaster, Pa.: The Science Press, 1929). A decade earlier, William T. Hornaday had sounded the same theme, for wildlife, in *Our Vanishing Wild Life: Its Extermination and Preservation* (New York: New York Zoological Society, 1913). David Fairchild's autobiography *The World Was My Garden* (Miami: Banyan Books, 1982; reprint of 1938 edition, Charles Scribner's Sons) also touches on Florida of this period. John C. Gifford's essential writings are contained in *On Preserving Tropical Florida,* compiled and with a biographical sketch by Elizabeth Orgen Rothra (Coral Gables, Fla.: University of Miami Press, 1972). Thomas Barbour's *That Vanishing Eden: A Naturalist's Florida* (Boston: Atlantic Monthly Press, 1945) picks up where Small left off in examining the environmental destruction of south Florida. Also dealing with south Florida is *A Naturalist in South Florida* (Coral Gables, Fla.: University of Miami Press, 1971) by Charlotte Orr Gantz. Elizabeth Austin edited *Frank M. Chapman in Florida: His Journals and Letters* in 1967 (Gainesville: University of Florida Press). Tracking back: Bernard Romans prepared *A Concise Natural History of East and West Florida* in 1775 (reprinted with an introduction by Rembert W. Patrick, (Gainesville: University of Florida Press, 1775). John James Audubon visited the state in the 1830s and provided descriptions in the first three volumes of his *Ornithological Biographie* (1831–35). John Muir crossed the peninsula in 1867 and recorded his impressions in *A Thousand Mile Walk to the Gulf* (Dunwoody, Ga.: Sellanraa, n.d., reprinted from Houghton Mifflin Company). W.E.D. Scott reported on the condition of Gulf coast rookeries in 1887 in *The Auk*. Archie Carr wrote movingly about vanishing sea turtles in *The Windward Road* in 1956 (Gainesville: University of Florida Press, 1979 reissue). Robert M. Ingle and G. G. Walton Smith offered a more technical account in *Sea Turtles and the Turtle Industry of the West Indies, Florida and the Gulf of Mexico, with Annotated Bibliography,* (Coral Gables, Fla.: University of Miami Press, 1949.)

Technical and scientific publications have come from universities, research stations, the water management districts, and the state geological and biological surveys, and more recently the Department of Natural Resources that subsumed them. The State Geological Survey has published its *Bulletin* for more than fifty years, detailing the topography, botany, and hydrology of Florida. Studies examined from all sources for this book are too numerous to elaborate, but following is a partial listing: C. Wythe Cooke, *Geology of Florida*, Bulletin 29, Florida Geological Survey, 1945; John H. Davis, Jr., *The Natural Features of Southern Florida, Especially the Vegetation and the Everglades*, Bulletin 25, Florida Geological Survey, 1943; Jack C. Rosenau, Glen L. Faulkner, Charles W. Hendry, Jr., and Robert Hull, *Springs of Florida*, Bulletin 31, Department of Natural Resources Bureau of Geology; William A. White, *The Geomorphology of the Florida Peninsula*, Bulletin 51, Department of Natural Resources Division of Geology, 1970; John Edward Hoffmeister, *Land from the Sea* (Coral Gables, Fla.: University of Miami Press, 1974). Linda C. Hendry, et al., *Florida's Vanishing Wildlife* (Florida Cooperative Extension Service, 1980); *Rare and Endangered Biota of Florida*, edited by Richard Franz (Gainesville: University of Florida Press, 1982); *Environments of South Florida, Present and Past II*, edited by Patrick J. Gleason (Miami: Miami Geological Society, 1974; revised edition, 1984); Daniel B. Beard, *Everglades National Park Project*, special report for National Park Service, 1938; *Final Environmental Impact Statement FES-78-7: Proposed Wilderness Recommendation, Everglades National Park*, Denver Service Center, National Park Service, 1978; Ingrid C. Olmsted, Lloyd L. Loope, and Charles E. Hilsenbeck, *Tropical Hardwood Hammocks of the Interior of Everglades National Park and Big Cypress National Preserve* (Homestead: Everglades National Park, South Florida Research Center, 1980); Erdman West and Lillian E. Arnold, *The Native Trees of Florida* (Gainesville: University of Florida Press, 1956); Frank Craighead, *The Trees of South Florida* (Coral Gables, Fla.: University of Miami Press, 1971); and S. David Webb, editor, *Pleistocene Mammals of Florida* (Gainesville: University of Florida Press, 1974).

Recent books blending natural history and public policy in various proportions include: *No Further Retreat: The Fight to Save Florida* (New York: Macmillan Company, 1971) by Raymond Dasmann; *The Florida Experience: Land and Water Policy in a Growth State* (Baltimore: The Johns Hopkins University Press, for Resources for the Future, 1976) by Luther Carter; *The Water Atlas of Florida*, produced in 1984 by the Institute of Science and Public Affairs at Florida State University; *Carrying Capacity for Man and Nature in South Florida* (Center for Wetlands, University of Florida) by Howard T. Odum and M. T. Brown; and various technical reports of the water management districts.

The Everglades have warranted scores of books, including some aforementioned. Others are: Marjory Stoneman Douglas, *The Everglades: River of Grass* (New York: Rinehart and Company, 1947); William B. Robertson, Jr., *Everglades: The Park Story* (Coral Gables, Fla.: University of Miami Press, 1959); Archie Carr, *The Everglades* (New York: Time-Life Books, 1973). Interesting historical accounts include those of: George Henry Preble, "A Canoe Expedition into the Everglades in 1842," in *Tequesta*, January 1946; Buckingham Smith, Esq., *The Everglades of Florida* in *Acts, Reports and Other Papers, State and National, Relating to the Everglades of the State of Florida and their Reclamation*, U.S. Congress, 1st Session, 62nd Congress, Senate Document No. 89; Hugh L. Willoughby, *Across the Everglades* (Philadelphia: J. B. Lippincott, 1900); Harry A. Kersey, *Pelts, Plumes, and Hides* (Gainesville: University of Florida Press, 1975); and, Calvin Stone's *Forty Years in the Everglades* (Tabor City, N.C.: W. Horace Wallace Atlantic Publishing Company, 1979). Orrin H. Pilkey, Jr., et al., have provided a thorough discussion of the ecology and environmental problems facing the Florida coasts and barrier islands in *Living with the East Florida Shore* and *Living with the West Florida Shore* (with Larry J. Doyle, serving as principal author) published by Duke University Press, (Durham, 1984).

Valuable material on citriculture and sugar cultivation is contained in the various publications of the Florida Citrus Commission, as well as: Louis W. Ziegler and Herbert S. Wolfe, *Citrus Growing in Florida* (Gainesville: University of Florida Press, 1961); John McPhee, *Oranges* (New York: Farrar, Straus and Giroux, 1966); and, J. Carlyle Sitterson, *Sugar Country: The Cane Sugar Industry in the South* (Westport, Conn.: Greenwood Press, 1973; reprint of 1953 edition, University of Kentucky Press). Arch F. Blakey's 1967 doctoral dissertation, "A History of the Phosphate Industry" (Florida State University) provides considerable detail on that undertaking. Joe A. Akerman, Jr., wrote *Florida Cowman, A History of Florida Cattle Raising* for the Florida Cattlemen's Association in 1976.

Among works on Florida's original settlers and early European colonization are: Bartolome Barrientos, *Pedro Menéndez de Avilés, Founder of Florida*, translated by Anthony Kerrigan (Gainesville: University of Florida Press, 1965); "The Narrative of Alvar Núñeza Cabeza de Vaca," edited by Frederick W. Hodge, in *Spanish Explorers in the Southern United States: 1528–1543* (New York: Barnes and Noble, 1965); "The Narrative of the Expedition of Hernando de Soto by the Gentleman of Elvas," edited by Theodore H. Lewis, in the same publication; *Jonathan Dickinson's Journal or God's Protecting Providence: Being the Narrative of a Journey from Port Royal in Jamaica to Philadelphia between August 23, 1696 and April 1, 1697*, edited by Evangeline Walker Andrews and Charles McLean Andrews (New Haven, Conn.: Yale University Press, 1945); Kathleen Deagan, "Sex, Status and Role in the Mestizaje of Spanish Colonial Florida" (Ph.D. dissertation, University of Florida, 1974); Jean Ribault, *The Whole and True Discouerye of Terra Florida*, edited by David L. Dowd (Gainesville: University of Florida Press, 1964; reprint of 1927 edition by Florida State Historical Society); Gonzalo Solis de Merás, *Pedro Menéndez de Avilés Memorial, 1567*, translated by Jeanette Thurber Connor (Gainesville: University of Florida Press, 1965; reprint from Florida State Historical Society, 1923); Stefan Lorant, *The New World: The First Pictures of America Made by John White and Jacques Lemoyne and Engraved by Theodore de Bry with Contemporary Narratives of the French Settlement in Florida, 1562–1565, and English Colonies in Virginia, 1585–1590* (New York: Duell, Sloan & Pearce, 1965); William Roberts, *An Account of the First Discovery and Natural History of Florida* (Gainesville: University of Florida Press, 1976); Francis Parkman, *France and England in North America* (Boston: Little, Brown, and Company, 1886); Federal Writers' Project, *The Spanish Missions of Florida* (St. Augustine, 1940); Lana Jill Loucks, "Political and Economic Interactions Between Spaniards and Indians" (Ph.D. dissertation, University of Florida, 1979); Barbara A. Purdy, *Florida's Prehistoric Stone Technology* (Gainesville: University of Florida Press, 1981); I. Randolph Daniel, Jr., and Michael Wisenbaker, *Harney Flats: A Florida Paleo-Indian Site* (Farmingdale, N.Y.: Baywood Publishing Company, 1987); John M. Goggin, *Indian and Spanish Selected Writings*, edited by Charles H. Fairbanks, Irving Rouse, and William C. Sturtevant (Coral Gables, Fla.: University of Miami Press, 1964); and, Charles H. Fairbanks, *Florida Indians* (Garland Publishing Company, 1974). Also on the Seminole is *Red Patriots* by Charles Coe (Gainesville: University of Florida Press, 1974; reprint of 1898 edition).

Glimpses of life in the territorial, antebellum, and Civil War periods are gleaned from a number of sources, including: George A. McCall, *Letters from the Frontier* (Gainesville: University of Florida Press, 1974; reprint of 1868 edition); Ellen Call Long, *Florida Breezes* (University of Florida Press, 1962; reproduction of 1883 edition); Walter Sidney Martin, *Florida During Territorial Days* (Athens: University of Georgia Press, 1944); John K. Mahon, *History of the Second Seminole War, 1835–1842* (Gainesville: University of Florida Press,

1967); John T. Sprague, *The Origin, Progress, and Conclusion of the Florida War, 1848* (Gainesville: University of Florida Press, 1964); Virginia Steele Wood, *Live-Oaking: Southern Timber for Tall Ships* (Boston: Northeastern University Press, 1981); *Florida Territory in 1844: The Diary of Master Edward C. Anderson*, edited by W. Stanley Hoole (Birmingham: University of Alabama Press, 1977); Julia Floyd Smith, *Slavery and Plantation Growth in Antebellum Florida: 1821–1869* (Gainesville: University of Florida Press, 1973); W. W. Davis, *The Civil War and Reconstruction in Florida* (New York: Columbia University Press, 1913); Mary Elizabeth Dickison, *Dickison and His Men: Reminiscences of the War in Florida* (Gainesville: University of Florida Press, 1962; reprint of 1890 edition); Joseph M. Richardson, *The Negro in the Reconstruction of Florida* (Tallahassee: Florida State University Press, 1965). John C. Powell provided his self-serving defense of the convict-lease system in *The American Siberia*, edited by William Warren Rogers (Gainesville: University of Florida Press, 1976; reprint of 1891 edition). Joshua R. Giddings, *The Exiles of Florida: Or, The Crimes Committed by Our Government Against the Maroons, Who Fled From South Carolina and Other Slave States, Seeking Protection Under Spanish Law* (Gainesville: University of Florida Press, 1964; reprint with Introduction by Arthur W. Thompson of 1858 edition), discusses causes of the Seminole War.

Histories of communities consulted for this book include: *Miami, U.S.A.* by Helen Muir (New York: Henry Holt and Company, 1953); *Miami* by T. D. Allman (Boston: Atlantic Monthly Press, 1987); *Miami* by Joan Didion (New York: Simon and Schuster, 1987); *Memoirs and History of Miami, Florida* by John Sewell (privately printed, ca. 1933); *Billion Dollar Sandbar: A Biography of Miami Beach* by Polly Redford (New York: E. P. Dutton, 1970); *Tropical Deco* by Laura Cerwinske (New York: Rizzoli, 1981); *Tampa: Yesterday, Today and Tomorrow* by Michael Bane and Mary Ellen Moore (Tampa: Mishler and King, 1981); *Tampa* by Karl H. Grismer (St. Petersburg: St. Petersburg Printing Company, 1950); *Key West, the Old and the New*, by Jefferson B. Browne (St. Augustine, Fla.: The Record Company, 1902); *A Guide to Key West* by the Federal Writers' Project (New York: Hastings House, 1949; second edition); *Key West: The Last Resort* by Chris Sherrill and Roger Aiello (Atlanta: Villa Press, 1978); "A History of Palatka" (manuscript, Palatka Historical Society); *The Miracle of Coral Gables* by Rex Beach (Coral Gables, Fla.: privately printed by George E. Merrick, 1926); and *The Last Resorts* by Cleveland Amory (New York: Harper and Brothers, 1952).

Material on more recent developments in the state was gleaned from major newspapers, including the *Orlando Sentinel, Miami Herald, Tampa Tribune, St. Petersburg Times*, and others, as well as local magazines, *Florida Sportsman*, and *Florida Trend*. *The New York Times, The Washington Post*, and *The Wall Street Journal* also run informative stories periodically. Books include: Leon Odell Griffith, *Ed Ball: Confusion to the Enemy* (Tampa: Trend House, 1975); Steve Birnbaum, *Walt Disney World* (Houghton Mifflin Company and Hearst Professional Magazines, 1987); *Keys to Florida's Future*, the Final Report of the State Comprehensive Plan Committee to the State of Florida, February 1987; *The Environmental Destruction of South Florida*, edited by William Ross McCluney (Coral Gables, Fla.: University of Miami Press, 1971); Alex Shoumatoff, *Florida Ramble* (New York: Harper & Row, 1974); John Rothchild, *Up for Grabs: A Trip Through Time and Space in The Sunshine State* (New York: Viking, 1985); *Statistical Abstract*, University of Florida Bureau of Economic and Business Research, a yearly compilation of census and economic data; and, Gerald Grow, *Florida Parks* (Tallahassee: Longleaf Publications, 1987; third edition).

Specific information on technical reports and other sources is available from the author by writing to him care of the publisher.

INDEX

CPSIA information can be obtained
at www.ICGtesting.com
Printed in the USA
LVOW12s1516120816

499572LV00004B/22/P